Preventing and Treating Bullying and Victimization

Preventing and Treating Bullying and Victimization

Edited by

Eric M. Vernberg
Bridget K. Biggs

UNIVERSITY PRESS

2010

Oxford University Press, Inc., publishes works that further
Oxford University's objective of excellence
in research, scholarship, and education.

Oxford   New York
Auckland   Cape Town   Dar es Salaam   Hong Kong   Karachi
Kuala Lumpur   Madrid   Melbourne   Mexico City   Nairobi
New Delhi   Shanghai   Taipei   Toronto

With offices in
Argentina   Austria   Brazil   Chile   Czech Republic   France   Greece
Guatemala   Hungary   Italy   Japan   Poland   Portugal   Singapore
South Korea   Switzerland   Thailand   Turkey   Ukraine   Vietnam

Published by Oxford University Press, Inc.
198 Madison Avenue, New York, New York 10016

www.oup.com

Library of Congress Cataloging-in-Publication Data

Preventing and treating bullying and victimization / edited by Eric M. Vernberg, Bridget K. Biggs.
p.   cm.
Includes bibliographical references and index.
ISBN-13: 978-0-19-533587-3
ISBN-10: 0-19-533587-2
1. Bullying.   2. Bullying—Prevention.   3. Bullying in schools.   4. Bullying in schools—
Prevention.   5. Aggressiveness.   I. Vernberg, Eric M.   II. Biggs, Bridget K.
BF637.B85P74 2010
302.3—dc22
2009028614

9   8   7   6   5   4   3   2   1

Printed in the United States of America
on acid-free paper

To my parents, F. John Vernberg and Winona B. Vernberg (E. M. V.)
To my parents, J. Dennis Biggs and Sheila J. Biggs (B. K. B.)

Acknowledgments

B ridget Biggs completed most of her work on this book while an Assistant Professor in the Clinical Child Psychology Program University of Kansas. The research discussed in Chapter 9 was funded by The Ontario Mental Health Foundation, The Social Sciences and Humanities Research Council, and National Crime Prevention Centre. The authors would like to gratefully acknowledge the contributions of Rebecca Loucks, Jun Hee Lee, Kathy Robideau, Leila Rahey, Danielle Shelley, and Audrey Cole.

Contents

Contributors

Daryaneh Badaly, Department of Psychology, University of Southern California, Los Angeles, California

Kendra B. Battaglia, Department of Psychology, Wheaton College, Wheaton, Illinois

Bridget K. Biggs, Assistant Professor of Psychology, College of Medicine, Mayo Clinic, Rochester, Minnesota

Wendy M. Craig, Department of Psychology, Queen's University, Kingston, Canada

Mary Elizabeth Curtner-Smith, Department of Human Development and Family Studies, College of Human Environmental Sciences, University of Alabama, Tuscaloosa, Alabama

Allison G. Dempsey, Department of Educational Psychology, University of Florida, Gainesville, Florida

Mylien T. Duong, Department of Psychology University of Southern California, Los Angeles, California

Kelly S. Flanagan, Department of Psychology, Wheaton College, Wheaton, Illinois

Fred Frankel, Department of Psychiatry and Biobehavioral Sciences, University of California at Los Angeles, Los Angeles, California

Amie E. Grills-Taquechel, Department of Psychology, University of Houston, Houston, Texas

Nancy G. Guerra, Department of Psychology, University of California at Riverside, Riverside, California

Arthur M. Horne, Department of Counseling and Human Development Services, University of Georgia, Athens, Georgia

Brynn M. Kelly, Department of Psychology, University of Southern California, Los Angeles, California

Becky Kochenderfer-Ladd, School of Social and Family Dynamics, Arizona State University, Tempe, Arizona

Gary W. Ladd, School of Social and Family Dynamics, Arizona State University, Tempe, Arizona

Heather McCuaig-Edge, Department of Psychology, Queen's University, Kingston, Canada

Ashley Murphy, Department of Psychology, Queen's University, Kingston, Canada

Pamela Orpinas, Department of Health Promotion and Behavior, University of Georgia, Athens, Georgia

Heather T. Pane, Department of Psychology, University of Houston, Houston, Texas

Anthony D. Pellegrini, Department of Educational Psychology, University of Minnesota, Twin Cities Campus, Minneapolis, Minnesota

Debra J. Pepler, Department of Psychology, York University and The Hospital for Sick Children, Toronto, Canada

Rosanna Polifroni, Department of Psychology, University of Houston, Houston, Texas

Malvin Porter, Department of Human Development and Family Studies, College of Human Environmental Sciences, University of Alabama, Tuscaloosa, Alabama

Cary J. Roseth, Department of Educational Psychology, Michigan State University, East Lansing, Michigan

Frank C. Sacco, President, Community Services Institute, Springfield, Massachusetts

David Schwartz, Department of Psychology, University of Southern California, Los Angeles, California

Anneliese A. Singh, Department of Counseling and Human Development Services, University of Georgia, Athens, Georgia

Peter K. Smith, Unit for School and Family Studies, Goldsmiths, University of London, United Kingdom

Eric A. Storch, Departments of Pediatrics and Psychiatry, University of South Florida, St. Petersburg, Florida

Stuart W. Twemlow, Professor of Psychiatry and Behavioral Sciences, Menninger Department of Psychiatry, Baylor College of Medicine, Houston, Texas

Eric M. Vernberg, Clinical Child Psychology Program, University of Kansas, Lawrence, Kansas

Kirk R. Williams, Department of Sociology, University of California at Riverside, Riverside, California

PART I

PERSPECTIVES ON BULLYING

1

Preventing and Treating Bullying and Victimization: An Evidence-Based Approach

Eric M. Vernberg and Bridget K. Biggs

Whether as a target, bystander, or perpetrator, adults of all ages typically recall some experience with bullying during their school years. Once viewed as an expected piece of the school landscape that must be tolerated or even valued for teaching life lessons, educators and mental health professionals have become increasingly aware and concerned about the negative effects of bully–victim problems on self-concept, emotions, interpersonal relationships, and academic performance. Also increasingly apparent is the devastating impact of severe, persistent bullying for some children and adolescents. Extreme cases leading to homicide or suicide grab headlines (deservedly so) and prompt lawsuits, which in turn have spurred many states to pass legislation requiring that bully–victim problems be addressed by schools in some fashion. Therein lies the big question: What can be done to make a difference?

Research evidence on bully–victim problems has accumulated rapidly in recent years. From this, there is little doubt that prolonged involvement in bullying, as a perpetrator, victim, or, not uncommonly, as both a perpetrator and target of bullying, conveys risk for many aspects of development. Much work has been done to understand how and why children and adolescents become involved in these problematic social interactions. Various methods for assessing the degree to which an individual or group of individuals are involved in bullying have also been developed. In addition, there have been numerous efforts to implement and evaluate intervention programs, ranging from whole-school prevention programs to more individual- or group-oriented approaches targeting children and adolescents who are already heavily involved in bullying.

As in many emerging areas of psychological science, many research efforts evolved more or less independently, with different groups or networks of researchers investigating bully–victim issues from a variety of conceptual frameworks and methodologies. Although this has produced a very large and rich body of knowledge, it has made it difficult to gain a comprehensive, integrated view of the overall evidence base. What is it we have learned from this flurry of scholarly activity? What guidance can be extracted for clinical scientists and practitioners, school officials, and others who work with the children, adolescents, and families that become caught up in bullying?

This book addresses these thorny questions by looking across the many disciplines engaged in research and intervention in this area with an eye toward describing and integrating current knowledge into a guide for evidence-based practices. In doing so, we aim to integrate the sometimes disparate perspectives from school, clinical, counseling, and developmental researchers and professionals to generate greater understanding of this complex problem and to enhance intervention approaches. There are three sections: *Perspectives on Bullying, Assessment and Intervention,* and *Strategies for Implementing Best Practices.* For each chapter, we asked contributors to address specific topics or issues with the goal of achieving strong coverage of the field overall. Ideally, this book appeals to a number of professionals, including clinical, child, developmental, counseling, and school psychologists; social workers; school counselors, school administrators, and educators; and public officials involved in setting policies that affect the resources and resolve to address this important topic. Although the chapters and recommendations were not intended to address directly parents' specific questions and concerns, parents and other concerned adults may find the content of this book helpful in gaining a broader and more complex understanding of bullying, which may be helpful in identifying whether their children are involved in bullying, for seeking help if needed, or for advocating for school and community efforts to address this common social problem. In this opening chapter, we describe some of the key concepts that have emerged.

Prevention and Treatment Efforts Benefit from an Evidence-Based Approach

This book addresses "what to do" questions from an *evidence-based* perspective (e.g., see American Psychological Association Task Force on Evidence-Based Practice, 2006). That is, we advocate basing prevention and intervention decisions on the information available from the systematic study of how and under what conditions bully–victim problems emerge and change over time, what methods reliably identify the presence of bully–victim problems, and what types of interventions are effective in preventing or reducing these problems. For readers who are unfamiliar with the evidence-based perspective, it may help to imagine you are faced with a diagnosis of cancer and the decision of how to treat it. Compared to a treatment recommendation based on the doctor's personal opinion of what should work or knowledge of what might have worked for one or two people, you would probably have greater confidence in a treatment approach that was based on knowledge about the development of the particular type of cancer you have as well as clinical trials that have shown the treatment to be more effective than other options across a substantial number of patients. A lot of information about bully–victim problems is available to the general public—one need only turn on the television, read a newspaper, or walk into a bookstore to be exposed to a wide range of opinions and speculations. Unfortunately, some sources promote myths about bullying that are not substantiated by observable fact. For example, one common belief is that bullying is a "normal" part of growing up that does not have a lasting effect on those who are bullied. This belief persists despite research that has demonstrated long-term negative outcomes associated with victimization from peers. Another myth is that significant problems with bullying occur only in schools that are atypical in some way, such as very disorganized or low-achieving schools. Instead, research indicates that bully–victim problems occur across the full spectrum of schools, even in orderly, upper-income, high-achieving schools. We advocate the evidence-based approach as a means of sorting through the abundance of information on bully–victim problems to determine what information has been observed across a substantial number of youth and has been studied and reviewed by other researchers as a way to reduce the possibility of bias or misinterpretation. Because we still have a lot to learn about bully–victim problems and how to intervene, an evidence-based perspective also involves a necessary degree of uncertainty. In this volume, we have asked authors to consider the current knowledge base and distill what this information tells us regarding how to intervene. We have asked authors to communicate the degree of certainty in their current conclusions relative to the quantity and quality of the currently available scientific evidence.

Bullying Is a Relationship-Based Form of Aggression

Because *bullying* has been part of our language for many years, the term lends itself to various interpretations and definitions. Almost everyone agrees that bullying involves the use of various forms of aggression to oppress, humiliate, or dominate others. The types of aggression used in bullying are quite diverse and include overt physical aggression (hitting, grabbing, chasing, or kicking), destruction or theft of property or belongings, relational aggression (spreading rumors, ostracizing, excluding from normal group activities), and general harassment (cruel teasing). If this were the extent of the definition, almost all acts of aggression among children could be labeled as bullying, and indeed this sometimes seems to occur. Many experts have argued for two additional stipulations (e.g., Olweus, 1993). First, bullying should be reserved for instances in which there is an imbalance of physical or social power between the bully and the victim, such that the victim cannot muster an effective defense against the bully (or bullies). This requirement provides an important rationale for adult or peer intervention. Second, bullying involves an ongoing relationship in which the bully (or bullies) repeatedly humiliates, dominates, or oppresses a less powerful victim.

Understandably, there is overlap between research on aggression and bullying. The contributors to this book give important guidance in integrating these related areas of research to yield practical conclusions and recommendations for practice. For example, Becky Kochenderfer-Ladd and Gary Ladd (Chapter 3) describe three patterns of aggression among often-identified groups of children who are bullied by peers. The first group is labeled *submissive victims* (sometimes referred to as passive victims), who seldom act aggressively and may even be selected by bullies because they are safe and rewarding targets (i.e., they do not fight back and display submissive behavior readily). The second group is labeled *aggressive victims*, as aggressive behavior by some children may represent reactive aggression (hot-headed, impulsive aggression) that follows repeated episodes of bullying by one or more classmates. *Bully victims* represent a third group of victims who often use coercion and proactive aggression (cool-headed, intentional aggression) in their interactions with peers, which in turn leads to rejection and ostracism by the larger peer group. These distinctions among different profiles of children who are bullied are important for tailoring intervention efforts to the specific factors that keep each of these three types of children caught up in a cycle of bullying relationships. Clearly, although some children may be primarily involved as either victims or bullies, some individuals are both perpetrators and recipients of aggression (Graham, Belmore, & Mize, 2006; Schwartz, 2000).

As pointed out by several authors in this volume, involvement in bully–victim problems is not limited to the aggressors and the victimized; rather, these social interactions occur in a complex social ecology. Acts of peer-directed aggression frequently occur in the presence of others, particularly other children or adolescents in the peer group. The responses of these onlookers, or bystanders, appear to influence whether the aggression continues (Salmivalli, Lagerspetz, Björkqvist, & Österman, 1996; Twemlow, Fonagy, & Sacco, 2004). For example, joining or "egging on" the aggressors may encourage them to continue their abuse. Alternatively, standing up for victims or ostracizing perpetrators of bullying could send a message that aggression is unacceptable in the peer group and discourage further offenses. All of these points illustrate the importance of looking beyond individuals as "bully" or "victim" to the broader social context and interpersonal dynamics in which bullying occurs.

Bully–Victim Problems Are Not Evenly Distributed

Although virtually any child or adolescent could become ensnared in a bully–victim relationship, we now know that certain personal characteristics increase risk for engaging in bullying, becoming a target of bullying, or both. Some of these characteristics reflect an individual's pattern of behavior with others, which may be influenced by the child's perceptions and attitudes as well as his/her emotional reactivity. For example, children who give in easily and withdraw when faced with various forms of aggression are more likely to become submissive victims. Children who are restless, disagreeable, and emotionally reactive to provocation are more likely to become aggressive victims. Kochenderfer-Ladd and Ladd (Chapter 3) describe such individual characteristics associated with peer victimization. Many of these behavioral characteristics emerge and become fairly stable in the early elementary grade years. Recognition of these behavioral risk factors has several important implications for intervention. One is an emphasis on prevention efforts that begin during the elementary school years. Another is taking a tiered approach to bully–victim problems, whereby higher-risk children receive greater monitoring and, when indicated, more intensive intervention or support (see Chapter 9).

Other risk factors for developing bully–victim problems are physical or health related. Allison Dempsey and Eric Storch (Chapter 5) show how health problems that reduce physical strength increase the risk of becoming a victim of bullying, as do health problems that provide an easy target for ridicule. These include health conditions such as cystic fibrosis, heart problems, cancer, craniofacial abnormalities, obesity, and cancer. Importantly, Dempsey and

Storch also explain how various emotional and behavioral disorders, including attention-deficit/hyperactivity disorder, conduct problems, depressive disorders, learning disabilities, and anxiety disorders, convey risk for bully–victim problems. In many ways, this chapter demonstrates the value of integrating bully–victim research from clinical child and pediatric psychology, which often focuses on psychopathology and health conditions, with research in developmental psychology, which less frequently focuses on diagnosable health or mental health conditions.

Behavioral styles that raise the risk of becoming a victim or bully do not develop in a vacuum. Rather, they arise from the interplay of child characteristics (e.g., emotional reactivity, behavioral inhibition, impulsivity) and social experiences at school, home, and in the community. Mary Elizabeth Curtner-Smith, Peter Smith, and Malvin Porter (Chapter 4) present key concepts linking family processes and involvement in bully–victim problems at school. Clearly, the use (or misuse) of power within the family provides a context for learning about how to manage issues of conflict, social coercion, and physical aggression in interpersonal relationships. Not surprisingly, children reared in families that rely heavily on power assertion and coercion as a way to get one's way tend to use similar tactics with peers at school, setting the stage for becoming a bully, aggressive victim, or bully victim. The connection between family processes and increased risk for becoming a victim is perhaps less intuitive and not as well studied. Researchers of these issues speculate that the risk for victimization is heightened when family dynamics impede the development of gender-specific competencies: autonomy and assertion for boys, social relatedness and connectivity for girls. Research in this area is in its early stages and has not yet made clear distinctions between the family factors that may differentiate children who respond to victimization submissively versus aggressively. Work in this area promises to provide much-needed information in the family socialization of children who frequently bully others, are victimized by bullies, or both.

Individual characteristics and the family processes that may shape their development are not even half the story. Several chapters in this volume describe the vast and complex picture of social contextual factors that influence the degree to which bullying occurs. David Schwartz, Brynn Kelly, Mylien Duong, and Daryaneh Badaly (Chapter 2) present a model for understanding the social context of bullying drawn largely from Urie Bronfenbrenner's ecological-contextual theory. This model recognizes that children and adolescents are influenced by the characteristics of social settings in which they participate directly (e.g., classrooms, peer networks, family), but it also acknowledges the influence of more subtle community and cultural factors (e.g., values, attitudes, policies) on interpersonal dynamics in these settings. Following this framework, Schwartz and his co-authors describe the factors within the peer group, school, community, and wider society and culture that scientific study has identified as important to understanding bully–victim problems.

Recognizing a Problem Is the First Step to Addressing It

One of the big discoveries from research on bully–victim problems is that parents and teachers are not necessarily aware of bullying. There are many reasons for this. Many youth who are teased, threatened, hit, or excluded by peers do not tell anyone else about the experience (Vernberg, Ewell, Beery, Freeman, & Abwender, 1995). Victimized children and adolescents may not disclose bullying for fear that adults will make things worse or because of embarrassment about what has happened. Chronically victimized children and adolescents may accept their role as something outside of their control or even as something they deserve in some way (Dill, Vernberg, Fonagy, Twemlow, & Gamm, 2004). Teachers may also vary in their awareness and concern about bullying among children in their classrooms (Biggs, Vernberg, Twemlow, Fonagy, & Dill, 2008; Mize, 2005). Somehow a "don't ask, don't tell" attitude seems to develop.

Dan Olweus, who is among the pioneers in the systematic study of bullying and efforts to address it, emphasized the importance integrating assessment into intervention efforts. For example, he observed that a school-wide survey of the prevalence of bullying and a subsequent presentation of the results not only provided a baseline measurement from which to determine progress but was also an important motivator for teachers and school staff to implement the intervention by raising awareness of the problem (Olweus, 1993). Since Olweus' earliest work, the number of available assessment tools and methods has expanded. Cary Roseth and Anthony Pellegrini (Chapter 8) provide an up-to-date description of the methods suited for school settings and offer practical guidance for conducting school-based assessments. Amie Grills-Taquechel, Rosanna Polifroni, and Heather Pane (Chapter 6) present methods for ascertaining involvement in bully–victim problems when working with individual children. Authors of both chapters advocate using multiple methods (e.g., questionnaires, diaries, observation) and getting information from multiple reporters (e.g., teachers, students, independent observers) in order to get the most complete picture.

Interventions Can Make a Difference, but Quality Matters

The number of studies evaluating the impact of bully–victim prevention programs has grown considerably in recent years. Wendy Craig, Debra Pepler, Ashley Murphy, and Heather McCuaig-Edge (Chapter 9) review 48 published studies that focused on school-based bully prevention programs and conclude that reductions in bullying so far are relatively modest. Almost three-quarters of these studies found some positive effects, and their examination of programs with more robust effects gives a picture of the types of efforts that contribute to meaningful changes. These authors argue that all schools need to find ways to protect students who are at increased risk of victimization from abuse and provide opportunities for them to develop positive peer relationships. They frame the challenge to schools as helping students understand that bullying involves the aggressive use of power in ways that are harmful to victims, bullies, and the social group as a whole. Considering the complexity of the problem, it is not surprising that these authors conclude that bullying prevention programs have the greatest chance of success if they target the problem at multiple levels of involvement and involve the whole school, parents, and the community.

Do all schools need to take action to prevent bullying? Nancy Guerra and Kirk Williams (Chapter 13) present data addressing the question of which characteristics of the school setting are associated with the prevalence of bullying among students. Their results underscore the importance of a school's culture in terms of the acceptability of aggression among students and school personnel. Interestingly, the attitudes toward aggression held by individuals in the school seem to matter more than the socioeconomic circumstances or racial and ethnic composition of the school's student body in determining the prevalence of bullying. These findings emphasize that bullying is an "equal opportunity" problem. Because of the importance of the prevailing attitudes toward aggression within a school's climate, it behooves all schools to be concerned about the climate promoted within their school community.

Anneliese Singh, Pamela Orpinas, and Arthur Horne (Chapter 10) provide practical guidance for implementing bullying prevention programs in schools. Like others in this volume, they emphasize that bullying is a relational problem influenced by the surrounding context. They frame the challenge of bullying prevention as promoting a respectful atmosphere in schools that is consistent with the values of individuals within that school. Their approach aims to empower students, teachers, administrators, and others to take action against bullying. The ideas in this chapter address the all-too-frequent implementation issues faced by many who have tried to start and sustain bullying prevention programs. Inadequate support at any level could lead to insufficient implementation or obstruct intervention efforts. Singh and colleagues provide practical ideas for getting all onboard.

The relational and contextual nature of bullying also has implications for policy. Schools provide a setting for learning about power relationships through interactions with peers, teachers, and other school personnel. Stuart Twemlow and Frank Sacco (Chapter 12) argue that schools would benefit from focusing more attention on the power dynamics operating within the school building and in the school system more broadly in making policy decisions and conducting the day-to-day business of running schools. For example, they point out ways that adults at school may inadvertently model the use of power to dominate students or other staff. These authors also suggest that schools may set the stage for marginalization of a subset of students by overemphasizing academic achievement and success in sports or other activities. In this scenario, less successful students receive multiple messages that they are less valued by adults and peers at school, which in turn creates easy targets for victimization by higher-status peers. This feeds into a cycle of domination, alienation, and retribution that sometimes produces serious acts of violence.

Clearly, gaining a school-wide commitment to reducing bully–victim problems is a critical step in bringing about change. At the same time, it simply is not realistic to think that whole-school approaches alone will be sufficient. In addition to studies of universal bully–victim prevention programs offered to everyone regardless of risk, research is needed to identify targeted interventions that help children and adolescents who are at risk for involvement and those who are already frequent bullies or victims. These interventions may involve referral to specialized group intervention or individualized treatment at school or with a mental health provider in the community. It is also possible that awareness of a child's involvement in bullying may arise in the context of individual or family treatment for another problem or a problem related to bullying (e.g., behavior problems) or victimization (e.g., internalizing problem such as anxiety or depression).

School-based bully–victim prevention programs seldom have the resources to offer much to parents beyond psychoeducational materials and perhaps referrals to local mental health providers. However, these providers may not have had much training in evidence-based approaches to addressing bully–victim problems. At this time, there is a paucity of well-studied individual and group interventions designed specifically for youth involved in bullying. Intervention efforts to this point have primarily focused on whole-school approaches, and rightly so. Most experts on bullying advocate a comprehensive approach that addresses the social context in which bullying occurs. Nonetheless, individual youth who are most intensely involved in bullying interactions may need additional attention.

Amie Grills-Taquechel, Rosanna Polifroni, and Heather Pane (Chapter 6) provide guidance regarding assessment and treatment for mental health practitioners working with individual children and their families, most typically in a clinic setting. Kelly Flanagan and Kendra Battaglia (Chapter 8) present options for group treatment for children identified as involved or at risk for involvement in bully–victim problems. The authors base many of their recommendations for addressing bullying on the vast amount of research on youth who are aggressive, generally speaking, and treatments that have been developed to reduce aggressive behavior. Importantly, Flanagan and Battaglia insist that caution be taken when considering group treatments for aggressive youth, because group treatments for aggression have at times led to *worse* problems, presumably because of the inadvertent modeling or encouragement of aggressive behavior among participants. Regarding victims, the authors of these chapters largely draw from research indicating that victimization is often associated with internalizing problems such as anxiety, depression, and loneliness, and that having a good quality friendship may provide protection from victimization. Their recommendations are primarily based on interventions designed to treat anxiety, depression, or social skills problems, although Flanagan and Battaglia also describe a few promising group interventions designed specifically for children involved in bullying. Schools are an ideal setting to offer these types of group interventions, because transportation, cost, and scheduling issues often present strong barriers to offering group interventions in outpatient mental health settings. However, schools typically do not have the personnel or expertise to provide these interventions on their own, making collaboration and pooling of resources an important step in addressing bully–victim problems.

Despite the potential challenges of offering group treatments in outpatient mental health settings, Fred Frankel (Chapter 11) gives a clear picture of what it takes to offer a group intervention aimed at helping isolated or socially rejected children and adolescents develop a close friendship. Many studies have found friendlessness to be a major issue for victimized children. His approach includes group sessions for children in conjunction with parallel group sessions for their parents. This is the type of innovative, evidence-based approach that could be used much more often within the overall framework of a comprehensive plan to address bully–victim problems.

As with universal, whole-school approaches, it is important to recognize that individual or group interventions in isolation seem unlikely to have much of an impact on bully–victim problems with the school overall. Rather, the promise lies with tiered approaches that combine whole-school efforts with targeted interventions for students with more intransigent bully–victim problems.

"Buy In" at Multiple Levels Is Crucial

Even the most comprehensive set of evidence-based practices for preventing and treating bully–victim problems will not have much impact if there is not widespread, sustained support for implementation on the part of teachers, school administrators, students, parents, and communities. Legislation can mandate that schools address bully–victim problems, but this does not necessarily lead to effective action. Anyone who tries to develop and implement bully–victim prevention programs in schools may learn that some teachers and building principals strongly support these efforts, some are mildly supportive, and others are passively (or even actively) opposed. Despite the successful reduction in bullying observed for some intervention programs (e.g., Fonagy et al., 2009), anecdotal and empirical evidence suggests that incomplete implementation of or participation in these programs can attenuate effects (Biggs et al., 2008; Twemlow et al., 2008). We have described a number of potential barriers to successful implementation of antibullying programs at multiple levels (i.e., culture, community, school, and individual) (Vernberg & Gamm, 2003). Successful implementation of the comprehensive interventions, which have the greatest empirical support, requires enthusiasm and sustained energy and resources from all levels. For example, societal norms favoring competition, aggression, and Social Darwinism can influence the degree to which the surrounding community—including community leaders, tax payers, school staff, parents, and students—will support a school-based program that emphasizes respect and discourages the use of aggression. Intervention efforts could be thwarted if norms and messages from the community regarding aggression and violence are at odds with those communicated at school. At the school level, administrators and teachers may believe that dealing with students' peer relationships is outside the educational mission of the school, despite compelling evidence that involvement in bullying (as perpetrator or victim) is associated with poorer academic engagement and achievement (Buhs, Ladd, & Herald, 2006; Graham et al., 2006) and that school-based violence prevention efforts have demonstrated improvements in students' standardized test scores (Fonagy, Twemlow, Vernberg, Sacco, & Little, 2005). A single administrator or teacher who actively opposes an intervention effort could do much to discourage its implementation; conversely, we have argued that the presence of a persuasive leader within the school or community could do much to ignite enthusiasm for a cooperative effort.

Consistent with the idea that cultural and societal values may exert influence through the various layers of the social fabric, many of the contributors to this book describe how concepts of bullying and victimization reflect underlying values related to compassion, social justice, and the use of power in social relationships. Many prevention and intervention programs for bullying rely on actions that are to be carried out throughout the school day and incorporated into the social fabric of the school. Singh and colleagues (Chapter 10) provide rationale and strategies for carrying out values-oriented discussions that help set the stage for meaningful interventions. From their perspective, these discussions must engage students as well as system administrators, building staff, and parents. Twemlow and Sacco (Chapter 12) focus on "myths" that often seem to interfere with the adoption and implementation of prevention and treatment strategies. Importantly, they offer counterarguments to these myths and describe strategies to garner the widespread awareness and understanding of bully–victim problems that drive meaningful change.

Let Knowledge Guide Action

We hold that research on bully–victim problems to this point has achieved several goals. First, it has raised awareness of the problem and its prevalence. Second, researchers have described the basic elements of the problem and characteristics of individuals involved. Third, growing awareness of bullying and its effects has fueled the search for effective interventions, particularly at the curriculum and whole-school levels. Finally, the connection is increasingly being made between bully–victim problems and other areas of research and practice that address issues of education, health, mental health, and child development. We propose that integration of knowledge from school, clinical, counseling, and developmental experts is essential for the future directions of this field. Such integration helps us understand better the nuances of these social phenomena, the issues related to developmental course of bully–victim dynamics and mental health, and increases the likelihood of having a positive impact at various levels, including individual, peer group, school, and community.

With this book, we have attempted to compile current knowledge about bully–victim problems to inform action. We are encouraged by the growing concern about this problem around the world and hope that actions to address bullying will be increasingly influenced by the growing body of scientifically based knowledge about this phenomenon and the interventions to address it. The contributing authors have taken seriously the task of providing the most up-to-date information and helping make sense of what this information means in terms of understanding bullying and what can be done to address it. Together, the chapters present a comprehensive picture of a complex problem. We hope readers find this book both informative and useful.

References

American Psychological Association Task Force on Evidence-Based Practice. (2006). Evidence-based practice in psychology. *American Psychologist, 61,* 271–285.

Biggs, B. K., Vernberg, E. M., Twemlow, S. W., Fonagy, P., & Dill, E. J. (2008). Teacher adherence and its relations to teacher attitudes and student outcomes in an elementary school-based violence prevention program. *School Psychology Review, 37,* 533–549.

Buhs, E. S., Ladd, G. W., & Herald, S. L. (2006). Peer exclusion and victimization: Processes that mediate the relation between peer group rejection and children's classroom engagement and achievement? *Journal of Educational Psychology, 98,* 1–13.

Dill, E. J., Vernberg, E. M., Fonagy, P., Twemlow, S. W., & Gamm, B. K. (2004). Negative affect in victimized children: The roles of social withdrawal, peer rejection, and attitudes towards bullying. *Journal of Abnormal Child Psychology, 32,* 159–173.

Fonagy, P., Twemlow, S. W., Vernberg, E. M., Nelson, J. M., Dill, E. J., Little, T. D., & Sargent, J. A. (2009). A cluster randomized controlled trial of child-focused psychiatric consultation and a school systems-focused intervention to reduce aggression. *Journal of Child Psychology and Psychiatry, 50,* 607–616.

Fonagy, P., Twemlow, S. W., Vernberg, E. M., Sacco, F. C., & Little, T. D. (2005). Creating a Peaceful School Learning Environment: The impact of an antibullying program on educational attainment in elementary schools. *Medical Science Monitor, 11,* 317–325.

Graham, S., Bellmore, A. D., & Mize, J. (2006). Peer victimization, aggression, and their co-occurrence in middle school: Pathways to adjustment problems. *Journal of Abnormal Child Psychology, 34,* 363–378.

Mize, J. (2005). *Predictors of discrepancies between teacher and child reports of aggression, victimization, and aggressive bystanding in elementary school.* Masters thesis, Clinical Child Psychology Program, University of Kansas, Lawrence, KS.

Olweus, D. (1993). *Bullying at school: What we know and what we can do.* Oxford, England: Blackwell Publishers.

Salmivalli, C., Lagerspetz, K., Björkqvist, K., & Österman, K. (1996). Bullying as a group process. Participant roles and their relations to social status within the group. *Aggressive Behavior, 22,* 1–15.

Schwartz, D. (2000). Subtypes of victims and aggressors in children's peer groups. *Journal of Abnormal Child Psychology, 28,* 181–192.

Twemlow, S. W., Biggs, B. K., Nelson, T. D., Vernberg, E. M., Fonagy, P., & Twemlow, S. W. (2008). Effects of participation in a martial art-based anti-bullying program on children's aggression in elementary schools. *Psychology in the Schools, 45,* 947–959.

Twemlow, S. W., Fonagy, P., & Sacco, F. C. (2004). The role of the bystander in the social architecture of bullying and violence in schools and communities. In J. Devine, J. Gilligan, K. A. Miczek, R. Shaikh, & D. Pfaff (Eds.), *Scientific approaches to youth violence prevention* (pp. 215–232). New York: New York Academy of Sciences.

Vernberg, E. M., Ewell, K. K., Beery, S. H., & Freeman, C. M. (1995). Aversive exchanges with peers and adjustment during early adolescence: Is disclosure helpful? *Child Psychiatry & Human Development, 26,* 43–59.

Vernberg, E. M., & Gamm, B. K. (2003). Resistance to violence prevention interventions in schools: Barriers and solutions. *Journal of Applied Psychoanalytic Studies, 5,* 125–138.

2

A Contextual Perspective on Intervention and Prevention Efforts for Bully–Victim Problems

David Schwartz, Brynn M. Kelly, Mylien T. Duong, and Daryaneh Badaly

I n this chapter, we discuss contextual factors that might influence the effectiveness of efforts to reduce the incidence of bully–victim problems in school peer groups. As we will contend, victimization in the peer group is a complex phenomenon that is embedded in a larger social environment. A focus on specific child vulnerabilities that might predict mistreatment by peers can be a useful starting point for intervention. Still, practitioners who seek a more complete understanding of the mechanisms underlying peer victimization will need to attend to powerful contextual influences such as peer group organization, school structure, neighborhood or community characteristics, and sociocultural setting.

We derive a guiding framework for our analysis from Bronfenbrenner's (1979) ecological systems theory. Bronfenbrenner posited that development is shaped by a series of transactions within and between layers of a child's environment (see Fig. 2.1). At the proximal level, a child's biological and psychological maturation is guided by social structures that include the family, peer group, school, and neighborhood. The child's experience is also affected by bidirectional relations between these structures. For example, the organization of the school peer group reflects features of the school and neighborhood as well as children's socialization in the home. In turn, peer relationships have a significant impact on the functioning of the school, community, and family. At a more distal level, these transactions are influenced by cultural beliefs, practices, and customs.

To illustrate the utility of Bronfenbrenner's perspectives for intervention, consider the case of a young boy who has emerged as a persistent victim of bullying. As a preliminary step, a practitioner might consider observing the boy

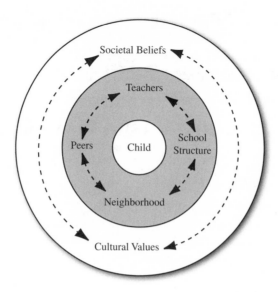

Figure 2.1 Ecological model of a child's environment.

and assessing his behavioral characteristics. Such an approach seems logical given that there are well-established links between particular classes of social behavior and a child's propensity to be mistreated by peers (Schwartz, Dodge, & Coie, 1993; Hodges & Perry, 1999). Nonetheless, the implications of the child's interactive style will likely be dependent on features of the peer group (i.e., peer group norms with regard to specific classes of social behavior), attitudes of the child's teacher toward bullying, and specific structural features of the school (e. g., class size, ethnic/racial composition). If the practitioner does not carefully consider these background features, any planned interventions may be unlikely to lead to a successful outcome. An ecological systems approach would encourage interventions that are informed by recognition of the larger context.

We begin our discussion by focusing on the immediate social contexts of the peer group, school (including adult caregivers in the school environment, as well as structural features of the school), and the surrounding neighborhood. Because the family and home environment are discussed elsewhere in this volume (Chapter 4) and in prior reviews (e.g., Schwartz, Toblin, Abou-ezzeddine, Tom, & Stevens, 2005), our emphasis is on these other proximal contextual factors. We will then move on to consider the influence of the wider cultural setting.

In keeping with the broader objectives of this volume, we emphasize the practical implications of an ecological systems perspective for intervention.

To this end, we offer a series of recommendations. Because research on contextual influences on victimization in the peer group is in an early stage of development, we adopt a cautious stance and are tentative in our conclusions.

Peers, Teachers, and the School as Contexts for Intervention
Guidelines for Intervention with the Peer Group

Initial attempts to understand the nature of bully–victim problems incorporated a view of bullying as either a process involving specific dyads of children (i.e., Dodge, Price, Coie, & Christopoulos, 1990; Olweus, 1978) or as persistent peer group aggression directed at individual targets (i.e., Pellegrini, Bartini, & Brooks, 1999; Perry, Kusel, & Perry, 1988; Schwartz, McFadyen-Ketchum, Dodge, Pettit, & Bates, 1998). For the most part, the emphasis was on children directly involved in incidents of bullying as either aggressors or victims. Nevertheless, aggression in school is an intricate system that includes bullies and victims as well as the surrounding peer group (Salmivalli, Lagerspetz, Björkqvist, Österman, & Kaukiainen, 1996; Salmivalli, 2001).

Assess Peer Reactions to Bullying Incidents

Consistent with our conceptualization of victimization as a process that is rooted in the larger peer group, a sizeable percentage of youth act as "reinforcers" and actively support or encourage potential aggressors (Salmivalli et al., 1996). Other children may serve a more passive role as "bystanders," who observe the interaction but do not intervene. Thus, victimization in the peer group can be contingent on the behavior of children who do not appear to be directly involved (Salmivalli et al., 1996; Sutton & Smith, 1999; Whitney & Smith, 1993).

Interestingly, the majority of dyadic bully–victim encounters occur in the presence of other children (Atlas & Pepler, 1998). Aggressors generally desist when these observing children protest (Hawkins, Pepler, & Craig, 2001). Unfortunately, in most cases, peers choose not to intervene on behalf of the victim (Craig, Pepler, & Atlas, 2000). Instead, the peer group is more likely to support the actions of the bully (Hawkins et al., 2001).

Successful interventions will need to move beyond an emphasis on children who have an immediate role in bully–victim interactions and toward an awareness of the full peer group. That said, readers should keep in mind that many questions about the role of the peer group remain unanswered. Are there settings in which peers are more or less likely to reinforce bullying behavior (Salmivalli & Voeten,

2004)? What attributes identify children who choose to adopt "bystander" or "reinforcer" roles (Salmivalli, 2001)? Can interventions be designed that successfully reduce bullying by altering the peer group social environment (Naylor & Cowie, 1999; Salmivalli, Kaukiainen, Voeten, & Sinisammal, 2004)?

Determine Whether the Peer Group Frowns upon or Supports Aggression

As one aspect of a focus on the role of peers, interventionists should attend carefully to the behavioral norms that characterize the peer group (see also Chapter 13). These norms can have critical implications for the social impact of bullying and other aggressive behaviors. Children who engage in bullying or other forms of aggression at a level that is inconsistent with the dominant values of the peer group may be viewed as "social misfits" and will be rejected as a result (Boivin, Dodge, & Coie, 1995; Wright, Giammarino, & Parad, 1986). On the other hand, bullying is less likely to predict negative social outcomes in settings where a relatively large percentage of children are aggressive (Chang, 2004; Stormshak et al., 1999). In these settings, peers may be supportive of such behaviors and bullies might even enjoy encouragement for their actions.

As an illustration, consider the fictionalized cases of two potential aggressors. George is a 12-year-old boy who attends a middle school that has a student body characterized by high rates of aggressive behavior problems. Among his peers, George enjoys the status of being "tough" and he is admired for his abilities as a fighter. George frequently picks on the smaller students in his grade. On one particular afternoon, he pushes one of his favorite targets into an open locker, and he is rewarded with laughter and slaps on the back from his classmates. George enjoys the positive attention he receives and feels motivated to continue his bullying behavior.

Dick is also a 12-year-old boy but he attends a much different kind of school. For the most part, Dick's classmates are not especially aggressive. In fact, physical confrontations between students at this school are relatively uncommon. Many of his peers view Dick as being a bully. For this reason, he is not well liked and has few friends at school. When Dick taunts or teases another child, he sometimes finds that observing peers object or try to intervene. As a result, Dick slowly abandons his aggressive ways and begins to find other strategies for interacting with his peers.

Pay Attention to the Presence of Aggressors

Aggressive tendencies among a child's peers could have more direct implications for determining bully–victim outcomes. Simply put, a child will not be at high risk for bullying if he or she is not in close proximity to potential aggressors. Consistent with this suggestion, Astor and colleagues reported that children are more likely to experience victimization in schools where peers are characterized by aggressive and disruptive behaviors (Astor, Benbenishty, & Marachi, 2004). Hanish, Ryan, Martin, and Fabes (2005) found that preschoolers were more likely to be bullied in classrooms with high aggression levels. In addition, there may be "contagion" effects with children engaging in aggressive behaviors as a reflection of exposure to aggressive role models in the peer group (Espelage, Holt, & Henkel, 2003; Hanish, Martin, Fabes, Leonard, & Herzog, 2005).

Be Aware of Group Norms That May Determine Who Is a "Social Misfit"
and at Risk for Victimization

The behavioral tendencies that are linked to victimization by peers might also be partially determined by classroom norms. Researchers have proposed a developmental progression through which specific classes of social behavior predict mistreatment by peers. In the hypothesized sequence, atypical behavioral styles (e.g., submissive/withdrawn or aggressive/reactive) are negatively evaluated by peers and, accordingly, lead to social rejection (Boivin, Hymel, & Bukowski, 1995; Schwartz, McFadyen-Ketchum, Dodge, Pettit, & Bates, 1999). This rebuff is then manifested in physical and verbal maltreatment by peers. This sequence notwithstanding, the association between children's social behavior and their acceptance or rejection by classmates will be dependent on the characteristics of the peer group (Stormshak et al., 1999; Wright et al., 1986). For this reason, we would not expect submissive or passive tendencies to increase risk for rejection and/or victimization by peers in settings where such behavioral styles are common.

Recognize That Friendships Can Help Protect against Victimization

Although there are factors within the peer group that might promote risk for victimization, peer relationships can also serve a protective role for youth who might otherwise emerge as persistent targets of bullying. In particular, friends might act as defenders or allies for children whose behavioral attributes could otherwise potentiate mistreatment by peers (Hodges, Boivin, Vitaro, & Bukowski, 1999; Hodges, Malone, & Perry, 1997). Friendship can also serve as a socializing context for children (Hartup & Stevens, 1997; Newcomb & Bagwell, 1995, 1996; Price, 1996). Interactions with friends are thought to enhance developing capacities (e.g., emotion regulation) that might allow a child to respond adaptively to provocative overtures from aggressors (Schwartz, Dodge, Pettit, Bates, & the Conduct Problems Prevention Research Group, 2000).

Evidence that friendship can mitigate risk for victimization has prompted the development of "befriending" interventions (Boulton, Trueman, Chau, Whitehand, & Amatya, 1999; Naylor & Cowie, 1999; Peterson & Rigby, 1999). The premise behind these efforts is that the peer group can be restructured to facilitate friendship formation for bullied youth. As efforts to prevent victimization in the peer group evolve to include a wider focus on the social context, it will be important to consider factors that reduce or increase opportunities for close dyadic affiliations between children. We suspect that there are features inherent in the organization of some peer groups (i.e., well-developed clique structures) that limit some children's opportunities for friendship. Likewise, some settings maybe facilitate interactions between friends.

Distinguish between Friendships with Well-Adjusted and Aggressive Peers

Another reason that the peer group environment is important to consider is that the behavioral characteristics of a child's friends can have critical implications for the outcomes that he or she experiences (Dishion & Dodge, 2005). Friends who are well adjusted and socially competent can serve as positive role models (Parker, Rubin, Price, & DeRosier, 1995), but affiliation with peers who are characterized by aggression or other behavior problems may accelerate trajectories toward negative outcomes (Laird, Pettit, Dodge, & Bates, 1999). Youth who form friendships with aggressive peers often experience increases in disruptive behavior (Lahey, Waldman, & McBurnett, 1999). Additionally, there is some evidence that friendships with aggressive or antisocial peers are relatively low in quality and lacking in important attributes such as closeness, security, and companionship (Dishion, Andrews, & Crosby, 1995; Poulin, Dishion, & Haas, 1999). The issue of friendship quality is notable because friendships that are high in negative features do not promote positive adjustment in school (Berndt, 1996).

The attributes of children's friends have rarely been considered in research on bully–victim problems. One exception is a recent study that examined differences between aggressive and nonaggressive friends in the link between victimization by peers and declines in academic performance over 2 years (Schwartz, Gorman, Dodge, Pettit, & Bates, 2008). Peer victimization was associated with academic declines only when children had either a large number of aggressive friends or a small number of nonaggressive friends.

That is, aggressive friends seem to exacerbate the negative impact of peer victimization, whereas nonaggressive friends appear to play a more ameliorative role. Furthermore, friendships might not necessarily serve as protective factors in schools where peers tend to be characterized by aggression or other maladaptive behaviors. Disengagement from the peer group or social withdrawal might buffer children against risk for bullying in high-risk urban settings (Hanish & Guerra, 2000).

As an illustration of our concerns regarding the attributes of children's friends, consider the fictionalized case of two adolescent girls, Sarah and Hillary. Sarah is Hillary's best friend, and the two girls spend much of their free time together. Occasionally, Sarah and Hillary find themselves talking about school. Sarah, who has always had very low grades, does not hesitate to share her very negative views about studying, homework, and teachers. One afternoon, Hillary confides in Sarah that she is often picked on at school. Sarah encourages Hillary to "ditch" school as much as possible and thus avoid aggressive peers. Sarah and Hillary continue to enjoy a close friendship, but Hillary begins to bring home disappointing report cards.

Summary Recommendations

The most efficient intervention programs will likely be those that view bully–victim interactions within the milieu of the wider peer group. Prevention efforts should continue to target deficits in the social skills of bullies and their victims but an awareness of the role of peers who serve as bystanders or reinforcers will also be critical. In addition, practitioners need to recognize that peer group norms may shape the extent to which bullies are supported for their aggressive behavior and can also help determine which children emerge as persistent victims. Finally, we would encourage interventionists to be cognizant of the role of friendships. Under some circumstances, a child's friends can serve as a powerful resource for interrupting the dynamic of peer group victimization. Conversely, affiliations with peers who serve as maladaptive socializing influences might actually exacerbate the impact of bullying.

Guidelines for Intervention with Teachers and Other Educational Professionals

The focus of our discussion up to this point has been the peer group, but adults in the school environment could also play a key role in the dynamics of bullying. Teachers, principals, and other school officials can significantly impact how often victimization occurs in the peer group. For this reason, many prevention programs explicitly acknowledge the role of adult authority figures and attempt to make changes in the school environment by altering the behavior of classroom teachers (e.g., Frey et al., 2005; Olweus, 2004). Although research on the role that teachers can play in intervention is arguably in an early stage of development, the available findings do highlight some issues that warrant close attention by practitioners.

Consider How School Professionals View Bullying

Given their vantage point at the head of the classroom, it is not surprising that many teachers have a sophisticated understanding of what behaviors actually constitute peer victimization. They not only recognize that physical and verbal aggression are forms of bullying (Craig, Henderson, & Murphy, 2000; Hazler, Miller, Carney, & Green, 2001), but they also attend to more subtle aspects of aggressive interactions, such as power imbalances and intent to harm (Naylor, Cowie, Cossin, de Bettencourt, & Lemme, 2006). Teacher's attitudes toward the students involved in bullying can depend on contextual factors and particular students' attributes (Arbeau & Coplan, 2007). In general, however, teachers do not approve of bullying and see it as an important issue for their schools (Boulton, 1997; Nicolaides, Toda, & Smith, 2002).

Understand School Professionals' Ability to Detect Bullying

Despite their capacity to recognize the multifaceted nature of bullying, teachers may not always be able to reliably detect individual incidents. Indeed, children report that their schoolteachers are largely unaware of bully–victim encounters (Houndoumadi & Pateraki, 2001). The unfortunate reality is that peer victimization tends to occur most frequently in unstructured situations that are not well supervised (Olweus, 1978). In fact, bullying is almost twice as likely to occur on the playground as it is in the classroom (Craig, Pepler, & Atlas, 2000). To complicate matters further, instructors are often unable to detect classroom-based bullying because they are not close enough to the incident or are attending to something else (Atlas & Pepler, 1998).

When school professionals are unable to observe bullying firsthand, it is possible that they can find out about it from the victims. Unfortunately, most bullied students do not tell any adults about their experiences, and when they do, they go to their parents more often than to their teachers (Houndoumadi & Pateraki, 2001; Smith & Shu, 2000). Boys and older students are especially hesitant to report peer problems to school professionals (Houndoumadi & Pateraki, 2001; Smith & Shu, 2000). By early adolescence, targeted youth report that they do not see adults at school as an important source of assistance (Rigby & Bagshaw, 2003).

Be Aware of the Possible Influences on Teachers' Intervention Decisions

Because a number of factors can limit teachers' awareness of bullying episodes, it is likely that they will only respond to a small percentage of bully–victim interactions (Craig, Pepler et al., 2000). The probability of a teacher intervening fluctuates as a function of where the bullying takes place, whether the teacher is in close proximity of the bullying incident, and whether the teacher is aware of the incident (Atlas & Pepler, 1998). When bullying occurs outside the classroom, teacher intervention is particularly unlikely.

Even when they do directly observe bullying, teachers may fail to act if they believe that intervention falls outside of their responsibilities as educators. Teachers clearly feel obligated to respond to conflicts between students in their own classrooms, but they are often uncertain about their role in other school contexts (Astor, Meyer, & Behre, 1999; Behre, Astor, & Meyer, 2001; Boulton, 1997; Meyer, Astor, & Behre, 2004). Ambiguous school policies can obfuscate the situation further. For example, teachers acknowledge reluctance to intervene when they are uncertain that the school will support their actions (Astor et al., 1999; Meyer et al., 2004; Mishna, Pepler, & Wiener, 2006). Thus, one possible goal for interventionists might be helping to clarify any ambiguous school polices.

Professionals should also recognize that fears regarding safety might factor into teachers' decisions about whether, and how, to intervene in bullying incidents. Although teachers generally report feeling secure during the school day, secondary school teachers tend to have more worries about their personal well-being than primary school teachers (Behre et al., 2001; Zeira, Astor, & Benbenishty, 2004). Consequently, secondary school teachers could be particularly hesitant to intervene in bullying and other acts of school violence (Astor et al., 1999). Moreover, primary school teachers report that if they worked with older students, fear of personal harm would decrease their chances of intervening (Meyer et al., 2004). It appears that teachers consider the age, size, and maturity of students when assessing the risk associated with conflict intervention (Behre et al., 2001).

Such concerns notwithstanding, most teachers are motivated to protect students from imminent harm (Behre et al., 2001; Meyer et al., 2004; Yoon,

2004) and will assess the level of risk that students face when making intervention decisions. In general, teachers view instances of physical and verbal victimization as more severe than relational victimization (Boulton, 1997; Craig, Henderson et al., 2000; Hazler et al., 2001; Yoon & Kerber, 2003). Teachers are most proactive when the victim is a persistent target (Boulton, 1997; Meyer et al., 2004; Nesdale & Pickering, 2006; Nicolaides et al., 2002) or when the aggressor has a negative reputation or substantial influence in the peer group (Nesdale & Pickering, 2006). Under these conditions, teachers may feel a heightened sense of responsibility because they perceive the victim to be at greater risk for current and future harm.

Distinguish Effective versus Ineffective Teacher Responses

Teachers who choose to intervene can use a variety of strategies. For example, they might attempt to punish bullies, contact parents, foster the development of coping skills in victimized youth, or conduct conflict resolution (Horne, Orpinas, Newman-Carlson, & Bartolomucci, 2004; Limber, 2004). It is not clear which of these options is most likely to prove effective or whether the usefulness of different methods is dependent on situational factors. The limited availability of information on the efficacy of specific response strategies is unfortunate because educators often ask for advice regarding effective intervention (Boulton, 1997). Teachers report wanting to know about procedures for determining the prevalence of bullying, techniques for talking with bullies and victims, activities for preventing and intervening in bullying, and methods for developing school-wide bullying policies (Nicolaides et al., 2002). Interventionists will likely find that many teachers welcome collaboration and assistance in dealing with bullying problems.

Teacher involvement can function to decrease conflict in the peer group, but such efforts can also backfire, to the detriment of the victim. Children indicate that teacher intervention has a positive impact only about half of the time (Fekkes, Pijpers, & Verloove-Vanhorick, 2005; Rigby & Bagshaw, 2003; Smith & Shu, 2000), and that adult assistance can exacerbate the problem under some conditions (Smith & Shu, 2000). Until we know more about the effectiveness of different response options and the circumstances under which success is most likely, it is difficult to advise teachers on how to best channel their efforts. In the meantime, a reasonable strategy might be for teachers to consult with victims about possible responses and to follow up about the success of any interventions that are employed.

Teachers generally recognize the multifaceted nature of bullying, are quite concerned about students who are mistreated by their peers, and would like to help if possible. For these reasons, practitioners will often find that school personnel are willing allies in prevention and intervention efforts. Despite their good intentions, teachers may have difficulty reliably detecting victimization in the peer group and most incidents will occur in settings in which adults are not readily present. Even when teachers are aware that a student is experiencing bullying, they might not know how to intercede successfully. Unfortunately, such uncertainty would be well founded given the dearth of available research. Because we know relatively little about what strategies are likely to succeed, practitioners should proceed with caution and be careful not to overstate their confidence in any recommendations offered to school personnel.

Guidelines for Evaluating Other Features of the School Environment

Relationships with adults and peers are important aspects of the school environment. As practitioners strive to prevent victimization in the peer group, they will also need to consider other organizational characteristics of the school context. Schools vary significantly with respect to average class size, size of the student body, ethnic/racial composition, and school attitudes and policies toward aggression. It will be important to assess the impact of these structural features on children's interactions with peers when planning interventions.

Pay Attention to School Size but Recognize That the Available
Findings Are Limited

It seems reasonable to hypothesize that large schools might foster anonymity among students. Under such conditions, vulnerable students might have difficulty establishing protective relationships with peers or adults at school. Large school sizes have also been linked to the development of aggressive behavior problems (Thomas, Bierman, & the Conduct Problems Prevention Research Group, 2006). Nonetheless, the findings regarding school size and victimization in the peer group are not yet decisive. Insofar as we are aware, there are no existing studies of this issue in North American schools. Moreover, research conducted in Israel and Sweden has provided initial evidence that bully–victim problems are equally common in large and small schools (Khoury-Kassabri, Benbenishty, Astor, & Zeira, 2004; Olweus, 1978).

Be Aware That Class Size May Matter

Research on class size has been somewhat more conclusive, although further exploration is clearly needed. In Israel, at least, children in larger classes tended to report higher rates of verbal and physical mistreatment by peers (Khoury-Kassabri et al., 2004). Busy classrooms can provide a management challenge for teachers so that bullying is not well controlled (Atlas & Pepler, 1998). Classrooms with high student-to-teacher ratios might exacerbate these difficulties.

Attend to the Implication of Ethnicity and Race

Teachers and other school personnel should also take into account the student's ethnicity, as well as the ethnic/racial composition of the student body. A disparity in power is inherent in bully–victim relationships (Dodge et al., 1990). The victim often lacks social resources or the capacity for self-defense (Olweus, 1978). Ethnic/racial background could have significant repercussions for the nature of this power imbalance (Graham & Juvonen, 2002). As a function of the weight of numbers, children from groups that are under-represented within a specific school could be at heightened risk for victimization (see Graham, 2006).

Intervening adults also need to bear in mind that the implications of a student's ethnicity will depend on the ethnic composition of the school as a whole. When schools feature a numerical balance among ethnic/racial subgroups, there will be less opportunity for power inequalities to occur. Compared to students in more homogeneous schools, youths who attend diverse schools report that they feel safer, are less lonely, and are victimized at lower rates (Juvonen, Nishina, & Graham, 2006). Thus, ethnic diversity can have a positive impact on efforts to mitigate the incidence of bullying.

Summary Recommendations

Structural factors such as classroom size and ethnic/racial composition of the student body are generally not amenable to change. It will behoove practitioners to incorporate an awareness of such contextual features in their intervention and prevention efforts. For example, programming that targets large classrooms will need to recognize the complexities associated with high student-to-teacher ratios. We believe that particular attention should be focused on the diversity of the school environment given compelling evidence of interactions between a child's own background and the composition of the larger peer group (Graham & Juvonen, 2002).

The Neighborhood and Community as Background Contexts for Intervention
Guidelines for Considering the Role of the Community

Bronfenbrenner's (1979) ecological systems theory holds that the structure of the surrounding community partially determines the functioning of the school, and the nature of peer group interactions within the school. From this perspective, effective intervention and prevention projects must not only include a focus on the school and immediate peer group but also reflect the complexities of the larger community. In fact, we would contend that careful evaluation of the neighborhood and community should be one of the first steps in the design of effective programs.

Assess Community Resources

Economic disadvantage has frequently been implicated in the development of aggression (Dodge, Pettit, & Bates, 1994; Kupersmidt, Griesler, DeRosier, Patterson, & Davis, 1995). Other community variables that may contribute to aggressive behavior include ethnic diversity (Aneshensel & Sucoff, 1996), residential instability (Sampson & Groves, 1989), and exposure to urban violence (Schwartz & Proctor, 2000).

Although there is research on the impact of neighborhood variables on aggression in schools, we know next to nothing about how community factors may play a role in the lives of youths who emerge as frequent victims of bullying. What little knowledge we have comes from a series of studies conducted with over 10,000 Arab and Jewish children attending schools in Israel (Benbenishty, & Astor, 2005; Khoury-Kassabri et al., 2004). In schools that contained large numbers of families from lower socioeconomic backgrounds, children reported relatively high levels of exposure to threats and moderate to serious violence. Other relevant indicators, such as community unemployment rates, were also linked with multiple forms of student-reported violence exposure.

What mechanisms may underlie the potential association between neighborhood economic disadvantage and children's experiences with victimization at school? While no studies have directly examined this question, we suspect that the stressors inherent in impoverished neighborhoods may be contributing factors. In these settings, children are likely to be exposed to shootings and other acts of extreme violence in the neighborhood (e.g., Richters & Martinez, 1993). Their home environments are often harsh and punitive (Dodge et al., 1994). Such experiences produce intense emotions that can interfere with children's developing capacities to manage their own emotions and relate with peers in an adaptive manner (Kelly, Schwartz, Gorman, & Nakamoto, 2008; Schwartz, Dodge, Pettit, & Bates, 1997; Schwartz & Proctor, 2000).

Be Cognizant of Neighborhood Factors That Might Propagate Aggressive Behavior

Interventionists should also be aware that the presence of peers who engage in aggression and other antisocial behaviors is a critical component of the bully–victim dynamic (Hanish, Martin et al., 2005). As we discussed earlier, a vulnerable child will not emerge as a target of mistreatment unless there are potential aggressors in the environment. Neighborhood factors (poverty, instability, unemployment) that are linked to high aggression levels in the school might therefore increase the probability that particular children will become subject to repeated bullying. These contextual features are important to consider even though the attributes of children who emerge as frequent victims of bullying are consistent across different settings (Bellmore, Witkow, Graham, & Juvonen, 2004; Graham & Juvonen, 2002; Hanish & Guerra, 2002; Toblin, Schwartz, Gorman, & Abou-ezzeddine, 2005).

Attend to Links between Community Organization and the Functioning of the School

Practitioners should recognize that the community context might also have implications for the functioning of the school as a whole. Students attending schools in economically advantaged neighborhoods tend to be relatively high achieving (Leventhal & Brooks-Gunn, 2000). The educational outcomes enjoyed by these students might partially reflect schools that have the resources to support educational and social programs. In contrast, schools in more underprivileged communities may need to devote a considerable amount of effort to addressing achievement deficits among their students. With this challenge on their hands, it may be difficult for teachers and administrators to find the time to tackle social problems such as bullying.

Summary Recommendations

As this brief discussion illustrates, the community and neighborhood are powerful contextual influences on the manifestation of bully–victim problems in school peer groups. Interventionists will need to recognize that some neighborhood features (e.g., economic disadvantage) can present significant challenges for the functioning of the school. The organization of the larger community and the surrounding neighborhoods will also have implications for the capacity of educators to participate in prevention or intervention programs. Because practitioners will generally need to work within the constraints of the community setting, it will be necessary to tailor interventions to the unique parameters of each specific environment.

Cultural and Societal Influences on Intervention

The values and beliefs inherent in a child's culture can shape development through an influence on the child's immediate surroundings (e.g., family, school, peer group). Of immediate relevance for bully–victim intervention programs is evidence that cultural values may affect how peers interpret and respond to a child's behavior. For example, consider the implications of shy or inhibited behavior in traditional Chinese cultures. Although such behavioral tendencies have been linked to rejection and victimization in Western settings (Hodges & Perry, 1999; Schwartz et al., 1993), a number of researchers have suggested that inhibited students may be well liked in the Chinese cultural context as a function of the influence of Confucian value systems (Chen, Rubin, & Sun, 1992). Practitioners who seek to mitigate problems related to bullying in schools will need to be alert to such processes.

Guidelines for Considering the Role of Culture
Understand That Bullying Is a Significant Issue across Cultures

A very basic first question that interventionists might consider is whether bully–victim problems occur with significant frequency across cultures. Reflecting, perhaps, the widespread nature of this phenomenon, researchers have focused on peer group victimization in many different cultural contexts (Smith et al., 1999). In each of the examined settings, a subgroup of children emerges as persistent victims of bullying. These findings seem to suggest that victimization in school peer groups is a problem that is not restricted to specific cultures but is more global in nature.

Recognize Conceptual Differences in How Children View Bullying across Cultures

As practitioners seek to develop programming that is culturally sensitive, a complicating factor will be that the behaviors children generally conceptualize as bullying differ across societies. In fact, the terminology used to refer to bullying in different languages varies in the extent to which it incorporates key features such as an imbalance of power in the bully–victim dyad, exclusion or indirect forms of aggression, and nonverbal behaviors (Smith et al., 2002). To complicate matters further, practitioners cannot assume that all children in a specific setting share the same cultural background and perspectives on bullying. Children differ in the degree to which they are oriented to the values of the dominant society (Bukowski & Sippola, 1998). Rather than relying on broad cultural generalities, we suggest that intervening adults may need to pay careful attention to the customs, beliefs, and practices that specific children have experienced.

Be Mindful That the Behaviors Involved in Bullying May Differ across Cultures

Moving beyond the issue of children's conceptualization of what constitutes bullying, a related set of issues focuses on the specific classes of aggression that are involved in bully–victim encounters. Do episodes of bullying involve the same kinds of behaviors across cultures? Both relational (e.g., gossiping, spreading rumors, and exclusion) and overt (e.g., hitting, pushing, verbal insults) subtypes of peer victimization have been observed in Western settings (Crick & Grotpeter, 1995). Nonetheless, it is clear that bullying in North American and European children's peer groups often involves physical aggression (Schwartz et al., 1993). On the other hand, bullying in Asian settings may tend to emphasize more social forms of aggression. In our own work, we have found that such forms of aggression are relatively common for both boys and girls in China and South Korea (Schwartz, Chang, & Farver, 2001; Schwartz, Farver, Chang, & Lee-Shin, 2002). Likewise, children who engage in aversive behavior in Hong Kong primary schools are more likely to be targeted for relational victimization than overt victimization (Tom, Schwartz, & Chang, 2005).

These preliminary findings suggest that relational forms of aggression are particularly likely to be a central aspect of victimization in Asian children's peer groups. If subsequent research confirms this pattern, we would speculate that larger societal influences shape the essential nature of bullying behavior. In some cultural contexts, children may be socialized to have very negative attitudes toward physical aggression. They may perceive relational bullying to be more acceptable than overt subtypes. It may also be the case that potential aggressors in collectivistic cultures view ostracism and exclusion as especially effective forms of bullying.

Identify the Behavioral Correlates of Victimization by Peers within the Cultural Context

Earlier in this chapter, we hypothesized that group norms can have significant implications for how children perceive and respond to the behaviors of their peers. The primary idea is that children who are social misfits and act in ways that do not conform to the norms established by their peers will emerge as targets of rejection and mistreatment (Wright et al., 1986). Based on this perspective, we might expect that, because norms can vary across cultures, the behavioral profiles of frequently bullied children might vary as well. Surprisingly, however, there appears to be considerable consistency in the behavioral attributes of victimized children across settings. In virtually every context examined thus far, the majority of bullied children are submissive, socially withdrawn, and exhibit low levels of prosocial behavior (Boivin et al., 1995; Boulton, 1999; Schwartz et al., 1993, 2002, Schwartz, Chang et al., 2001). Aggression and overreactivity have also been linked to victimization by peers in a number of settings (Hanish & Guerra, 2004; Olweus, 1978; Perry et al., 1988; Schwartz, 2000; Schwartz, Proctor, & Chien, 2001; Xu, Farver, Schwartz, & Chang, 2003).

We must qualify these findings by noting that our conclusions are based on relative comparisons within contexts. Children who are submissive or withdrawn in comparison to their peers are at risk for bullying in many different cultures. Nonetheless, the behaviors that are viewed as submissive in Asian children's peer groups will not necessarily correspond to submissive behavior for North American children. For this reason, we would encourage practitioners to recognize that a persistently victimized child in one setting may not display behavioral tendencies that are identical to victimized children in other settings.

There is also compelling evidence for cross-cultural differences when it comes to children's academic functioning. In North America and Europe, associations between victimization in the peer group and negative academic outcomes are modest (Juvonen, Nishina, & Graham, 2000; Nishina, Juvonen, & Witkow, 2005; Schwartz, Gorman, Nakamoto, & Toblin, 2005; Schwartz et al., 2008). The corresponding effects in Mainland China, South Korea, and Hong Kong appear to be large (Nakamoto & Schwartz, in press). This pattern of findings might reflect the cultural emphasis on achievement in many Asian cultures (Lee & Larson, 2000; Stevenson et al., 1990). Chinese and South Korean children who do poorly in school may be devalued by their peers because of a societal emphasis on academic excellence.

Look for Factors (such as Friendship) That May Protect
Vulnerable Youth in Different Settings

As noted earlier, research conducted in Western settings suggests that friendship can protect vulnerable children from bullying by peers (Hodges et al., 1997; Schwartz et al., 1999). There is some limited evidence for a similar pattern in South Korean and Chinese children's peer groups (Abou-ezzeddine et al., 2007), although we are not yet in a position to make any firm conclusions. The findings that are available highlight the need for practitioners to search for potential buffering mechanisms that are relevant within the cultural context.

Summary Recommendations

It is apparent that victimization in school peer groups is a serious issue in many different cultural contexts. Indeed, we are inclined to believe that this phenomenon is nearly universal in scope. Moreover, there does seem to be some consistency in the behavioral profiles of bullied children across settings, at least on a relative basis. Still, culture remains a powerful background factor that affects the manifestation of bully–victim problems through an influence on more immediate processes (e.g., peer group social norms). We encourage practitioners to carefully assess the sociocultural context and to be aware of the values and beliefs that characterize the involved children.

Concluding Remarks

Bronfenbrenner's (1979) ecological systems theory portrayed development as a process that is shaped by transactions across layers of a child's environment. From this perspective, an understanding of context becomes critical for professionals who seek to reduce the incidence of bully–victim problems in school peer groups. To intervene effectively, the practitioner must consider the immediate social influences in a youth's life (school, peer, family, and neighborhood) as well as dynamic links between each of these aspects of the sociocultural environment. Bronfenbrenner also regarded culture, society, and historical epoch as broader contextual features that impact all aspects of a child's social world.

Guided by Bronfenbrenner's ecological systems model, our objective in this chapter was to present a contextual perspective on intervention and prevention with persistently bullied youths. We sought to consider the role of the peers, teachers, and other adults in the school setting; the structural features of the school, the community, and neighborhood; and the larger cultural backdrop. Our efforts in this regard were complicated by the limited availability of relevant empirical findings. Nonetheless, we have highlighted a number of specific areas that we believe warrant attention from practitioners (see Table 2.1). We hope that these recommendations will facilitate the immediate work of those who seek to develop relevant programs, but we recognize that further testing and development may lead to more refined guidelines.

In our view, systematic consideration of sociocultural environments in which bully–victim problems occur will be a crucial task for interventionists. There will, of course, be a host of difficult issues for both planning and implementation that will need to be surmounted. These potential barriers

Table 2.1.
Key Points Regarding the Sociocultural Context of Bully–Victim Problems

What the practitioner needs to know...
... *about the peer group.*

☑ Victimization can be contingent on the behavior of children who may not appear to be directly involved in bullying but act as reinforcers or bystanders, so be aware of peer reactions to bullying incidents.

☑ Children are more likely to experience victimization in schools where peers are aggressive and group norms support aggression.

☑ Proximity to aggressors increases the risk of children acting aggressively.

☑ Pay attention to children who display atypical behavior styles compared to peer norms. They may be viewed as social misfits and experience victimization.

☑ Friendships can mitigate the risk for victimization. Look carefully for children who lack close friends.

(continued)

Table 2.1
(Continued)

☑ Aggressive friends seem to exacerbate the negative impact of peer victimization, whereas well-adjusted friends appear to have a more ameliorative role.

. . . about teachers and the school.

☑ Most teachers understand the complex nature of bullying.

☑ Bullying can be difficult for school professionals to detect.

☑ Teachers are often uncertain about how and when they should intervene, especially when considering ambiguous school policies, concerns for their own safety, and the risk of current and future harm to the victim.

☑ Teacher responses to bullying can function to decrease conflict in the peer group but may also backfire to the detriment of the victim.

☑ School and class sizes could potentially impact bully–victim problems.

☑ Children from groups who are underrepresented in the classroom may be at heighted risk for victimization.

. . . about the neighborhood.

☑ Growing up in economically disadvantaged neighborhoods may put children at risk for exposure to violence, negative home environments, and other stressors that may negatively impact a child's social and emotional development.

☑ Poverty and related factors may place youth at risk for the development of aggressive behavior.

☑ It can be difficult for teachers and administrators in schools of underprivileged communities to find the time to tackle social problems such as bullying.

. . . about the role of culture.

☑ Peer victimization has been documented in many cultures and is likely a pervasive phenomenon.

☑ Culture and language may impact children's conceptions of bullying.

☑ Cultural norms may influence the behavioral expression of bullying. Where there are strong sanctions on physical aggression, or where great importance is placed on interpersonal relationships, children may choose to aggress by relational, rather than by physical or verbal means.

☑ When children do not behave in line with the values of their culture, they may be at heightened risk for victimization by peers.

☑ Pay attention to different factors, such as friendship, that may protect vulnerable youths in different cultural settings.

notwithstanding, the payoff could be an enhanced understanding of the underlying social processes as well as a strong foundation for intervention efforts.

References

Abou-ezzeddine, T., Schwartz, D., Chang, L., Lee-Shin, Y., Farver, J., & Xu, Y. (2007). Positive peer relationships as moderators of risk for victimization in Chinese and South Korean children's peer groups. *Social Development, 16*, 106–127.

Aneshensel, C. S., & Sucoff, C. A. (1996). The neighborhood context and adolescent mental health. *Journal of Health & Social Behavior, 37*, 293–310.

Arbeau, K.A., & Coplan, R. J. (2007). Kindergarten teachers' beliefs and responses to hypothetical prosocial, asocial, and antisocial children. *Merrill-Palmer Quarterly, 53*, 291–318.

Astor, R. A., Benbenishty, R., & Marachi, R. (2004). Violence in schools. In P. A. Meares (Ed.), *Social work services in schools* (pp. 149–182). Boston: Allyn and Bacon.

Astor, R. A., Meyer, H. A., & Behre, W. J. (1999). Unowned places and times: Maps and interviews about violence in high schools. *American Educational Research Journal, 36*, 3–42.

Atlas, R. S., & Pepler, D. J. (1998). Observations of bullying in the classroom. *The Journal of Educational Research, 92*, 86–97.

Behre, W. J., Astor, R. A., & Meyer, H. A. (2001). Elementary- and middle-school teachers' reasoning about intervening in school violence: An examination of violence-prone school subcontexts. *Journal of Moral Education, 30*, 131–153.

Bellmore, A., Witkow, M., Graham, S., & Juvonen, J. (2004). Beyond the individual: The impact of ethnic context and classroom behavioral norms on victims' adjustment. *Developmental Psychology, 40*, 1159–1172.

Benbenishty, R., & Astor, A. R. (2005). *School violence embedded in context.* New York: Oxford University Press.

Berndt, T. J. (1996). Exploring the effects of friendship quality on social development. In W. M. Bukowski, A. F. Newcomb, & W. W. Hartup (Eds.), *The company they keep: Friendship in childhood and adolescence* (pp. 346–365). New York: Cambridge University Press.

Boivin, M., Dodge, J. D., & Coie, J. D. (1995). Individual-group similarity and peer status in experimental play groups of boys: The social misfit revisited. *Journal of Personality and Social Psychology, 69*, 269–279.

Boivin, M., Hymel, S., & Bukowski, W. M. (1995). The roles of social withdrawal, peer rejection, and victimization by peers in predicting loneliness and depressed mood in children. *Development and Psychopathology, 7*, 765–786.

Boulton, M. J. (1997). Teachers' views on bullying: Definitions, attitudes and ability to cope. *British Journal of Educational Psychology, 67*, 223–233.

Boulton, M. J. (1999). Concurrent and longitudinal relations between children's playground behavior and social preference, victimization, and bullying. *Child Development, 70,* 944–954.

Boulton, M. J., Trueman, M., Chau, C., Whitehand, C. & Amatya, K. (1999). Concurrent and longitudinal links between friendship and peer victimization: Implications for befriending interventions. *Journal of Adolescence, 22,* 461–466.

Bronfenbrenner, U. (1979). *The ecology of human development: Experiments by nature and design.* Cambridge, MA: Harvard University Press.

Bukowski, W. M., & Sippola, L. K. (1998). Diversity and the social mind: Goals, constructs, culture, and development. *Developmental Psychology, 34,* 742–746.

Chang, L. (2004). The role of classroom norms in contextualizing the relations of children's social behaviors to peer acceptance. *Developmental Psychology, 40,* 691–702.

Chen, X., Rubin, K. H., & Sun, Y. (1992). Social reputation and peer relationships in Chinese and Canadian children: A cross-cultural study. *Child Development, 63,* 1336–1343.

Craig, W. M., Henderson, K., & Murphy, J. G. (2000). Prospective teachers' attitudes toward bullying and victimization. *School Psychology International, 21,* 5–21.

Craig, W. M., Pepler, D. J., Atlas, R. (2000). Observations of bullying on the playground and in the classroom. *International Journal of School Psychology, 21,* 22–36.

Crick, N. R., & Grotpeter, J. K. (1995). Relational aggression, gender and social-psychological adjustment. *Child Development, 66,* 710–722.

Dishion, T. J., Andrews, D. W., & Crosby, L. (1995). Antisocial boys and their friends in early adolescence: Relationship characteristics, quality, and interactional processes. *Child Development, 66,* 139–151.

Dishion, T. J., & Dodge, K. A. (2005). Peer contagion in interventions for children and adolescents: moving towards an understanding of the ecology and dynamics of change. *Journal of Abnormal Child Psychology, 33,* 395–400.

Dodge, K. A., Pettit, G. S., & Bates, J. E. (1994). Socialization mediators of the relation between socioeconomic status and child conduct problems. *Child Development, 65,* 649–665.

Dodge, K. A., Price, J. M., Coie, J. D. & Christopoulos, C. (1990). On the development of aggressive dyadic relationships in boys' peer groups. *Human Development, 33,* 260–270.

Espelage, D. L., Holt, M. K., & Henkel, R. R. (2003). Examination of peer-group contextual effects on aggression during early adolescence. *Child Development, 74,* 205–220.

Fekkes, M., Pijpers, F. I. M., & Verloove-Vanhorick, S. P. (2005). Bullying: Who does what, when and where? Involvement of children, teachers and parents in bullying behavior. *Health Education Research, 20,* 81–91.

Frey, K. S., Hirschstein, M. K., Snell, J. L., Van Schoiack Edstrom, L., MacKenzie, E. P., & Broderick, C. J. (2005). Reducing playground bullying and supporting beliefs: An experimental trial of the Steps to Respect Program. *Developmental Psychology, 41*, 479–491.

Graham, S. (2006). Peer victimization in school: Exploring the ethnic context. *Current Directions in Psychological Science, 15*, 317–321.

Graham, S., & Juvonen, J. (2002). Ethnicity, peer harassment and adjustment in middle school: An exploratory study. *Journal of Early Adolescence, 22*, 173–199.

Hanish, L. D., & Guerra, N. G. (2000). Predictors of peer victimization among urban youth. *Social Development, 9*, 521–543.

Hanish, L. D., & Guerra, N. G. (2002). A longitudinal analysis of patterns of adjustment following peer victimization. *Development and Psychopathology, 14*, 69–89.

Hanish, L. D., & Guerra, N. G. (2004). Aggressive victims, passive victims, and bullies: Developmental continuity or developmental change? *Merrill Palmer Quarterly, 50*, 17–38.

Hanish, L. D., Martin, C. L., Fabes, R. A., Leonard, S., & Herzog, M. (2005). Exposure to externalizing peers in early childhood: Homophily and peer contagion processes. *Journal of Abnormal Child Psychology, 33*, 267–281.

Hanish, L. D., Ryan, P., Martin, C. L., & Fabes, R. A. (2005). The social context of young children's peer victimization. *Social Development, 14*, 2–19.

Hartup, W. W. & Stevens, N. (1997). Friendships and adaptation in the life course. *Psychological Bulletin, 121*, 355–370.

Hawkins, D. L., Pepler, D., & Craig, W. M. (2001). Peer interventions in playground bullying. *Social Development, 10*, 512–527.

Hazler, R. J., Miller, D. L., Carney, J. V., & Green, S. (2001). Adult recognition of school bullying situations. *Educational Research, 43*, 133–146.

Hodges, E. V. E., Boivin, M., Vitaro, F., & Bukowski, W. M. (1999). The power of friendship: Protection against an escalating cycle of peer victimization. *Developmental Psychology, 35*, 94–101.

Hodges, E. V. E., Malone, M. J., & Perry, D. G. (1997). Individual risk and social risk as interacting determinants of victimization in the peer group. *Developmental Psychology, 33*, 1032–1039.

Hodges, E. V. E., & Perry, D. G. (1999). Personal and interpersonal antecedents and consequences of victimization by peers. *Journal of Personality and Social Psychology, 76*, 677–685.

Horne, A. M., Orpinas, P., Newman-Carlson, D., & Bartolomucci, C. L. (2004). Elementary school Bully Busters Program: Understanding why children bully and what to do about it. In D. L. Espelage & S. M. Swearer (Eds.), *Bullying in American schools: A social-ecological perspective on prevention and intervention* (pp. 297–325). Mahwah, NJ: Erlbaum.

Houndoumadi, A., & Pateraki, L. (2001). Bullying and bullies in Greek elementary schools: Pupils' attitudes and teachers'/parents' awareness. *Educational Review, 53,* 19–26.

Juvonen, J., Nishina, A., & Graham, S. (2000). Peer harassment, psychological adjustment, and school functioning in early adolescence. *Journal of Educational Psychology, 92,* 349–359.

Juvonen, J., Nishina, A., & Graham, S. (2006). Ethnic diversity and perceptions of safety in urban middle schools. *Psychological Science, 17,* 393–400.

Kelly, B. M., Schwartz, D. Gorman, A. H., & Nakamoto, J. (2008). Community violence exposure and children's subsequent peer rejection: The mediating role of emotion dysregulation. *Journal of Abnormal Child Psychology, 36,* 175–185.

Khoury-Kassabri, M., Benbenishty, R., Astor, R. A. & Zeira, A. (2004). The contributions of community, family, and school variables to student victimization. *American Journal of Community Psychology, 34,* 187–204.

Kupersmidt, J. B., Griesler, P. C., DeRosier, M. E., Patterson, C. J., & Davis, P. W. (1995). Childhood aggression and peer relations in the context of family and neighborhood factors. *Child Development, 66,* 360–375.

Lahey, B. B., Waldman, I. D., & McBurnett, K. (1999). The development of antisocial behavior: An integrative model. *Journal of Child Psychology and Psychiatry and Allied Disciplines, 40,* 669–682.

Laird, R. D., Pettit, G. S., Dodge, K. A., & Bates, J. E. (1999). Best friendships, group relationships, and antisocial behavior in early adolescence. *Journal of Early Adolescence, 19,* 413–437.

Lee, M., & Larson, R. (2000). The Korean 'examination hell': Long hours of studying, distress, and depression. *Journal of Youth and Adolescence, 29,* 249–271.

Leventhal, T. & Brooks-Gunn, J. (2000). The neighborhoods they live in: Effects of neighborhood residence upon child and adolescent outcomes. *Psychological Bulletin, 126,* 309–337.

Limber, S. P. (2004). Implementation of the Olweus Bullying Prevention Program in American schools: Lessons learned from the field. In D. L. Espelage & S. M. Swearer (Eds.), *Bullying in American schools: A social-ecological perspective on prevention and intervention* (pp. 351–363). Mahwah, NJ: Erlbaum.

Meyer, H. A., Astor, R. A., & Behre, W. J. (2004). Teachers' reasoning about school fights, contexts, and gender: An expanded developmental domain approach. *Aggression and Violent Behavior, 9,* 45–74.

Mishna, F., Pepler, D., & Wiener, J. (2006). Factors associated with perceptions and responses to bullying situations by children, parents, teachers, and principals. *Victims and Offenders, 1,* 255–288.

Nakamoto, J. & Schwartz, D. (in press). Is peer victimization associated with academic achievement? A Meta-analytic review. *Social Development.*

Naylor, P., & Cowie, H. (1999). The effectiveness of peer support systems in challenging school bullying: The perspectives and experiences of teachers and pupils. *Journal of Adolescence, 22*, 467–479.

Naylor, P., Cowie, H., Cossin, F., de Bettencourt, R., & Lemme, F. (2006). Teachers' and pupils' definitions of bullying. *British Journal of Educational Psychology, 76*, 553–576.

Nesdale, D., & Pickering, K. (2006). Teachers' reactions to children's aggression. *Social Development, 15*, 109–127.

Newcomb, A. F., & Bagwell, C. L. (1995). Children's friendship relations: A meta-analytic review. *Psychological Bulletin, 117*, 306–347.

Newcomb, A. F., & Bagwell, C. L. (1996). The developmental significance of children's friendship relations. In W. M. Bukowski, A. F. Newcomb, & W. W. Hartup (Eds.), *The company they keep: Friendship in childhood and adolescence* (pp. 289–321). New York: Cambridge University Press.

Nicolaides, S., Toda, Y., & Smith, P. K. (2002). Knowledge and attitudes about school bullying in trainee teachers. *British Journal of Educational Psychology, 72*, 105–118.

Nishina, A., Juvonen, J., & Witkow M. (2005). Sticks and stones may break my bones, but names will make me sick: The consequences of peer harassment. *Journal of Clinical Child and Adolescent Psychology, 34*, 37–48.

Olweus, D. (1978). *Aggression in the schools: Bullies and their whipping boys.* Washington, DC: Hemisphere.

Olweus, D. (2004). Olweus bullying prevention program: Design and implementation issues and a new national initiative in Norway. In P. K. Smith, D. Pepler, & K. Rigby (Eds.), *Bullying in schools: How successful can interventions be?* (pp. 13–36). Cambridge, England: Cambridge University Press.

Parker, J. G., Rubin, K. H., Price, J. M., & DeRosier, M. E. (1995). Peer relationships, child development, and adjustment: A developmental psychopathology perspective. In D. Cicchetti & D. J. Cohen (Eds.), *Developmental psychopathology, Vol. 2: Risk, disorder, and adaptation* (pp. 96–161). New York: Wiley.

Pellegrini, A. D., Bartini, M., & Brooks, F. (1999). School bullies, victims, and aggressive victims: Factors relating to group affiliation and victimization in early adolescence. *Journal of Educational Psychology, 91*, 216–224.

Perry, D. G., Kusel, S. J., & Perry, L. C. (1988). Victims of peer aggression. *Developmental Psychology, 24*, 807–814.

Peterson, L. & Rigby, K. (1999). Countering bullying at an Australian secondary school with students as helpers. *Journal of Adolescence, 22*, 481–492.

Poulin, F., Dishion, T. J., & Haas, E. (1999). The peer influence paradox: Friendship quality and deviancy training within male adolescent friendships. *Merrill-Palmer Quarterly, 45*, 42–61.

Price, J. M. (1996). Friendships of maltreated children and adolescents: Contexts for expressing and modifying relationship history. In W. M. Bukowski, A. F. Newcomb, &

W. W. Hartup (Eds.), *The company they keep: Friendship in childhood and adolescence* (pp. 262–288). New York: Cambridge University Press.

Richters, J. E., & Martinez, P. (1993). The NIMH community violence project: I. Children as victims of and witnesses to violence. In D. Reiss, J. E. Richters, M. Radke-Yarrow, & D. Scharff (Eds.), *Children and violence* (pp. 7–21). New York: Guilford.

Rigby, K., & Bagshaw, D. (2003). Prospects of adolescent students collaborating with teachers in addressing issues of bullying and conflict in schools. *Educational Psychology, 23,* 535–546.

Salmivalli, C. (2001). Group view on victimization: Empirical findings and their implications. In J. Juvonen & S. Graham (Eds.), *Peer harassment in school: The plight of the vulnerable and victimized* (pp. 398–419). New York: Guilford Press.

Salmivalli, C., Kaukiainen, A., Voeten, M., & Sinisammal, M. (2004). Targeting the group as a whole: The Finnish anti-bullying intervention. In P. K. Smith, D. Pepler, & K. Rigby (Eds), *Bullying in schools: How successful can interventions be?* (pp. 251–273). New York: Cambridge University Press.

Salmivalli, C., Lagerspetz, K., Björkqvist, K., Österman, K., & Kaukiainen, A. (1996). Bullying as a group process: Participant roles and their relations to social status within the group. *Aggressive Behavior, 22,* 1–15.

Salmivalli, C., & Voeten, M. (2004). Connections between attitudes, group norms, and behavior in bullying situations. *International Journal of Behavioral Development, 28,* 246–258.

Sampson, R. J. & Groves, W. B. (1989). Community structure and crime: Testing social-disorganization theory. *American Journal of Sociology, 94,* 774–780.

Schwartz, D. (2000). Subtypes of victims and aggressors in children's peer groups. *Journal of Abnormal Child Psychology, 28,* 181–192.

Schwartz, D., Chang, L., & Farver, J. M. (2001). Correlates of victimization in Chinese children's peer groups. *Developmental Psychology, 37,* 520–532.

Schwartz, D., Dodge, K. A., & Coie, J. D. (1993). The emergence of chronic peer victimization in boys' play groups. *Child Development, 67,* 1755–1772.

Schwartz, D., Dodge, K. A., Pettit, G. S., & Bates, J. E. (1997). The early socialization of aggressive victims of bullying. *Child Development, 68,* 665–675.

Schwartz, D., Dodge, K. A., Pettit, G. S., Bates, J. E., & the Conduct Problems Prevention Research Group (2000). Friendship as a moderating factor in the pathway between early harsh home environment and later victimization in the peer group. *Developmental Psychology, 36,* 646–662.

Schwartz, D., Farver, J. M., Chang, L., Lee-Shin, Y. (2002). Victimization in South Korean children's peer groups. *Journal of Abnormal Child Psychology, 32,* 113–125.

Schwartz, D., Gorman, A. H., Dodge, K. A., Pettit, G. S., & Bates, J. E. (2008). Friendships with peers who are low or high in aggression as moderators of the link between peer victimization and declines in academic functioning. *Journal of Abnormal Child Psychology, 36,* 719–730.

Schwartz, D., Gorman, A. H., Nakamoto, J., & Toblin, R. L. (2005). Victimization in the peer group and children's academic functioning. *Journal of Educational Psychology, 97*, 425–435.

Schwartz, D., McFadyen-Ketchum, S. A., Dodge, K. A., Pettit, G. S., & Bates, J. E. (1998). Peer victimization as a predictor of behavior problems at home and in school. *Development and Psychopathology, 10*, 87–100.

Schwartz, D., McFadyen-Ketchum, S. A., Dodge, K. A., Pettit, G. S., & Bates, J. E. (1999). Early behavior problems as a predictor of later peer group victimization: Moderators and mediators in the pathways of social risk. *Journal of Abnormal Child Psychology, 27*, 191–201.

Schwartz, D., & Proctor, L. J. (2000). Community violence exposure and children's social adjustment in the school peer group: The mediating roles of emotion regulation and social cognition. *Journal of Consulting and Clinical Psychology, 68*, 670–683.

Schwartz, D., Proctor, L. J., & Chien, D. (2001). The aggressive victim of bullying: Emotional and behavioral dysregulation as a pathway to victimization by peers. In J. Juvonen & S. Graham (Eds.), *School-based peer harassment: The plight of the vulnerable and victimized* (pp. 147–174). New York: Guilford Press.

Schwartz, D., Toblin, R. L., Abou-ezzeddine, T., Tom, S., & Stevens, K. I. (2005). Difficult home environments and the development of aggressive victims of bullying. In. K. Kendall-Tackett & S. Giacomoni (Eds.), *Child victimization: Maltreatment, bullying and dating violence; prevention and intervention* (pp. 11.2–11.9). Kingston, NJ: Civic Research Institute.

Smith, P. K., Cowie, H., Olafsson, R. F., Liefooghe, A. P. D., Almeida, A., Araki, H., et al. (2002). Definitions of bullying: A comparison of terms used, and age and gender differences, in a fourteen-country international comparison. *Child Development, 73*, 1119–1133.

Smith, P. K., Morita, Y., Junger-Tas, J., Olweus, D., Catalano, R., & Slee, P. (1999). *The nature of school bullying: A cross-national perspective*. London: Routledge.

Smith, P. K., & Shu, S. (2000). What good schools can do about bullying: Findings from a survey in English schools after a decade of research and action. *Childhood: A Global Journal of Child Research, 7*, 193–212.

Stevenson, H. W., Lee, S., Chen, C., Lummis, M., Stigler, J., Fan, L., et al. (1990). Mathematics achievement of children in China and the United States. *Child Development, 61*, 1053–1066.

Stormshak, E. A., Bierman, K. L., Bruschi, C., Dodge, K. A., Coie, J. D., & Conduct Problems Prevention Research Group. (1999). The relation between behavior problems and peer preference in different classroom contexts. *Child Development, 70*, 169–182.

Sutton, J., & Smith, P. K. (1999). Bullying as a group process: An adaptation of the participant role approach. *Aggressive Behavior, 25*, 97–111.

Thomas, D. E., Bierman, K. L., & the Conduct Problems Prevention Research Group. (2006). The impact of classroom aggression on the development of aggressive behavior problems in children. *Development and Psychopathology, 18*, 471–487.

Toblin, R. L, Schwartz, D., Gorman, A. H., & Abou-ezzeddine, T. (2005). Social-cognitive and behavioral attributes of aggressive victims of bullying. *Journal of Applied Developmental Psychology, 26*, 325–346.

Tom, S. R., Schwartz, D., & Chang, L. (2005, April). Victimization in Hong Kong children's peer groups. In D. Schwartz (Chair), *Correlates of acceptance/rejection, and peer victimization for Chinese children: Evidence from research conducted across contexts.* Symposium presented at the Biennial Meetings of the Society for Research in Child Development, Atlanta, GA.

Whitney, I., & Smith, P. K. (1993). A survey of the nature and extent of bullying in junior/ middle and secondary schools. *Educational Research, 35*, 3–25.

Wright, J. C., Giammarino, M., & Parad, H. W. (1986). Social status in small groups: Individual-group similarity and the social "misfit." *Journal of Personality and Social Psychology, 50*, 523–536.

Xu, Y., Farver, J. M., Schwartz, D., & Chang, L. (2003). Identifying aggressive victims in Chinese children's peer groups. *International Journal of Behavioral Development, 27*, 243–253.

Yoon, J. S. (2004). Predicting teacher interventions in bullying situations. *Education and Treatment of Children, 27*, 37–45.

Yoon, J. S., & Kerber, K. (2003). Bullying: Elementary teachers' attitudes and intervention strategies. *Research in Education, 69*, 27–35.

Zeira, A., Astor, R. A., & Benbenishty, R. (2004). School violence in Israel: Perceptions of homeroom teachers. *School Psychology International, 25*, 149–166.

3

A Child-by-Environment Framework for Planning Interventions with Children Involved in Bullying

Becky Kochenderfer-Ladd and Gary W. Ladd

Curtis was an 8th grade honors student. For over 3 years, almost on a weekly basis, Curtis came home from school in tears. Students banged his head against a locker or tripped him in the hallways. They knocked things out of his hands, and when he picked them up, they knocked them down again. His favorite books were stolen, and kids poured chocolate milk on his favorite shirt. His bicycle had been vandalized twice and the name-calling grew worse every day. When he had a broken foot, the other kids kicked the cast. One day Curtis went to a school counselor, extremely upset and talking about suicide. The counselor reported talking to Curtis until he seemed calmer and sent him home with some literature and the number of a suicide hotline. They were supposed to meet the next morning. That night, 14-year-old Curtis went to his bedroom and shot himself to death. He was found by his 5-year-old brother. (Adapted from Greene, 1993)

Jared High was 12 years old when older students bullied him in his middle school. The bullying came to a head when a well-known bully assaulted Jared inside his middle school gym. Because of the bullying and the assault, Jared began to show signs of depression, which included lack of sleep and emotional outbursts. On the morning of September 29, 1998, just 6 days after his 13th birthday, Jared called his father at work to say good-bye. While on the phone with him, Jared shot himself, dying instantly. (http://www.bullypolice.org/brenda.html)

In these sad, and unfortunately true, stories of Curtis Taylor and Jared High, we see the pain and suffering of children who are forced to face bullies every day at school with no hope of relief and with no person with whom they can share their pain. We also see the serious consequences of years of abuse. Although not all victimized children commit suicide, untold numbers do or are depressed enough to think about it or attempt it (see http://www.bullypolice.org, founded by Brenda High).

This is all the more alarming when one considers that peer abuse begins early in children's school careers and, for some, persists over many years. For example, we (Kochenderfer & Ladd, 1996a) estimated that about 20% to 23% of kindergarten children experience moderate to severe victimization, and in a subsequent study, we followed these children into 3rd grade and found that between 5% to 10% had been chronically abused during this time period (Kochenderfer-Ladd & Wardrop, 2001). Moreover, although the percent of children who are bullied appears to decline with age (e.g., 20%–23% of elementary school children compared to 5% to 13% of middle and high school students; Craig, 1997; Ladd & Kochenderfer-Ladd, 2002; Nansel et al., 2001), the stability of victimization increases. For example, in a longitudinal study in which we followed children from kindergarten to 3rd grade, the 12-month stability coefficients that were calculated across grades increased from .24 to .41 (Kochenderfer-Ladd, 2003). Moreover, for children ages 9 to 12, stability coefficients have been found to increase from .30 and .71 (Boivin, Hymel & Bukowski, 1995; Hawker, 1997).

As reflected in the real-life examples of Curtis and Jared, children who are regularly targeted by bullies are at risk for severe psychological adjustment problems, including loneliness, depression, anxiety, and low self-esteem (see Hawker & Boulton, 2000, for a meta-analytic review). In addition, victimized children are also at risk for school problems, including absenteeism, truancy, dropping out, and the development of negative school attitudes (Kochenderfer & Ladd, 1996a, 1996b; Reid, 1989; Slee, 1994).

Child and Environment Model

Child and environment models have guided much of our research and we have organized the contents of this chapter in a way that is consistent with this perspective. We believe that frameworks of this type are not only valuable for hypothesis generation but are also useful for organizing what is known about bullying and victimization, and for guiding the development of individual and school-wide interventions or prevention programs for children. Specifically, a child and environment model, such as the one shown in Figure 3.1, draws attention to many aspects of the child and his or her social environments that

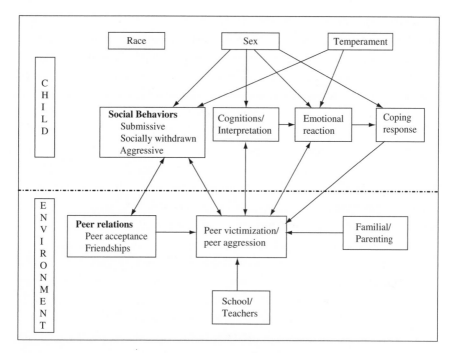

Figure 3.1 Child-by-environment model of school bullying.

may need to be considered when planning interventions that are designed to stop the cycle of bullying and victimization.

In the following sections, we will consider each aspect of the model, beginning with child characteristics that have been linked with victimization, and then turning to environmental factors that may increase or decrease the likelihood that children will become involved in bulling or victimizing interactions. It is our contention that the variables depicted in the model, and the pathways that link these variables, are suggestive of opportunities for intervention, or junctures where it may be beneficial to focus intervention efforts. For example, consider the interaction of the child and his or her environment, which is reflected in the cyclical relationships between children's exposure to peer aggression, their cognitive and emotional responses to victimization, and their subsequent coping responses. In this context, the child's coping strategies are likely to be successful or unsuccessful at reducing victimization and, therefore, instrumental in determining whether cycles of bullying and victimization are sustained or repeated. Thus, if this model were used to guide prevention efforts, it would suggest that it is important to focus on how children respond to bullying episodes (e.g., the child's cognitive interpretations and emotional reactivity) and how these reactions lead children to construct more or less competent or effective coping responses. Furthermore, the model highlights a variety of sources, including prior experiences with peers, familial or parenting practices, as well as child characteristics, such as race or sex that should be considered when planning intervention strategies with individual children.

Child Characteristics

In this section, we present evidence linking children's social behaviors, temperament/emotionality, and social cognitions to vulnerability for bullying and peer victimization. In addition, we discuss several issues that need to be considered when coaching children in how to cope or respond to aggressive peers.

Sex of Child

Research on sex differences provides little evidence for the belief that boys are more likely to be victimized than girls; rather, established prevalence rates appear similar for both sexes (Alsaker & Valkanover, 2001; Charach, Pepler & Ziegler, 1995; Perry, Hodges, & Egan, 2001; Underwood, 2003). Moreover, while there is some evidence to suggest that boys and girls might be at risk for different types of victimization, the overall pattern of findings is mixed. Nevertheless, when sex differences are detected it appears that bullies are more likely to use physical aggression against boys and indirect, or social forms of, aggression against girls (Crick & Bigbee, 1998). In contrast to these findings, however, Kochenderfer and Ladd (1997) found that among severely victimized children, both boys and girls were equally at risk for multiple types of aggression, including physical, verbal, indirect, and general forms of teasing (i.e., "getting picked on"). Thus, when considering the sex of child when intervening in bullying situations, it may be less important to consider dimensions such as prevalence or frequency than it is to consider what constitutes socially appropriate forms of behavior within boys and girls groups. That is, as we discuss later, some forms of coping strategies are more or less likely to be effective for boys and girls.

Social Behavioral Risk Factors

While great care is needed to avoid blaming victims for their abuse, researchers have found that some children are more vulnerable to bullying because of their behavioral tendencies. For example, as reviewed below, submissiveness, withdrawn behavior, and aggression have all been linked to the emergence and stability of victimization. Still, it is important to note that not all children who display these behaviors are bullied—nor do all victims evidence these behavioral propensities—but rather it is the interaction between children's characteristics and features of their social milieu (e.g., permissive, "bully-friendly" environments; Olweus, 1991) that makes some children especially vulnerable to peer abuse.

Submissive, Passive Victims

With the cautionary note presented above, consider the following case of a 9-year-old victimized boy:

> I try hard not to catch his eye in class, but it's like he's pulling me, it's an awful feeling. I'm helpless and when I do look at him he gives me this look and I know what it'll be like at recess, and what's going to happen to my lunch money. (Ross, 1996)

Here we see a boy who is unable to defend himself against a bully who has been persistently harassing him during recess (apparently an unattended or unmonitored area) and taking his lunch money. In all likelihood, he has long given up fighting to retain his money, and instead he surrenders it quickly in the hope that doing so will bring an end to his pain and humiliation. This is a typical view of victims—that is, victims are portrayed as children who are passive and quick to give into bullies' demands. In fact, researchers do find that nonaggressive victims are more common than aggressive victims (of whom we will turn to later; Ladd & Kochenderfer-Ladd, 2002; Olweus, 1978, Schwartz, 2000). Not only are such victims submissive, but they also tend to be socially withdrawn (Gazelle, 1999; Ladd & Burgess, 1999; Perry, Kusel, & Perry, 1988; Schwartz et al., 1998); moreover, these behavioral tendencies predict increases in victimization over time (Hodges & Perry, 1999; Schwartz, Dodge, & Coie, 1993).

It has been argued that bullies seek out submissive and socially withdrawn children because they are "easy marks" and do not pose much threat of retaliation or getting them into trouble (Perry, Willard, & Perry, 1990; Veenstra et al., 2007). Such arguments are supported by observational data, including observational research on the causes of aggression. Patterson, Littman, and Bricker (1967), for example, found that aggressive children sought out targets who would acquiesce to their demands, who rewarded them with signs of distress, and who would not fight back.

Furthermore, socially withdrawn children may be vulnerable to being bullied because of their social isolation. However, it is not always clear which comes first, the solitary behavior or the victimization. On one hand, socially withdrawn children may be especially vulnerable because, as they are often alone and have no friends who can defend them, they are "easy marks" for bullies (Hodges, Malone, & Perry, 1997). For example, in his column about Curtis Taylor, Bob Greene (1993) reports:

> . . . He didn't really have any friends to turn to; in fact, once when he did make friends, they soon joined the group of kids who were tormenting him. He blamed himself for the other kids not liking him, and he did not like himself very much . . .

But it is unlikely that simply being alone leaves children open to peer harassment. Instead, it is more likely that socially withdrawn children also emanate an anxious vulnerability that makes them attractive targets to bullies (Perry et al., 1988).

On the other hand, it is not difficult to imagine that a child who once was socially outgoing would either withdraw from peers after being bullied or would be forced into isolation because peers were afraid to associate with them out of fear of being bullied themselves. For example, in the following case, we see an early maturing girl who is not only being victimized because of her new physical maturity, but who is also being isolated from girls who feared being harassed in a similar fashion. In this case, social withdrawal, or solitude, seems to be a consequence rather than an antecedent of bullying.

> Marie began developing physically more quickly than her classmates. Older students who rode the school bus with her began to tease her about her development and told her she was getting bustier than her classmates because she wanted sex. They teased her about being sexual, calling her "horny" and "whore." Other female students began to avoid her, so they wouldn't be teased in a similar fashion, and they told Marie to leave them alone because they didn't want to be around someone who wanted sex. Marie had no way to defend herself against these attacks, and felt alone and isolated. (Ross, 1996)

Aggressive Victims versus Bully Victims

Though the majority of victims tend to be characterized by submissive/withdrawn social behavior, a proportion of victims have been identified as aggressive victims or as bully victims (Kochenderfer-Ladd, 2003; Perry et al., 1988; Schwartz, Dodge, Pettit, & Bates, 1997). It is important for those intervening with bullies and victims to be aware of the distinction between aggressive victims and bully victims because it is likely that differences exist in the causes of their behavior and in the types of intervention strategies that would be effective with each type of child. To highlight the differences, we describe two hypothetical boys: Joshua, an 8-year-old aggressive victim whose aggression is in response to being victimized, and Aaron, a 12-year-old who was a bully victim when he was 10 years old who bullied to regain a sense of control.

> *Joshua*: "Well, there are a lot of mean kids at school. They come out on the playground just looking for a fight. They grab my backpack or whatever I have with me—and if I don't have anything for them to mess with, they start saying horrible things to me. I don't want to fight them, but I have to—it is the only way to get them to stop."

> *Aaron*: "When I was 10, I was really small—I mean even smaller than the girls. Kids would call me all kinds of names about being "puny" and they thought it was a lot of fun to pick on me and beat me up because I couldn't fight back—I wouldn't stand a chance. I hated it. So whenever they beat me up real bad, I would find some kid even smaller than me—like in kindergarten or something—and really let him have it. But, the next year, I was a lot bigger and no one beat me up anymore; so I stopped bullying small kids."

As can be seen by comparing these two cases, the biggest distinction is between whether the boys' aggression is reactive (i.e., response to provocation) or proactive (i.e., cold, calculated, aimed at obtaining a goal). In fact, in cases such as Joshua's, his willingness to use aggression may have identified him as a potential target. For example, Olson (1992) found that children who initiated aggressive peer interactions at the onset of preschool subsequently emerged as the recipients of peers' *unprovoked* aggression; that is, they became actively victimized and their own aggression became mostly reactive in nature. Moreover, aggressive victims tend to be more restless, disagreeable, disruptive, argumentative, hot-tempered, and emotionally dysregulated than other groups of children (see Kumpulainen et al, 1998; Olweus, 1978; Perry, Hodges, & Egan, 2001; Schwartz, Proctor, & Chien, 2001). In turn, these aversive social behaviors incite other children to respond to them with hostility and aggression (Perry, Perry, & Kennedy, 1992; Pope & Bierman, 1999; Schwartz et al., 2001). Aggressive victims' difficulty regulating their intense emotions often is manifested in the form of uncontrolled angry outbursts, and these outbursts often serve to escalate conflict and prolong aggressive interactions. Thus, aggressive victims have been referred to as "ineffectual aggressors," "high conflict victims," or even "provocative victims" because they appear to provoke their aggressors and reward bullies with signs of emotional distress and ineffective counterattacks (Olweus, 1978; Perry et al., 1990). Thus, when intervening with an aggressive victim, such as Joshua, the foci may be on identifying the source of his impulsivity, helping him control his emotions, and finding other, more socially appropriate and less attention-provoking ways of responding to bullies.

In contrast, bullies and bully victims share the common feature of using proactive aggression to gain control, power, and tangible rewards from their victims. In other words, bullies and bully victims are intentional in their use of aggression, carefully selecting their targets and organizing their attacks (see Bijttebier & Vertommen, 1998; Perry et al., 1990). As with bullies in general, it is important to identify: *(1)* the underlying cause of aggressive behavior, *(2)* the need that they are trying to fulfill, or *(3)* the objectives that they are trying to achieve.

Temperament, Emotional Arousability, and Regulation

Children's emotionality has also been linked to peer victimization. In particular, when intervening with bullies and victims, special attention needs to be given to children's emotional reactivity—that is, how quickly and intensely individuals feel emotions—as well as their ability to regulate or control their emotions (emotion regulation skills). Investigators find that these two components interact with each other in ways that may be either adaptive or maladaptive (Eisenberg et al., 1993; Rubin, Coplan, Fox, & Calkins, 1995). For example, children who are high on emotional reactivity but can regulate, or control, their intense emotion tend to be better adjusted than children who are highly reactive but have difficulty regulating their emotions. Moreover, it is these latter children who tend to be victimized because they experience "debilitating emotional arousal" (e.g., Rubin, Bukowski, & Parker, 1998); that is, these children are not only high on emotional reactivity, but they also have difficulty regulating their emotions (Schwartz et al., 2001). Furthermore, emotional dysregulation has been implicated in the stability of the harassment because bullies tend to find victimized children's emotional displays reinforcing (Perry et al., 1990).

In addition to emotional reactivity and regulation, our own research suggests that it is also important to consider the type of emotion that victims are experiencing. In other words, it is not sufficient to know that a child is overwhelmed emotionally, but we need to know if they are beset by fear, anger, embarrassment, and so forth. For instance, we found that not only do victimized children experience more intense negative emotional reactions (e.g., fear and anger) to peer aggression than infrequently victimized, or nonvictimized peers, but the type of emotional response predicts whether they use adaptive or maladaptive coping strategies (Kochenderfer-Ladd, 2004). For example, bullied children who reported feeling scared or embarrassed were more likely to seek advice, which, in turn, predicted conflict resolution, reduction in peer victimization, and fewer internalizing problems. In contrast, those who reported feeling angry were not only less likely to ask for help, but they were also more likely to seek revenge, which was, in turn, associated with increases in victimization. Moreover, anger was the most common emotional response to peer harassment across sex (i.e., for both boys and girls) and age (kindergarten through 5th graders). Thus, children who are bullied may need to learn how to control their anger and refrain from revenge-seeking coping responses. They may need to be trained in to use other strategies, such as conflict resolution, ignoring or walking away, or seeking adult intervention.

Social Cognitions

Researchers have also investigated whether victims have dysfunctional ways of viewing themselves, their peers, or their interactions with peers (see Ladd, 2005). Specifically, it has posited that victimization may be related to differences in the ways children interpret and respond to peers' social behaviors. Consistent with this proposition, Schwartz et al. (1998) found that aggressive victims tend to display hostile attributional biases; that is, they interpret ambiguous events as hostile. For instance, when a child is hit with a ball and there are no obvious clues about the intent of the child who threw the ball, he assumes it was done purposefully to hurt him as opposed to assuming that it was an accident. However, it is reasonable to suspect that, after being repeatedly excluded and victimized, children come to see danger even when it is not present. In other words, because peers often do intend to harm these children, intervention efforts may need to focus on encouraging children to make positive, or at least benign, interpretations of peers' intentions so as to prevent the development of hostile attribution biases (cf., Hudley & Graham, 1993).

In comparison, there is little evidence to suggest that nonaggressive victims suffer from these types of information-processing errors. Thus, it is not clear if nonaggressive victims hold any particular biases. However, in young children, anxious social withdrawal, a characteristic of many nonaggressive victims, has been linked with *under*attributing peer hostile intent, whereas social withdrawal due to peer exclusion has been associated with hostile attribution biases (Harrist, Zaia, Bates, Dodge, & Pettit, 1997).

It may also be beneficial to incorporate into interventions procedures that help victims develop constructive attributions about why they have been targeted for peer abuse. Specifically, attribution theory maintains that when individuals experience certain events, especially unexpected or undesirable ones, they are motivated to search for rationale to explain why such those events, or outcomes, occurred (Weiner, 1986). Applying an attribution theory framework to the study of peer victimization, Graham and Juvonen (1998, 2001) focused on two distinct patterns of attribution that victimized children tend to endorse as explanations for their harassment. Specifically, they examined a pattern of characterological self-blame (CSB) that consists of causes based on internal, stable, and uncontrollable characteristics (e.g., because of "how I am"; such as being weak or small) and another pattern referred to as behavioral self-blame (BSB) that involves internal, unstable, controllable causes (e.g., because of something "I did"). Rather than finding that victims tended to endorse characterological or behavioral characteristics more frequently, they found victims endorsed both self-blaming attributions more than nonvictims and that self-blame was associated with more internalizing problems (i.e., loneliness, anxiety).

In another study examining the attributions of victimized children, Clifford (2008) found that children made a variety of attributions that were atypical of those found on existing measures—and that did not fit easily into the categories of attributions defined within classic attribution theory (i.e., locus of control, stability, or controllability). Specifically, she asked 4th grade children open-ended questions regarding why they might be disliked or picked on by peers and created a Likert-scale measure from their responses. She found that children's responses factored consistently (over a 2-year period) into five content areas: (1) jealousy (e.g., because the other kid is jealous of me); (2) mutual antipathy (e.g., because we do not like each other); (3) behavior (e.g., because I did something stupid), (4) not being cool (e.g., because I do not wear cool clothes); and (5) being different (e.g., because I look different from them). Moreover, consistent with her hypothesis that children's attributions tell us something about their perceived status within the peer group—or the degree to which they feel apart of the peer group (belongingness hypothesis; see Baumeister & Leary, 1995). Clifford (2008) found that attributions reflecting a low sense of belonging (i.e., not being cool) were associated with higher levels of loneliness. In contrast, those reflecting high status (i.e., jealousy) or neutral status (i.e., mutual antipathy) predicted lower expressed loneliness. Interestingly, while a direct positive path was found from "being different" to loneliness, if children believed they are picked on because of differences that also lead them to think their peers were jealous of them, such attributions reduced their risk for loneliness.

These findings suggest that children have beliefs about why they might be victimized, whether accurate or not, that could be used to guide interventions. For instance, efforts could either being aimed at *(1)* altering the attributions to be more accurate, *(2)* replacing personal or especially hurtful attributions with more benign ones, or *(3)* modifying the cause to lessen the risk for being bullied or teased. For example, while collecting data in an elementary school, one of the teachers shared with us that a boy in her class had been harassed because he wore suspenders (a cause that could possibly fall in the category of "not being cool"; see Clifford, 2008). Although his mother was reluctant to let her son go to school without suspenders because she feared his pants would fall down, she finally agreed. The teacher was happy to report not only did his pants not fall down, but the other kids stopped teasing him.

Coping Strategies

There is a growing body of research on children's strategies for coping with bullying. Moreover, victimized children do not appear to be limited in the variety of strategies they employ. For instance, Smith, Shu, and Madsen (2001) found that victimized children report crying, telling bullies to stop, and asking an adult or friend for assistance; however, all these strategies were associated with greater frequency and duration of their peer victimization. In comparison, Kochenderfer and Ladd (1997) found that certain strategies, such as "having a friend help" and "fighting back," altered the probability of future victimization. In particular, boys who reported seeking help from a friend were less likely to suffer further victimization, whereas those who responded by fighting back were more likely to remain victimized.

Unfortunately, researchers have found that even the use of socially appropriate or typically effective coping strategies is not sufficient to ensure reduced risk for victimization. For example, Kochenderfer-Ladd and Skinner (2002) found that, although problem solving, cognitive distancing, and seeking support were effective strategies among children reporting low levels of victimization, these same strategies appeared ineffective among frequently victimized children. Such findings highlight the need to monitor the effectiveness of coping strategies for victimized children. This is especially critical as researchers tend to recommend strategies that have been shown to reduce bullying in their overall samples rather than focusing on what works for severely victimized children. For example, Salmivalli, Karhunen, and Lagerspetz (1996) found that among 12- to 13-year-old boys, "nonchalance" was effective at deterring future victimization; however, it was not clear if the most severely victimized children were as successful at acting nonchalantly as their less frequently victimized peers.

Moderators of Coping: Sex

As noted earlier, the effectiveness of coping strategies appears to depend on the sex of the victim and the severity of the harassment. In fact, main effects of coping on reducing risk for future victimization are rare—in almost every study, either sex or victimization severity—or both—moderate main effects. It has been suggested that the effectiveness of various coping strategies is linked to socially appropriate or sex-typed expectations for boys and girls (Kochenderfer-Ladd & Skinner, 2002). For example, boys may not only be expected to handle bullying incidences alone, but efforts to discuss victimization and to seek assistance may be met with reproach or disapproval. In comparison, girls tend to be socialized to focus and rely on their relationships (Maccoby & Jacklin, 1974); thus, sharing painful experiences and talking about how it made them feel might be more acceptable and adaptive for females.

Moderators of Coping: Severity of Victimization

Similarly, the effectiveness of children's strategies has been linked to the severity of their victimization. In other words, when intervening with bullied children, it is critical to remember that they are dealing with less controllable, more severe types of peer abuse than children who experience transient or less harmful forms of harassment. Moreover, victimized children differ in the social resources (i.e., peer reputations, social power or influence, social skills) they have to respond to bullies. For although problem solving reduces victimization for most children, among severely *victimized* children, problem solving is associated with stable victimization and peer rejection (Kochenderfer-Ladd & Skinner, 2002). Unfortunately, it is not clear whether victims' coping is ineffective because of their lower group status or if it is because they implement them ineffectually. For instance, Perry, Willard, and Perry (1990) contend that victimized children are not very influential in their peer relations; that is, they do not hold much sway over their peers or pose much threat to their persecutors. Moreover, when responding to peer abuse, they tend to react either too passively or too aggressively (Perry et al., 1992; Schwartz et al., 2001). Thus, victimized children tend to either implement strategies ineffectively or use inappropriate strategies. In so doing, others may erroneously believe that they are *provoking* the abuse as opposed to trying to stop it—and when victims are perceived to cause their own harassment, children are less sympathetic and tend to hold such victims in low regard (Graham & Juvonen, 1998, 2001). Consequently, victimized children may need special coaching on how to implement recommended strategies, as well as social supports that will empower them to influence peers. For example, adults need to back up victimized children's attempts to stop bullying on their own by providing serious consequences to children who refuse to stop bullying.

Moderators of Coping: Sex by Severity of Bulling

Because sex by severity of bullying interaction effects are typically found when examining the effectiveness of coping strategies, the following sections deal with these two special considerations in tandem. Moreover, we also make special note of findings in which, although a particular coping strategy may not necessarily reduce vulnerability to harassment, it nevertheless has been linked with healthier psychological adjustment.

Consistent with the argument that boys are expected to deal with peer conflicts alone, Kochenderfer-Ladd and Skinner (2002) found that victimized boys who attempted to resolve peer problems on their own were less lonely and reported fewer social problems, whereas those who sought social support tended to be more lonely. Moreover, victimized boys who seek social support are more likely to experience peer rejection (Chung & Asher, 1996). However, for *nonvictimized* boys, seeking social support was linked with greater peer preference (Kochenderfer-Ladd & Skinner, 2002). It is possible that the assistance victimized boys receive differs either qualitatively or quantitatively from that obtained by nonvictimized boys. For example, investigators have reported that nonvictimized and victimized boys vary in their access to supportive peers (e.g., protective friends; see Hodges, Boivin, Vitaro, & Bukowski, 1999) or sympathetic, helpful adults (Hoover, Oliver, & Hazler, 1992). Thus, it can not be assumed that victimized boys have social networks that will support their attempts to seek help.

In contrast to findings for victimized boys, Kochenderfer-Ladd and Skinner (2002) found that seeking social support by asking for help and advice protected victimized girls from social problems (i.e., being clingy or not getting along with peers). Thus, intervention efforts that identify factors that may prevent victimized girls from seeking assistance may prove helpful. For instance, are they lacking supportive peers and adults? If so, would they be willing or able to take advantage of intervention programs that included a social support system—or are there other obstacles preventing them from using this strategy?

Although some researchers have found that acting nonchalantly is effective at reducing subsequent victimization (Salmivalli et al., 1996), our own research suggests that this is primarily true for children who are infrequently harassed, but not for severely victimized boys (Kochenderfer-Ladd & Skinner, 2002). Moreover, emotional distancing does not appear to be effective at buffering victims from maladjustment. For example, victimized boys who reported distancing coping exhibited greater signs of anxiety. It could be surmised that victimized boys who try to convince themselves that their peer problems "are no big deal" or "don't matter" are nonetheless aware of the likelihood of future abuse, as well as their inability to prevent its occurrence. As a result, such feelings of helplessness while anticipating the next attack could conceivably be manifested as depressed and anxious behaviors. Likewise, girls who used this strategy were lonelier and evidenced greater social problems than those who did not. It was suggested that by pretending peer problems do not happen, girls may be precluded from sharing their experiences with others, thereby missing the opportunity to have such experiences validated. Alternatively, if distancing coping replaced attempts to prevent future difficulties, these girls may have inadvertently intensified such problems.

However, despite being associated with greater anxiety for boys, distancing appeared to protect victimized boys from peer rejection. In other words, Kochenderfer-Ladd and Skinner (2002) found that by downplaying the seriousness of peer conflicts or pretending nothing happened, victimized boys who reported distancing were as well liked as *non*victimized boys who coped in this manner. This finding suggests that boys may be expected to act nonchalantly, or unaffected, in the face of difficult peer interactions (i.e., "save face") and the greater social preference attained could be interpreted as peer approval for how these victimized boys handled peer conflicts. Still, until further studies are conducted on the effectiveness of distancing for coping with peer conflicts, this potential buffering benefit needs to be weighed against the potential for exacerbating boys' risk for anxiety or depression.

Although it seems reasonable to speculate that aggressive responses to bullying may be acceptable or adaptive for boys, no support was found for such a hypothesis. In fact, "fighting back" tends to contribute to the chronicity or escalation of bullying (e.g., Kochenderfer & Ladd, 1997). Thus, rather than being adaptive, it could be that by "losing one's cool" and getting angry, boys may deny sympathetic peers the opportunity to show their support of a perceived injustice.

Although somewhat ignored by researchers thus far, there are many other ways that children may cope to either reduce their risk for future victimization and/or allow them to maintain a healthy sense of self-worth and belonging in the face of harassment. For example, counselors and practitioners may need to suggest immediate behavioral coping strategies that are specific to peer victimization, such as staying clear of bully hangouts (e.g., unattended restrooms, remote playground areas) or seeking out areas near safe groups of children. Similarly, there have been anecdotes that involvement in sports or other extracurricular activities and religious beliefs and affiliations are effective at reducing risk for bullying or protecting victims from psychological distress. Additionally, it is most likely that *combinations* of strategies will prove most effective at reducing children's risk for bullying. For instance, teaching victims not to blame themselves while simultaneously practicing how to respond to bullies with a nonchalant attitude. Moreover, helping victims problem solve by generating multiple ideas for why bullies might be targeting them, how they can effectively involve peers or teachers in protecting them, or how to avoid bullies may all be necessary to reduce vulnerability to bullying.

Combinations of Child Characteristics

In previous sections, we described various child characteristics (e.g., emotionality, behavioral propensities, cognitions, and coping styles) that are associated with involvement in bullying as a bully, a victim—or both. In this section, we briefly describe how these characteristics may interact with one another to influence how the child will respond to being bullied. Specifically, we present findings from a study we recently conducted that examined how children's emotions, cognitions, and behavioral tendencies tend to cluster together in victimized children (Kochenderfer-Ladd, 2005).

Consistent with previous studies in which both aggressive and nonaggressive victims are identified (Pellegrini, Bartini, & Brooks, 1999; Perry et al., 1990; 1992; Schwartz, 2000; Schwartz et al., 2001), our study of 389 ethnically diverse (38% Latino; 46.80% Caucasian; 4.40% African American; 3.60% Native

American; 6.20% biracial; and 1.00% Asian/Pacific Islander and "Other") first and third grade children ($M = 7$ years 9 months) also identified both of these behavioral subtypes. However, when children's emotional responses and cognitive perceptions were considered, additional subtypes also were detected. For example, aggressive victims could be further distinguished by their emotionality and self-blaming cognitive style. In particular, of the 39 aggressive victims, 25 of them clustered into an angry aggressive victim group characterized by intense anger responses and low tendency to blame themselves, whereas the remaining 14 clustered together as a group labeled aggressive vulnerable victims. This latter group was characterized by high levels of all the emotional reactions assessed, including, anger, fear, hurt, and embarrassment along high levels of self-blame. Moreover, evidence suggested that these two aggressive victim groups cope differently with bullying. For example, aggressive *angry* victims were more likely to retaliate on their own; however, by 3rd grade, aggressive *vulnerable* victims were just as likely to strike back. Furthermore, aggressive vulnerable victims (boys) were more likely to have friends help them get revenge. Moreover, the presence of vulnerable emotions and cognitions appeared to make otherwise aggressive victims more amenable to seeking assistance from both adults and friends alike.

The emergence of a group of aggressive vulnerable victims has important implications for those intervening with victimized children. Specifically, aggressive vulnerable victims may be particularly ineffective in coping with bullying until they learn how to control their intense emotional reactions. In other words, because of the combination of angry and vulnerable emotions, they may have difficulty planning and implementing competent responses to bullying; thus, their efforts may be disorganized and futile. In fact, it may be that these particular aggressive victims reflect Perry et al.'s (1992) "ineffectual fighters"— children who are ". . . emotionally aroused . . . escalate conflicts . . . usually end up losing the battle amid exaggerated displays of frustration and distress" (p. 310). In contrast, angry aggressive victims appear to have more focused emotional reactions, which may lead them to be more single-purposed in their coping strategies, and thus more effective at stopping their victimization.

In addition to the two clusters of aggressive victims, we also identified three nonaggressive victim clusters: asocial vulnerable, emotional, and nondescript. The asocial vulnerable victim cluster consisted of children ($n = 16$) who preferred to be alone, reported vulnerable emotions (fearful, hurt feelings, and embarrassed), and blamed themselves for being bullied. In comparison, the emotional victims ($n = 16$) were not asocial, but they expressed anger in addition to the vulnerable emotions. Moreover, these children were less likely to blame themselves. Although asocial vulnerable and emotional victims did not differ significantly in their coping strategies or their risk for the development of adjustment problems, their unique characteristics offer possible courses of action for intervention. For example, emotional victims may need special guidance in anger management, whereas the vulnerable victims may benefit from attribution retraining (i.e., so they place the blame appropriately on the bully and those who do nothing to stop the bullying and not on themselves).

Lastly, the nondescript victim group ($n = 48$) serves as a reminder that other factors are involved in children's risk for bullying that have, thus far, not been as fully examined. For example, gender variant behaviors (e.g., boys engaging in feminine activities or behaviors; see Kreiger, 2005) and racial or ethnic differences (e.g., Markham, 2006) have been implicated as risk factors for victimization. Thus, while we hope that this review and overarching framework of common child risk factors will serve as an initial guide for planning interventions, it is important to keep the individual child and circumstances in mind.

Environment Characteristics

Although environmental/ecological factors are considered in depth in Chapter 2, we include a brief overview to demonstrate how schools, family experiences, and peer contexts contribute to the emergence and stability of the bullying phenomenon. We also briefly examine how parenting styles can either reduce or increase children's involvement in bullying as either victimizers or victims.

School Environments

Because most bullying behavior occurs in school (as opposed to going to or from school), most anti-bullying programs have been designed to be implemented within that context (Olweus, 1993a; Smith & Shu, 2000). Moreover, such prevention and intervention programs tend to focus on *(1)* raising awareness about the consequences of bullying on children's social, emotional, and psychological adjustment; *(2)* training teachers, administrators, and other school personnel how to recognize bullying and intervene right away; and *(3)* ensuring schools have developed enforceable codes of conduct (e.g., Olweus, 1991; Pepler, Craig, Zeigler, & Charach, 1994). For example, recess on the playground seems to be particularly conducive to victimization as adult supervision is typically inadequate for watching for students' bullying behavior. Specifically, Olweus (1993b) found a moderate negative correlation ($r = -.45$) between teacher–student ratio at recess and the occurrence of victimization. Moreover, although victims of bullying report that teachers are effective when they intervene, many students report that teachers are typically unaware of the bullying that occurs among their students (Bauman & Del Rio, 2005; Smith & Shu, 2000). These findings are consistent with Olweus (1993a), who found that about 40% of elementary school Scandinavian students and 60% of their junior high counterparts report that that their teachers rarely intervene in bullying. Similarly, Hoover, Oliver, and Hazler (1992) found that 66.4% of their American sample claimed that school personnel respond poorly to bullying. Such findings support the necessity of raising awareness of bullying and providing teachers and school personnel and staff with adequate training for intervening swiftly and effectively as soon as it is detected.

Even though anti-bullying programs train teachers to intervene with bullies and victims, and encourage them to adopt strategies to effectively manage bullying within their classrooms (e.g., Olweus, 1991), researchers caution that teachers tend to overestimate their abilities to detect bullying as well as their effectiveness in intervening (Limber, 2002; Yoon & Kerber, 2003). Moreover, if teachers' intervention efforts are inconsistent or ineffective, their assistance may be problematic for victims. For example, Smith and Shu (2000) reported that confiding in a teacher led to more difficulties for a number of victims in their study. Nevertheless, when teachers intervene in a timely, consistent, and decisive manner their efforts are usually effective (Olweus, 1991).

Not surprisingly then, teachers are often given a central role in the management and prevention of peer victimization (Craig, Henderson, & Murphy, 2000; Nicolaides, Toda, & Smith, 2002; Yoon & Kerber, 2003). However, teachers vary widely in what they consider to be bullying behaviors, as well as in what they deem serious aggressive behaviors that warrant adult intervention (Olweus, 1993a; Siann, Callaghan, Lockhart, & Rawson, 1993. For example, Yoon and Kerber (2003) studied teachers' feelings of sympathy for victims along with their efficacy for handling bullying episodes and found that teachers believed that verbal and physical aggression were more serious forms of victimization than social exclusion, and thus, expressed more sympathy for children who were the targets of verbal and physical aggression. In turn, they were more likely to intervene when they felt sympathetic. In addition, Yoon (2004) found that teachers not only intervene when they feel greater sympathy for the victim, but also when they felt greater self-efficacy in dealing with peer victimization.

In our research (Kochenderfer-Ladd & Pelletier, 2008; Troop & Ladd, 2002), we have found that teachers are less likely to intervene if they view bullying as normative behavior, but they are more likely to intervene if they endorse assertion ("if children stand up for themselves, they will not get bullied") or avoidance ("if children stay away from bullies, they will not be bullied") beliefs. Moreover, teachers' beliefs influenced the ways that they intervened, such that teachers holding avoidant beliefs were more likely to separate involved students. In turn, this strategy was associated with decreased levels of peer victimization in their classrooms (Kochenderfer-Ladd & Pelletier, 2008). In contrast, teachers who endorsed normative beliefs were less likely to punish acts of aggression (Troop & Ladd, 2002).

In conclusion, evidence clearly implies that the school environment as well as the quantity and quality of teacher involvement in bully–victim interactions influence the frequency of bullying in schools and classrooms; thus, even children who display vulnerable characteristics may be protected from bullying if they are fortunate enough to be in a school or classroom with caring, attentive adults. However, findings also clearly suggest that more studies are needed to investigate how individual teachers choose to manage bullying among their students to improve their level of intervention as well as effectiveness (Olweus, 1993b; Smith & Shu, 2000; Yoon, 2004).

Familial Influences

Factors that influence the emergence of bullying have also been associated with family environments (see also Chapter 4). Evidence from multiple lines of investigation demonstrate the link between early family relationships and parenting practices and children's later involvement in bullying as either the aggressor or the victim. In general, the premises that researchers investigated were drawn from larger models of family socialization (see Parke & Buriel, 1998) and tend to focus on parent–child attachment relationships (Troy & Sroufe, 1987); dimensions or parenting styles such as parental control and responsiveness (Finnegan, Hodges, & Perry, 1998); and children's exposure to conflictual or abusive family conditions and parent–child interaction (Schwartz et al., 1993). We briefly highlight those links that may prove especially invaluable when considering how to best intervene with children involved in bullying.

Caregiver–Child Attachment Styles

In a study conducted by Troy and Sroufe (1987), the emergence of bullying was studied in a sample of 4- and 5-year-old preschoolers whose attachment histories had been identified at 12 and 18 months. They found that victimized children often had histories of anxious/resistant attachment with their care-givers. However, such children were only vulnerable to peer victimization when paired with playmates who had avoidant attachment histories; that is, they were not bullied by securely attached children or by other peers with anxious/resistant attachment histories. In contrast, preschoolers with anxious/avoidant attachment histories tended to be negative in their interactions with whomever they were paired—even securely attached agemates. Moreover, when paired with other preschoolers with similar anxious/avoidant attachment histories, they vacillated between being the victimizer and the victim.

Such findings not only offer support for the argument that victimized children display an anxious vulnerability around peers, but they further suggest a possible reason for their anxiety. Specifically, anxious children may come to school with internal working models based on their attachment histories with caregivers (see Bowlby, 1973) that leave them either uncertain as to how peers will treat them or expecting to be treated poorly. Moreover, this link between children's insecure attachment histories and peer victimization may be partially mediated by children's withdrawn behavior. For instance, children's insecure attachment to caregivers in early childhood is predictive of social withdrawal from peers in middle childhood (for a review see Rubin & Burgess, 2001). Thus, children's insecure attachment to caregivers may contribute to socially withdrawn behavior in the peer group, which, in turn, may increase vulnerability for peer victimization.

Parenting Styles

Several aspects of parenting styles have also been implicated in children's vulnerability to peer victimization, such as maternal overprotectiveness, overly warm or enmeshed mother–child interactions, parental control and coercion, as well as paternal rejection (Bowers, Smith, & Binney, 1994; Finnegan et al., 1998; Ladd & Kochenderfer-Ladd, 1998; Olweus, 1993c). However, whereas insecure attachment was found to be a risk factor for both boys and girls, the associations with parenting styles tend to be gender specific. It is has been argued that parenting behaviors that threaten boys' agentic or girls' communal skill development undermine children's confidence to engage in socially appropriate interactions (e.g., culturally accepted gender-role behavior; see Finnegan et al., 1998). In turn, this lack of confidence may manifest in feelings of inferiority and anxious behaviors (e.g., passive victims)—or frustration and defiant behaviors (e.g., aggressive victims). In fact, evidence does seem to support such arguments. For example, for boys, maternal overprotectiveness, intense closeness, father negativity, and poor identification with father are concurrently and predictively related to victimization, perhaps because these parenting styles impede the development of autonomy and independence valued in boys' peer groups (Finnegan et al., 1998; Ladd & Kochenderfer-Ladd, 1998). For girls, mothers' coercive behavior, emotional control, and lack of responsiveness is associated with victimization (Finnegan et al., 1998; Rigby, 1993), conceivably because it interferes with the intimate communication and connectedness characteristic of girls' relationships.

Family Systems Perspectives

Evidence from a family systems perspective also links family characteristics to children's risk for victimization. For example, enmeshed or overly close and dependent family relationships may place children at risk for peer victimization by impeding the development of autonomy and self-defense competency (Bowers et al., 1994; Smith, Bowers, Binney, & Cowie, 1993). However, an alternate family systems hypothesis is that children may learn the role of aggressor or victim, or both, within conflictual family relationships. Consistent with this hypothesis, aggressive victimized boys tend to have family histories that included physical abuse, harsh restrictive disciplinary styles, and exposure to violence between adults in the home (Schwartz et al., 1993; Schwartz et al., 1997). Other studies also suggest that abusive family conditions may be associated with vulnerability to peer victimization (see Duncan, 1999). However, it should be noted that researchers know relatively little about the home life of passive victims, as studies do not find that they come from abusive or violent homes (Schwartz et al., 1997). Thus, counselors need to refrain from assuming victimized children come from broken, or troubled, homes and work with parents to ensure their children's safety.

Peer Group Context

Finally, there is evidence that characteristics of the peer culture either increase or decrease the likelihood of individual children being targeted for victimization, or exacerbate or buffer the effects of other risk factors (e.g., child characteristics, such as aggressiveness). Although it has been proposed that it is the combination of behavioral and relational risk factors that renders children vulnerable to peer victimization (Hodges et al., 1997; Ladd, 2005), most researchers focus on understanding how peer victimization relates to children's social status in their peer groups or their participation in friendships, as opposed to interactions between the child and their particular peer culture. For example, studies consistently show that peer rejection and friendlessness are associated with peer victimization (Hodges & Perry, 1999; Pellegrini et al., 1999; Perry et al., 1988).

Nevertheless, evidence has shown that friendships (i.e., number of reciprocated friendships) can serve as a protective factor even when children display behavioral risk factors (Hodges et al., 1997). However, friendships deter victimization only to the extent that friends are capable of providing protection. Thus, it is important to identify the friends of victimized children to see if they can be included in intervention efforts. For instance, on one hand, having aggressive friends tends to reduce children's risk for victimization. But, on the other hand, nonaggressive victims tend to have friends who are not well equipped to protect them because they tend to be weak, withdrawn, submissive, and victimized themselves (see Hodges & Perry, 1999). In fact, in this latter case, counselors may need to also target victimized children's friends for intervention as well.

In addition to understanding the friendship network of bullies and victims, practitioners may also be informed by knowing the child's status within his or her peer group. In fact, there is some indication that peer rejection is a stronger predictor of victimization than lacking friends (Hodges & Perry, 1999; Pellegrini et al., 1999). Peer rejection has been identified as an especially vulnerable position in the peer group because even nonaggressive peers do not tend to sympathize with rejected children when they are victimized (Hodges & Perry, 1999; Perry et al., 1990). Additionally, dislike may fuel bullies' desire to harm the victim, and the victim's weak social position may create an opportunity for bullies to assert social dominance. Also, being picked on by a bully may signal to other peers that it is acceptable to mistreat victimized children (Buhs & Ladd, 2001). Whatever the underlying processes, it is clear that being negatively regarded by the peer group and lacking supportive peer relationships contribute to children's vulnerability to victimization.

Conclusions

On April 16, 2002, my son, 14-year-old Jon Gettle, left his home during the night, walked 200 yards to his middle school and hung himself outside the 8th grade hallway. His note said, "Bullying is a problem." (http://www.bullycide.org/testimonials.html)

Indeed, bullying is a problem. Moreover, as a society and as individual professionals working with children, we need to do more than punish bullies and support victims. As this chapter attests to, we need to intervene at both the child and the environment levels simultaneously. In fact, not only do we as counselors, school psychologists, social workers, school administrators, and educators have critical roles to play in preventing and reducing bullying, but parents, bullies, victims, and peer bystanders also have important roles to play in stopping this form of violence that is directed against children. For all those who wish to address this problem, the following steps are recommended:

- Raise awareness of the prevalence and consequences of school bullying and the urgency with which it needs to be addressed and stopped in our schools
- Ensure that all reports of bullying are taken seriously, regardless of the form of victimization (physical, relational, verbal, threats, taunts, etc.) and for all children (i.e., whether it is a male or female victimizer or a male or female victim)
- Be aware of children who may be especially vulnerable for peer abuse because of their sensitivity (i.e., submissiveness, passive, withdrawn, isolated) or apparent insensitivity (i.e., aggressive, hyperactive/ distractible)
- Recognize how strongly victimized children feel their emotions as well as how difficult it may be for them to control them. Victims may not be able to control intense emotions when in the throes of being bullied. Therefore, rather than emphasizing emotional control, it may be more productive to teach victims coping strategies that are consistent with their temperament—and work to protect them from further abuse.
- Ask children why they think they are being bullied, help them understand that it is not their fault, and explain that others (parents, teachers, school administrators, other school staff) are responsible for ensuring their safety and well-being
- Teach children many different types of coping strategies and keep in mind that not all strategies are effective or appropriate within their particular peer culture (e.g., boys and girls often live by different sets of "peer-approved" social norms)
- Communicate concerns about the supervision and monitoring of "bully-friendly" places such as the playground, hallways, lunchrooms, and so forth to school administrators
- Become an ally with teachers in the campaign to rid classrooms and schools of bullying. Educate persons who work with children about what

bullying is and why it requires their immediate attention. Work to ensure the safety of children who are known to be bullied.

- Help schools develop anti-bullying rules and social norms, and create clear policies about the consequences of bullying for peer aggressors and their parents
- Offer parenting classes for parents of bullies and victims (or, if you are a parent, take advantage of such classes that are offered in your community)
- Provide for, or be prepared to refer bullies and their parents to family crisis counseling, especially in cases where families are experiencing domestic violence, marital discord, or other serious problems (or, if you are a parent, seek out such assistance—for yourself as well as for your children)
- Help children form healthy, positive, peer relationships and encourage them to stay near peers who are likely to ensure their safety (during recess, free periods, etc.)

References

Alsaker, F. D., & Valkanover, S. (2001). Early diagnosis and prevention of victimization in kindergarten. In J. Juvonen & S. Graham (Eds.), *Peer harassment in school: The plight of the vulnerable and victimized* (pp. 175–195). New York: The Guilford Press.

Bauman, S., & Del Rio, A. (2005). Knowledge and beliefs about bullying in schools: Comparing pre-service teachers in the Unites States and the United Kingdom. *School Psychology International, 26*, 428–442.

Baumeister, R.F., & Leary, M.R. (1995). The need to belong: Desire for interpersonal attachments as a fundamental human motivation. *Psychological Bulletin,* 117, 497–529.

Bijttebier, P., & Vertommen, H. (1998). Coping with peer arguments in school-age children with bully-victim problems. *British Journal of Educational Psychology, 68,* 387–394.

Boivin, M., Hymel, S., & Bukowski, W. M. (1995). The roles of social withdrawal, peer rejection, and victimization by peers in predicting loneliness and depressed mood in children. *Development and Psychopathology, 7,* 765–785.

Bowers, L., Smith, P. K., & Binney, V. (1994). Perceived family relationships of bullies, victims and bully/victims in middle childhood. *Journal of Social and Personal Relationships, 11,* 215–232.

Bowlby, J. (1973). *Attachment and loss, Vol. 2: Separation.* New York: Basic Books.

Buhs, E. S., & Ladd, G. W. (2001). Peer rejection as antecedent of young children's school adjustment: An examination of mediating processes. *Developmental Psychology, 37,* 550–560.

Charach, A., Pepler, D., & Ziegler, S. (1995). Bullying at school: A Canadian perspective. *Education Canada*, Spring, 12–18.

Chung, T., & Asher, S. R. (1996). Children's goals and strategies in peer conflict situations. *Merrill-Palmer Quarterly, 42*, 125–147.

Clifford, C. (2008). Children's attributions for peer rejection: Links to peer victimization and internalizing problems. In C. Clifford's (Chair), *Children's attributions for peer victimization.* Paper symposium presented at the biennial meetings of the Society for Research in Adolescence, Chicago, IL.

Craig, W. (1997). A comparison among self-, peer- and teacher-identified victims, bullies and bully/victims: Are victims an under-identified risk groups? In B. Kochenderfer (Chair), *Research on bully/victim problems: Agendas from several cultures.* Symposium conducted at the biennial meeting of the Society for Research in Child Development, Washington, DC.

Craig, W. M., Henderson, K., & Murphy, J. G. (2000). Prospective teachers' attitudes toward bullying and victimization. *School Psychology International, 21*, 5–21.

Crick, N. R., & Bigbee, M A. (1998). Relational and overt forms of peer victimization: A multi-informant approach. *Journal of Consulting and Clinical Psychology, 66*, 337–347.

Duncan, R. (1999). Maltreatment by parents and peers: The relationship between child abuse, bully victimization, and psychological distress. *Child Maltreatment, 4*, 45–55.

Eisenberg, N., Fabes, R. A., Bernsweig, J., Karbon, M., Poulin, R., & Hanish, L. (1993). The relations of emotionality and regulation to preschoolers' social skills and sociometric status. *Child Development, 64*, 1418–1438.

Finnegan, R. A., Hodges, E. V. E., & Perry, D. G. (1998). Victimization by peers: Associations with children's reports of mother–child interaction. *Journal of Personality & Social Psychology, 75*, 1076–1086.

Gazelle, H. (1999). *Solitude and risk in late childhood: Identifying solitary subgroups that differ in severity and specificity of risk.* Poster presented at the 1999 biennial meeting of the Society for Research in Child Development, Albuquerque, NM.

Graham, S., & Juvonen, J. (1998). A social cognitive perspective on peer aggression and victimization. In R. Vasta (Ed.), *Annals of Child Development* (pp. 23 – 70). London: Jessica Kingsley.

Graham, S., & Juvonen, J. (2001). An attributional approach to peer victimization. In J. Juvonen & S. Graham (Eds.), *Peer harassment in school: The plight of the vulnerable and victimized* (pp. 332–351). New York: The Guilford Press.

Greene, B. (April 19, 1993). Why weren't you his friends? *Chicago Tribune.* Retrieved from http://www.chicagotribune.com.

Harrist, A. W., Zaia, A. F., Bates, J. E., Dodge, K. A., & Pettit, G. S. (1997). Subtypes of social withdrawal in early childhood: Sociometric status and social-cognitive differences across four years. *Child Development, 68*, 278–294.

Hawker, D. S. J. (1997). *Socioemotional maladjustment among victims of different forms of peer aggression.* Unpublished doctoral dissertation, Keele University, UK.

Hawker, D. S. J., & Boulton, M. J. (2000). Twenty years' research on peer victimization and psychosocial maladjustment: A meta-analytic review of cross-sectional studies. *Journal of Child Psychology & Psychiatry & Allied Disciplines, 41,* 441–455.

High, B. Bully Police USA: A Watchdog Organization Advocating for Bullied Children and Reporting on State Anti-Bullying Laws. (n.d.). *Jared's story.* Retrieved February 28, 2008, from http://www.bullypolice.org/brenda.html

Hodges, E. V. E., Boivin, M., Vitaro, F., & Bukowski, W. M. (1999). The power of friendship: Protecting against an escalating cycle of peer victimization. *Developmental Psychology, 35,* 94–101.

Hodges, E. V. E., Malone, M. J., & Perry, D. G. (1997). Individual risk and social risk as interacting determinants of victimization in the peer group. *Developmental Psychology, 33,* 1032–1039.

Hodges, E. V. E., & Perry, D. G. (1999). Personal and interpersonal antecedents and consequences of victimization by peers. *Journal of Personality and Social Psychology, 76,* 677–685.

Hoover, J. H., Oliver, R., & Hazler, R. J. (1992). Bullying: Perceptions of adolescent victims in the Midwestern USA. *School Psychology International, 13,* 5–16.

Hudley, C., & Graham, S. (1993). An attributional intervention to reduce peer-directed aggression among African-American boys. *Child Development, 64,* 124–138.

Kochenderfer-Ladd, B. (2005, August). Attributions, emotions and coping: Children's responses to peer aggression. In Wolke, D., & Menesini (Chairs), *Emotions, moral cognitions and bullying.* Paper symposium presented at the XIIth European Conference on Developmental Psychology, Canary Islands.

Kochenderfer, B. J., & Ladd, G. W. (1996a). Peer victimization: Cause or consequence of children's school adjustment difficulties? *Child Development, 67,* 1305–1317.

Kochenderfer, B. J., & Ladd, G. W. (1996b). Peer victimization: Manifestations and relations to school adjustment in kindergarten. *Journal of School Psychology, 34,* 267–283.

Kochenderfer, B. J., & Ladd, G. W. (1997). Victimized children's responses to peers' aggression: Behaviors associated with reduced versus continued victimization. *Development and Psychopathology, 9,* 59–73.

Kochenderfer-Ladd, B. (2003).Identification of aggressive and asocial victims and the stability of their peer victimization. *Merrill-Palmer Quarterly,* 401–425.

Kochenderfer-Ladd, B. (2004). The role of emotions in adaptive and maladaptive coping with peer victimization. *Social Development, 3,* 329–349.

Kochenderfer-Ladd, B., & Pelletier, M. E. (2008). Teachers' views and beliefs about bullying: Influences on classroom management strategies and students' coping with peer victimization. *Journal of School Psychology, 46,* 431–453.

Kochenderfer-Ladd, B., & Skinner, K. (2002). Children's coping strategies: Moderators of the effects of peer victimization? *Developmental Psychology, 38,* 267–278.

Kochenderfer-Ladd, B., & Wardrop, J. L. (2001). Chronicity and instability of children's peer victimization experiences as predictors of loneliness and social satisfaction trajectories. *Child Development, 72,* 134–151.

Kreiger, T. (2005, April). *Gender-typed activities as predictors of peer rejection and peer victimization.* Poster presented at the biennial meetings of the Society for Research in Child Development, Atlanta, GA.

Kumpulainen, K., Räsänen, E., Henttonen, I., Almqvist, F., Kresanov, K., Linna, S. L., Moilanen, I., Phiha, J. Puura, K., & Tamminen, T. (1998). Bullying and psychiatric symptoms among elementary school-age children. *Child Abuse and Neglect, 22,* 705–717.

Ladd, G. W. (2005). *Children's peer relations and social competence: A century of progress.* London: Yale University Press.

Ladd, G. W., & Burgess, K. B. (1999). Charting the relationship trajectories of aggressive, withdrawn, and aggressive/withdrawn children during early grade school. *Child Development, 70,* 910–929.

Ladd, G. W., & Kochenderfer-Ladd, B. (1998). Parenting behaviors and parent-child relationships: Correlates of peer victimization in kindergarten. *Developmental Psychology, 34,* 1450–1458.

Ladd, G. W., & Kochenderfer-Ladd, B. (2002). Identifying victims of peer aggression from early to middle childhood: Analysis of cross-informant data for concordance, estimation of relational adjustment, prevalence of victimization, and characteristics of identified victims. *Psychological Assessment, 14,* 74–96.

Limber, S. (2002, May 3). *Addressing youth bullying behaviors.* Paper presented at the Educational Forum on Adolescent Health: Youth bullying. Retrieved January, 13, 2006, from http://www.ama-assn.org/ama1/pub/upload/mm/39/youthbullying.pdf

Maccoby, E., & Jacklin, C. (1974). *The psychology of sex differences.* Stanford, CA: Stanford University Press.

Markham, C. (2006, April). Children's attributions for peer rejection: Links to peer victimization and internalizing problems. In Kochenderfer-Ladd, B. (Chair), *Diverse perspectives in the study of peer victimization: Cultural, behavioral, emotional and cognitive considerations.* Paper symposium presented at the annual meetings of American Educational Research Association, San Francisco, CA.

Nansel, T. R., Overpeck, M., Pilla, R. S., Ruan, W. J., Simons-Morton, B., & Scheidt, P. (2001) Bullying behaviors among us youth: Prevalence and association with psychosocial adjustment. *Journal of American Medical Association, 285,* 2094–2100.

Nicolaides, S., Toda, Y., & Smith, P. K. (2002). Knowledge and attitudes about school bullying in trainee teachers. *British Journal of Educational Psychology, 72,* 105–118.

Olson, S. L. (1992). Development of conduct problems and peer rejection in preschool children: A social systems analysis. *Journal of Abnormal Psychology, 29,* 327–350.

Olweus, D. (1978). *Aggression in the schools: Bullies and whipping boys.* Washington, DC: Hemisphere (Wiley).

Olweus, D. (1991). Bully/victim problems among schoolchildren: Basic facts and effects of a school based intervention program. In D. Pepler & K. Rubin (Eds.), *The development and treatment of childhood aggression* (pp. 411–448). Hillsdale, NJ: Erlbaum.

Olweus D. (1993a). *Bullying at school: What we know and what we can do.* Oxford, England: Blackwell Publishers.

Olweus, D. (1993b). Bullies on the playground: The role of victimization. In C. H. Hart (Ed.), *SUNY series, children's play in society. Children on playgrounds: Research perspectives and applications* (pp. 85–128). Albany, NY: SUNY Press.

Olweus, D. (1993c). Victimization by peers: Antecedents and long-term outcomes. In K. H. Rubin & J. B. Asendorpf (Eds.), *Social withdrawal, inhibition, and shyness in childhood* (pp. 315–341). Hillsdale, NJ: Erlbaum.

Parke, R. D., & Buriel, R. (1998). Socialization in the family: Ethnic and ecological perspectives. In W. Damon (Series Ed.) and N. Eisenberg (Vol. Ed.), *Handbook of child psychology, Vol. 3: Social, emotional, and personality development* (5th ed., pp. 463–552). New York: John Wiley and Sons.

Patterson, G. R., Littman, R. A., & Bricker, W. (1967). Assertive behavior in children: A step toward a theory of aggression. *Monographs of the Society for Research in Child Development, 113*(5), 1–43.

Pellegrini, A. D., Bartini, M., & Brooks, F. (1999). School bullies, victims and aggressive victims: Factors relating to group affiliation and victimization in early adolescence. *Journal of Educational Psychology, 91*, 165–176.

Pepler, D.J., Craig, W. M., Zeigler, S. & Charach, A. (1994). An evaluation of an antibullying intervention in Toronto schools. *Canadian Journal of Community Mental Health, 13*, 95–110.

Perry, D. G., Hodges, E. V. E., & Egan, S. K. (2001). Determinants of chronic victimization by peers: A review and a new model of family influence. In J. Juvonen & S. Graham (Eds.), *Peer harassment in school: The plight of the vulnerable and victimized* (pp. 73–104). New York: The Guilford Press.

Perry, D. G., Kusel, S. J., & Perry, L. C. (1988). Victims of peer aggression. *Developmental Psychology, 24*, 807–814.

Perry, D. G., Perry, L. C., & Kennedy, E. (1992). Conflict and development of antisocial behavior. In C. U. Shantz & W. W. Hartup (Eds.), *Conflict in child and adolescent development* (pp. 301–329). New York: Cambridge University Press.

Perry, D. G., Williard, J. C., & Perry, L. C. (1990). Peers' perceptions of the consequences that victimized children provide aggressors. *Child Development, 61*, 1310–1325.

Pope, A. W., & Bierman, K. L. (1999). Predicting adolescent peer problems and antisocial activities: The relative roles of aggression and dysregulation. *Developmental Psychology, 35*, 335–346.

Reid, K. (1989). Bullying and persistent school absenteeism. In D. P. Tattum & D. A. Lane (Eds.), *Bullying in schools*. Stoke-on-Trent, England: Trentham.

Rigby, K. (1993). School children's perceptions of their families and parents as a function of peer relations. *The Journal of Genetic Psychology, 154,* 501–513.

Ross, D. M. (1996). *Childhood bullying and Teasing: What school personnel, other professionals, and parents can do.* Alexandria, VA: American Counseling Association.

Rubin, K. H., Bukowski, W. M., & Parker, J. G. (1998). Peer interactions, relationships, and groups. In N. Eisenberg (Ed.), *Handbook of child psychology* (Vol. 3, pp. 619–700). New York: Wiley.

Rubin, K. H., & Burgess, K. B. (2001). Social withdrawal and anxiety. In M. W. Vasey & M. R. Dadds (Eds.), *The developmental psychopathology of anxiety.* (pp. 407–434). New York: Oxford University Press.

Rubin, K. H., Coplan, R. J., Fox, N. A., & Calkins, S. D. (1995). Emotionality, emotion regulation, and preschoolers' social adaptation. *Development and Psychopathology, 7,* 49–62.

Salmivalli, C., Karhunen, J., & Lagerspetz, K. (1996). How do the victims respond to bullying? *Aggressive Behavior, 22,* 99–109.

Schwartz, D. (2000). Subtypes of victims and aggressors in children's peer groups. *Journal of Abnormal Child Psychology, 28,* 181–192.

Schwartz, D., Dodge, K. A., & Coie, J. D. (1993). The emergence of chronic peer victimization in boys' play groups. *Child Development, 64,* 1755–1772.

Schwartz, D., Dodge, K. A., Coie, J. D., Hubbard, J. A., Cillessen, A. H. N., Lemerise, E. A., & Bateman, H. (1998). Social-cognitive and behavioral correlates of aggression and victimization in boys' play groups. *Journal of Abnormal Child Psychology, 26,* 431–440.

Schwartz, D., Dodge, K. A., Pettit, G. S., & Bates, J. E. (1997). The early socialization of aggressive victims of bullying. *Child Development, 68,* 665–675.

Schwartz, D., Proctor, L. J., & Chien, D. H. (2001). The aggressive victim of bullying: Emotional and behavioral dysregulation as a pathway to victimization by peers. In J. Juvonen & S. Graham (Eds.), *Peer harassment in school: The plight of the vulnerable and victimized* (pp. 147–174). New York: The Guilford Press.

Siann, G., Callaghan, M., Lockhart, R., & Rawson, L. (1993). Bullying: Teachers' views and school effects. *Educational Studies, 19* (4), 307–321.

Slee, P. T. (1994). Situational and interpersonal correlates of anxiety associated with peer victimization. *Child Psychiatry and Human Development, 25,* 97–107.

Smith, P. K., Bowers, L., Binney, V., & Cowie, H. (1993). Relationships of children involved in bully/victim problems at school. In S. Duck (Ed.), *Learning about relationships, Vol 2.* (pp. 184–212). London: Sage Publications.

Smith, P. K., & Shu, S. (2000). What good schools can do about bullying: Findings from a survey in English schools after a decade of research and action. *Childhood, 7,* 193–212.

Smith, P. K., Shu, S., & Madsen, K. (2001). Characteristics of victims of school bullying: Developmental changes in coping strategies and skills. In J. Juvonen & S. Graham

(Eds.), *Peer harassment in school: The plight of the vulnerable and victimized* (pp. 332–351). New York: The Guilford Press.

Troop, W. P., & Ladd, G. W. (2002). *Teachers' beliefs regarding peer victimization and their intervention practices.* Poster presented at the Conference on Human Development, Charlotte, NC.

Troy, M., & Sroufe, L. A. (1987). Victimization among preschoolers: Role of attachment relationship history. *Journal of the American Academy of Child and Adolescent Psychiatry, 26,* 166–172.

Underwood, M. K. (2003). *Social aggression among girls.* New York: Guilford Press.

Veenstra, R., Lindenberg, S., Zijlstra, B. J. H., De Winter, A. F., Verhulst, F. C., & Ormel, J. (2007). The dyadic nature of bullying and victimization: Testing a dual-perspective theory. *Child Development, 78,* 1843–1854.

Weiner, B. (1986). An attributional theory of motivation and emotion. New York: Springer-Verlag.

Yoon, J. S. (2004). Predicting teacher interventions in bullying situations. *Education and Treatment of Children, 27* (1), 37–45.

Yoon, J. S., & Kerber, K. (2003). Bullying: Elementary teachers' attitudes and intervention strategies. *Research in Education, 69,* 27–35.

4

Family-Level Perspective on Bullies and Victims

Mary Elizabeth Curtner-Smith, Peter K. Smith, and Malvin Porter

Recently, a news article appeared in the *Tuscaloosa News*, the local newspaper for Tuscaloosa, Alabama (Cummings, 2008), reporting the responses of children interviewed about their experiences with bully–victim problems. One boy, a 14-year-old enrolled in the 7th grade who used to get in trouble for constant bullying, said, "I used to go around school and pick on people for no reason." His school guidance counselor stated, "The thing that struck me cold was that he knew it wasn't right, but he would just choose his next target." The assistant principal at the middle school where the former bully is enrolled offers the following explanation for why children like this 7th grader bully, "They [children who bully] don't know how to talk because at home, fighting is the only way."

The theme that "fighting is the only way" to solve social conflicts in families of bullies is further illustrated by findings from a recent research project aimed at examining how mothers socialize their young children for bullying and victimization. In this study, low-income African American mothers of 4-year-old children were presented with two series of hypothetical vignettes (Curtner-Smith, 2007). In the first series of vignettes, mothers imagined that their children were victims of various forms of bullying. In the second series of vignettes, mothers imagined that their children engaged in various forms of bullying. After each vignette, mothers were asked, "What advice would you give to your child?" or "What would you do if your child engaged in this behavior?"

One mother's response to imagining her child engaging in overt physical bullying was, "I'd probably spank her if she do that. I'd spank her and I'd tell her that, um, not to hit no one because she won't want no one to hit her."

Following are two mothers' responses when asked, "What advice would you give to your child if he had been hit by another child for no reason?":

Mother 1: "Well, I always told him if somebody hit him for no obvious reason, then he's always allowed to hit somebody back. Just basically, if a child hits you [first], it's okay to hit back. I would not have taught him to do it first."

Mother 2:"Well, if my kid came home after getting beaten up by another kid, then my kid would get two beatings that day: one from the other kid and one from me. I would have to beat my kid for getting beaten up cause that's the only way I can teach him to stick up for himself."

Finally, the theme that "fighting is the only way" to solve social conflict was recently illustrated in real life, as opposed to responses to hypothetical vignettes. The Associated Press (2007) reported a story about a mother living in Tampa, Florida, who actually directed her 9-year-old daughter to fight a bully. The incident was recorded on the school bus surveillance video. The video shows the mother ". . . leading her daughter onto the bus and saying, 'Where's the girl who slapped my girl?' A 10-year-old girl raised her hand, the trio go to the back of the bus, and a fight breaks out. According to a police report, witnesses said Muldrow [the mother] told her 9-year-old daughter to 'take care of her business.' The bus driver can be heard on the videotape calling for help on the radio as Muldrow watches the girls scuffle. No one was seriously hurt. 'Hold on,' she tells the bus driver at one point. 'I didn't want this to happen.' She then went back to the fight and a few moments later pulls her daughter out of the fray, which continues as she walks off the bus."

This chapter focuses on how maladaptive family processes contribute to the development and persistence of bully–victim problems among children and adolescents. Once these processes are identified, then interventionists can employ a variety of formats such as psychoeducational workshops for large groups of parents, as well as family systems therapy for individual families with children who are bullies, victims, or aggressive victims. The aim of these intervention programs is to help change the maladaptive family processes that contribute in a theoretically causal way to children's bully–victim problems.

We begin by asserting several basic propositions that have strong implications for interventions aimed at helping such children. First, some family processes increase the likelihood that a child or adolescent will bully others. Some family processes more strongly predict physical overt bullying, whereas others more strongly predict relational bullying, and these vary by child gender. Second, a different set of family processes increases the likelihood that a child or adolescent will be the frequent target of bullying. Third, some family processes increase the likelihood that a child will be both a bully and a victim. Fourth, changing the maladaptive family processes within the families of children who are bullies, victims, or aggressive victims should increase the efficacy of anti-bullying programs. Therefore, comprehensive anti-bullying intervention and prevention programs should include a focus on assessing a child's role in bully–victim problems (i.e., bully, victim, or aggressive victim) and changing the family processes so that they promote more positive outcomes for these children.

In this chapter, we present research-based family profiles of children in each role (bully, victim, and aggressive victim) and offer implications for intervention. We also describe implications for effective family-level interventions for children with bully–victim problems. Finally, we propose practical considerations for including family interventions as part of comprehensive bully–victim programs.

Family Processes and Children's Bully–Victim Problems

Most studies linking family processes to children's bullying behaviors have simply sought to describe the family backgrounds of bullies and victims. Moreover, most studies have been conducted with samples of elementary school–aged children or adolescents and have attempted to identify how family processes contribute to overt, physical bullying, particularly among boys. Recent interest in the etiological role that family processes play in children's bullying, both physical and relational, have led investigators to include samples of both boys and girls, as well as younger children who range in age from 3 to 5 years. Consequently, there is a growing body of literature on how parents socialize their children to engage in bully–victim problems. A fair amount of research exists on the family processes related to children's bullying behavior, but more exists on children's aggressive behavior, externalizing behaviors, and conduct disorders. Given that bullying is often assessed along with other forms of children's aggressive and deviant behaviors, in this chapter we will also reference the broader literature on family processes among aggressive children. Relatively less is known about the family processes of victims than of bullies, and unfortunately, even fewer studies have identified the family processes linked to children who are both bullies and victims.

Family Profile of Children Who Bully

A rather large set of maladaptive family process variables contributes to children's aggressive, bullying behavior. These include angry, hostile parent–child interactions; low parent–child involvement, warmth, and affection; harsh, power-assertive discipline that is sometimes inconsistent and lax, and at other times involves the heavy use of psychological control; and low parent monitoring. Antecedents to these family process variables are likely parental depression and anger, low parental empathy for child, and strong parental valuing of aggression.

Angry, Hostile Parent–Child Interactions

Parental anger that is directed at children is often a manifestation of parental depression and stress, and leads to ineffective discipline (Patterson & Forgatch, 1990). Parental anger directed at children also conveys the message that the child is unacceptable and unworthy of parental love and that the parent is rejecting the child. In two separate studies, Renk, Phares, and Epps (1999) found that parental anger was related to clinical levels of parental depression, and that children whose parents scored higher on trait anger and anger expression within the family engaged in more internalizing and externalizing behavior problems. According to Patterson's model of coercive family interactions, children's coercive exchanges with their depressed, angry mothers amplify in intensity with each coercive interchange, and each interchange places children at risk for aggressive, antisocial behavior, including physical bullying of peers. Patterson and colleagues go so far as to refer to the homes of these children as training grounds for aggression.

Low Parental Warmth, Involvement, and Affection

Parental warmth at all ages of children's development is important for promoting positive child outcomes. It includes expressions of affection, nurturance, love, kindness, acceptance, positive regard, and care. Some experts even refer to parental warmth and nurturance as the single most important dimension in parenting because if children do not feel cherished and loved, then there is little else that parents can do to influence their children (Skinner, Johnson, & Synder, 2005). Many studies find that the family relationships of aggressive children, including bullies, are lacking in warmth or affection. A longitudinal study predicting preschool children's externalizing behaviors from toddler temperament, peer conflict, and maternal negativity found that low maternal warmth and high maternal negativity (irritability, annoyance) were related to observations of aggressive peer interactions initiated by toddlers at age 2 years (Rubin, Burgess, Dwyer, &

Hastings, 2003). Moreover, the relationship between age 2 aggressive initiated interactions and age 4 externalizing problems, which includes fighting with other children, was strongest for children whose mothers were the most negative and least warm. Low maternal warmth or affection also was a strong socialization predictor of children's peer nominations for aggression in the study by Dodge, Pettit, and Bates (1994). Similarly, Deater-Deckard, Ivy, and Petrill (2006) assessed 3- to 8-year-old children and their mothers; mothers reported on children's externalizing behaviors, which included bullying or peer aggression, their warm feelings for their children, and their disciplinary strategies. Observers also reported on maternal warmth during the home interview. Harsh parenting was more strongly related to child externalizing problems when mothers lacked warm feelings for their children; harsh parenting by mothers who otherwise felt warmly toward their children was not strongly linked to children's externalizing problems.

Parent involvement, which is sometimes included in assessments of warmth, refers to the amount of time and activities that parents and children share together. Children who spend considerable amounts of time with their parents engaged in fun, pleasurable activities have more opportunities to experience parental warmth and affection than children who spend little time with their parents. Several studies find that parents' lack of involvement with their children is related to children's aggressive behaviors (Flouri & Buchanan, 2003; Loeber & Stouthamer-Loeber, 1986; Loeber, Farrington, Stouthamer-Loeber, & Van Kamman, 1998).

Attachment refers to an enduring reciprocal emotional bond between parent and child that transcends space, time, and even death (Ainsworth, 1989). During infancy, children develop expectations for the quality of care they receive from parents. These expectations develop into internal working models that the child has for parent, self, and relationships. Children who experience sensitive, synchronous (i.e., correctly timed), warm caregiving develop a sense of security and are able to explore the environment. In contrast, children who experience parental responses that are intrusive, inconsistent, or ill timed for meeting the child's needs develop a sense of insecurity (Nievar & Becker, 2007). The quality of the parent–child attachment relationship serves as a prototype for the quality of relationships that children expect to experience throughout the life span (Ainsworth, 1989). Thus, children in secure attachment relationships with their parents expect to experience positive, rewarding relationships with others. In contrast, children in insecure attachment relationships come to expect negative or unfulfilling relationships with others. There are two types of insecure attachment relationships. Children in insecure-resistant relationships tend to be clingy and whiney and are very dependent upon their mothers. This attachment quality is generally associated with inconsistent care-giving. Children in insecure-avoidant relationships show little distress when separated from their mothers and often ignore their mothers during times of reunion. Mothers of insecure-avoidant children have been observed to be either disengaged from their children or overly intrusive such that the child has to turn away. A fourth category of disorganized attachment (Main, Kaplan, & Cassidy, 1985) describes children who are the most distressed upon separation, confused upon reunion, and exhibit behaviors that appear to be a combination of resistant and avoidant.

Children's bullying behaviors have been linked to the quality of parent–child attachment relationships. Troy and Sroufe (1987) conducted a study of urban poor children in the United States. The investigators assessed children's attachment quality to mothers when children were 18 months old. Years later, when children were 4 to 5 years old, the children were observed during dyadic same-sex play sessions. The 14 dyads were categorized for victimization behavior. Troy and Sroufe found that insecure pairs (both resistant and avoidant) were more likely to show patterns of victimization in play, whereas children with a secure attachment history were able to avoid being a victim or bullying others. This research was limited to a small sample and should be regarded as exploratory.

A study using the Parent/Child Reunion Inventory (Marcus, 1991) examined how quality of parent–child attachment was related to physical and relational bullying in U.S. preschool-aged children. Insecure mother–child attachment was related to physical and relational bullying among girls, but not among boys. Father–child insecure attachment was related only to boys' relational aggression. Research in the wider area of aggression indicates that insecure attachment predicts more aggressive and difficult peer relationships. A U.S. study found that girls, but not boys, who were classified as insecure-avoidant at 18 months had more externalizing difficulties with peers at age 4 years (Fagot & Kavanaugh, 1990). An English study reported that insecurely attached boys became more aggressive and externalizing with their peers at 4 years, whereas insecurely attached girls became more dependent (Turner, 1991). Another U.S. study with 5- to 6-year-old children found that boys, but not girls, with insecure attachment histories, became more aggressive with peers (Cohn, 1990).

Finnegan, Hodges, and Perry (1996) did not use classic measures of the parent–child attachment relationship, but did find that 9- to 13-year-old children who engaged in avoidant coping, which the authors defined as a denial of need for mother and avoidance of her during stress, were also more likely to evince externalizing behaviors. Broadly similar results were obtained in a follow-up of the sample 1 year later (Hodges, Finnegan, & Perry, 1999). Myron, Smith, and Sutton (unpublished manuscript) carried out a study with children aged 8–11 years in England. They used the Separation Anxiety Test, which yields more detailed attachment subtypes, especially for insecure attachment. Their data show that ringleader bullies are especially high in anger, but have restricted feelings, believe they are self-sufficient, and dismiss the importance of relationships in their lives. Their self-sufficiency is their way of protecting themselves from rejection from an unsatisfactory attachment figure. The investigators suggest that this type of child may be very likely to take his frustration into the classroom.

Harsh Discipline That Is Also Inconsistent and Lax

Parents of bullies tend to prefer harsh methods of discipline, which include frequent use of corporal punishment and psychological control (Olweus, 1994). A study of 10- to 15-year-olds who scored positive for adjustment difficulties found that parents' use of corporal punishment was related to higher levels of bullying behaviors (Ohene, Ireland, McNeely, & Borowsky, 2006). In the broader literature on children's aggression, most studies find that parental use of corporal punishment predicts children's engagement in physical aggression (Dodge et al., 1994; Loeber et al., 1998; Strassberg, Dodge, Pettit, & Bates, 1994; Straus, 2001). Moreover, the association between parental corporal punishment and children's engagement in physical aggression increases with child age (Loeber et al., 1998). Straus (2001) also concluded that corporal punishment is linked to negative child development outcomes. In fact, Straus, Sugarman, and Giles-Sims (1997) postulate a causal link between corporal punishment, even mild corporal punishment, and increases in children's aggression, depression, and psychological distress. They base their rationale for a causal relationship because the links between corporal punishment and negative child development outcomes persist even when accounting for variations in race, socioeconomic status, gender of child, and quality of relationship with parents.

Not all studies of corporal punishment link it to increases in negative child development outcomes, however. Baumrind, Larzelere, and Cowan (2002) found that mildly administered corporal punishment was not related to increased aggression or depression in a small sample of children. Findings investigating the effects of corporal punishment on African American children are equivocal. Deater-Deckard, Dodge, Bates, and Pettit (1996) and Gunnoe and Mariner (1997) found in separate studies that rates of African American children's behavior problems decreased over time among those whose mothers reported using corporal punishment. In contrast, other studies find that both African American children and European American children who receive corporal punishment engage in higher rates of behavior problems (McLoyd & Smith, 2002; Stormshak, Bierman, McMahon, & Lengua, 2000).

Psychological control is a type of control that attempts to coerce children into doing something against their will by inducing excessive child guilt, leveling harsh criticism at the child, or expressing shame in the child. Psychological control is rejecting of the child, and therefore, it undermines the parent–child bond (Barber, 1996). Recently, investigators have begun to examine the links between parents' use of psychological control to children's engagement in relational aggression. The two are theoretically linked because both involve damage or threat of damage to a social relationship (Casas et al., 2006). Several studies have found that parents' use of psychological control is associated with relational aggression, particularly in girls (Nelson & Crick, 2002). Casas et al. (2006) studied children aged 2.5 to 5 years living in the Midwestern United States. They found that maternal psychological control and paternal psychological control were related to girls' relational bullying. Only father's use of love withdrawal was related to boys' relational bullying.

Effective discipline involves setting clear limits and rules, and it is most effective when parents respond contingently to rule violations (Snyder & Stoolmiller, 2002). Effective discipline and good monitoring begin early in parent–child relationships and continue to influence children's peer associations throughout childhood and adolescence. Inconsistency in parents' expectations for child compliance or unpredictable discipline may be related to poor peer relations. Pettit and colleagues hypothesize that unpredictable discipline may lead children to feel a lack of control; therefore, they may develop maladaptive social skills. Inconsistent discipline, or more precisely, waxing and waning between expecting child compliance to rules and being permissive by allowing children to break rules has been related to bullying behaviors (Olweus, 1980) and delinquency (Loeber & Stouthamer-Loeber, 1986).

Low Parental Monitoring

Parental monitoring refers to "... parental awareness of all aspects of an adolescent's [or a younger child's] life and development, including activities in and outside the home, friendships and other relationships, progress in school, and health-related behaviors" (Capaldi, 2003). Parental monitoring begins when the child is a newborn and lasts until the child is in young adulthood. The ways in which parents monitor their children change as children age. For example, parents keep infants and very young children within sight to monitor their activities. As children become preschoolers, they may be able to be out of the parent's range of vision for short periods of time, but they are still required to be in a certain location such as in another room within the family home. Most parents allow school children to venture outside of the house to play with friends in the neighborhood, but they place conditions on how far away from home or exactly where the children can go, with whom they may play, and when they are to be home. In the United States, many parents equip their school children with two-way walkie talkies or cell phones as a means to monitor their children's whereabouts and activities.

In a longitudinal study of boys aged 7 to 14 years in an urban area of the United States, poor parental monitoring or supervision was related to boys' physical aggression across all age groups (Loeber et al., 1998). Poor parental monitoring also was related to boys' engagement in more antisocial behavior such as drug use and theft. Other large scale studies conducted in the United States that examine the development of antisocial behaviors over time also point to the contribution of poor parental monitoring and children's poor peer relations (Leve, Pears, & Fisher, 2002). Similarly, unsupervised peer contacts that are unmonitored by parents have been found to be related to adolescents' externalizing problems (Pettit, Bates, Dodge, & Meece, 1999).

Parental Depression and Anger

Individual parent personality characteristics such as depression and anger or "hot temper" are important predictors of children's aggressive bullying behavior (Curtner-Smith, 2000). A longitudinal study conducted in England found that postnatal maternal depression when the child was 3 months old was related to more distressing, noncontingent mother–infant interactions and to poor infant self-regulation. Eleven years later, maternal depression during the child's infancy, noncontingent mother–infant interactions, and poor infant self-regulation were related to more aggressive, violent child behavior (Hay, Pawlby, Angold, Harold, & Sharp, 2003). A classic study linking mothers' parenting to children's aggression by Patterson (1980) at the Oregon Social Learning Center found that depressed mothers were more likely to be poor monitors of their children's whereabouts, peer associations, and activities. Mothers also tended to overreact to their children's negative behaviors while failing to recognize their children's positive behaviors, even when independent observers identified positive behaviors in the children. Moreover, mothers who engaged in more frequent coercive interactions with their children became even more depressed as a result of the coercive mother–child interchanges. Maternal depression manifests itself in less responsive and less sensitive caregiving (Cohn, Campbell, Matias, & Hopkins, 1990; Garber & Martin, 2002) and is related to intrusive, disengaged, hostile, erratic, unpredictable, and rejecting parenting (Driscoll & Easterbrooks, 2007; Goodman, Adamson, Riniti, & Cole, 1994). In addition, depressed mothers tend to be less consistent at enforcing rules, and they provide less positive guidance and structure for their children (Goodman & Brumley, 1990). Garber and Martin (2002) overview the research regarding how the negative cognitive set of depressed mothers influences parenting behaviors, and ultimately children's negative cognitions and behaviors. They conclude that children exposed to parenting that is rejecting, critical, and low in warmth tend to internalize their parents' views into negative self-schemas that include being unworthy of love or attention.

Low Parental Empathy for Child

Empathy (both parental empathy for child and child empathy for others) is beginning to gain more attention by investigators because of the causal role it plays in inhibiting children's aggressive behaviors and motivating children's prosocial behaviors. Zhou et al. (2002) contend that empathy is an important inhibitor of aggression because it motivates people to behave in ways that will not be hurtful to others. Parenting behaviors that foster children's empathy include those that are responsive to the child's emotional needs, allow the child to express emotions, and encourage the child's sensitivity to others. Findings from a longitudinal study conducted by Zhou et al. (2002), which included elementary-school aged children and their mothers, confirmed the theoretical links between parenting, children's empathy, and children's social functioning. In particular, the study found that high levels of parental warmth and "positive expressiveness" (i.e., the expression of positive emotions in front of children) were related to high levels of children's empathy. In turn, children's empathy was related to fewer teacher-reported child externalizing behaviors. Likewise, Culp and colleagues (2003) conducted an observational study of Head Start children's bullying. They found that mothers who lacked warmth and empathy, as assessed by vignettes that tapped mothers' reactions to child distress on the computer-presented parenting dilemmas (CPPD; Hubbs-Tait, Culp, Culp, & Miller, 2002), were more likely to have children who were observed bullying on the playground. Finally, in another U.S. study, of mothers of 4- to 5-year-old children in a Head Start program, Curtner-Smith et al. (2006) found that maternal empathy as measured by the empathy subscale of the Adolescent-Adult Parenting Inventory (AAPI; Bavolek, 1984) was the strongest predictor of children's overt and relational bullying behavior. The AAPI empathy subscale contains items that assess how mothers view the role of children. Specific items include "children should keep their views to themselves," "children should do as they are told," and "children should not expect too much from their parents." Although these items may tap into parents' values about being responsive to children's emotional needs and allowing children to express emotions, the items clearly fail at assessing parental empathy for a child, which is a combination of vicariously sharing another's emotion and understanding another's emotions, thoughts, and motives (Kilpatrick, 2005).

Previous research efforts have focused on defining empathy as the vicarious sharing of another's emotions. Studies that have attempted to develop reliable measures of parental empathy based on this definition have been plagued with problems; most notably, these measures failed to discriminate between abusive parents and nonabusive parents (for a review, see Kilpatrick, 2005). Kilpatrick proposes that a broader definition of parental empathy should include both vicarious emotion sharing between parent and child, and positive child-focused parent emotions such as compassion, sympathy, urge to nurture, and love. Collectively, these make up the construct of *empathic parenting*. Kilpatrick found that her measure of parental empathy, the PEM, which is based on empathic parenting, successfully classified 94% of known abusive parents in her study of 103 parents.

Eisenberg and Valiente (2002) reviewed Hoffman's theory of moral internalization. According to Hoffman (2000), parents' disciplinary encounters with children serve as the primary context in which children have the opportunity to learn the moral message, "Do not hurt others." This is because in many disciplinary encounters, the child has acted or has the potential to act in a way that hurts another. The parent intervenes and tries to change the child's behavior. Hoffman identified three classes of disciplinary techniques: inductive reasoning, power assertion, and love withdrawal. In inductive reasoning, parents emphasize the effects of the child's behavior on others. Examples of inductive reasoning statements made by a parent would be, "You hurt Sally when you hit her! No hitting; hitting hurts!" "How would you feel if you were the only girl in your class not invited to Susie's birthday party?" and "You hurt your sister's feelings when you wouldn't let her join in the game. She feels really left out now." Power-assertive techniques, in contrast, are punitive and rely on the parent's powerful status over the child to take away a possession, impose a loss of privilege that is unrelated to the misdeed, or administer physical punishment. These actions are typically communicated in the form of direct commands or threats. Finally, love-withdrawal techniques involve the withdrawal of parental affection or attention from the child and include enforced separations or isolating the child. Parental expressions of anger or disapproval of the child for engaging in the undesirable behavior are also included in this class of disciplinary techniques.

Of the three classes of disciplinary techniques, inductive reasoning is most strongly linked to children's empathy, empathy-based guilt, and internalization of norms for prosocial, caring behaviors. In contrast, power-assertive techniques have been found to be related to low levels of child empathy, empathy-based guilt, and a lack of internalized norms for prosocial caring behaviors (Eisenberg & Valiente, 2002; Krevans & Gibbs, 1996). A study of Caucasian U.S. preschool-aged children found that those whose parents practiced more power-assertive parenting techniques, particularly corporal punishment, had lower parent ratings of empathy. In addition, inconsistent parental discipline was related to low levels of child empathy, but only for children who were rated by teachers as behaviorally uninhibited (i.e., fearless, thrillseekers) (Cornell & Frick, 2007). The links between love-withdrawal disciplinary techniques and children's empathy, empathy-based guilt, and prosocial behavior are inconsistent. Statements of parents' disappointment may have some positive associations with inducing children's empathy-based guilt and prosocial behaviors, but other forms of love withdrawal (expressions of anger, witholding of affection) are related to low levels of empathy-based guilt and low levels of prosocial behaviors (Krevans & Gibbs, 1996).

Empathy is typically viewed as two dimensional. First there is, cognitive empathy, which refers to the ability to recognize the emotions of others, and second, there is affective empathy, which refers to sharing the feelings of others. The role of empathy as a facilitator of prosocial helping behavior and an inhibitor of aggressive behavior in children is important. Highly empathic individuals both recognize and feel the pain of others. Hence, empathic individuals try to relieve the distress of others either for altruistic reasons, or for selfish reasons (helping another in distress relieves their own distress). Despite literature on the theoretical links between low empathy and bullying, only a few studies have sought to empirically demonstrate those links. For example, Endresen and Olweus (2002) found bullying behavior and low affective empathy were related for both boys and girls in Norwegian adolescents.

Sutton, Smith, and Swettenham (1999) assessed understanding of another's mental state or emotions, a measure that is similar to cognitive empathy, in British children aged 7 to 10 years. Children classified by peers as bullies scored *higher* on understanding or recognizing another's emotions (cognitive empathy) than children classified as reinforcers of bullies' behaviors and assistants to bullies. The authors suggest that the ability to recognize another person's emotions might help bullies plan and engage in more hurtful bullying behavior and in recruiting other children to bully.

Jolliffe and Farrington (2006) examined the cognitive, affective, and total empathy scores of British adolescents in relation to their self-reports of bullying. Females who bullied scored lower than females who did not bully on the measures of affective and total empathy, but not for cognitive empathy. Thus, it appears that female bullies can recognize another person's distress, but they do not necessarily feel the pain of another person. Male bully scores on each of the three measures of empathy (cognitive, affective, and total) were not significantly different from male nonbully scores. The data were also analyzed to determine if empathy varied by type of bullying; males who bullied violently (engaging in physical assault, threatening, taking things away) had significantly lower total empathy scores than males who bullied less violently (engaging in name-calling, racial name-calling, indirect relational bullying), and there was a tendency for girls who bullied violently and for girls who engaged in relational bullying to have lower affective and total empathy scores than females who did not bully.

Empathy deficits, particularly affective empathy deficits, appear to be characteristic of children who bully frequently. Empathy is fostered in young children by parents' use of inductive reasoning discipline strategies; thus, it is not surprising that we find that parents of bullies tend to rely more on power-assertive discipline strategies rather than inductive reasoning strategies. Consequently, an important family-level intervention for families with children who bully would be training parents to use inductive reasoning strategies as an alternative to corporal punishment and other more harsh, punitive forms of discipline.

Strong Parental Valuing of Aggression

Some evidence suggests that maternal values of aggression are typical of mothers of children who bully. Dodge and colleagues (1994) studied children in the Midwestern and Southeastern United States. Teachers and peers completed child assessments when children were enrolled in kindergarten and grades 1, 2, and 3. Data on the mother–child relationship were collected during the summer prior to the child's kindergarten year during a home visit. One assessment completed by mothers was the "Culture Questionnaire," assessing mother's values regarding the use of aggression to solve problems. Sample items included, "Sometimes a physical fight might help my child have a better relationship with other children," "If my child were teased by other kids at school, I would want my child to defend him/herself even if it meant hitting another child," and "If I found out my child hit another child, I would be very disappointed, no matter what the reason." Maternal values of aggression were strongest for African American mothers, even after statistically controlling for socioeconomic status, and for mothers of sons. Moreover, maternal values of aggression were correlated with teacher reports of children's externalizing behavior, which includes bullying behavior.

Loeber and Stouthamer-Loeber (1986) performed a meta-analysis on the relation of family factors to juvenile conduct problems and delinquency. Their analyses supported the link between parental deviant values, such as parents' tolerance of children's delinquency and their encouragement of children's aggression, and children's delinquency and aggressive behaviors. Likewise, maternal values of aggression have been found to be related to peer and teacher reports of boys' bullying (Olweus, 1980). In particular, mothers' permissiveness for sons' aggressive behavior directed toward mother, peers, or siblings was predictive of boys' aggressiveness (i.e., starts fights with peers, protests against teachers, and verbally hurts peers) across two separate samples of Swedish boys.

A study of 10- to 14-year-old children who scored positive for adjustment difficulties (i.e., externalizing behaviors, internalizing behaviors, and/or poor attentional skills), found that parents' stated expectations for how their children should respond to physical peer provocation (e.g., "It's okay for your child to hit if someone pushes him") was unrelated to children's self-reported bullying. However, children's perception of parental approval regarding aggressive retaliation (e.g., "My family would want me to hit back if someone hits me") was positively related to children's bullying (Ohene et al., 2006).

Two separate U.S. studies examined mothers' responses to hypothetical vignettes in which they imagined their young children as victims of physical bullying and relational bullying (Curtner-Smith, 2007; Werner, Senich, & Przepyszny, 2006). Both studies found that mothers were more upset or concerned when their children were victims of physical bullying than when their children were victims of relational bullying. In fact, mothers in one study did not seem at all concerned with instances of relational bullying (Curtner-Smith, 2007). In both studies, mothers were more likely to say they would intervene for instances involving physical aggression than for instances involving relational aggression. Another U.S. study of mothers of older children also finds that mothers seem more tolerant of relational aggression than of physical aggression (Stockdale, Haungaduambo, Duys, Larson, & Sarvela, 2002).

Parents' role as advisors or consultants to their children about peer relations has been studied for the past two decades (Ladd, 2005). For example, Laird, Pettit, Mize, and Lindsey (1994) found that preschool-aged children residing in the United States who had more frequent conversations with their parents about peer relationships had children who were perceived by peers as more likeable. Mothers in the same study reported that common topics of mother–child conversations involved giving advice to their children about how to initiate a friendship and how to deal with bullying. Other studies find that the quality of advice or social problem-solving strategies that parents suggest in response to hypothetical peer conflicts is related to children's peer aggression or bullying. For example, a U.S. study of preschool-aged children found that mothers who suggest prosocial strategies for how to deal with hypothetical peer provocations and rebuffs tend to have children who are rated as less aggressive by teachers than mothers who suggest neutral or unfriendly strategies (Mize & Pettit, 1997). A study with a similar line of research involved aggressive and nonaggressive Finnish adolescent boys and both their mothers and fathers (Pakaslahti, Asplund-Peltola, & Keltikangas-Jarvinen, 1996). Social problem-solving strategies were measured by presenting parents with six social conflict situations that are typically encountered by adolescents. These social conflict situations ask parents to imagine that their sons commit illegal or immoral behavior after being pressured into it by peers. Examples included "to get friends, the son has to engage in a housebreaking attempt with a gang," "a violent boy has blackmailed the son into bringing money or cigarettes," and "during a school examination, the son is forced into giving the correct answers to other students." Nonaggressive boys had mothers and fathers who were more willing to discuss and advise their sons through the social problems, whereas aggressive boys had mothers and fathers who were more likely to punish and deny or divert responsibility for their sons' behavior.

Family Profile of Passive (Submissive) Victims

Much more research is needed before firm conclusions can be drawn about how families play a role in the etiology of children's victimization, either passive victimization or aggressive victimization. Nonetheless, the following characteristics and family processes have been identified among families of victimized children, and many of the findings lend some support to the notion that parenting behaviors that impede children's gender-specific social competencies place children at risk for victimization. A body of literature suggests that parenting processes may contribute to the development of children's passive, submissive individual traits, which place some children at risk to become passive victims. For example, parental overprotection appears to contribute to victimization of boys because it impedes the development of boys' assertiveness and autonomy. For girls, parental rejection and hostility seems to contribute to victimization because they impede girls' sense of social relatedness. Other family risk factors for children's victimization include low parent involvement/low family support, insecure attachment history, intrusive-demandingness, low parental responsivity, and harsh parenting that includes corporal punishment.

Most of the research on peer victimization has focused on individual characteristics that place children at risk for chronic victimization. In addition, most of the research has focused on studying individual characteristics of children who are passive victims. These characteristics include being weak or submissive in appearance, low in self-esteem, calm and withdrawn in temperament, high in anxiety, afraid to assert themselves, and having a physical trait that sets them apart and makes them a target for victimization, such as wearing glasses with thick lenses or speaking with a lisp (Hodges, Malone, & Perry, 1997; Perry, Hodges, & Egan, 2001). Unfortunately, many victims experience peer rejection (Boulton & Underwood, 1992; Curtner et al., 1993; Olweus, 1993) and have fewer friends than nonvictimized children (Boulton & Underwood, 1992; Curtner et al., 1993; Hodges et al., 1997).

A longitudinal investigation of Canadian children demonstrated that neither early emotional difficulties, which were measured by maternal reports of child appearing sad, fearful, worried, anxious, nervous, or tense, nor early signs of hyperactivity, both of which were assessed when children were 17 months old, were associated with peer victimization when children were preschool age (Barker et al., 2008). The authors concluded that emotional difficulties of older school-aged victimized children are a consequence rather than an antecedent of young children's peer victimization. Other studies, however, are based on the assumption that characteristics of being anxious, submissive, and withdrawn precede children's victimization and act as risk factors. Clearly, more longitudinal research is needed to identify the antecedents and consequences of young children's victimization.

Regardless of whether children's individual characteristics of being anxious, withdrawn, and passive precede or following victimization, the major challenge for parents of victimized children, particularly for parents of children who are passive victims, is to help children cope with the emotional difficulties that are associated with the victimization experience, to teach their children how to deal with bullies in an appropriately assertive way, and to help their children make and maintain friendships. The latter socialization task is just as important as the first two given that children who have at least one friend are less likely to be victimized (Hodges, Boivin, Vitaro, & Bukowski, 1999; Pellegrini, Bartini, & Brooks, 1999). Parents of aggressive victims, however, have much greater challenges, which are to deter their children's tendency to retaliate with aggression, teach their children to be appropriately assertive when dealing with bullies, and to socialize their children for social competence within the larger peer group.

Research on children's victimization has focused more on identifying individual characteristics of victims and less on parenting processes that may be linked to children's victimization. Considering the two types of victim status: passive victims and aggressive victims, it is quite likely that different parenting processes predict different types of victim status. Unfortunately, most research on this topic has neglected to distinguish between children who are passive victims and children who are aggressive victims, or research has focused solely on family processes of passive victims. Because passive victims tend to be submissive, withdrawn, and afraid to assert themselves, a few investigators such as Finnegan, Hodges, and Perry (1996, 1998) and Ladd and Kochenderfer-Ladd (1998) examined parenting behaviors that have been linked to these individual child characteristics.

The prevailing theory is that there are gender-specific social competencies, and that parenting behaviors which impede the development of these gender-specific social competencies make children vulnerable to victimization (Perry et al., 2001). Finnegan et al. (1998) identify the major social competency for boys as the establishment of autonomy and assertion within the peer group. Parenting behaviors that are likely to impede boys' development of autonomy and assertion include parental overprotection and discouragement of autonomy. Finnegan et al. argue that when parents are overprotective of boys and discourage their autonomy, boys become less likely to engage in behaviors that help defend their position within the social dominance hierarchy of peer groups. These behaviors include rough and tumble play, risk taking, exploration, assertion, and conflict management skills. Moreover, the investigators speculate that boys' inability to defend themselves during peer conflicts leads them to feel weak relative to peers. The self-perception of weakness leads these boys to behave in ways that make them a target for victimization.

A corresponding yet different process explains the links between parenting, individual child development, and peer victimization among girls. For girls, the major social competency is "connectedness within close relationships." Parenting behaviors that convey maternal disinterest and rejection are likely to impede girls' social connectedness to significant others. When parents, particularly mothers, threaten girls' connectedness by being rejecting, girls feel unworthy of love and fail to develop relationship-nurturing behaviors such as empathy, sharing, cooperation, and play caregiving. Finnegan et al. speculate that girls who feel unloved are incapable of relating closely with others; therefore, they are devalued within the peer group and vulnerable to victimization.

Parental Overprotection/Intense Emotional Closeness

Having an overprotective mother places boys, but not girls, at risk for victimization (Bowers, Smith, & Binney, 1994; Finnegan et al., 1998; Ladd & Kochenderfer-Ladd, 1998; Olweus, 1978). In a classic study of Swedish male bullies and their victims, Olweus (1978) found that mothers of victimized boys treated their sons as younger than the boys' age and were overcontrolling of the boys' spare time. Ladd and Kochenderfer-Ladd (1998) observed U.S. kindergarten-aged children; boys who engaged in interactions with their mothers that were indicative of an unusually emotionally intense relationship (sitting close together, and lots of positive touching, cuddling, smiling) were more likely to self-report high victimization by peers. This relationship between emotionally close behaviors and victimization was not significant for girls. Similarly, Finnegan et al. (1998) found that American boys, but not girls, aged 9 to 12 years who described their mothers as overprotective and who reported being afraid and compelled to submit to their mothers during conflict were more likely to be victimized, suggesting that parenting practices that impede the development of boys' autonomy is linked to peer victimization.

Insecure-Resistant Attachment History

Several studies have demonstrated that preschool- and school-aged children with histories of insecure-resistant attachment histories during infancy are more likely to be victimized than children with secure attachment histories during infancy (Jacobson & Wille, 1986; LaFreneiere & Sroufe, 1985;

Troy & Sroufe, 1987). Jacobson and Wille (1986) assessed security of attachment to mother among 18-month-old children. When children were 2 years old and again when they were 3 years old, the children were observed during a 25-minute free play session with an unfamiliar playmate who was securely attached to his or her mother. Children with anxious-resistant attachment with their mothers were less likely than secure children to receive positive initiations by the securely attached playmate. Moreover, anxious-resistant children were more likely than secure children to withdraw without defending self when the playmate engaged in agonistic behaviors. Likewise, Troy and Sroufe (1987) found that insecure-resistant 4- to 5-year-old children were more likely to be victimized during dyadic play than children whose quality of attachment to mothers was secure. In a similar study, LaFreniere and Sroufe (1985) found that insecure-resistant children were lower in social dominance and social participation than either secure or insecure-avoidant children.

Finnegan et al. (1998) studied 11-year-old U.S. children and found that girls, but not boys, who perceived their mothers as rejecting (characteristic of mothers who share an insecure attachment relationship with their children, particularly an insecure-resistant attachment relationship), were more likely to be nominated by classmates as victims. They concluded that parenting behaviors such as maternal rejection, which impedes girls' feelings of connectedness or closeness to their mothers, places them at risk for victimization. In a separate study, the same authors (Finnegan et al., 1996) found that boys' preoccupied coping, defined as having a strong need for mother, but unable to be soothed by her, was related to victimization. Thus, it appears that an insecure attachment bond, particularly an insecure-resistant bond, which is fostered by chaotic, inconsistent caregiving, is a risk factor for children's victimization.

Low parent involvement/low family support

Parental involvement includes the time parents and children engage in shared activities, how available parents are to assist children through emotionally difficult times, how interested parents are in children's school work and extracurricular activities, how much parents help their children plan for the future, and how much responsibility parents take for seeing that their children's physical needs are met. Among families with school-aged children and adolescents, low parent involvement and low family support have been related to victimization. Flouri and Buchanan (2002) surveyed boys aged 13–19 years in the United Kingdom; low father involvement with sons predicted boys' extreme victimization. In a study of Swiss adolescents aged 13–15 years, low parent support was mildly associated with bullying victimization and with criminal victimization (bodily injury, robbery, sexual assault) among both boys and girls (Perren & Hornung, 2005). Spriggs, Iannotti, Nansel, and Haynie (2007) studied U.S. adolescents and found that low parent–school involvement (e.g. helping with homework) predicted victim status among whites and African Americans, but not among Hispanics. Additionally, white adolescents who did not live with both biological parents were more likely to be victims. The investigators speculated that living with both biological parents provided each parent more opportunities to be involved with their children. No relationship was found for family structure and victim status among African Americans or Hispanics; however, African American and Hispanic victims were more likely than white victims and children not involved in bully–victim problems to have difficulty or feel uneasy about talking to parents regarding issues that really bother them.

Parental involvement may protect children from victimization in three ways. First, parents who seek to be involved with their children convey the message that their children are important and worthy of parental time and interest, and this message likely bolsters children's self-esteem and self-confidence. Children who are high in self-esteem and self-confidence are less likely to be targets of bullying because they have the confidence and social skills to be assertive and to stand up for themselves. Second, involved parents are likely to be better monitors of their children's peer associations and activities, which means they are better able to detect when their children are having social difficulties. Consequently, involved parents may be more likely to offer emotional support and guidance to their children who are occasionally victimized. Third, not only are involved parents more likely to detect when their children are victims of bullying, but because of the emotional support found between involved parents and their children, children who are targets of occasional bullying may be more likely to seek the advice and counsel of their parents on how to deal with peer difficulties.

Poor Parent–Child Communication

Quality of communication (as opposed to level of emotional intimacy shared in communication, which is an aspect of parental involvement) also has been found to predict young children's victimization. In particular, intrusive-demandingness and parental responsivity have been documented in families of young victimized children. Intrusive-demandingness refers to how much a parent interrupts a child (i.e., intrudes) or overrides a child's initiatives (i.e., makes demands). Parental responsivity refers to how quickly, consistently, and appropriately parents respond to children's verbalizations and nonverbal behaviors. Ladd and Kochenderfer-Ladd (1998) made home observations of mothers and their kindergarten-aged children engaging in a series of semistructured tasks. Mothers high in intrusive-demandingness and low in responsivity were more likely to have girls, but not boys, who self-reported peer victimization. Ladd and Kochenderfer-Ladd argue that intrusive-demanding parenting socializes children to be compliant and dependent rather than independent and assertive. In contrast, parental responsiveness conveys to children that parents are interested and "provides children with feedback that may allow them [the children] to infer a sense of control and influence over others...." (p. 1452). Thus, high levels of intrusive-demandingness and low levels of maternal responsivity interfere with girls' social connectedness to others, which places them at risk for victimization.

Harsh Overreactive Parenting

Harsh parenting not only predicts bullying behavior, but it also predicts victimization. Another finding of the Finnegan et al. (1998) study described earlier was that mothers' hostility predicted victimization status for 9- to 12-year-old girls. In addition, a study of 10- to 15-year-olds in the Midwestern United States found that youth who reported receiving corporal punishment or physical discipline were more likely to report being victimized during the past school term (Ohene et al., 2006).

Barker et al. (2008) found that mothers who reported engaging in harsh parenting when children were 17 months of age had children who increased in their victimization throughout the preschool years, kindergarten year, and 1st grade year. Harsh parenting emerged as an especially strong predictor of children's victimization among children who scored very high in victimization across the preschool, kindergarten, and early elementary school years. For these children, harsh parenting when the children were very young (feeling angry toward, shouting at, and spanking the 17-month-old child when the child was particularly fussy) remained predictive of victimization across the years even after statistically controlling for children's aggressive behavior. Barker et al. conclude that victimization for children, especially children who receive high rates of victimization over several years, actually begins in the home and is perpetrated by parents.

Family Profile of Aggressive Victims

As previously mentioned, aggressive victims are children who are not only the recipients of bullying but also engage in high rates of bullying behaviors. They may often retaliate against the very children who bullied them, or they may bully other children who are lower in social dominance. These children are very emotionally dysregulated, hot tempered, and easily provoked (Olweus, 1978). Families of aggressive victims have not been studied extensively, but the available research gives at least a preliminary view. A landmark study of the family backgrounds of male aggressive victims ranging in age from 8 to 9 years was conducted by Schwartz, Dodge, Pettit, and Bates (1997). They found that aggressive victims were more likely than other children (i.e., children classified as either bullies, victims, nonbullies/nonvictims) to have experienced parenting during the preschool years that was so harsh, hostile, and punitive that it was perceived by the investigators as abuse. Moreover, the aggressive children's mothers reported highly conflictual interactions between adult members of the household (spouses or partners), which included overt physical violence.

In many ways, the parenting processes in families with aggressive victims are likely to be more similar to the parenting processes in families of bullies given the aggressive tendencies and other externalizing behaviors that are common among aggressive victims. However, one major difference between the family backgrounds of aggressive victims and the family backgrounds of either bullies or victims is that the family processes of families of aggressive victims have been labeled as physically and emotionally abusive. Families of aggressive victims often appear to experience very harsh, angry, explosive hostility (between parents and between parent and child), physical abuse/ interpersonal violence between parents, and physical abuse of children.

Implications for Effective Family-Level Interventions
Help for Families of Children Who Bully

The body of literature on the family profiles of children who bully reveals many points for interventions. Prior to beginning an intervention, counselors, therapists, and family life educators need to give careful consideration to the sequence of topics addressed in intervention. For example, it would likely do little good to try to promote warmth and affection without first giving parents some skills for managing their children's aggressive behaviors. Values clarification activities that contrast physical punishment with discipline that leads by example could be implemented with parents. Additionally, specific skills for managing children's behavior would include having age-appropriate expectations for behavior and setting and enforcing limits. Parents can learn to enforce limits by using either natural or logical consequences. Natural consequences are those that happen without parental intervention. For example, if a child leaves her soccer ball in the rain, it will get wet and eventually be ruined. Logical consequences are those that are logically related to the child's misdeed and do not involve physical punishment. An example of a logical consequence would be to have the child go to bed 10 minutes early if he is late getting up in the morning. Reciprocal discipline is a type of logical consequence that involves making reparations for a transgression. For instance, if a child breaks a sibling's toy, then the child could perform some extra chores around the house to earn the money to pay for the toy.

Early in the intervention program, interventionists need to identify parents who may be depressed, have difficulty with expressing anger, and/or who feel hopeless about the future. These parents may need some extra support and cognitive therapy to help them change their self and other perceptions to become more positive.

Parents and children may need an interventionist's help in creating opportunities for fun, warmth, and enjoyment. Perhaps this could even be a weekly assignment that parents report on during each intervention session. Opportunities for experiencing pleasure, warmth, and enjoyment, particularly if these are repeated over time should aid in promoting parent–child attachment bonds. Secure attachments are promoted during times of shared positive affect (joy) between parent and child (Schore, 2005).

Empathy training that helps parents engage in more empathic positive parenting should help foster children's empathy. Important topics would be to try to get parents to understand their child's point of view, even if they disagree with that view, developing compassion for the child, and learning to forgive and accept children. Finally, parents need to be educated about the different types of children's bullying behaviors and the long-term consequences for engaging in bullying. Parents may need to learn specific ways they can promote their child's social competence, such as monitoring their child's peer activities and creating opportunities for play with more socially competent children. Parents also may need some training in how to express disapproval or disappointment when children engage in aggression, when and how to intervene in their children's peer conflicts, and how to directly coach their children to become more socially competent.

Help for Families of Submissive Victims

Although the body of research regarding parental contributions to children's victimization is just emerging, several points for intervention can be identified. First, mothers of sons can be taught parenting skills that encourage them to be less overprotective and more promoting of boys' autonomy. Mothers of daughters can be taught parenting skills that encourage them to be more accepting of, warm toward, and involved and connected with their children. Parents of both sons and daughters can be taught how to be more open to opportunities for communicating in nonjudgmental ways with their children about issues that are of concern or worry to children. Parents may also help their children engage in assertiveness training activities that may help fend off a bully's provocation, and parents can directly coach their children in how to handle a bully.

Help for Families of Aggressive Victims

Some parents of aggressive victims will likely need assistance in dealing with anger or hostility, and they may benefit from being taught alternatives to corporal punishment as ways of guiding children's behavior and inducing child compliance. Parents of aggressive victims may be especially in need of help in dealing with the problem of family violence.

Practical Considerations

Family-level intervention that is integrated into a school-based bully–victim program should help to maximize the efficacy of the intervention for children involved in bully–victim problems (Ahmed & Braithwaite, 2004). Several practical considerations arise when thinking about how to integrate family-level intervention within the school setting. The first consideration regards format. The various formats of family-level interventions include large-group, small-group, and individual family education/therapy, which can take place in an office located at the school, in an office located at the interventionist's place of practice, or in the family home (Powell & Cassidy, 2007). The ideal size for a small group of parents ranges between 5 to 7, which allows for high levels of interaction among group members. The intensity of interaction among group members whose purpose is to experience therapeutic change is usually very high. Likewise, the intensity among family members in family education/

therapy, whether it takes place in an office or the family home, can be very high. Consequently, interventionists who run small groups or lead family education/therapy sessions need to be highly skilled at managing the emotionally charged sessions. Home visits can be particularly helpful because they allow the interventionist to observe family interaction and teach new interaction skills within the family's natural setting.

A second consideration regarding programs for families with children involved in bully–victim problems is how to encourage parent participation. It is likely that parents of passive victims, especially mothers of boys because these mothers tend to be overprotective, will want to attend psychoeducational programs or groups that will enable them to help their children. Parents of bullies and parents of aggressive victims, however, may be very resistant to the idea of attending either small-group or family education/therapy sessions. It may be beneficial for schools to develop a policy that requires parent attendance in family-level intervention programs before children who have been expelled because of their bullying are allowed to return to school.

Small groups for parents of bullies, parents of aggressive victims, and parents of passive victims need to be run separately for two reasons. First, parents of children in each group have different needs and different sets of parenting skills that need to be learned. Additionally, parents of aggressive victims may need individual therapy to address issues of anger and interpersonal violence in their marital or partner relationships as well as in the parent–child relationships. Second, running separate groups for the sets of parents (parents of bullies, parents of aggressive victims, and parents of passive victims) helps minimize the potential for conflict between parents of bullies and parents of victims.

Interventionists need to be aware of when interventions harm rather than help. Outcome studies of intervention programs involving small groups of antisocial youth find that the programs can have iatrogenic effects. That is, the children in the programs actually increase the frequency and severity of their antisocial behaviors by talking with each other about the rules they violated (Dishion, McCord, & Poulin, 1999). In a similar way, parents of bullies and parents of aggressive victims who share their experiences with parenting their children may learn negative, harsh parenting behaviors from each other, and they may reinforce each other's values for harsh, hostile parenting.

Programs that target families with children age 8 years and younger may produce the greatest change in reducing harsh, hostile parenting and in increasing warm, involved, sensitive parenting that promotes secure parent–child attachments (Karoly et al., 1998). Likewise, early intervention/

prevention programs that aim to reduce young children's bullying behavior and increase their prosocial behavior may be more effective than interventions for families with older youth and adolescents. Change takes time, and once parents make positive gains in changing their parenting behaviors, children may act out more to test new limits (Patterson & Narrett, 1990). Change is possible, however, even for children and families who are the most difficult to reach.

References

Ahmed, E., & Braithwaite, V. (2004). Bullying and victimization: Cause for concern for both families and schools. *Social Psychology of Education, 7,* 35–54.

Ainsworth, M. D. (1989). Attachments beyond infancy. *American Psychologist, 44,* 709–716.

Associated Press (2007). *Mother accused of directing fight on bus,* May 9, 2007.

Barber, B. (1996). Parental psychological control: Revisiting a neglected construct. *Child Development, 67,* 3296–3319.

Barker, E. D., Boivin, M., Brendgen, M., Fontaine, N., Arseneault, L., Vitaro, F., Bissonette, C., & Tremblay, R. E. (2008). The predictive validity and early predictors of peer victimization trajectories in preschool. *Archives of General Psychiatry, 65,* 1185–1192.

Baumrind, D., Larzelere, R., & Cowan, A. (2002). Ordinary physical punishment, is it harmful? Comment on Gershoff (2002). *Psychological Bulletin, 128,* 580–589.

Bavolek, S. J. (1984). *Adult-adolescent parenting inventory.* Eau Claire, WI: Family Development Resources.

Boulton, M. J., & Underwood, K. (1992). Bully/victim problems among middle school children. *British Journal of Educational Psychology, 62,* 73–87.

Bowers, L., Smith, P. K., & Binney, V. (1994). Perceived family relationships of bullies, victims, and bully/victims in middle childhood. *Journal of Social and Personal Relationships, 11,* 215–232.

Capaldi, D. M. (2003). Parental monitoring: A person-environment interaction perspective on this key parenting skill. In A. C. Crouter & A. Booth (Eds.), *Children's influence on family dynamics* (pp. 171–179). Mahwah, NJ: Erlbaum.

Casas, J. F., Weigel, S. M., Crick, N. R., Ostrov, J. M., Woods, K. E., Jansen Yeh, E. A., & Huddleston-Casas, C. A. (2006). Early parenting and children's relational and physical aggression in the preschool and home contexts. *Applied Developmental Psychology, 27,* 209–227.

Cohn, D.A. (1990). Child-mother attachment of six-year-olds and social competence at school. *Child Development, 61,* 152–162.

Cohn, J. F., Campbell, S. B., Matias, R., & Hopkins, J. (1990). Face-to-face interactions of postpartum depressed and nondepressed mother-infant pairs at 2 months. *Developmental Psychology, 26,* 15–23.

Cornell, A. H., & Frick, P. H. (2007). The moderating effects of parenting styles in the association between behavioral inhibition and parent-reported guilt and empathy in preschool children. *Journal of Clinical Child and Adolescent Psychology, 36*, 305–318.

Culp, A. M., Culp, R. E., Horton, C., Curtner-Smith, M. E., Palermo, F., & Culp, K. C. (2003). *Head Start children's playground aggression and teachers' and maternal reports.* Poster presented at the annual meeting of Division 37: Child, Youth, and Family Services. American Psychological Association, Toronto, Canada.

Cummings, M. (2008). *Halting bullies. Tuscaloosa News,* Tuscaloosa, AL (Tuesday April 29).

Curtner, M. E., O'Rear, M. R., Herr, D. G., Dawson, J., McWilliams, K., & Williams, S. (1993). *School-age bullies and victims: Others' and self perceptions, problematic situations, and social networks.* Paper presented at the Biennial Meetings of the Society for Research in Child Development, New Orleans, LA. Abstract published in proceedings.

Curtner-Smith, M. E. (2000). Mechanisms by which family processes contribute to school-age boys' bullying. *Child Study Journal, 30,* 169–186.

Curtner-Smith, M. E. (2007, July). *Developmental versus power assertive strategies mothers say they would use to help their children deal with bully/victim problems.* Research Colloquium, Goldsmiths, University of London.

Curtner-Smith, M. E., Culp, A. M., Culp, R., Scheib, C., Owen, K., Tilley, A. Murphy, M., Parkan, L., & Coleman, P. W. (2006). Mothers' parenting and young economically disadvantaged children's relational and overt bullying. *Journal of Child and Family Studies, 15,* 177–189.

Deater-Deckard, K., Dodge, K., Bates, J., & Pettit, G. S. (1996). Physical discipline among African American and European American mothers: Links to children's externalizing behaviors. *Developmental Psychology, 32,* 1065–1072.

Deater-Deckard, K., Ivy, L., & Petrill, S. A. (2006). Maternal warmth moderates the link between physical punishment and child externalizing problems: A parent-offspring genetic analysis. *Parenting: Science and Practice, 6,* 59–78.

Dishion, T. J., McCord, J., & Poulin, F. (1999). When interventions harm: Peer groups and problem behavior. *American Psychologist, 54,* 755–764.

Dodge, K. A., Pettit, G. S., & Bates, J. E. (1994). Socialization mediators of the relation between socioeconomic status and child conduct problems. *Child Development, 65,* 649–665.

Driscoll, J. R., & Easterbrooks, M. A. (2007). Young mothers' play with their toddlers: Individual variability as a function of psychosocial factors. *Infant and Child Development, 16,* 649–670.

Eisenberg, N., & Valiente, C. (2002). Parenting and children's prosocial and moral development. In Marc H. Bornstein (Ed.), *Handbook of parenting. Vol. 5. Practical issues in parenting* (2nd ed., pp. 111–142). Mahwah, NJ: Erlbaum.

Endresen, I. M., & Olweus, D. (2002). Self-reported empathy in Norwegian adolescents: Sex differences, age trends, and relationship to bullying. In D. Stipek & A. Bohart

(Eds.), *Constructive and destructive behavior. Implications for family, school, and society* (pp. 147–165). Washington, DC: American Psychological Association.

Fagot, B. I., & Kavanagh, K. (1990). The prediction of antisocial behavior from avoidant attachment classifications. *Child Development, 61,* 864–873.

Finnegan, R. A., Hodges, E. V. E., & Perry, D. G. (1996). Preoccupied and avoidant coping during middle childhood. *Child Development, 67,* 1318–1328.

Finnegan, R. A., Hodges, E. V. E., & Perry, D. G. (1998). Victimization by peers: Associations with children's reports of mother-child interaction. *Journal of Personality and Social Psychology, 75,* 1076–1086.

Flouri, E., & Buchanan, A. (2002). Life satisfaction in teenager boys: The moderating role of father involvement and bullying. *Aggressive Behavior, 28,* 126–133.

Flouri, E., & Buchanan, A. (2003). The role of mother involvement and father involvement in adolescent bullying behavior. *Journal of Interpersonal Violence, 18,* 1–11.

Garber, J., & Martin, N. C. (2002). Negative cognitions in offspring of depressed parents: Mechanisims of risk. In S. H. Goodman and I. H. Gotlib (Eds.), *Children of depressed parents: Mechanisms of risk and implications for treatment* (pp. 121–153). Washington DC: American Psychological Association.

Goodman, S. H., Adamson, L. B., Riniti, J., & Cole, S. (1994). Mothers' expressed attitudes: Associations with maternal depression and children's self-esteem and psycho-pathology. *Journal of the American Academy of Child and Adolescent Psychiatry, 33,* 1265–1274.

Goodman, S. H., & Brumley, H. E. (1990). Schizophrenic and depressed mothers: Relational deficits in parenting. *Developmental Psychology, 26,* 31–39.

Gunnoe, M. L., & Mariner, C. L. (1997). Toward a developmental contextual model of the effects of parental spanking on children's aggression. *Archives of Pediatric Adolescent Medicine, 151,* 768–775.

Hay, D. F., Pawlby, S., Angold, A., Harold, G. T., & Sharp, D. (2003). Pathways to violence in the children of mothers who were depressed postpartum. *Developmental Psychology, 39,* 1083–1094.

Hodges, E. V. E., Boivin, M., Vitaro, F., & Bukowski, W. M. (1999). The power of friendship: Protection against an escalating cycle of peer victimization. *Developmental Psychology, 35,* 94–101.

Hodges, E. V. E., Finnegan, R. A., & Perry, D. G. (1999). Skewed autonomy-relatedness in preadolescents' conceptions of their relationships with mother, father, and best friend. *Developmental Psychology, 35,* 737–748.

Hodges, E. V. E., Malone, M. J., & Perry, D. G. (1997). Individual risk and social risk as interacting determinants of victimization in the peer group. *Developmental Psychology, 33,* 1032–1039.

Hoffman, M. L. (2000). *Empathy and moral development: Implications for caring and justice.* Cambridge, England: Cambridge University Press.

Hubbs-Tait, L., Culp, A. M., Culp, R. E., & Miller, C. E. (2002). Relation of maternal cognitive stimulation, emotional support, and intrusive behavior during Head Start to children's kindergarten cognitive abilities. *Child Development, 73,* 110–131.

Jacobson, J. L., & Wille, D. E. (1986). The influence of attachment pattern on developmental changes in peer interaction from the toddler to the preschool period. *Child Development, 57,* 338–347.

Jolliffe, D., & Farrington, D. P. (2006). Examining the relationship between low empathy and bullying. *Aggressive Behavior, 32,* 540–550.

Karoly, L. A., Greenwood, P. W., Everingham, S. S., Hoube, J., Kilburn, M. R., Rydell, C. P., Sanders, M., & Chiesa, J. (1998). *Investing in our children: What we know and don't know about the costs of early childhood interventions.* Santa Monica, CA: Rand Corporation.

Kilpatrick, K. (2005). The parental empathy measure: A new approach to assessing child maltreatment risk. *Abnormal Journal of Orthopsychiatry, 75,* 608–620.

Krevans, J., & Gibbs, J. C. (1996). Parents' use of inductive discipline: Relations to children's empathy and prosocial behavior. *Child Development, 67,* 3263–3277.

Ladd, G. W. (2005). *Children's peer relations and social competence: A century of progress.* New Haven, CT: Yale University Press.

Ladd, G. W., & Kochenderfer-Ladd, B. J. (1998). Parenting behaviors and parent-child relationships: Correlates of peer victimization in kindergarten? *Developmental Psychology, 34,* 1450–1458.

LaFreniere, P. J., & Sroufe, L. A. (1985). Profiles of peer competence in the preschool: Interrelations between measures, influence of social ecology, and relation to attachment history. *Developmental Psychology, 21,* 56–89.

Laird, R. D., Pettit, G. S., Mize, J., & Lindsey, E. (1994). Mother-child conversations about peers: Contributions to competence. *Family Relations, 43,* 425–432.

Leve, L. D., Pears, K. C., & Fisher, P. A. (2002). Competence in early development. In J. B. Reid, G. R. Patterson, & J. Snyder (Eds.), *Antisocial behavior in children and adolescents: A developmental analysis and model for intervention* (pp. 45–64). Washington DC: American Psychological Society.

Loeber, R., Farrington, D. P., Stouthamer-Loeber, M., & Van Kamman, W. B. (1998). *Antisocial behavior and mental health problems: Explanatory factors in childhood and adolescence.* Mahwah, NJ: Erlbaum.

Loeber, R., & Stouthamer-Loeber, M. (1986). Family factors as correlates and predictors of juvenile conduct problems and delinquency. In M. Tonry and N. Morris (Eds.), *Crime and justice: Vol. 7. An annual review of research* (pp. 29–149). Chicago: University of Chicago Press.

Main, M., Kaplan, N., & Cassidy, J. (1985). Security in infancy, childhood, and adulthood: A move to the level of representation. In I. Bretherton & E. Waters (Eds.), *Growing points of attachment theory and research. Monographs of the Society for Research in Child Development, 50,* nos 1–2.

Marcus, R. F. (1991). The attachments of children in foster care. *Genetics, social, and general psychology monographs, 117*, 365–394.

McLoyd, V., & Smith, J. (2002). Physical discipline and behavior problems in African American, European American, and Hispanic children: Emotional support as a moderator. *Journal of Marriage and the Family, 64*, 40–53.

Mize, J., & Pettit, G. S. (1997). Mothers' social coaching, mother-child relationship style, and children's peer competence: Is the medium the message? *Child Development, 68*, 312–332.

Myron, R., Smith, P. K., & Sutton, J. (unpublished manuscript). The association between bully and victim roles in school and the nature of attachment in middle childhood. Submitted for publication.

Nelson, D. A., & Crick, N. R. (2002). Parental psychological control: Implications for childhood physical and relational aggression. In B. Barber (Ed.), *Intrusive parenting: How psychological control affects children and adolescents* (pp. 161–189). Washington, DC: American Psychological Association (APA) Books.

Nievar, M. A., & Becker, B. J. (2007). Sensitivity as a privileged predictor of attachment: A second perspective on De Wolff and IJzendoorn's meta-analysis. *Social Development, 17*, 102–114.

Ohene, S., Ireland, M., McNeely, C., & Borowsky, I. W. (2006). Parental expectations, physical punishment, and violence among adolescents who score positive on a psychosocial screening test in primary care. *Pediatrics, 117*, 441–447.

Olweus, D. (1978). *Aggression in the schools: Bullies and their whipping boys.* Washington, DC: Hemisphere.

Olweus, D. (1980). Familial and temperamental determinants of aggressive behavior in adolescent boys: A causal analysis. *Developmental Psychology, 16*, 644–660.

Olweus, D. (1993). Victimization by peers: Antecedents and long-term outcomes. In K. H. Rubin & J. B. Asendorpf (Eds.), *Social withdrawal, inhibition and shyness in childhood* (pp. 315–341). Hillsdale, NJ: Erlbaum.

Olweus, D. (1994). Bullying at school: Long-term outcomes for victims and an effective school-based intervention program. In L. R. Huesmann (Ed.), *Aggressive behavior: Current perspectives* (pp. 97–130). New York: Plenum Press.

Pakaslahti, L., Asplund-Peltola, R., & Keltikangas,-Jarvinen, L. (1996). Parents' social problem-solving strategies in families with aggressive and non-aggressive boys. *Aggressive Behavior, 22*, 345–356.

Patterson, G. R. (1980). Mothers: The unacknowledged victims. *Monographs for the Society for Research in Child Development, 45* (5,Serial No. 180).

Patterson, G. R., & Forgatch, M. S. (1990). Initiation and maintenance of process disrupting single-mother families. In G. R. Patterson (Ed.), *Depression and aggression in family interaction* (pp. 209–245). Hillsdale, NJ: Erlbaum.

Patterson, G. R., & Narrett, C. M. (1990). The development of a reliable and valid treatment program for aggressive young children. *International Journal of Mental Health, 19*, 19–26.

Pellegrini, A. D., Bartini, M., & Brooks, F. (1999). School bullies, victims, and aggressive victims: Factors relating to group affiliation and victimization in early adolescence. *Journal of Educational Psychology, 91*, 216–224.

Perren, S., & Hornung, R. (2005). Bullying and delinquency in adolescence: Victims' and perpetrators' family and peer relations. *Swiss Journal of Psychology, 64*, 51–64.

Perry, D. G., Hodges, E. V. E., & Egan, S. K. (2001). Determinants of chronic victimization by peers. In J. Juvonen & S. Graham (Eds.), *Peer harassment in school* (pp. 73–104). New York & London: Guilford Press.

Pettit, G. S., Bates, J. E., Dodge, K. A., & Meece, D. (1999). The impact of after-school peer contact on early adolescent externalizing problems is moderated by parental monitoring, perceived knowledge of neighbourhood safety, and prior adjustment. *Child Development, 70*, 768–778.

Powell, L. H., & Cassidy, D. (2007). *Family life education: Working with families across the life span* (2nd ed.). Long Grove, IL: Waveland Press.

Renk, K., Phares, V., & Epps, J. (1999). The relationship between parental anger and behavior problems in children and adolescents. *Journal of Family Psychology, 13*, 209–227.

Rubin, K. H., Burgess, K. B., Dwyer, K. M., & Hastings, P. D. (2003). Predicting preschoolers' externalizing behaviors from toddler temperament, conflict, and maternal negativity. *Developmental Psychology, 39*, 164–176.

Schore, A. N. (2005). Attachment, affect regulation, and the developing right brain: Linking developmental neuroscience to pediatrics. *Pediatrics in Review, 26*, 204–217.

Schwartz, D., Dodge, K. A., Pettit, G. S., & Bates, J. E. (1997). The early socialization of aggressive victims of bullying. *Child Development, 68*, 665–675.

Skinner, E., Johnson, S., & Synder, T. (2005). Six dimensions of parenting: A motivational model. *Parenting Science and Practice, 5*, 175–235.

Snyder, J., & Stoolmiller, M. (2002). Reinforcement and coercion mechanisms in the development of antisocial behavior: The family. In J. B. Reid, G. R. Patterson, and J. Synder (Eds.), *Antisocial behavior in children and adolescents: A developmental analysis and model for intervention* (pp. 65–122). Washington, DC: American Psychological Society.

Spriggs, A. L., Iannotti, R. J., Nansel, T. R. & Haynie, D. L. (2007). Adolescent bullying involvement and perceived family, peer and school relations: Commonalities and differences across race/ethnicity. *Journal of Adolescent Health, 41*, 283–293.

Stockdale, M. S., Haungaduambo, S., Duys, D., Larson, K., & Sarvela, P. D. (2002). Rural elementary students', parents, and teachers' perceptions of bullying. *American Journal of Health Behavior, 26*, 266–277.

Stormshak, E. A., Bierman, K. L., & McMahon, R. J., Lengua, L. J. (2000) Parenting practices and child disruptive behavior problems in early elementary school. *Journal of Clinical Child Psychology, 29*, 17–29.

Strassberg, Z., Dodge, K. A., Pettit, G. S., & Bates, J. E. (1994). Spanking in the home and children's subsequent aggression toward kindergarten peers. *Development and Psychopathology, 6*, 445–461.

Straus, M. A. (2001). *Beating the devil out of them: Corporal punishment in American families and its effects on children.* New Brunswick, NJ: Transaction Publishers.

Straus, M. A., Sugarman, D. B., & Giles-Sims, J. (1997). Spanking and antisocial behavior of children. *Archives of Paediatrics and Adolescent Medicine, 152,* 761–767.

Sutton, J., Smith, P. K., & Swettenham, J. (1999). Social cognition and bullying: Social inadequacy of skilled manipulation. *British Journal of Developmental Psychology, 17,* 435–450.

Troy, M., & Sroufe, L.A. (1987). Victimization among preschoolers: Role of attachment relationship history. *Journal of the American Academy of Child and Adolescent Psychiatry, 26,*166–172.

Turner, P. (1991). Relations between attachment, gender and behavior with peers in preschool. *Child Development, 62,* 1475–1488.

Werner, N. E., Senich, S., & Przepyszny, K. A. (2006). Mothers' responses to preschoolers' relational and physical aggression. *Applied Developmental Psychology, 27,*193–208.

Zhou, Q., Eisenberg, N., Losoya, S., Fabes, R. A., Reiser, M., Guthrie, I. K., Murphy, B., Cumberland, A., & Shepard, S. A. (2002). The relations of parental warmth and positive expressiveness to children's empathy-related responding and social functioning: A longitudinal study. *Child Development, 73,* 893–915.

5

Psychopathology and Health Problems Affecting Involvement in Bullying

Allison G. Dempsey and Eric A. Storch

This chapter focuses on bully–victim problems among children and adolescents who have clinically significant psychopathology or physical health conditions. Let us begin with the following example of Daniel (not his real name), a 7th grade student with whom one author (AGD) worked for several months.

Daniel's guidance counselor referred him to the psychologist due to problems with academics and peer relationships. Daniel's grades had been slipping and his teacher was concerned that he was exhibiting what she described as bizarre behavior. Daniel frequently hummed or mumbled to himself during classes and in the hallways and would sway his head when he sat still. His teachers reported that he occasionally made strange statements in class that were off topic. Daniel had a family history of bipolar disorder and schizophrenia. In addition, he experienced dysgraphia, a type of learning disability that involves difficulty in writing, and so he used a portable typing machine in all his classes.

When the psychologist first met with Daniel, Daniel reported that everything was fine and that he just had a difficult time concentrating in some classes. In addition, he reported that he had some friends and had no problems with his peers. However, after speaking with Daniel's teachers and guidance counselor, the psychologist learned that Daniel was extremely withdrawn from other students. In addition, Daniel's teacher explained that he was a "sad" child with no friends who had a difficult time relating to his peers. The school guidance counselor reported that Daniel's mother had made several complaints that Daniel was physically bullied by other students. The school had responded by moving one of the repeated bullies to another classroom. Incidentally, the bully was also receiving family therapy from another psychologist on the school district's psychology team to address behaviors related to the child's diagnosis of conduct disorder. However, the guidance counselor justified the bully's actions by saying that Daniel was an odd child and that middle school students always pick on the child who cannot get along with others.

The psychologist asked Daniel specific questions about his experiences with his peers. He revealed that every day he had things thrown at him in the halls, pencils jabbed in his neck during classes, and was verbally taunted when the teachers were not listening. On several occasions he had returned home with bruises on his arms and shins from being kicked or pushed in the hallways and cafeteria. Daniel explained that other students teased him because he had to use a machine in class and that they laughed at him when he hummed. After several sessions with the psychologist Daniel admitted that he was usually afraid to attend school because of the daily harassment he received. The constant peer harassment in classes when the teachers' backs were turned also interfered with his ability to concentrate and finish his assignments, thus exacerbating his academic difficulties. Furthermore, the negative interactions with peers contributed to feelings of anxiety related to social situations.

The above example illustrates several of the key points that will be discussed in this chapter. We describe three basic propositions that have strong implications for interventionists. First, some physical and mental health conditions raise the likelihood that a child or adolescent will be a target of bullying. In the case of Daniel, atypical behavior, likely associated with severe psychopathology, and a learning disability caused Daniel to stand out from his peers and made him an easily identifiable target to bullies. Second, physical and mental health conditions often amplify the impact of bullying. In these instances, bullying may contribute to a worsening of psychological symptoms or health-related behaviors and outcomes. Daniel's daily experiences of verbal and physical bullying interfered with his ability to succeed in the classroom and also compounded his preexisting mental health condition with symptoms of anxiety related to social situations. Third, some disorders, especially those involving antisocial behaviors and cognitions, increase the likelihood that a child or adolescent will bully others. In the case of Daniel, one of his most frequent and aggressive bullies had a diagnosis of conduct disorder—a condition associated with antisocial behaviors (American Psychiatric Association, 2000). It is our intention that by reading this chapter, the reader will develop the following knowledge and skills:

1. Understand the populations of children that are at an increased likelihood for being bullied and for engaging in bullying of others.

2. Appreciate the need to monitor children with medical and mental illnesses for their involvement in bullying and provide appropriate interventions when necessary.
3. Engage in interventions that promote positive interactions with empathetic peers and that build resiliency in children who are victims of bullying.
4. Engage in interventions that provide immediate and consistent consequences for children who are bullies.
5. Carefully consider the use of classroom education interventions to dispel myths and to encourage children to talk with their peers about their conditions.

Individual Characteristics That Influence Involvement in Bullying

A key component in the definition of bullying is an imbalance of power between the bully and the victim (Olweus, 2003). The establishment of dominance may be a reason that bullies seek to demonstrate their power over others. According to the social dominance theory hypothesis, youth in late childhood to early adolescence—when rates of bullying are at their highest—establish their positions in social hierarchies by demonstrating their power, or dominance, over their peers via agonistic methods, such as bullying (Pellegrini & Bartini, 2000). For example, middle school boys often establish their place in a social hierarchy based on physical stature and athleticism; the bigger, stronger, and most attractive males tend to emerge at the top of the hierarchy because they are the most likely to draw the attention of females. To demonstrate that they are bigger and stronger than their peers, the boys frequently verbally and physically bully peers that they perceive as physically weaker. When selecting a victim to bully, an aggressor will search for a peer that he or she can readily identify as weak to ensure the victim can be easily overpowered.

Physical strength, however, is not the only characteristic that may be used to identify "weakness" in students. Bullies, who seek to elicit submissive reactions from peers, such as fear, crying, aggression, or helplessness, identify weaknesses in students based upon easily identifiable features that differentiate victims from their peers. Such features may include differences in emotional functioning and social and cognitive deficits. Therefore, children and adolescents with medical or psychological conditions that result in differences in appearance and cognitive and psychosocial functioning have an increased vulnerability to peer victimization. The next section will provide an overview of the association between peer victimization and the most common forms of childhood chronic health conditions (e.g., obesity, asthma, diabetes) and psychological disorders (depression, anxiety, disruptive behavior disorders).

Chronic Health Conditions

Emerging research has demonstrated that various pediatric populations are at an increased likelihood to be victims of bullying. Indeed as many as one-third of students with a chronic illness report being verbally or physically bullied due to their medical condition (Mukherjee, Lightfoot, & Sloper, 2000). Physical characteristics that differentiate pediatric populations from their peers may cause bullies to easily identify and select children with health problems as their targets.

Many chronic childhood illnesses have associated features that result in changes to physical appearance. These physical differences may marginalize children from their peers and cause them to become targets of bullying more frequently than other students. For example, children undergoing chemotherapy to treat various forms of cancer usually experience alopecia (hair loss), changes in weight, and facial swelling. Children with cystic fibrosis often have a small stature, as well as malformations of their fingertips, called "clubbing." Children with chronic heart conditions may also demonstrate stunted growth and swelling of toes and fingers and irregular skin coloring. Children with craniofacial abnormalities frequently have noticeable facial disfiguration.

Children and adolescents may also exhibit behaviors associated with their illnesses that cause their peers to view them as weak or different. Many children may be excused from classes regularly to visit the nurse's office to take medications or engage in other components of their treatment regimen. Children may also be unavailable to participate in in-school and/or extracurricular activities or events due to the need to engage in treatments, refrain from physical activities, or attend doctor appointments after school. Chronic illnesses can also be associated with the need for prolonged absences from school due to hospitalizations and worsening of symptoms. These frequent absences can cause children to miss important social events and opportunities to build friendships with their peers.

Finally, children with chronic health conditions also may exhibit comorbid social problems (e.g., withdrawal), psychopathology (e.g., depression, anxiety, acute stress), and deficits in cognitive functioning (e.g., processing or attention deficits) and academic performance (e.g., poor grades related to frequent absences, grade retention) that place them at increased risk for victimization. The association between preexisting mental health conditions and involvement in bullying will be discussed in the next section. Although there is research to suggest that higher rates of bullying occur among populations of children with low-incidence pediatric conditions, we will focus the next section on research regarding peer victimization among pediatric conditions that are commonly observed in schools. The following section will provide a brief description of research linking the most prevalent chronic medical problems (obesity, asthma, and diabetes/endocrine disorders) observed in student populations to involvement in peer victimization as aggressors or victims.

Obesity

Obesity, one of the most researched chronic illnesses in children, is a growing problem for children and adolescents. National surveys indicate that the prevalence of obesity among children and adolescence is on the rise (Ogden, Flegal, Carroll, & Johnson, 2002). In a society that values fitness and athleticism in both boys and girls, being overweight or obese is an easily identifiable physical feature that isolates children from other students and places them at risk for being targets of bullying.

The negative stigmatization related to high body weight is present even in early childhood and continues through adolescence. Children have been shown to make negative judgments about peers based on body shape when they first begin schooling. Obese children may be perceived as less athletic and less physically attractive than their peers and fellow students may be less willing to befriend overweight/obese children (Goldfield & Chrisler, 1995) or become romantically involved with them (Pearce, Boergers, & Prinstein, 2002). Social isolation not only may place obese youth at risk for being bullied, it may also cause or amplify feelings of poor self-worth and depression.

Due to the high prevalence of weight-related stigmatization from an early age, overweight and obese youth may be more vulnerable to chronic bullying because of the highly visible nature of obesity. Indeed, verbal teasing by peers about body weight is a particular problem for overweight children and adolescents, and it exists across gender and ethnic groups. Weight-related teasing may be especially salient among overweight and obese youth because bullies tend to select methods of aggression that they know will elicit emotional or fearful reactions from their victims and, in turn, victims are most likely to react to vulnerable issues. However, verbal aggression is not the only form of bullying by which overweight/obese children and adolescents are bullied.

Obese children experience more physical, verbal, and relational bullying than their peers. Recent research indicates that approximately one in four overweight or obese children and adolescents reports clinically significant levels of peer victimization—significantly higher than prevalence rates of victimization among the general population of students (Storch et al., 2007). In addition, the children and adolescents who experienced higher levels of victimization also indicated that they engaged in less physical activity and experienced more depression, anxiety, loneliness, internalizing symptoms, and externalizing behaviors.

Interestingly, obese girls have a higher likelihood of being victims of bullying than do obese boys. Obese girls are nearly 250% more likely than non-overweight girls to be chronic victims of peer aggression, whereas obese boys are only 175% more likely to be victims than non-overweight boys (Janssen, Craig, Boyce, & Pickett, 2004). Gender differences extend beyond prevalence of bullying and are also observed for the type of bullying experienced. Increased body mass index (BMI), an indication of obesity status, is associated with increased verbal, physical, and relational victimization, including both exclusion and rumor/lie spreading for girls, but only associated with increased physical victimization and exclusion for boys.

These significant gender differences in victimization type and frequency among overweight and obese children and adolescents may be due to gender differences in the stigmatization of being overweight. Potentially, overweight females are selected for victimization because they are more insecure regarding their body type. Females place a high importance on being thin, and thus, obese girls may be more likely to be victimized, especially vis-à-vis weight-related teasing, because of the chances that victimization will elicit an emotional reaction and demonstrate weakness. In contrast, males place less stigmatization on being thin and more emphasis on athleticism and strength. Using physical victimization may be a common technique against overweight males because it allows bullies to demonstrate physical and athletic dominance.

Body mass also predicts perpetration of bullying. In a study of Canadian adolescents (Janssen et al., 2004), overweight and obese females were more than four times as likely as their female peers to engage in verbal aggression related to peers' ethnicity. In addition, obese girls were more than five times more likely than their female peers to engage in physical bullying. Body mass index was unrelated to perpetration of bullying in males. Interestingly, the authors have observed this pattern in their work with obese clients. It frequently appears that obese children acknowledge that they are at risk for being bullied and so preemptively victimize their peers to exhibit their physical and emotional dominance first. Thus, it is important when working with these children to teach them more positive and adaptive ways of avoiding being bullied or to build resiliency against being bullied so that they do not choose to act out in aggressive ways.

Asthma

Asthma is another common medical condition among school-aged children and adolescents and can range from being minor and well-controlled to severe. Children with well-controlled asthma may not exhibit behaviors that differentiate them from their peers, whereas children with severe asthma may exhibit several symptoms associated with their condition and treatment, including leaving class to take medications, refraining from physical activity, and prolonged school absences. To date, very little research has been conducted on the relationship between asthma and involvement in bullying. Of the studies that have been conducted, findings regarding the existence of differences in social experiences and relationships among children with and without asthma are mixed, with some studies finding that children with asthma are at an increased risk for peer victimization and others finding no social differences between asthmatic children and their healthy peers (e.g., Swahn & Bossarte, 2006; Zbikowki & Cohen, 1998). For example, among a large, nationally representative sample of high school students, students who reported that they experienced an asthma episode within the past year also reported higher rates of peer victimization than did students without an asthma episode (Swahn & Bossarte, 2006). However, in other studies of children with chronic asthma, peers did not report significant differences in popularity or acceptability of befriending other children with asthma (Zbikowski & Cohen, 1998).

These differences may be partially explained by the severity of asthma symptoms among the participating children and adolescents in the studies. As we previously explained, bullies select victims based upon signs of identified weakness. Therefore, children with poorly controlled asthma may be at a higher risk of being bullied than children with less severe asthma symptoms because their health condition is more visible and interferes with their functioning (e.g., athleticism, school absences, and performance). In contrast, children with controlled asthma may not be readily identifiable or show differences in athletic or academic performance from their peers and may not be viewed as weak. In support of this hypothesis, one study comparing children with asthma to same-aged peers found no differences among the two groups on social skills, but it did find that children with more severe, and thus identifiable, asthma were less preferred as companions and were more likely to self-report feelings of loneliness (Graetz & Shute, 1995). Although the study did not examine differences in bullying experiences between children with well-controlled and severe asthma, it indicated that children with severe asthma felt more marginalized than their peers, which would likely put them at increased risk for being bullied.

Diabetes and Other Endocrine Disorders

Endocrine disorders include any deficits of the endocrine system, which is responsible for the secretion of hormones. Both type I and type II diabetes are disorders of the endocrine system. Type I diabetes—commonly referred to as childhood or juvenile diabetes—is an autoimmune disorder that develops in healthy children and is not reversible by diet and exercise; type II diabetes is associated with obesity and is frequently reversible by diet and exercise. We will include a discussion of type I diabetes in this section, as it often develops in otherwise healthy children, whereas type II diabetes is usually associated with obesity—a topic discussed in the previous section.

Though children with type I diabetes frequently do not exhibit physical symptoms of their disorder that differentiate them from peers, they may be more likely to be selected as targets of peer victimization because of treatment-related behaviors that make them stand out from their peers, such as differential diet, need for insulin shots, and blood-glucose checks. These treatment-related behaviors may serve to make them easily identifiable targets to bullies and place the children at risk for being bullied. In support of this concept, in a study comparing over 30 children with type I diagnoses to a control group of peers matched on gender and age, children with diabetes reported more relational, but not overt victimization, and less perceived social support from their peers (Storch et al., 2004a).

Children with type I diabetes may also be concerned that their treatment-related behaviors cause them to stand out from their peers and lead them to perceive that they receive lower levels of social support than other students. In one study, 35% of children newly diagnosed with diabetes indicated beliefs that their peers would judge them more favorably if they had not been diagnosed (Jacobson et al., 1986). Poor social support is problematic for children with diabetes because decreased social support and diabetes-related bullying are related to aspects of treatment adherence and depression, loneliness, and social anxiety (Bearman & La Greca, 2002; Storch, Heidgerken et al., 2006; Storch et al., 2004a).

Endocrine disorders also include other medical conditions that result in physical symptoms that differentiate children from their peers, including short stature and delayed puberty. In a sample of 93 children with readily visible (e. g., short stature, delayed puberty) and without readily visible (type I diabetes and hypothyroidism) endocrine disorders, approximately one-third of children reported experiences of overt and relational peer victimization that exceeded clinical cutoff, indicating that they were chronic victims of bullying (Storch et al., 2004b). Differences among victimization rates between the two groups of children were not examined, nor were differences in the type of victimization experienced. The children that reported being bullied also were more likely to indicate that they experienced depression, social anxiety, and loneliness and parent reports of externalizing behavior problems. Interestingly, victimization was more strongly related to symptoms of psychopathology, including self-reported depressive symptoms and parent-reported internalizing symptoms and externalizing behavior problems, for children without readily visible endocrine disorders than with them, suggesting that resiliency to the victimization differed between the two groups. In fact, despite the common assumption that deficits in growth hormone release (resulting in short stature) is related to victimization, studies have neglected to find differences in the peer relationships of short stature children in comparison to their peers (Sandberg & Voss, 2002; Voss & Sandberg, 2004).

Summary of Bullying among Pediatric Illness Populations

Evidence supporting the relationship between common pediatric illnesses and peer victimization is mixed. These findings suggest that chronic medical conditions are linked to higher rates of being bullied when the medical conditions are associated with a negative stigmatization, such as obesity, or if they are related to feelings of heightened social awareness and concern about negative judgment from peers.

For children with medical conditions, bullying can also be more stressful than for children without medical conditions. Many children with chronic illnesses view school as a chance to normalize their lives and focus on something other than their illness. In such cases, attending school may actually serve as a retreat from focusing on the illness and treatment. Indeed, many children express their excitement to return to school after prolonged hospitalizations. When such children return to school and are bullied, attending school may lose its positive aspects and even be avoided. Thus, the children no longer view school as a positive way of distracting themselves from their illness and feeling like "normal" children. Furthermore, when children are teased or bullied specifically due to features of their illness, attending school may actually amplify a child's focus on the aspects of the illness that make him or her different than others—further isolating the child and causing increased stress.

Learning Disabilities

Learning disabilities are a category of cognitive disorder that may place children at increased risk for being victims of bullying. The experience of a learning disability may be easily identifiable to peers because fellow students observe when another student struggles in a class. Academic problems may then be perceived by bullies as a sign of weakness that makes a child an easy target. Consistent with this idea, children who experience a learning disability are more likely than their nondisabled peers to experience peer neglect (ignoring and isolation), rejection (La Greca & Stone, 1990), and peer victimization (Nabuzoka, 2003). In the case of Daniel, his dysgraphia made him stand out from his peers because he was required to use assistive technology in his classes instead of writing assignments by hand. Daniel reported that he received taunts from peers about using the machine and consequently opted to leave the machine at home or in his locker on several occasions due to embarrassment.

Experiences of being bullied may serve as an additive effect of the already negative psychosocial outcomes associated with learning disabilities, thus placing children at an even higher risk for future academic and psychosocial problems. In Daniel's case, failure to bring the machine to classes caused him to submit incomplete assignments and receive lower grades than he would likely have otherwise been assigned if he had used the assistive technology.

Many children with learning disabilities are educated in general education classrooms, whereas others receive specialized instruction in self-contained classrooms. Critics of self-contained classrooms argue that children miss important social interactions and may be easily identified by their peers as victims of bullying because they attend "social classes." Similarly, critics of mainstream classrooms argue that children with learning disabilities continue to be easily spotted because they struggle academically and require the help of special education personnel in the generalized classrooms, which also may cause them to become targets of bullying. Research into this debate does little to resolve this conflict, as it reveals that children and adolescents with moderate learning disabilities in reading, mathematics, or science are bullied regardless of their academic placement (Norwich & Kelly, 2004). Among students served in either mainstreamed settings or special schools, 83% reported that they were either physically or verbally bullied by their peers in their school and neighborhood, and 49% said they were teased specifically about their learning disability. That is, the children continue to be identified as easy targets of bullying whether they are educated in mainstreamed or self-contained classroom. Additionally, self-contained classrooms do not shelter children from opportunities to bully, as much of the bullying occurred outside of school. One girl who participated in the study explained, "I was picked on more...because I couldn't read...I'm not sure...they call me thick, thick...um, dumb," (p. 56). As this quote aptly illustrates, the experiences of learning disabilities in the classroom is an easily identifiable trait to other peers and is a "weakness" that bullies frequently opt to exploit to demonstrate power and dominance.

Interestingly, some research also suggests that the proportion of children with learning disabilities that bully others is higher than the proportion of bullies form nondisabled samples (Nabuzoka, 2003). One potential explanation is that some children with learning disabilities may assert dominance over others through bullying to compensate for their academic difficulties. However, other studies find no significant trend between learning disabilities and bullying behavior (for a review, see Mishna, 2003). It is possible that the mixed findings are due to the relatively high comorbidity rate of learning disabilities with behavioral disorders that are associated with perpetration of bullying. A discussion of psychological and behavioral disorders associated with involvement in bullying in the roles of bullies and victims is provided later in the chapter. Another explanation for the mixed findings could be that age of children with a learning disability affects their involvement in bullying. It could be expected that as children with severe, untreated learning disabilities grow older, they become more detached from school and increasingly likely to engage in bullying to demonstrate power and dominance.

Psychological and Behavior Disorders

Saneka (not her real name) is a 14-year-old 7th grader who is an athlete on the track team, a good B student, and somewhat socially timid. She has a prior diagnosis of depression, has received counseling from the school counselor for a year, and her mood was relatively stable with psychotropic medication until recently when she became the target of a bully. She has a single mother who is disabled with cerebral palsy and attends Saneka's games but often has very awkward body postures and movement. Due to the debilitating nature of her mother's illness, Saneka has a large responsibility at home for daily cooking, cleaning, and some care-related tasks for her mother. Saneka is often tired in school and withdrawn from peers.

A group of three girls have begun mocking Saneka's mother's movement and making comments about this so that Saneka can hear. Saneka will not make eye contact and responds with instant tears. Assertiveness skills have been added to Saneka's counseling goals. The girls have also begun to socially isolate Saneka during lunch and other activities; they also instant message jokes about her. The leader of the bullying group is a cheerleader who has engaged in these kinds of activities in prior years, often changing the target of her harassment. The bully has received several suspensions, counseling, and her schedule is being changed to avoid some class contact with Saneka (although this has not been completely successful).

It has been well established that a strong and consistent link between victimization and various forms of psychopathology exists. As we have repeatedly emphasized in this chapter, bullies seek to readily identify weaknesses in victims that will elicit an emotional reaction. Children with preexisting psychological disorders, such as Seneka, therefore, are easily identifiable targets for bullies because children and adolescents who appear emotionally unstable may already stand out from their peers. It is difficult to determine whether some psychological and behavioral problems precede bullying experiences or result from them. As was discussed in previous chapters, research that tracks children's social and emotional functioning over an extended period of time indicates that peer victimization precedes the development of symptoms of depression and anxiety in many students. However, it is also likely that the experience of depression and/or anxiety is associated with behaviors that serve to marginalize students from their peers (e.g., social withdrawal, crying, and avoidance of social situations) and increase the likelihood that they are bullied by fellow students. In the case of Seneka, both of these appear to be in play. Seneka already had a diagnosis of depression prior to the bullying and was timid and withdrawn from her peers. A group of bullies identified this weakness and also chose to bully Seneka related to a topic for which they knew she would exhibit high emotional reactivity. Though her depressive symptoms had been in remission with the help of therapy and psychotropic medication, symptoms reemerged after the bullying experiences began.

In this section, we illustrate that preexisting psychological and behavioral conditions place children at risk for involvement in bullying. Due to the "chicken or the egg" problem when explaining the relationship between psychological disorders and involvement in bullying, we will focus our discussion on psychological and behavioral problems that likely develop independently of bullying experiences, such as obsessive-compulsive disorder (OCD) and attention-deficit/hyperactivity disorder (ADHD). Though both conditions have a strong organic etiology, it is possible, although rare, that the expression of symptoms can be triggered by a bullying experience. The following excerpt illustrates this example as it describes one case of childhood OCD in which bullying apparently triggered the onset of OCD symptoms (Storch et al., 2005). The case report is as follows:

> At symptom onset, Max engaged in only one ritual, which was to go home after being bullied and immediately take a shower. The shower served to reduce his overall level of anxiety by "cleansing" himself of the bullies' remarks. With time, Max began avoiding wearing clothing that he wore on days he had been bullied because the clothing was "contaminated" by the insults. Avoidance of "contaminated" objects and situations expanded to include places (e.g., his living room, the dining room table, the family cars) and objects (e.g., a blanket on the sofa that he would use when studying) that were perceived by Max to be linked to bullying experiences. Max's use of rituals also expanded to include clearing his throat when he had a thought associated with bullying, as well as re-starting activities (e.g., reading a sentence, washing his hands, or getting dressed) whenever he had a bullying-related cognition. (p. 42)

Obsessive-Compulsive Disorder

Obsessive-compulsive disorder involves the presence of pervasive obsessive thoughts and compulsive behaviors that cause distress, are time consuming, or interfere with normal functioning of daily living. This disorder has a strong biological/organic etiology and so it is perceived to develop independently of peer victimization experiences. Children diagnosed with OCD typically display noticeable ritual behavior, such as hand washing, counting, or avoiding peers or situations due to fears of contamination. Similar to the case of Daniel, who was targeted for bullying partly due to atypical behaviors (i.e., humming and swaying), children with OCD may become targets of bullying because of their anxiety and ritual behaviors if they display them in school. Such behaviors differentiate them from their peers and place them at risk for being targeted by bullies. Research has demonstrated that children that exhibit OCD symptoms indicate more frequent peer victimization (Storch, Ledley et al., 2006) than children without OCD symptoms.

However, it has been the experience of one author through his clinical work with children diagnosed with OCD that children usually are aware that their compulsions may place them at risk for bullying. To compensate for this, the children attempt to keep their disorder private by avoiding engaging in compulsive behavior while at school and instead engaging in elaborate rituals after school. As can be expected, the need to immediately return home and engage in the ritualistic behavior prevents the children from engaging in after-school activities and social interactions—both which serve as protective factors from bullying and for building resiliency in children who are bullied. Additionally, children with OCD may entirely avoid social interactions to avoid any chance of peer rejection. Therefore, along with treating the OCD, the therapist may also want to work with the bullied child to increase positive social interactions with other children to build resiliency.

Stress and Somatization

The experience of somatic symptoms, such as abdominal pain, nausea, sore throats, and headaches, is another anxiety-related problem for many school-aged children and adolescents. The experience of somatic symptoms is often unaccounted for by a medical condition, and thus is thought to stem from the internalization of stress from multiple environments. School problems, which include negative interactions with other students in the school environment, are more strongly associated with the experience of somatic symptoms than is stress in the home (Walker, Smith, Garber, & Van Slyke, 1997). Furthermore, these symptoms may prohibit children from attending school, and thus further exacerbate problems with academics and social interactions.

Children who experience somatic symptoms may be easily identifiable targets for bullies because of their high stress patterns that isolate them from their peers. Indeed, children who experience chronic somatic pain are three times more likely than their peers to experience bullying (Srabstein, McCarter, Shao, & Huang, 2006). It is difficult to determine whether bullying or development of somatic complaints precedes the other. For some bullied children, school may become an aversive environment, and to cope they develop psychosomatic complaints as a way to obtain positive attention from adults and escape from the school environment. For other children, somatic symptoms may result from something other than negative peer experiences (e.g., stress at home, difficulty with academics) and make the children appear weak and prone to whining in front of their peers. These behaviors may then cause these children to be singled out as targets for bullying.

Attention-deficit/hyperactivity disorder is a widely diagnosed disorder among school-aged children and adolescents. Children with ADHD tend to be involved in bullying as bullies, victims, and bully–victims more often than their peers. Low self-control may partially explain the relationship between ADHD and bullying behavior (Unnever & Cornell, 2003). That is, children who are unable to control their behavioral impulses (low self-control) are more likely to bully other children in comparison to their peers with average or above average levels of self-control. However, children who take medication to treat the symptoms of ADHD did not exhibit more bullying than their peers. This potentially indicates that medication for ADHD may serve to help children control aggressive behavioral impulses and therefore refrain from bullying their peers.

Finally, more severe forms of disruptive behavior disorders have also been found to place children at risk for involvement in bullying. One study using a sample of Greek adolescents (ages 12 to 15 years) examined the relationship between DSM-IV symptoms of conduct disorder and oppositional defiant disorder (Kokkinos & Panayiotou, 2004). Adolescents who displayed symptoms of oppositional defiant disorder were more likely than their peers to report being victims of bullying, and children with conduct disorder were more likely than their peers to be bully-victims.

A colleague recounted the following case example that illustrates the link between ADHD and perpetration of bullying behavior and also demonstrates a school intervention using a response to intervention (RTI) framework (see Fig. 5.1). As a Tier I intervention, the school implemented a bullying prevention program that consisted of a classroom curriculum for all students and a strict bullying policy that consisted of immediate and consistent consequences for engagement in bullying behavior.

> Carl was a 10-year-old 4th grader with a diagnoses of ADHD, predominately hyperactive/impulsive type, who did not receive his prescribed medication due to parental objections. Carl also expressed anger control problems related to a recent degenerative health diagnosis that left his father unable to walk or work. Carl exhibited increasing anger and irritability due to his father's inability to play with him and lack of conversation that was associated with pain related to the condition. Carl also had a quick temper and engaged in impulsive and increasingly frequent acts of bullying others through intimidation over a period of 2 years.

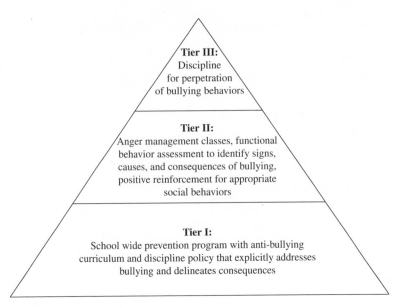

Figure 5.1 A sample response to intervention model to address bullying among children with disruptive behavior disorders.

Carl received Tier II RTI services for a year that included a positive reinforcement plan for appropriate social skills and biweekly counseling sessions to teach him anger management. Despite these interventions, his behaviors continued to escalate in severity, resulting in multiple fights and several in-school suspensions. Therefore, a functional behavioral assessment (FBA) was conducted over 1 week with 7 hours of observations across settings. Results indicated his intimidation characteristics followed a progression of blinking, tightening posture with firm jaw set, flat facial demeanor, eye glaring, turning red, raising his body posture over other children, and making threatening comments. He engaged in the behavior when he wanted something or wished to control the actions of other students. Tier II RTI was implemented with weekly individual counseling to further address anger management, a more comprehensive behavior management plan was provided, and the family was asked to consult a physician as well as begin family counseling.

The above example illustrates several important factors that practitioners should keep in mind when working with children with disruptive behaviors who engage in bullying. First, difficulties at home or school may cause the children to experience intense feelings of anger and desire to assert control over their environment. Coupled with a predisposition for impulsivity, these children may impulsively bully their peers when they feel angry or a loss of control. In such cases, interventions should include anger management training, as well as recommendations for family therapy. A second important feature of the case is that school personnel should take actions to understand situations in which the bullying behavior may occur and signs that the student will likely engage in bullying. Recognition of these factors is essential for intervention because the teacher has opportunities to *(a)* reward the child from refraining from bullying behavior in scenarios in which he or she would normally engage in bullying; *(b)* immediately intervene to remind the child not to bully and redirect him or her to a different activity; and *(c)* monitor the child for engagement in bullying and implement immediate consequences when bullying does occur.

Summary of Bullying among Children with Learning and Psychological Disorders

Similar to children with chronic medical conditions, children with learning and psychological disorders are at an increased likelihood for becoming victims of bullying due to identifiable symptoms and behaviors that bullies perceive as potential weaknesses. When working with children with preexisting mental conditions who report that they are bullied, it is important to assess the nature of these peer exchanges. Children with preexisting mental health conditions, such as depression or conduct problems, may have a "negative filter" in which they process information with a negative bias. That is, they may interpret the actions of other children to be more negative/hostile than intended. In addition, they may shift their focus to the negative peer interactions during their day and selectively ignore positive interactions. In such cases, it is important to work with these children using cognitive-behavioral therapy to coach them to alter these negative cognitive patterns and to learn to recognize and acknowledge positive interactions.

Children with learning and behavioral disorders may also be at an increased likelihood for bullying perpetration. Children with a predisposition to act impulsively may engage in bullying to act out anger, receive attention, or achieve control over a situation. Similar to working with any bully, it is essential that school personnel employ immediate and consistent consequences when bullying occurs. Additionally, it may be beneficial to take actions to prevent bullying by identifying situations in which the children with ADHD act on bullying impulses and the physical and behavioral symptoms that precede the bullying.

Effects of Bullying on Children with Psychopathology and Health Problems

Bullying is a potentially significant problem because it may exacerbate a child's experience or likelihood of experiencing psychopathology, including depressive symptoms. In turn, it has been well established that psychological adjustment is directly related to a child's adherence to treatment regimen (Storch, Heidgerken et al., 2006; Storch et al., 2007) and overall health (Kovacs, Goldston, Obrosky, & Iyengar, 1992). In addition, positive peer relationships are associated with more positive adaptation to disease and adherence to treatment regimens, which is directly related to a child's health (for a review, see La Greca, Bearman, & Moore, 2002). For these reasons, it has been recommended that intervention programs for children with chronic illnesses specifically address their relationships with peers to achieve more positive health outcomes (La Greca, 1990).

Being bullied may be more harmful to children with learning disabilities and mental health disorders than other children because their coping skills are already stressed dealing with other concerns in their environment. For example, children with depression or anxiety may already lack adequate coping skills for handling stress. The addition of problems with peer relationships adds another layer of strain into their lives and further taxes their already deficient coping skills. Thus, a child with a preexisting mental health condition may exhibit worsened outcomes in relation to bullying than a child without such a preexisting condition.

Much of our work with children with psychiatric and pediatric illnesses when dealing with the school setting has focused on peer issues. In the case of pediatric illnesses, children often struggle with worries about how to tell their peers and with being teased due to symptoms of their illnesses or secondary side effects, such as frequent absences, leaving classes to take medications, or inability to participate in specific activities. Children who are teased about these symptoms or behaviors sometimes take steps to avoid being seen as different than their peers.

One of the authors frequently works with children with cystic fibrosis to address a number of issues related to having a chronic illness. When meeting children and adolescents with the condition, the author routinely asks about peers' reactions to physical symptoms of the disorder. Frequently, children will reveal that their peers tease them for physical differences due to their condition, such as smaller stature, delayed puberty, and clubbing of the fingers. Several children have revealed painful memories of peers audibly complaining about sitting near them or accusing the child of being contagious for frequent bouts of coughing. In some cases these negative experiences have been so traumatic that the children will attempt to avoid school due to fear and embarrassment.

When working with children who exhibit school avoidance or oppositional behavior related to attending school, children should always be questioned about their relationships with peers. However, simply asking children, "Are you bullied?" is usually not effective in achieving an accurate depiction of their peer relationships because children may not (a) understand what bullying is, or (b) want to admit they are bullied for fear that they will appear weak to the adults. In fact, many children may be embarrassed to admit to their own parents that they are bullied because they are afraid that it will disappoint their parents or make them sad. Instead, it may be helpful to ask children about specific behaviors. Because of this fear, it is important to emphasize that you understand that the behaviors occur with a lot of children and that it is okay to share them with you. Below is a list of sample questions that may be helpful when asking children about their experiences with being bullied:

- A lot of children with cystic fibrosis tell me that they sometimes feel embarrassed around other children because of their illness. Some have even told me that other students lean away or tease them when they cough, make comments about their fingers, or laugh at them for having to leave class to take their medications. Do things like this ever happen to you?
- I know it can be very difficult to return to school after being absent for so long. What did other students say to you when you came back? What was it like to be around other students?
- I know in middle/elementary school there are sometimes children who are mean to their classmates. Can you tell me about some of these kids in your school? Have they ever done anything mean to you?
- Tell me about what you've told other children about your condition. How do they react? Are there things about it that they make comments about that hurt your feelings?

Children with pediatric and mental health conditions often experience a sense of loneliness, and therefore they may find it comforting that other children share similar experiences. Learning that other children have similar experiences can provide children with a sense of empowerment and diminish feelings of isolation. Indeed, patients often report that they enjoy communicating with other patients because they understand the struggles of coping with a chronic physical/mental health condition. One way that they may learn this and be able to share their experiences with their peers is through websites hosted by an organization that is specific to their condition. Many of these websites have the following resources that may be helpful: (a) guides to talking to their peers about their conditions to reduce myths; and (b) chat rooms or message boards on which children with the conditions can converse with one another to share their experiences and to build friendships. We have included a list of such websites in Table 5.1 that we know have these resources. This certainly is not an exhaustive list, and we encourage you to help children and families seek resources that are relevant to their illnesses/conditions if they are not listed here.

Another intervention that has been shown to be helpful in elementary-aged children with medical illnesses is to host a session in which a psychologist, pediatrician, or other health representative works with the child, parents, and school to provide a classroom presentation to educate the child's classmates about the condition. This can be helpful in dispelling any myths that classmates (and teachers) may have about the child's condition that perpetuate bullying, such

Table 5.1
Resources for Children with Chronic Health Conditions

Website	Address	Resources	Interactive?
Kids health Teen health	http://kidshealth. org http:// teenhealth.org	Provides information about a range of chronic illnesses and potential problems at school (including bullying). There are separate sites for kids, teens, and parents.	No
Brave Kids	http://bravekids. org	Provides information about a range of illnesses and includes a message board for youth to engage in online discussions. The site also allows the user to search for local support groups for youth and parents.	Yes
Pediatric Network	http:// pediatricnetwork. org	Provides links to online forums/ communities for children and adolescents with pediatric illnesses. The site also allows users to locate support groups in their geographical regions.	Yes

as beliefs that the child is contagious. We offer caution, however, in carefully weighing the risks and benefits of this form of intervention, especially when the child experiences a mental health condition. Such interventions may be helpful when working with children whose conditions cause them to exhibit easily noticeable symptoms or behaviors (as in the case of stuttering, obsessive-compulsive disorder), but they may draw negative attention and marginalization to children whose condition did not cause them to engage in behaviors or routines that are atypical from their peers. In a personal memoir detailing his personal experience with OCD as a teenager (Kant, 2008), Kant discusses the decision to share a diagnosis of OCD with classmates. In the following statement, he addresses the potential pros and cons of telling other children about his mental health condition:

> On [the] one hand, not everyone needs to know the details of your personal life. In addition, some people are less than enlightened when it comes to mental illness. There might be some backlash, such as gossip or teasing. On the other hand, the only way to overcome the stigma attached to mental illness is by educating people, and one of the best ways of doing that is simply by sharing your story. While you might run into some mean-spirited response, you're also likely to encounter many compassionate ones. (p. 67)

For children with less noticeable conditions, interventions may not need to take place at the classroom level and instead should only focus on the individual level. For example, children with depression may withdraw from their peers and refrain from seeking interaction or involvement in group activities as a symptom of their depression. In such as case, the school should work with mental health–care workers to treat the child's depression and encourage involvement in previously enjoyed activities that involve positive interactions with small or large groups of peers. Interventions for children with anxiety disorders should include work with mental health–care workers to address their concerns about relating with peers and to repeatedly rehearse and reflect upon engagement in interactions with nonthreatening classmates (e.g., those highest in empathy and social skills).

Implications for Practice

Bullying is frequently a mechanism through which children attempt to establish their dominance over others by demonstrating their physical, academic, social, or emotional strength (Pellegrini & Long, 2002). Bullies attempt to select victims whose "weaknesses" can be easily identified and exploited. Therefore, children with medical, cognitive, learning, or psychological disabilities frequently draw the attention of bullies because they have readily identifiable features that differentiate them from their peers. Schools should carefully monitor children with such conditions to determine whether school bullies target them. In addition, some children with disorders tend to bully others at higher rates than their nondisabled peers. Such bullying behaviors may be used to compensate for perceived personal weaknesses or result from a lack of self-control. Such bullies may benefit from counseling services that target self-esteem and attempt to improve self-control strategies.

- Regardless of whether children with special needs are placed in mainstreamed or self-contained academic environments, teachers should monitor students for involvement in bullying and take action when necessary.
- School intervention plans for children with chronic medical and psychological illnesses should place an emphasis on strategies to encourage positive peer interactions.
- A discussion of individual characteristics and a celebration of diversity in classrooms may increase the acceptability of individual differences.
- Children who exhibit symptoms of ADHD, impulsivity, and limited self-control may benefit from behavioral interventions in which they are taught self-control and anger management strategies and more adaptive ways of achieving a sense of control/mastery over their environment.
- Teachers and school mental health workers can also work to prevent incidents of bullying among children with behavior problems through the use of functional behavioral assessments (FBAs). These may help to identify factors that trigger bullying behavior, physical/behavioral signs that the child exhibits immediately prior to engaging in bullying, and consequences that serve to reinforce bullying behavior. Using this information, teachers can learn to recognize when bullying behaviors are likely to occur and intervene before the student engages in bullying. They also need to implement immediate and consistent consequences when bullying does occur.
- Evidence-based psychotherapeutic and/or pharmacological treatments may be appropriate when levels of distress experienced by victimized youth are high and when impulsivity perpetuates engagement in bullying among children with disruptive behavior disorders.

References

American Psychiatric Association. (2000). *Diagnostic and statistical manual of mental disorders* (4th ed., text revision). Washington, DC: Author.

Bearman, K. J., & La Greca, A. M. (2002). Assessing friend support of adolescents' diabetes care: The Diabetes Social Support Questionnaire–Friends Version. *Journal of Pediatric Psychology, 27,* 417–428.

Goldfield, A., & Chrisler, J. C. (1995). Body stereotyping and stigmatization of obese persons by first graders. *Perceptual and Motor Skills, 81,* 909–910.

Graetz, B., & Shute, R. (1995). Assessment of peer relationships in children with asthma. *Journal of Pediatric Psychology, 20,* 205–216.

Jacobson, A. M., Hauser, S. T., Wertlieb, D., Wolfsdorf, J. I., Orleans, J., & Vieyra, M. (1986). Psychological adjustment of children with recently diagnosed diabetes mellitus. *Diabetes Care, 9,* 323–329.

Janssen, I., Craig, W. M., Boyce, W. F., & Pickett, W. (2004). Associations between overweight and obesity with bullying behaviors in school-aged children. *Pediatrics, 113,* 1187–1194.

Kant, J. D. (2008). *The thought that counts: A firsthand account of one teenager's experience with obsessive-compulsive disorder.* New York: Oxford University Press.

Kokkinos, C. M., & Panayiotou, G. (2004). Predicting bullying and victimization among early adolescents: Associations with disruptive behavior disorders. *Aggressive Behavior, 30,* 520–533.

Kovacs, M., Goldston, D., Obrosky, D. S., & Iyengar, S. (1992). Prevalence and predictors of pervasive noncompliance with medical treatment among youths with insulin-dependent diabetes mellitus. *Journal of the American Academy of Child & Adolescent Psychiatry, 31,* 1112–1119.

La Greca, A. M. (1990). Social consequences of pediatric conditions: Fertile area for future investigation and intervention? *Journal of Pediatric Psychology, 15,* 285–307.

La Greca, A. M., Bearman, K. J., & Moore, H. (2002). Peer relations of youth with pediatric conditions and health risks: Promoting social support and healthy lifestyles. *Journal of Developmental & Behavioral Pediatrics, 23,* 1–10.

La Greca, A. M., & Stone, W. L. (1990). LD status and achievement: Confounding variables in the study of children's social status, self-esteem, and behavioral functioning. *Journal of Learning Disabilities, 23,* 32–37.

Mishna, F. (2003). Learning disabilities and bullying: Double jeopardy. *Journal of Learning Disabilities, 36,* 336–347.

Mukherjee, S., Lightfoot, J., & Sloper, P. (2000). The inclusion of pupils with a chronic health condition in mainstream school: What does it mean for teachers? *Educational Research, 42,* 59–72.

Nabuzoka, D. (2003). Teacher ratings and peer nominations of bullying and other behavior of children with and without learning difficulties. *Educational Psychology, 23,* 307–321.

Norwich, B., & Kelly, N. (2004). Pupils' views on inclusion: Moderate learning difficulties and bullying in mainstream and special schools. *British Educational Research Journal, 30,* 43–65.

Ogden, C. L., Flegal, K. M., Carroll, M. D., & Johnson, C. L. (2002). Prevalence and trends in overweight among US children and adolescents, 1999–2000. *Journal of the American Medical Association, 288,* 1728–1732.

Olweus, D. (2003). A profile of bullying at school. *Educational Leadership, 60,* 12–17.

Pearce, M. J., Boergers, J., & Prinstein, M. J. (2002). Adolescent obesity, overt and relational peer victimization, and romantic relationships. *Obesity Research, 10,* 386–393.

Pellegrini, A. D., & Bartini, M. (2000). A longitudinal study of bullying, victimization, and peer affiliation during the transition from primary school to middle school. *American Educational Research Journal, 37,* 699–725.

Pellegrini, A. D., & Long, J. D. (2002). A longitudinal study of bullying, dominance, and victimization during the transition from primary school through secondary school. *British Journal of Developmental Psychology, 20,* 259–280.

Sandberg, D. E., & Voss, L. D. (2002). The psychosocial consequences of short stature: A review of the evidence. *Best Practice & Research Clinical Endocrinology & Metabolism, 16,* 449–463.

Srabstein, J. C., McCarter, R. J., Shao, C., & Huang, Z. J. (2006). Morbidities associated with bullying behaviors in adolescents: School based study of American adolescents. *International Journal of Adolescent Medicine and Health, 18,* 587–596.

Storch, E. A., Heidgerken, A. D., Adkins, J. W., Cole, M., Murphy, T. K., & Geffken, G. R. (2005). Peer victimization and the development of obsessive-compulsive disorder in adolescence. *Depression and Anxiety, 21,* 41–44.

Storch, E. A., Heidgerken, A. D., Geffken, G. R., Lewin, A. B., Ohleyer, V., Freddo, M., et al. (2006). Bullying, regimen self-management, and metabolic control in youth with type I diabetes. *The Journal of Pediatrics, 148,* 784–787.

Storch, E. A., Ledley, D. R., Lewin, A. B., Murphy, T. K., Johns, N. B., Goodman, W. K., et al. (2006). Peer victimization in children with obsessive-compulsive disorder: Relations with symptoms of psychopathology. *Journal of Clinical Child and Adolescent Psychology, 35,* 446–455.

Storch, E. A., Lewin, A., Silverstein, J. H., Heidgerken, A. D., Strawser, M. S., Baumeister, A., et al. (2004a). Peer victimization and psychosocial adjustment in children with Type 1 diabetes. *Clinical Pediatrics, 43,* 467–471.

Storch, E. A., Lewin, A. B., Silverstein, J. H., Heidgerken, A. D., Strawser, M. S., Baumeister, A., et al. (2004b). Social-psychological correlates of peer victimization in children with endocrine disorders. *The Journal of Pediatrics, 145,* 784–789.

Storch, E. A., Milsom, V. A., DeBraganza, N., Lewin, A. B., Geffken, G. R., & Silverstein, J. H. (2007). Peer victimization, psychosocial adjustment, and physical activity in overweight and at-risk-for-overweight youth. *Journal of Pediatric Psychology, 32,* 80–89.

Swahn, M. H., & Bossarte, R. M. (2006). The associations between victimization, feeling unsafe, and asthma episodes among US high-school students. *American Journal of Public Health, 96,* 802–804.

Unnever, J. D., & Cornell, D. G. (2003). Bullying, self-control, and ADHD. *Journal of Interpersonal Violence, 18,* 129–147.

Voss, L. D., & Sandberg, D. E. (2004). The psychological burden of short stature: Evidence against. *European Journal of Endocrinology, 151,* S29–33.

Walker, L. S., Smith, C. A., Garber, J., & Van Slyke, D. A. (1997). Development and validation of the pain response inventory for children. *Psychological Assessment, 9,* 392–405.

Zbikowski, S. M., & Cohen, R. (1998). Parent and peer evaluations of the social competence of children with mild asthma. *Journal of Applied Developmental Psychology, 19,* 249–266.

PART II

ASSESSMENT AND INTERVENTION

6

Methods for Assessing and Treating Bully–Victim Problems for Individual Children and Adolescents

Amie E. Grills-Taquechel, Rosanna Polifroni, and Heather T. Pane

The study of bullying and peer victimization in childhood and adolescence has been gaining increased interest over the past several years. Bullying behaviors occur directly (e.g., hitting, teasing), as well as indirectly (e.g., spreading rumors) or relationally (e.g., attempts to damage others' relationships). Sadly, today's youth often experience relational-type bullying via technological devices (Harmon, 2004). Instant messaging, e-mail, text messages, and Internet sites (e.g., http://www.myspace.com) have all become additional venues for bullying, with the same overwhelming psychosocial implications.

As described in previous chapters, the prevalence of bullying has been found to be particularly concerning among today's youth (Grills, 2003; Grills & Ollendick, 2002; Nansel et al., 2001; Perry, Kusel, & Perry, 1988). Not only are the heightened prevalence and occurrence of bullying/victimization a worry, but also of considerable concern are the consistently reported findings of associated mental (Hawker & Boulton, 2000) and physical health (Williams, Chambers, Logan, & Robinson, 1996) consequences of such experiences. In all, these findings point to the relevance of understanding bullying issues for practitioners who work with youth. Importantly, clinicians should also have skills for assessing bullying and related problems, as well as for including relevant intervention strategies into treatment programs.

This chapter focuses first on presenting different methods of assessing bullying problems in youth, followed by a discussion of commonly associated difficulties and different treatment options for children involved in bullying. Unfortunately, little attention has been given to how best to assess and address bullying-related behaviors on an individual level; therefore, we draw on extant research and available information that can be applied in the context of individual treatment. This includes assessment and treatment methods used in school and other group settings, as well as interventions designed to address aggression/externalizing and internalizing behavior problems. Ideally, such individualized treatment strategies would be incorporated in a larger school-based intervention/prevention program (as discussed in other chapters of this book). Such an approach would potentially allow for the targeting of all those students involved with bullying, as well as promote greater inclusion of important sources of information and intervention (i.e., teachers, peers, school personnel).

Methods for Assessing Bullying Involvement

A variety of assessment methods are available to clinicians for evaluating bullying/victimization behaviors, including observations, questionnaires and surveys, and clinical interviews (also see Cornell, Sheras, & Cole, 2006; Crothers & Levinson, 2004). Each of these methods offers important information pertaining to the child's behavior and could be reported on by multiple informants (e.g., parents, teachers, child, and peers) when possible for the clinician to gather such varied information.

Self-Report Questionnaires and Surveys

Self-report measures are among the most frequently utilized methods of assessing bullying-related behaviors. Self-report measures are particularly beneficial as they can be used to collect information from a variety of sources generally in a short-period of time. By utilizing psychometrically sound measures, reliable reports of bullying and related constructs may be obtained. However, clinicians should be cautious when using student self-reports as they may be biased for reasons such as social desirability. For example, we have found that, early in treatment, youth are sometimes reluctant to report bullying based on suspected consequences from school or home, or victimization based on shyness and embarrassment. A number of self-report measures are available for children to complete, and they vary with regard to such aspects as the timeline specified (e.g., in the past week), the different forms of bullying evaluated (e.g., physical, relational), and the specifics of the experiences. Several examples of self-report measures that are widely used for assessing child bully–victim experiences are described below.

The Revised Olweus Bully/Victim Questionnaire (Olweus, 1996; Solberg & Olweus, 2003) contains 40 items (including several subquestions for several of the 36 main questions) designed to assess various aspects of bully–victim problems. Part I assesses experiences of being bullied, whereas Part II assesses bullying behaviors against others by the child. Children indicate their answers for each question using a 5-point Likert scale. This measure has been used with youth from the 3rd to 12th grades and takes approximately 10–15 minutes to complete.

The Reynolds Bullying Victimization Scales for Schools (Reynolds, 2003) is a set of three self-report measures designed for use in school or clinical settings: *(1)* The Bully Victimization Scale (46 items) assesses bullying others and being victimized (i.e., overt and relational) in or near school settings over the past month; *(2)* The Bully Victimization Distress Scale (35 items) assesses students' psychological distress related to being bullied in the past month; and *(3)* The School Violence Anxiety Scale (29 items) assesses anxiety related to potential violence based on feelings about overt peer aggression, relational aggression, and being unsafe in school. Each scale is rated on a 4-point Likert scale, takes approximately 10 minutes to complete, and can be used with children from the 3rd through 12th grades.

The Multidimensional Peer Victimization Scale (Mynard & Joseph, 2000) has 16 items that measure peer victimization in terms of negative physical actions (e.g., punched me), negative verbal actions (e.g., swore at me), social manipulation (e.g., tried to make my friends turn against me), and attacks on property (e.g., tried to break something of mine). This scale is intended for use with children aged 11–16 and questions are rated on a 3-point Likert scale with the complete scale typically taking less than 10 minutes to complete.

The Bully Survey–Student Version (Swearer, 2001; Swearer & Cary, 2003) is a self-report questionnaire that is divided into three sections for assessment of victim, bystander, and bully behaviors. Each section is preceded by a "yes"/ "no" screening question to determine whether the child has been bullied, has seen another child being bullied, or been a bully to others. If the child responds negatively, he or she is asked to move on to the next section. If the child responds affirmatively to a screener question, he or she is asked to continue answering more specific questions within that section. Additional questions pertain to where and how the bullying occurred, who bullied them or whom they bullied most often, how the bullying affected them, why they think the bullying occurred, and who was aware of the problem. Finally, all children are asked to complete a fourth section that assesses general attitudes toward bullying behaviors. Classification of each child's bully status can be made upon completion of this measure (i.e., bully-only, victim-only, bully-victim, or not-involved). This measure was designed for use with children in 3rd to 12th grades and takes approximately 10–15 minutes to complete.

The Peer Victimization Scale (Neary & Joseph, 1994) assesses victimization in the form of negative physical and verbal actions with six items that can be embedded within the Self-Perception Profile for Children (Harter, 1985). Each item is antithetical in format, and children are asked to select which phrase better describes them and then rate it as "really true" or "sort-of true." This scale has been utilized with children aged 8–12 years (Callaghan & Joseph, 1995; Grills & Ollendick, 2002; Neary & Joseph, 1994) and takes approximately 5 minutes to complete.

The Peer Experiences Questionnaire is a self-report questionnaire that includes scales on victimization of self and victimization of others over the past 3 months, attitudes toward aggression, and bystander responses (perceived adult sanctions, helpful bystanding, aggressive bystanding). The entire measure takes approximately 20–25 minutes to complete. This measure was initially designed for children from the 7th to 12th grades (Vernberg, Jacobs, & Hershberger, 1999). A downward extension of this scale has been developed and used with elementary school children (Dill, Vernberg, Fonagy, Twemlow, & Gamm, 2004, Fonagy et al., 2009).

The Revised Peer Experiences Questionnaire (Prinstein, Boergers, & Vernberg, 2001) has 36 items pertaining to aggression and victimization in the school context. Overt and indirect forms of bullying/aggression, as well as prosocial behaviors, are measured in terms of behaviors directed at oneself and those directed at others. Children indicate their answers for each question using a 5-point Likert scale. This measure has been used with youth from the 7th to 12th grades, and it takes approximately 10–15 minutes to complete.

The University of Illinois Aggression Scales (Espelage & Holt, 2001; Espelage, Holt, & Henkel, 2003) are three self-report measures that assess behaviors from the past month and are rated on a 5-point Likert scale. These scales were designed for use with children from the 6th to 8th grades, and each takes approximately 5 minutes to complete. The University of Illinois Bully Scale is a modified version of the Aggression Scale (Orpinas & Frankowski, 2001) and includes nine items designed to assess the extent of indirect bullying engaged in by youth. The University of Illinois Fight Scale is a five-item self-report questionnaire that assesses the extent of physical fighting experienced by youth. The University of Illinois Victimization Scale is a four-item measure that assesses the frequency of peer victimization experienced by youth.

Other Informant Reports of Bullying Problems

Assessment of student bully–victim behaviors from the vantage point of teachers, parents, and peers can also be of significant value for clinicians. For example, children often spend a great deal of their waking weekday hours at school where teachers can be privy to observations of student interactions. In addition to broad-band measures that include a few items pertaining to bullying/aggression and victimization (e.g., the Child Behavior Checklist; Achenbach & Rescorla, 2001), there are also a few teacher-report questionnaires devised to specifically evaluate these behaviors. Examples of the latter type of scales include The Bully Survey–Teacher version (Swearer, 2001) and the Social Behavior Rating Scale (teacher-report; Schwartz, Chang, & Farver, 2001). In contrast, parent reports of their child's bullying-related behaviors are often captured on the former types of scales (i.e., more global measure of child behavior like the Child Behavior Checklist). Although information from peers/classmates may also be helpful, obtaining such information would typically not be feasible or essential within the context of individual child assessment and treatment.

Observations

Observation methods offer a way for clinicians to directly gather information about the child's bullying behaviors, contextual influences, frequency of behaviors, and interpersonal interactions (see also Chapter 7). Observation assessments can be made by a variety of informants (e.g., teachers, counselors) in a variety of settings (e.g., classroom, cafeteria, playground), and, of note, offer a rather inexpensive method of assessment (as compared to using copyrighted measures). Bullying-related behaviors could be assessed by observing and coding negative verbal and physical behaviors directed toward other students, while victimization could be measured by observing those targeted by bullying, as well as observing related behaviors such as social isolation and withdrawal (Crothers & Levinson, 2004). Although observations offer direct viewing and coding of children's behaviors (as opposed to relying on others' reports), they may also only provide a limited sample of behaviors, particularly since they must often be collected over a brief period of time. Further, some clinicians find it helpful to not let their clients know that they are being observed as this may alter their behaviors and thus result in inaccurate conclusions regarding the frequency and extent of bully-related behaviors (Olweus, 1993a). Nonetheless, we have found that, when observations can occur over a period of time (e.g., over a 1–2 hour period) and from a distance (e.g., on the playground or sitting across the room in a cafeteria), children often lose track of the observer and begin to engage in more typical behaviors. Overall, including observations is strongly recommended for clinicians if time and feasibility permits, as they are a valuable way to gain insight into not only your client's own behavior but how others behave toward him or her.

Interviews

Interviews can also be used for gathering more comprehensive and detailed information about bullying behaviors, coping strategies, internalizing/externalizing difficulties resulting from such experiences, relationship perceptions, and individual interpersonal styles common among bullies and victims. However, since specific bullying interviews are not currently available, more traditional diagnostic interviews could be substituted. There are several diagnostic interviews available for use with children (Grills-Taquechel, Polifroni, & Fletcher, 2008), though these are commonly too costly and time consuming for a clinician in an individual setting. Therefore, clinicians may find it helpful to take a modular approach to using structured interview components, by selecting specific interview modules to use based on predetermined risk areas. For example, if it has been reported that the child is regularly crying at school, then the depression module would be appropriate to administer along with other related domains.

Functional Behavioral Assessment

In addition to determining the existence and frequency of bullying behaviors and/or peer victimization for a given client, it is important to conduct a functional behavioral assessment of the problem specific to your client. That is, identifying the typical antecedents (i.e., settings and circumstances in which bullying occurs) and consequences (i.e., what happens as a result of the aggressive behavior) will provide clues to the function of bullying and help identify targets for intervention. For example, through questionnaire, observation, and interview you learn that a client is frequently teased by a classmate when the teacher leaves the room and the tormenter gets other kids to laugh at your client who responds with tears and name-calling. If this is the typical pattern, entertainment and peer esteem (on the part of the bully) may be the possible function of the bullying behavior. Logical targets for intervention include contacting the school regarding improving classroom supervision and discipline and working with your client to improve emotion regulation under provocation and to practice nonchalance or other responses that might be more effective.

Common Correlates and Treatment Recommendations for Children Who Bully

For children engaging in bullying behaviors, clinicians need to take immediate steps to reduce such behaviors, particularly for those who are engaging in harmful, aggressive, and violent acts. If these behaviors are left unattended, the child is at greater risk for developing other problems such as criminality, delinquency, academic failure, externalizing behaviors (e.g., oppositional defiant and conduct disorders), and substance abuse (Coie, Lochman, Terry, & Hyman, 1992; Ollendick, Weist, Borden, & Greene, 1992). Thus, the first step clinicians should take in treatment should be targeting these behaviors and either helping the child manage them or, in the best case, extinguishing them. As there are not currently empirically supported treatments for individuals with bullying problems, we provide an overview of key issues and objectives based on related literature on youth aggression and our own clinical experience.

Key Issues/Objectives to Address: Bully or Aggressive Victim Interventions

When devising an individualized treatment plan for a child who bullies or who is an aggressive victim, a clinician should consider and address the following factors related to the child's functioning and maintenance of his or her maladaptive bullying behaviors (see also Chapter 3): behavioral and cognitive difficulties related to aggression, association of bullying behaviors specific psychopathology (e.g., oppositional defiant disorder), child gender, and family environmental factors.

The major objectives of an intervention for a child who bullies are to decrease anger and aggression and to increase prosocial and adaptive behaviors as deemed appropriate. Keeping this in mind, we will now further discuss each of these four areas and how to consider and integrate them while planning treatment for a child who bullies.

Addressing Behavioral and Cognitive Difficulties Related to Aggression

Aggressive behavior is the "bully trademark." The majority of children who bully are engaging in some form of aggression toward another individual.

Typically, two types of aggression are described for children (i.e., Dodge & Coie, 1987). Reactive aggression is an angry response to a perceived threat. In these instances, aggression is geared toward retaliation and is oftentimes motivated by anger, irritation, or the misinterpretation of others' behavior as hostile. Conversely, proactive, or instrumental, aggression is unprovoked and is typically aimed at influencing another person (e.g., bullying another student at school). The proactively aggressive child has an intention to manipulate his or her social environment and, in some instances, these behaviors are used as a means to achieve a desired social or relational goal (Crick & Dodge, 1996; Dodge & Coie, 1987). Clinicians should carefully consider the types of aggressive behaviors a client in formulating an intervention.

It has also been suggested that childhood aggression is associated with an underlying biased or inaccurate social information processing system (Dodge, 1980). That is, if a child is aggressive, especially if he or she is reactively aggressive, he or she is likely to feel threatened by even nonthreatening or ambiguous interactions with others (Dodge, 1980; Feldman & Dodge, 1987). Similarly, aggressive children often show limited problem-solving abilities during difficult social situations. They are typically unable to generate as many solutions to problems as other children and tend to think of hostile or ineffective actions (Dodge & Schwartz, 1997). Aggressive children are also more likely than other children to evaluate the outcomes of hostile responses positively (e.g., aggression will reduce adverse situations) and may not perceive their behaviors as harmful to others (Slaby & Guerra, 1988).

Aggression may also be accompanied by anger and impulsivity, characteristics that often lead to disinhibition of potentially harmful responses (Lochman, Nelson, & Sims, 1981). In addition, aggression is often reinforced and maintained by positive outcomes (i.e., the child gets what s/he wants; Dodge & Schwartz, 1997). This may become the lens through which such children view the world, with the outcome of pervasive aggressive responses across situations (Dodge, 1980). Thus, children who act aggressively by bullying others may not recognize the destructiveness of their behaviors or may determine that the positive outcomes obtained (e.g., getting one's way) outweigh the negative (e.g., getting suspended from school). In these instances, it is important for the clinician to gather information about these areas to help direct intervention choices.

Given that children who exhibit aggressive/bullying tendencies often experience behavioral and cognitive difficulties pertaining particularly to their relationships with peers, cognitive-behavioral therapy (CBT) techniques appear most appropriate for working with such children. Within the framework of CBT, aggression can be viewed as the behavioral consequence of distorted cognitive processing of perceived threat and/or provocation and the expectation that aggressive behavior will pay off (perhaps because it has in the past). Key components of CBT for childhood aggression include *(1)* cognitive components such as cognitive restructuring and problem-solving skills, *(2)* behavioral modification strategies to replace aggression with prosocial behaviors, *(3)* social skills training, and *(4)* anger management/impulse control strategies.

When intervening with an aggressive/bullying child, clinicians should assess and subsequently address all relevant types of social information processing deficits (i.e., hostile attribution bias, limited problem-solving skills, evaluations of aggressive behavior outcomes, and thinking through options before acting). For example, if a client thinks others are always threatening him or her, the clinician can work with the child to consider "evidence" for or against such thinking, as well as help the child come up with alternative ways of viewing others' behavior. Problem solving can also be integrated into such an intervention by helping the child determine different courses of action for interacting with peers. For instance, if the child typically chooses physical aggression to get his or her way with peers, the clinician could use Socratic discussion to identify the pros and cons of such behavior, followed by discussion of the best overall approach for obtaining the desired goal while limiting negative consequences. The broader goal of this type of intervention would be to teach your client how to use these problem-solving techniques on his or her own in a variety of situations. Thus, while specific examples can be worked through with the clinician in session, homework assignments should be incorporated into treatment to help promote practice by the child and generalization to diverse settings.

The main behavioral aspects of treating aggression with CBT target prosocial behaviors and anger management (Coie, Underwood, & Lochman, 1991; Webster-Stratton & Hammond, 1997). Important behavioral information to obtain at the outset of CBT is a functional assessment of the child's specific behavioral goals and what influences are serving as maintenance factors of the aggression (Colvin, Kameenui, & Sugai, 1998). Colvin and colleagues (1998) suggest that the behavioral task at hand is to teach the child an efficient replacement behavior without changing their behavioral goal. That is, as a clinician you need to understand what the child is achieving from his or her behavior and then discuss other behavioral ways for him or her to meet that desired goal. In addition, behavior modification strategies, such as positive reinforcement and behavior charts, can be used to support replacement of inappropriate behavioral choices with appropriate ones (e.g., asking for toys instead of just taking them).

To increase the use of prosocial behaviors, social skills training is often incorporated into treatment (Lochman, Wayland, & White, 1993). Social skills training may include helping children inhibit behaviors that may limit their interactions with others. For example, if your client engages in relational bullying he or she is unlikely aware of how to make and/or keep friends without manipulation or bullying techniques. The child may also be unaware that his/her behaviors are what are destructive to his/her friendships, instead attributing loss or lack of friends to others' behaviors. In addition, prosocial behavioral responses and problem-solving skills may be increased by encouraging the child to consider alternative ways of solving problems in difficult social situations (Coie et al., 1991). Asking children to consider being on the receiving end of their behaviors (or times when they have been on the receiving end of similar behaviors) with role play is often helpful in these instances.

As aggressive children may also experience aroused anger in difficult situations, anger and impulse control components may also be helpful to include in the treatment of a bullying child (Lochman et al., 1981). In general, these approaches usually involve some variant on the theme of stop, think, and relax. Thus, the child is first taught to identify his or her cues for anger (e.g., feeling hot, angry thoughts, shaking fists) and to "stop" or pause (e.g., counting to 20) when these are noticed. The next step typically includes having the child use cognitive strategies, such as those previously identified, to think through the situation. Finally, the child is taught anger-reduction techniques, such as relaxation.

The use of CBT as an intervention for aggressive behaviors has proven to be efficacious in a number of studies. Treatment manuals with empirical support for reducing aggressive behaviors include Anger Coping Therapy (Lochman et al., 1981; Lochman, Burch, Curry, & Lampron, 1984), the Social Relations Intervention Program (Lochman, Coie, Underwood, & Terry, 1993), and Coping Power (Lochman & Wells, 2004). Although these interventions have been tested as group treatments, the key components from them (e.g., problem-solving strategies, cognitive restructuring, anger management, and social skills training) could also be used with individual children. Thus, clinicians may follow a similar type of treatment when they have clients who are bullies or adapt the group manuals to better fit the needs of the individual client.

Additional treatments that have been found to be efficacious for youth with externalizing problems, generally speaking, also offer alternative components for working with bullies. For example, Problem Solving Skills Training (Kazdin, Esveldt-Dawson, French, & Unis, 1987a, b), Assertiveness Training (Huey & Rank, 1984), and Group Anger Control Training with Stress Inoculation (Feindler, Marriott, & Iwata, 1984) have all demonstrated positive findings and are denoted as probably efficacious treatments for school-aged children and adolescents (Brestan & Eyberg, 1998). While these treatments were not specifically designed with "bullies" in mind, because aggressive and externalizing behaviors are prevalent among the bully population, utilizing these interventions would seem particularly beneficial.

Additional Considerations for Intervening with Bullies
Comorbidity

It is important to note that in addition to aggressive behaviors, bullying has been linked with other co-occurring behavioral and/or psychosocial problems. These types of behaviors are important to assess/consider because they may interfere with targeted treatment goals that are directly related to the bullying. As might be expected, bullying behaviors have often been associated with externalizing disorders, such as attention-deficit/hyperactivity disorder (Unnever & Cornell, 2003), as well as oppositional defiant disorder (ODD) and conduct disorder (CD; Kumpulainen, Räsänen, & Kaija, 2001). In addition, Kaukiainen, Salmivalli, and Lagerspetz (2002) suggested that because some children with learning disabilities have poor social skills, misinterpret verbal communication, and display aggressive tendencies, they may take on a bullying role in the classroom. Additionally, comorbid depressive symptoms have been identified, likely due to the shared irritability and emotion regulation difficulties commonly inherent with depressive problems in youth (Biggam & Power, 1999, Craig, 1998).

Gender

It is also important to consider potential gender differences when applying intervention strategies with youth identified as bullies. For example, girls often engage in greater relational forms of bullying, while boys engage in more direct, physical aggression (Lagerspetz, Bjorkqvist, & Peltonen, 1988; Whitney & Smith, 1993). Thus, increased focus on interpersonal relationship difficulties and social skills training may be warranted for girls, whereas for boys the initial focus of treatment may need to target the reduction of harmful, physical behaviors, as well as teaching alternative responses to physical violence.

Under most circumstances, the involvement of parents in the treatment process is important when working with children. The case of bullying is no exception with research findings suggesting that the family environment can play an influential role in children's involvement with such behaviors (Farrington & West, 1993; Landy & Menna, 2006). Family factors to assess and address in treatment may include parental history of bullying (Farrington and West, 1993); high tolerance for aggression, harsh and/or ineffective discipline strategies (Rican, Klicperova, & Koucka 1993; Rigby, 1994), poor communication, few opportunities or intolerance for expression of emotions and ideas (Rigby, 1994; Stevens, De Bourdeauhuij, & Van Oost, 2002), and low family cohesiveness (Stevens et al., 2002). Further description of family factors associated with bullying behavior can be found in Chapter 5.

Given the connection between family functioning and bullying, parental involvement in the treatment of children engaged in aggressive and/or bullying behavior is important either through family therapy and/or parent training in behavior management techniques. The few studies that have implemented family treatment plans for children identified as bullies have illustrated positive and significant associations between parental involvement and reductions of bullying behaviors (Landy & Menna, 2006; Nickel, Luley, & Krawczyk, 2006).

In conclusion, extant literature on bullying and related domains offers several potential intervention strategies for targeting these behaviors with children and their families. Based on this review, it appears that important areas to target with a child identified as a bully include social information processing and problem-solving skills; social skills; emotion regulation (e.g., anger and impulsivity control); and behavioral modification. Children should not only be encouraged to practice skills during sessions but also outside treatment, with the assistance of worksheets or other aids. In addition, specified rewards for homework completion by parents and the therapist as well as directed child–therapist discussion in the following session about the past week's experiences should be used. The inclusion of parent/family intervention components appears to be additionally beneficial when working with bullying youth.

Common Correlates and Treatment Recommendations for Victimized Children

Recent research has focused on social-cognitive models that can illuminate the interconnected pathways of environmental factors (e.g., peer and parent–child relationships) and individual child factors (e.g., interpretation of bullying behavior) that may lead to or protect against psychological symptoms among victims of bullying. Similar to treatment planning for a child who bullies, when devising an individualized treatment plan for victimized children several issues should be considered, including behavioral and cognitive difficulties related to internalizing symptoms; peer relationship problems; and familial environmental factors.

The major objectives of an intervention are to decrease avoidance and isolation of the victimized child, and to increase self-esteem, social skills, and problem-solving skills. In addition, evaluation of the areas noted above, along with specific internalizing symptoms, can help the clinician determine which additional interventions may be appropriate for inclusion in individual treatment.

Behavioral and Cognitive Difficulties Related to Internalizing Symptoms

Whereas difficulties with aggression are common among bullies, internalizing symptoms are among the most frequently discussed for bullied children. Numerous investigations have revealed increased anxiety concerns among youth who report being bullied (e.g., Craig, 1998; Grills, 2003; Grills & Ollendick, 2002; Hawker & Boulton, 2000; Swearer, Song, Cary, Eagle, & Mickelson, 2001). For example, while anxiety has been implicated as a correlate of all aspects of bullying, children who are the recipients of bullying have been found to evidence the greatest impairment (Swearer, Grills, Haye, & Cary, 2004). Several causal pathways have been posited in an attempt to explain this relation. One such theory is based on the assumption that particular children appear to be singled out as "victims" and experience repeated peer attacks. If you are treating a victim of bullying, you are likely to see this pattern and, therefore, it is critical to evaluate the history of victimizing behaviors experienced by the client across classrooms, grades, peers, and so forth. Due to this repeated exposure to potentially harmful situations, it has been proposed that bullied children may become hypervigilant to their surroundings and the opinions of others (Grills & Ollendick, 2002; Roth, Coles, & Heimberg, 2002). Over time, these concerns may result in a specific or social phobia or a more generalized anxiety state and may present in the form of increased somatic anxiety symptoms (Rigby, 1999) or other physical health complaints (Williams et al., 1996), and school-related difficulties (e.g., school refusal, absenteeism, discontent/fear of school; Kumpulainen et al., 1998; Ross, 1996).

Research has also revealed significant relations between peer victimization and depressive symptoms (Callaghan & Joseph, 1995; Craig, 1998; Grills,

2003; Kumpulainen et al., 1998; Neary & Joseph, 1994; Olweus, 1993b, 1993c) and suicidal behaviors (Kaltiala-Heino, Rimpela, Marttunen, Rimpela, & Rantanen, 1999; Olweus, 1991). Relatedly, bullied youth tend to report lower self-worth and to display more signs of loneliness (Callaghan & Joseph, 1995; Grills, 2003; Grills & Ollendick, 2002; Hawker & Boulton, 2000; Neary & Joseph, 1994; Prinstein et al., 2001; Ross, 1996; Swearer et al., 2001, 2004). Although all children involved in bullying have been found to report concurrent depressive symptoms, bullied children typically report lower self-worth than their bullying and uninvolved peers, who tend not to differ from one another (Andreou, 2000; Boulton & Underwood, 1992). It has been suggested that bullied children may develop a cognitive style characterized by thoughts of helplessness regarding their ability to effect change in their environment both in the present and future (Roth et al., 2002). Furthermore, children who are repeatedly exposed to bullying without assistance from classmates or school personnel may develop a sense of hopelessness, come to view the world negatively, and find it difficult to identify positive events occurring in their lives (Grills, 2003; Swearer et al., 2004). Attribution style has also been suggested as a cognitive factor that may influence the development of depressive symptoms in bullied youth. For example, a child's attributional style could lead to either an internal (self-focused) or external (bully-focused) interpretation and explanation of a negative event, such as being victimized by a bully. A self-focused attribution of being victimized might entail the youth believing that the bullying is due to a personal defect or shortcoming—something that they cannot control. It seems likely that this type of attributional style would lead to worse psychological outcomes as compared to an external, bully-focused, or situational attributional style (i.e., the youth attributes the bullying to a cause or situation unrelated to him or her). Several studies have supported this notion by finding that depressive symptoms are associated with critical self-referent attributions for ambiguous peer cues (Prinstein, Cheah, & Guyer, 2005) and with ineffective coping styles (Bijttebier & Vertommen, 1998; Craig, 1998; Grills, 2003).

Unfortunately, internalizing symptoms may also promote continued bullying from others. For example, Salmivalli, Karhunen, and Lagerspetz (1996) found bullying was more likely to continue against children whose response appeared anxious or helpless (e.g., crying). In contrast, children who responded in a calm or unaffected manner were less likely to continue being bullied. Thus, children's responses to being bullied should be evaluated, ideally by both interview and observational means. Similarly, children with internalizing problems may miss out on normative social developmental encounters because of anxiety about them or lack of motivation to engage in them. Over time, these missed opportunities may limit the child's social network and skills, problems that may place him or her at greater risk for both being bullied and experiencing further internalizing symptoms (Grills, 2003; Kaltiala-Heino et al., 1999; Swearer et al., 2001). These findings point to the importance of including aspects of interventions that target these domains, such as social skills and assertiveness training.

To address internalizing symptoms among victimized youth, there are several techniques identified from the extant treatment literature that clinicians can apply. For example, the Coping Cat (Kendall & Hedtke, 2006) is an empirically supported treatment that has been developed for children with generalized anxiety symptomatology. Treatment manuals designed for children with social anxiety, such as *Cognitive Behavioral Group Treatment for Adolescents* (Albano, Marten, Holt, Heimberg, & Barlow, 1995) or *Social Effectiveness Therapy for Children and Adolescents* (Beidel, Turner, & Morris, 2003) may also be pertinent to the treatment of bullied children. Likewise, efficacious treatments from the child depression literature (Kaslow & Thompson, 1998; Stark, Sander, Yancy, Bronik, & Hoke, 2000), such as interpersonal or cognitive-behavioral therapies, could be utilized to supplement interventions with victimized youth. Moreover, as internalizing symptoms may contribute to the maintenance of negative behaviors from bullies, exposing children to others through structured activities (e.g., extracurricular) would also be an important intervention component to include. This may reduce anxiety ignited by social interactions (Beidel & Turner, 1998), as well as provide behavioral activation for depressed youth.

These treatments include several techniques to help target the client's internalizing experiences, as well as peer relationships. Examples of such techniques include relaxation training, cognitive restructuring, problem-solving skills, role playing, and behavioral exposures. From the previously discussed findings of difficulties often reported by bullied children, it is also apparent that additional cognitive and behavioral skills (i.e., attribution style, coping skills, self-esteem, perceived helplessness and hopelessness) should be assessed and targeted. Relaxation training can be helpful for reducing anxiety symptoms in general, and specifically related to being bullied. Cognitive restructuring can be used to address negative attributions, both specific to bullying and more generally to address internalizing symptoms. Problem solving and assertiveness training with practice (role plays) are also often particularly important with victimized clients as their avoidance of social situations and their lack of assertiveness likely contribute to their vulnerability and risk of repeated victimization experiences. Assertiveness training and social problem solving may allow victimized children to develop and implement alternative responses to bullies and/or alternative coping strategies, which may reduce the frequency with which the bullying occurs (Salmivalli, 1999; Salmivalli et al., 1996).

These strategies can also be particularly helpful with a client who is experiencing hopelessness (Stark et al., 2000) as a result of the bullying he or she has experienced. Furthermore, as researchers have identified a number of difficulties associated with low self-esteem, this should also be a focus of individual treatment with victimized children. Indeed, social skills and self-esteem-building strategies (Barrett, Webster, & Wallis, 1999; Larkin & Thyer, 1999) appear to be important aspects of intervention with bullied youth (as noted below), as involvement in positive peer interactions may foster the development of friendships as well as reduce the likelihood of further bullying attacks.

Additional Considerations for Intervening with Victims
Peer Relationship Problems

It has long been acknowledged that the quality of peer relationships is associated with psychosocial adjustment in children and youth (Bagwell, Bender, & Andreassi, 2005; Kingery & Erdley, 2007). Several studies have found peer acceptance to be associated with positive social skills and adaptive emotional functioning, whereas peer rejection and neglect have been associated with internal distress and behavioral problems (LaGreca & Fetter, 1995; Parker & Asher, 1987). Relatedly, quality of friendships has been identified as having an influence on children's psychosocial functioning. Friendship quality can be said to increase concurrently with the following characteristics: helping behavior, support, intimacy, security, affection, low levels of conflict, and companionship (Bowker, 2004; Martin & Smith, 2002; Phillipsen, 1999; Schneider, Fonzi, Tani, & Tomada, 1997; Simpkins, Parke, & Flyr, 2006). Further, friendships are highly influential in the realms of children's self-worth and self-efficacy (Boulton & Underwood, 1992; Kupersmidt, Coie, & Dodge, 1990; Ledley, Storch, & Coles, 2006; Rubin, Dwyer, & Booth-LaForce, 2004), areas that have previously been noted to be deficient in bullied youth.

If positive friendships are absent or limited, a bullied child or adolescent may be prone to poorer psychological outcomes that can, as previously described, lead to recurrent victimization. Research has established that bullied youth tend to experience increased isolation and lack of support from peers

(Ross, 1996), as well as lower social acceptance and perceived competence (Callaghan & Joseph, 1995; Grills, 2003; Neary & Joseph, 1994). For example, peers have been found to reject (socially) victimized children and to describe them as "shy" and "seeking help" (Perry et al., 1988; Whitney & Smith, 1993).

In contrast, positive relationships with other children have been identified as a protective factor among victimized children (Grills, 2003; Prinstein et al., 2001). Clinicians should, therefore, take the child's social competence and connectedness, as well as the quality of existing friendships into account when devising a treatment plan for bullied youth (see also Chapter 11). Further, it is recommended that clinicians consider social skills training to help their clients increase the quality and perhaps quantity of their friendships. For example, LaGreca and Fetter (1995) have identified several skills important for positive peer interactions (i.e., showing enjoyment of interactions, greeting, joining, inviting, conversation, sharing/cooperation, complimenting/giving positive feedback, and conflict resolution) and each of these can be assessed and addressed as applicable with bullied children. Indeed, many bullied clients may need help learning and using the aforementioned positive peer interactions skills. In such cases, the clinician should not only model the appropriate and inappropriate skills/behaviors but also engage the child in role plays and practice these skills in session. Following repeated practice, the child can then try these new skills with a peer; however, it may first be important to identify certain classmates/peers that are receptive to your client in order to increase the likelihood that he or she will succeed. Further supporting the inclusion of these techniques, children identified as high risk for being bullied have been found to respond favorably to social skills training (Hanish & Guerra, 2000).

Family Environment

Evaluating family patterns during your initial assessments may be useful as research has found that the family environment of bullied children tends to be characterized by parental overprotectiveness, less warmth, and rejection (Finnegan, Hodges, & Perry, 1998). Smokowski and Kopasz (2005) posit that parents of victims tend to be overprotective because they are aware of their child's anxiety. The authors also suggest that such parents become overly involved in their children's activities to compensate for their children's social difficulties. Parents of victims have also been found to report more avoidant coping strategies and higher levels of internalizing symptoms for themselves (Stevens et al., 2002; Veenstra et al., 2005). Thus, it may be useful to include parenting components when treating bullied children that help their parents learn to be supportive and encouraging of their child, without overcompensating. For instance, clinical treatment should involve strengthening the parent–child relationship and creating a more positive familial environment. Including parents can also be important for educating them on the intervention components (e.g., cognitive restructuring, encouraging social activities) so that they can continue to work on these aspects after the intervention has been completed. Further, parental involvement is especially important for helping the child to practice his or her new skills outside of the session and for creating an additional source of reinforcement for the child's efforts.

Additional Remarks on Interventions for Children Involved in Bullying

Two final points seem pertinent to the present discussion of individualized assessment and treatment planning for children involved in bullying. The first of these pertains to the generalization of skills from individualized treatment to other environments, while the second comments on the state of the individualized treatment literature base.

When working one on one with a child who bullies and/or has experienced peer victimization, it is of utmost importance to formulate a plan for skill generalization outside of therapy. The ability of the child to use learned social, problem-solving, and other related skills at school and at home can directly influence how successful the individualized treatment is for the child (e.g., Bierman, 2004). This rolling over of skills into naturalistic settings and sustenance of such adaptive behaviors in all environments can be a difficult goal to accomplish with child-focused therapy due in part to the necessity of collaboration between the therapist and other adults intimately involved in the child's life (e.g., parents/guardians and teachers). However, certain practical components utilized during treatment can facilitate the child's gradual extension of skills from the therapy room to these other settings. Such additive components include homework assignments, practice of social situations in therapy sessions and naturalistic settings, and therapist-facilitated creation of new social opportunities for the child (Bierman, 2004). In addition, the therapist can accomplish collaboration with parents/guardians and teachers by educating them about the skills taught to the child during therapy sessions and how they can support the child in his or her attempts to use these skills at home or school. Although difficulties may arise, the benefits of skill generalization more than compensate for the potential hassles. It is crucial for the child to be competent in using learned skills in the real world beyond individualized therapy so that such an intervention, aimed at combating maladaptive psychosocial trajectories of the bully, bully-victim, or victim, will have greater success.

As noted at the beginning of this chapter, the majority of effective interventions for bullying problems are school-based programs that are established on the assumption that it is easier to change the environment than the individual and that prevention is better than intervention (Horne, Orpinas, Newman-Carlson, & Bartolomucci, 2004). While these tenets are true, it is also important to address the psychological distress and maladjustment of individual children and adolescents. This seems particularly true given the number of problematic behaviors commonly associated with both bullying and victimization. Although there are a limited number of efficacious interventions created specifically for youth who are victimized by their peers, a variety of treatment options that have been established as effective for particular psychological symptoms or related social and cognitive problems are available for clinicians to employ. Many examples of these have been discussed in this chapter, and additional examples of nonindividualized (i.e., group and universal) treatments can be found in Chapters 9 and 10.

References

Achenbach, T. M., & Rescorla, L. A. (2001). *Manual for the Child Behavior Checklist/6–18*. Burlington: University of Vermont Department of Psychiatry.

Albano, A. M., Marten, P. A., Holt, C. S., Heimberg, R. G., & Barlow, D. H. (1995). Cognitive-behavioral group treatment for social phobia in adolescents: A preliminary study. *The Journal of Nervous and Mental Disease, 183,* 649–656.

Andreou, E. (2000). Bully/victim problems and their association with psychological constructs in 8–12-year old Greek schoolchildren. *Aggressive Behavior, 26,* 49–56.

Bagwell, C. L., Bender, S. E., & Andreassi, C. L. (2005). Friendship quality and perceived relationship changes predict psychosocial adjustment in early adulthood. *Journal of Social and Personal Relationships, 22,* 235–254.

Barrett, P. M., Webster, H. M., & Wallis, J. R. (1999). Adolescent self-esteem and cognitive skills training: A school-based intervention. *Journal of Child and Family Studies, 8,* 217–227.

Beidel, D. C., & Turner, S. M. (1998). *Shy children, phobic adults: Nature and treatment of social phobia*. Washington, DC: American Psychiatric Association.

Beidel, D. C., Turner, S. M., & Morris, T. L. (2003). *Social effectiveness therapy—child version: Therapist's guide.* Toronto: Multi-Health Systems, Inc.

Bierman, K. L. (2004). *Peer rejection: Developmental processes and intervention strategies.* New York: The Guilford Press.

Biggam, F. H., & Power, K. G. (1999). Social problem-solving skills and psychological distress among incarcerated young offenders: The issue of bullying and victimization. *Cognitive Therapy and Research, 23,* 307–326.

Bijttebier, P., & Vertommen, H. (1998). Coping with peer arguments in school-age children with bully/victim problems. *British Journal of Educational Psychology, 68,* 387–394.

Boulton, M. J., & Underwood, K. (1992). Bully/victim problems among middle school children. *British Journal of Educational Psychology, 62,* 73–87.

Bowker, A. (2004). Predicting friendship stability during early adolescence. *Journal of Early Adolescence, 24,* 85–112.

Brestan, E. V., & Eyberg, S. M. (1998). Effective psychosocial treatments of conduct-disordered children and adolescents: 29 years, 82 studies, and 5,272 kids. *Journal of Clinical Child Psychology, 27,* 180–189.

Callaghan, S., & Joseph, S. (1995). Self-concept and peer victimization among schoolchildren. *Personality and Individual Differences, 18,* 161–163.

Coie, J. D., Lochman, J. E., Terry, R., & Hyman, C. (1992). Predicting early adolescent disorder from childhood aggression and peer rejection. *Journal of Consulting and Clinical Psychology, 60,* 783–792.

Coie, J. D., Underwood, M., & Lochman, J. E. (1991). Programmatic intervention with aggressive children in the school setting. In D. J. Pepler & K. H. Rubin (Eds.), *The development and treatment of childhood aggression* (pp. 389–410). Hillsdale, NJ: Erlbaum.

Colvin, G., Kameenui, E., J., & Sugai, G. (1998). Reconceptualizing behavior management and school-wide discipline in general education. *Education and Treatment of Children, 16,* 361–381.

Cornell, D. G., Sheras, P. L., & Cole, J. C. M. (2006). Assessment of bullying. In S. R. Jimerson & M. J. Furlong (Eds.), *Handbook of school violence and school safety: From research to practice* (pp. 191–209). Mahwah, NJ: Erlbaum.

Craig, W. M. (1998). The relationship among bullying, victimization, depression, anxiety, and aggression in elementary school children. *Personality and Individual Differences, 24,* 123–130.

Crick, N. R., & Dodge, K. (1996). Social-information processing mechanisms in reactive and proactive aggression. *Child Development, 67,* 993–1002.

Crothers, L. M., & Levinson, E. M. (2004). Assessment of bullying: A review of methods and instruments. *Journal of Counseling and Development, 82,* 496–503.

Dill, E. J., Vernberg, E. M., Fonagy, P., Twemlow, S. W., & Gamm, B. K. (2004). Negative affect in victimized children: The roles of social withdrawal, peer rejection, and attitudes towards bullying. *Journal of Abnormal Child Psychology, 32,* 159–173.

Dodge, K. (1980). Social cognition and children's aggressive behavior. *Child Development,* *51,* 162–170.

Dodge, K. A., & Coie, J. D. (1987). Social information processing factors in reactive and proactive aggression in children's peer groups. *Journal of Personality and Social Psychology, 53,* 1146–1158.

Dodge, K. A., & Schwartz, D. (1997). Social information processing mechanisms in aggressive behavior. In D. M. Stoff, J. Breiling, & J. D. Maser (Eds.), *Handbook of antisocial behavior* (pp. 171–180). Hoboken, NJ: John Wiley & Sons Inc.

Espelage, D. L., & Holt, M. K. (2001). Bullying and victimization during early adolescence: Peer influences and psychosocial correlates. *Journal of Emotional Abuse, 2,* 123–142.

Espelage, D. L., Holt, M. K., & Henkel, R. R. (2003). Examination of peer-group contextual effects on aggression during early adolescence. *Child Development, 74,* 205–220.

Farrington, D. P., & West, D. J. (1993). Criminal, penal and life histories of chronic offenders: Risk and protective factors and early identification. *Criminal Behaviour and Mental Health, 3,* 492–523.

Feindler, E. L., Marriott, S. A., & Iwata, M. (1984). Group anger control training for junior high school delinquents. *Cognitive Therapy and Research, 8,* 299–311.

Feldman, E., & Dodge, K. A. (1987). Social information processing and sociometric status: Sex, age, and situational effects. *Journal of Abnormal Child Psychology, 15,* 211–227.

Finnegan, R. A., Hodges, E. V. E., & Perry, D. G. (1998). Victimization by peers: Associations with children's reports of mother-child interaction. *Journal of Personality and Social Psychology, 75,* 1076–1086.

Fonagy, P., Twemlow, S. W., Vernberg, E. M., Nelson, J. M., Dill, E. J., Little, T. D., et al. (2009). A cluster randomized controlled trial of child-focused psychiatric consultation and a school systems-focused intervention to reduce aggression. *Journal of Child Psychology and Psychiatry, 50,* 607–616

Grills, A. E. (2003). *Long-term relations among peer victimization and internalizing symptoms in children.* Unpublished dissertation, Virginia Polytechnic Institute and State University, Blacksburg.

Grills, A., & Ollendick, T. (2002). Peer victimization, global self-worth, and anxiety in middle school children. *Journal of Clinical Child and Adolescent Psychology, 31,* 59–68.

Grills-Taquechel, A. E., Polifroni, R., & Fletcher, J. M. (2008). Interview and report writing. In J. L. Matson, F. Andrasik, & M. L. Matson (Eds.), *Assessing childhood psychopathology and developmental disabilities.* New York: Springer.

Hanish, L. D., & Guerra, N. G. (2000). Children who get victimized at school: What is known? What can be done? *Professional School Counseling, 4,* 113–119.

Harmon, A. (2004, August 26). Internet gives teenage bullies weapons to wound from afar. *The New York Times.* Retrieved October 1, 2007, from http://query.nytimes.com/gst/fullpage.html?res=9E00E6D8133EF935A1575BC0A9629C8B63.

Harter, S. (1985). *Manual for the self-perception profile for children*. Denver, CO: University of Denver.

Hawker, D. S. J., & Boulton, M. J. (2000). Twenty years' research on peer victimization and psychosocial maladjustment: A meta-analytic review of cross-sectional studies. *Journal of Child Psychology and Psychiatry and Allied Disciplines, 41*, 441–455.

Horne, A. M., Orpinas, P., Newman-Carlson, D., & Bartolomucci, C. L. (2004). Elementary School Bully Busters Program: Understanding why children bully and what to do about it. In D. L. Espelage & S. M. Swearer (Eds.), *Bullying in American schools: A social-ecological perspective on prevention and intervention* (pp. 297–325). Mahwah, NJ: Erlbaum.

Huey, W. C., & Rank, R. C. (1984). Effects of counselor and peer-led group assertive training on Black adolescent aggression. *Journal of Counseling Psychology, 31*, 95–98.

Kaltiala-Heino, R., Rimpela, M., Marttunen, M., Rimpela, A., & Rantanen, P. (1999). Bullying, depression, and suicidal ideation in Finnish adolescents: School survey. *British Medical Journal, 319*, 348–351.

Kaslow, N. J., & Thompson, M. P. (1998). Applying the criteria for empirically supported treatments to studies of psychosocial interventions for child and adolescent depression. *Journal of Clinical Child Psychology, 27*, 146–155.

Kaukiainen, A., Salmivalli, C., & Lagerspetz, K. (2002). Learning difficulties, social intelligence and self-concept: Connections to bully-victim problems. *Scandinavian Journal of Psychology, 43*, 269–278.

Kazdin A. E., Esveldt-Dawson, K., French, N. H., & Unis, A. S. (1987a). Effects of parent management training and problem-solving skills training combined in the treatment of antisocial child behavior. *Journal of the American Academy of Child and Adolescent Psychiatry, 26*, 416–424.

Kazdin, A. E., Esveldt-Dawson, K., French, N. H., & Unis, A. S. (1987b). Problem-solving skills training and relationship therapy in the treatment of antisocial child behavior. *Journal of Consulting and Clinical Psychology, 55*, 76–85.

Kendall, P. C., & Hedtke, K. A.. (2006). *Cognitive-behavior therapy for anxious children: Therapist manual, 3rd ed*. Available from http://www.workbookpublishing.com.

Kingery, J. N., & Erdley, C. A. (2007). Peer experiences as predictors of adjustment across the middle school transition. *Education and Treatment of Children, 30*, 73–88.

Kumpulainen, K., Räsänen, E., Henttonen, I., Almqvist, F., Kresanov, K., Linna, S. L. et al. (1998). Bullying and psychiatric symptoms among elementary school-age children. *Child Abuse and Neglect, 22*, 705–717.

Kumpulainen, K., Räsänen, E., & Kaija, P. (2001). Psychiatric disorders and the use of mental health services among children involved in bullying. *Aggressive Behavior, 27*, 102–110.

Kupersmidt, J. B., Coie, J. D., & Dodge, K. A. (1990). The role of poor peer relationships in the development of disorder. In S. R. Asher & J. D. Coie (Eds.), *Peer rejection in childhood*. New York: Cambridge University Press.

Lagerspetz, K. M., Bjorkqvist, K., & Peltonen, T. (1988). Is indirect aggression typical of females? Gender differences in aggressiveness in 11- to 12-year-old children. *Aggressive Behavior, 14*, 403–414.

LaGreca, A. M., & Fetter, M. D. (1995). Peer relations. In A. R. Eisen, C. A. Kearney, & C. E. Schaefer (Eds.), *Clinical handbook of anxiety disorders in children and adolescents.* Lanham, MD: Jason Aronson Inc.

Landy, S., & Menna, R. (2006). An evaluation of a group intervention for parents with aggressive young children: Improvements in child functioning, maternal confidence, parenting knowledge and attitudes. *Early Child Development and Care, 176*, 605–620.

Larkin, R., & Thyer, B. A. (1999). Evaluating cognitive-behavioral group counseling to improve elementary school students' self-esteem, self-control and classroom behavior. *Behavioral Interventions, 14*, 147–161.

Ledley, D. R., Storch, E. A., & Coles, M. E. (2006). The relationship between childhood teasing and later interpersonal functioning. *Journal of Psychopathology and Behavioral Assessment, 28*, 33–40.

Lochman, J., Coie, J., Underwood, M., & Terry, R. (1993). Effectiveness of a Social Relations Intervention Program for aggressive and nonaggressive, rejected children. *Journal of Consulting and Clinical Psychology, 61*, 1053–1058.

Lochman, J. E., Burch, P. R., Curry, J. F, & Lampron, L. (1984). Treatment and generalization effects of cognitive-behavioral and goal-setting interventions with aggressive boys. *Journal of Consulting and Clinical Psychology, 52*, 915–916.

Lochman, J. E., Nelson, W. M., & Sims, J. P. (1981). A cognitive behavioral program for use with aggressive children. *Journal of Clinical Child Psychology, 10*, 146–148.

Lochman, J. E., Wayland, K. K., & White, K. J. (1993). Social goals: Relationship to adolescent adjustment and to social problem-solving. *Journal of Abnormal Child Psychology, 21*, 135–151.

Lochman, J. E., & Wells, K. C. (2004). The coping power program for preadolescent aggressive boys and their parents: Outcome effects at the 1-year follow-up. *Journal of Consulting and Clinical Psychology, 72*, 571–578.

Martin, J. J., & Smith, K. (2002). Friendship quality in youth disability sport: Perceptions of a best friend. *Adapted Physical Activity Quarterly, 19*, 472–482.

Mynard, H., & Joseph, S. (2000). Development of the multidimensional peer victimization scale. *Aggressive Behavior, 26*, 169–178.

Nansel, T. R., Overpeck, M., Pilla, R. S., Ruan, W. J., Simons-Morton, B., & Schedit, P. (2001). Bullying behaviors among US youth: Prevalence and association with psychosocial adjustment. *Journal of the American Medical Association, 285*, 2094–2100.

Neary, A., & Joseph, S. (1994). Peer victimization and its relationship to self-concept and depression among school children. *Personality and Individual Differences, 16*, 183–186.

Nickel, M., Luley, J., & Krawczyk, J. (2006). Bullying girls—changes after brief strategic family therapy: A randomized, prospective, controlled trial with one-year follow-up. *Psychotherapy and Psychosomatics, 75*, 47–55.

Ollendick, T. H., Weist, M. D., Borden, M. C., & Greene, R. W. (1992). Sociometric status and academic, behavioral, and psychological adjustment: A five year longitudinal study. *Journal of Consulting and Clinical Psychology, 60,* 80–87.

Olweus, D. (1991). Bully/victim problems among school children: Basic facts and effects of a school based intervention program. In D. Pepler and K. Rubin (Eds.), *The development and treatment of childhood aggression.* Hillsdale, NJ: Erlbaum.

Olweus, D. (1993a). *Bullying at school: What we know and what we can do.* Oxford, England: Blackwell Publishers.

Olweus, D. (1993b). Bullies on the playground: The role of victimization. In C. Hart (Ed.), *Children on playgrounds.* New York: SUNY Press.

Olweus, D. (1993c). Victimization by peers: Antecedents and long-term consequences. In K. H. Rubin and J. B. Asendorpf (Eds.), *Social withdrawal, inhibition, and shyness in childhood.* Hillsdale, NJ: Erlbaum.

Olweus, D. (1996). *Revised Olweus Bully/Victim Questionnaire.* Mimeo. Bergen, Norway: Research Center for Health Promotion, University of Bergen.

Orpinas, P., & Frankowski, R. (2001). The Aggression Scale: A self-report measure of aggressive behavior for young adolescents. *Journal of Early Adolescence, 21,* 50–67.

Parker, J. G., & Asher, S. R. (1987). Peer relations and later personal adjustment: Are low accepted children at risk? *Psychological Bulletin, 102,* 357–389.

Perry, D. G., Kusel, S. J., & Perry, L. C. (1988). Victims of peer aggression. *Developmental Psychology, 24,* 807–814.

Phillipsen, L. C. (1999). Associations between age, gender, and group acceptance and three components of friendship quality. *Journal of Early Adolescence, 19,* 438–464.

Prinstein, M. J., Boergers, J., & Vernberg, E. M. (2001). Overt and relational aggression in adolescents: Social-psychological adjustment of aggressors and victims. *Journal of Clinical Child Psychology, 30,* 479–491.

Prinstein, M. J., Cheah, C. S. L., & Guyer, A. E. (2005). Peer victimization, cue interpretation, and internalizing symptoms: Preliminary, concurrent, and longitudinal findings for children and adolescents. *Journal of Clinical Child Psychology, 34,* 11–24.

Reynolds, W. M. (2003). *Bully victimization: Reynolds Scales for Schools Manual.* San Antonio, TX: The Psychological Corporation.

Rican, P., Klicperova, M., & Koucka, T. (1993). Families of bullies and their victims: A children's view. *Studia Psychologica, 35,* 261–266.

Rigby, K. (1994). Psychosocial functioning in families of Australian adolescent school-children involved in bully/victim problems. *Journal of Family Therapy, 16,* 173–187.

Rigby, K. (1999). Peer victimisation at school and the health of secondary school students. *British Journal of Educational Psychology, 69,* 95–104.

Ross, D. M. (1996). *Childhood bullying and teasing: What school personnel, other professionals, and parents can do.* Alexandria, VA: American Counseling Association.

Roth, D. A., Coles, M. E., & Heimberg, R. G. (2002). The relationship between memories for childhood teasing and anxiety and depression in adulthood. *Journal of Anxiety Disorders, 16,* 149–164.

Rubin, K. H., Dwyer, K., & Booth-LaForce, C. (2004). Attachment, friendship, and psychosocial functioning in early adolescence. *Journal of Early Adolescence, 24,* 326–356.

Salmivalli, C. (1999). Participant role approach to school bullying: Implications for intervention. *Journal of Adolescence, 22,* 453–459.

Salmivalli, C., Karhunen, J., & Lagerspetz, K. M. J. (1996). How do the victims respond to bullying? *Aggressive Behavior, 22,* 99–109.

Schneider, B. H., Fonzi, A., Tani, F., & Tomada, G. (1997). A cross-cultural exploration of the stability of children's friendships and predictors of their continuation. *Social Development, 6,* 322–339.

Schwartz, D., Chang, L., & Farver, J. M. (2001). Correlates of victimization in Chinese children's peer groups. *Developmental Psychology, 37,* 520–532.

Simpkins, S. D., Parke, R. D., & Flyr, M. L. (2006). Similarities in children's and early adolescents' perceptions of friendship qualities across development, gender, and friendship qualities. *Journal of Early Adolescence, 26,* 491–508.

Slaby, G. R., & Guerra, N. G. (1988). Cognitive mediators of aggression in adolescent offenders: Assessment. *Developmental Psychology, 24,* 580–588.

Smokowski, P. R., & Kopasz, K. H. (2005). Bullying in school: An overview of types, effects, family characteristics, and intervention strategies. *Children & Schools, 27,* 101–110.

Solberg, M. E., & Olweus, D. (2003). Prevalence estimation of school bullying with the Olweus Bully/Victim Questionnaire. *Aggressive Behavior, 29,* 239–268.

Stark, K. D., Sander, J. B., Yancy, M. G., Bronik, M. D., & Hoke, J. A. (2000). Treatment of depression in childhood and adolescence: Cognitive-behavioral procedures for the individual and family. In P. C. Kendall (Ed.), *Child and adolescent therapy: Cognitive-behavioral procedures* (pp 173–234). New York: The Guilford Press.

Stevens, V., De Bourdeaudhuij, I., & Van Oost, P. (2002). Relationship of the family environment to the children's involvement in bully/victim problems at school. *Journal of Youth and Adolescence, 31,* 419–428.

Swearer, S. M. (2001). *Bully Survey—Youth version (BSY).* Available at www.targetbully.com.

Swearer, S. M., & Cary, P. T. (2003). Perceptions and attitudes toward bullying in middle school youth: A developmental examination across the bully/victim continuum. *Journal of Applied School Psychology, 19,* 63–79.

Swearer, S. M., Grills, A. E., Haye, K. M., & Cary, P. T. (2004). Internalizing problems in students involved in bullying and victimization: Implications for intervention. In D. L. Espelage & S. M. Swearer (Eds.), *Bullying in American schools: A social-ecological perspective on prevention and intervention* (pp. 63–83). Mahwah, NJ: Erlbaum.

Swearer, S. M., Song, S. Y., Cary, P. T., Eagle, J. W., & Mickelson, W. T. (2001). Psychosocial correlates in bullying and victimization: The relationship between depression, anxiety, and bully/victim status. *Journal of Emotional Abuse, 2,* 95–121.

Unnever, J. D., & Cornell, D. G. (2003). Bullying, self-control, and ADHD. *Journal of Interpersonal Violence, 18,* 129–147.

Veenstra, R., Lindenberg, S., Oldehinkel, A., De Winter, A. F., Verhulst, F., & Ormel, J. (2005). Bullying and victimization in elementary schools: A comparison of bullies, victims, bully/victims, and uninvolved preadolescents. *Developmental Psychology, 41,* 672–682.

Vernberg, E. M., Jacobs, A. K., & Hershberger, S. L. (1999). Peer victimization and attitudes about violence during early adolescence. *Journal of Clinical Child Psychology, 28,* 386–395.

Webster-Stratton, C., & Hammond, M. (1997). Treating children with early-onset conduct problems: A comparison of child and parent training interventions. *Journal of Consulting and Clinical Psychology, 65,* 93–109.

Whitney, I., & Smith, P. K. (1993). A survey of the nature and extent of bullying in junior/ middle and secondary schools. *Educational Research, 35,* 3–25.

Williams, K., Chambers, M., Logan, S., & Robinson, D. (1996). Association of common health symptoms with bullying in primary school children. *British Medical Journal, 313,* 17–19.

7

Methods for Assessing Bullying and Victimization in Schools and Other Settings: Some Empirical Comparisons and Recommendations

Cary J. Roseth and Anthony D. Pellegrini

T his chapter focuses on methods for gauging the nature and extent of bullying and victimization in schools and other settings. We begin by making the point that bullies and victims represent heterogeneous groups and, as a result, require different methods of assessment and intervention. We then provide a brief description of assessment methods, using empirical examples from our own research to show how different assessment methods are linked to different types of information. We conclude by arguing that choosing an assessment method plays a critical role in deciding whether (and where) intervention is needed and in measuring the impact of interventions.

Heterogeneity among Bullies and Victims

Bullying is a common and persistent problem around the world (Smith, Morita, et al., 1999). Unfortunately, this is not new information, as research in Asia (Morita et al., 1999), Europe (Salmivalli, Huttunen, & Lagerspetz, 1997; Smith & Sharp, 1994), and North America (Espelage & Swearer, 2004; Juvonen & Graham, 2001) has documented the all too frequent story of youngsters systematically "victimizing" less powerful peers by repeatedly using harmful actions such as physical, verbal, relational, and indirect aggression (Boulton & Smith, 1994; Crick & Grotpeter, 1995; Espelage, Bosworth, & Simon, 2000; Smith & Sharp, 1994).

Popular stereotypes characterize bullies as oafish and simple minded. This view fits neatly with the social skills model of aggression (Crick & Dodge, 1994), the premise being that aggressive children generally and bullies specifically lack social cognitive skills in processing social information. These children tend to respond in a hostile manner to ambiguous social situations and so doing use aggression reactively rather than instrumentally to solve social problems. For example, Johnny may lash out and hit another child in response to having milk accidentally spilled on him at lunch. Peers may also provoke Johnny on purpose, teasing him until he lashes out explosively. In either case, Johnny's use of reactive aggression in response to ambiguous social situations encourages dislike among his peers. Over time, this dynamic ultimately results in Johnny becoming friendless, lonely, or a member of small, peripheral groups of similarly unpopular, aggressive children (Dodge & Coie, 1998; Rubin, Bukowski, & Parker, 2006). Preventive interventions based on the deficit model of bullying emphasize social skill acquisition and addressing social-cognitive biases.

The problem with the deficit model is that many bullies are not rejected. To the contrary, some bullies enjoy high status and support from the peer group (Rodkin & Hodges, 2003; see also Hawley, Little, & Rodkin, 2007). Recent research suggests that these bullies are rather calculating in their behavioral strategies, strategically targeting certain children for specific ends (e.g., Pellegrini, 2002; Pellegrini, Bartini, & Brooks, 1999). Rather than using aggression reactively, these bullies employ a form of proactive and instrumental aggression to victimize their peers in the service of accessing resources, be it a place in line or a peer's attention, such as attaining and maintaining social dominance (e.g., Pellegrini, 1998; Pellegrini, 2002; Pellegrini et al., 1999; Pellegrini, Roseth, et al., 2007; Roseth, Pellegrini, Bohn, Van Ryzin, & Vance, 2007). Rather than lack social skills, these bullies employ quite sophisticated social cognitive skills in the form of "theory of mind," or social perspective taking (Sutton, Smith, & Swettenham, 1999a, 1999b). They discriminate about whom they target, focusing their victimization on those children who do not fight back and who do not receive support from peers (Salmivalli, Lagerspetz, Bjorkqvist, Osterman, & Kaukiainen, 1996). And, in contrast to the stereotype of the rejected, "oafish" bully, these socially skilled bullies enjoy moderate to high levels of social status and are well integrated into their peer ecologies (Farmer et al., 2002; Pellegrini, 2002; Pellegrini et al., 1999; Rodkin, Farmer, Pearl, & Van Acker, 2000).

The fact that some bullies receive positive support from peers while others are rejected highlights the danger of assuming that "all popular children are prosocial, or that all rejected children are aggressive" (Rodkin & Hodges, 2003, p. 387). Such an assumption risks focusing only on those bullies lacking social skills, and so doing leaves intact mainstream peer support for bullying and victimization. These two groups—socially rejected and socially supported bullies—require different intervention strategies. And, as we shall see next, these groups also call for different methods of assessment.

Methods of Studying Bullying and Victimization

The vast majority of research on bullying and victimization has been conducted with questionnaires and other forms of informant ratings (Pellegrini, 1998). While these are useful tools for studying aggression and other infrequently occurring behaviors with a large number of subjects, the method is also severely limited, as our understanding of the events is limited by what informants choose to tell us. This limitation may be particularly problematic for bullying and victimization, as informants (e.g., children and school authorities) may be less than forthcoming with the facts. The extent to which a given data source captures the reality of bullying and victimization is the common question underlying each of the various methods used to study the phenomenon.

The next sections provide a brief description of the various assessment methods used to study bullying and victimization. The goal here is to ensure that all readers share a common starting place in considering the practical considerations for using the various methods.

Self-Report Scales and Surveys

Self-report scales and surveys tell us about an individual's perception of his or her experiences and are often the preferred method for researchers and school personnel (see also Chapter 6). Most commonly, self-report involves asking students directly how often they engaged in bullying behaviors like name-calling, teasing, rumor spreading, exclusion, and physical fighting. For victimization, students are asked how often they were recipients or targets of these bullying behaviors. Bullies and victims are identified as those individuals whose composite score places them at the extreme end of the perpetrating or receiving continuums (see also Chapter 6).

Generally speaking, children are asked to focus on a specified period of time (e.g., last 30 days) and must be assured that their reports will remain confidential. Some self-report surveys also solicit information about the locations where bullying occurs, who engaged in the bullying, and how school personnel responded (e.g., Olweus, 1993). Commonly used self-report measures include Olweus' (1993) classic scales of bullying and victimization and the University of Illinois Aggression Scales (Espelage, Holt, & Henkel, 2003).

Peer and Teacher Ratings and Nomination Tasks

Peer ratings and teacher questionnaires are typically used to collect normative information on bullying and victimization. Schwartz (Schwartz, Pettit, Dodge, & Bates, 1997) and Perry (Perry, Kusel, & Perry, 1988) have developed different peer nomination procedures that have been widely used and shown to be reliable indicators of bullies and victims. In our own research we have used a teacher rating scale, developed by Dodge and Coie (1987) to identify aggressive middle school youngsters (Pellegrini & Bartini, 2000; Pellegrini et al., 1999) and preschoolers (Pellegrini, Roseth et al., 2007; Roseth et al., 2007).

Sociometric methods, another form of peer nomination, represent powerful techniques for identifying high- and low-status children, friends and close associates, and for providing a rudimentary map of the social ecology of children's peer groups. Following the summary offered by Rodkin and Hodges (2003), the most common sociometric method involves asking children to nominate *(a)* three kids you *like the most* (LM) and *(b)* three kids you *like the least* (LL). Combining the results of these questions yields two indices of social status: *(a) social preference,* or LM minus LL ratings, and *(b) social impact,* or LM plus LL ratings. Children with low social preference and average (or greater) social impact are labeled *rejected,* and children with high social preference and impact are labeled *popular* (Coie, Dodge, & Coppotelli, 1982). Recent research suggests that sociometric methods provide invaluable information about different kinds of bullies, those that are supported by their peers and those that are rejected (see also Farmer et al., 2002; Rodkin et al., 2000).

Behavioral Observations

Observational methods represent the "gold standard" of bullying and victim assessment as they provide the most objective account of the actual nature and frequency of these events. Like gold, however, such data are expensive to collect, requiring highly reliable coding by unbiased observers across a variety of settings and time. There are also ethical considerations on where and when observational data may be collected. It has long been known, for example, that bullying is most likely to occur in the absence of adult supervision, such as the locker room, hallway, bathroom, and other "less visible" areas of the school. Obvious privacy concerns make data collection in these areas inappropriate, even as objective information about bullying victimization is desperately needed.

Direct behavioral observations of children and adolescents involve clearly articulated measures of behavior and reliable sampling by unbiased observers. Repeated training and reliability checks are also necessary to avoid observer "drift" and to maintain high reliability standards across the duration of a long-term study (Pellegrini, 2004). For example, in our work with preschoolers (Pellegrini, Roseth et al., 2007; Pellegrini, Long, Roseth, Bohn, & Van Ryzin, 2007) and adolescents (Pellegrini & Long, 2002, 2003) we typically observed children in numerous school settings across the whole school day and the entire school year. Further, and importantly, reliability checks and re-training of observers occurred during alternative months across the whole school year. Craig and Pepler (1997) provide another example of observational data collection by videotaping aggressive and socially competent elementary school children on the playground.

Indirect Assessment Methods

In our own work, we have also used indirect methods of observational data collection. Indirect methods, such as diaries, have the advantage of sampling those areas (e.g., lavatories and locker rooms) that are typically out of bounds for direct observers but frequently afford aggression. Thus, the assumption is made that, by virtue of being completed by the focal subjects, indirect observations are indicative of a "private" perspective on aggression/bullying. Direct observations, in contrast, are objectively conducted in public view, and consequently they represent a "public" or normative perspective on the phenomena. Herein lies the strengths and weaknesses of indirect observation, at once providing invaluable information about the "unseen" aspects of bullying and victimization while also being limited in terms of being *perceived* rather than objective accounts of experience. Like other forms of self-report measures, indirect observations may also be limited by social desirability, or respondents' tendency to report only what they want others to know.

Methodological Issues

The next section provides a general discussion of the methodological issues associated with the various ways of assessing bullying and victimization. We emphasize four points. First, practitioners and researchers alike must know the strengths and limitations of the various measurement options. Second, multimodal approaches are critical, especially for high-stakes assessment. Third, different age groups may require different assessment techniques. Fourth, ethical concerns with different methods must be considered.

Strengths and Limitations

Collecting information on the frequency, intensity, perpetrators, and targets of aggressive acts in schools is notoriously difficult. Aggressive acts are usually committed in places and at times when there are few adult witnesses (Craig & Pepler, 1997; Craig, Pepler, & Atlas, 2000; Olweus, 1993). Additionally, aggressive acts, relative to all other behaviors observed during the school day, occur at low frequencies (e.g., Humphreys & Smith, 1987; Pellegrini, 1988), making them very difficult to observe directly. For these reasons researchers typically utilize some form of informant rating of students (Caspi, 1998), such as students' self-reports, peer rating/nominations, and teacher questionnaires. The extensive experience that peer and teacher informants have with the students usually enables them to identify aggressive youngsters with some degree of accuracy (Dodge & Coie, 1998). It is also considerably less expensive to administer questionnaires en masse to groups of youngsters and teachers than to spend months in the field observing a low-frequency event.

The fact that different data sources offer different kinds of information makes it all the more important to recognize distinctions among data sources and the sorts of information each generates. For example, self-report measures tell us about an individual's perception of his or her experiences. On the other hand, normative information on aggression and victimization can be derived from peers and teachers (Cairns & Cairns, 1986). In our early work with early adolescents (e.g., Pellegrini & Bartini, 2000), we also required that research associates who spent 10 weeks directly observing each child complete these teacher rating scales. We found that teachers' and researchers' ratings of youngsters' aggression was significantly, though only moderately, correlated ($r = .50, p < .01$). In practical terms, this means that there was an overlap of only 25% between teachers' and observers' ratings.

The lack of a greater overlap between these ratings may have been due to a number of factors. First, the teachers and research associates may have been differentially deliberate in their completion of the checklists. This conclusion is not, however, supported by the similar and relatively high reliability coefficients on this measure for both teachers (Cronbach's $alpha = .88$) and research associates (Cronbach's *alpha* = .85). A second reason for the modest intercorrelation may have been teachers being more biased than the research associates. Specifically, the teachers, while consistent in their ratings of youngsters (as indicated by the reliability coefficients), may have scored youngsters in a way that was less consistent with the ways in which the youngsters viewed themselves, relative to research associates' ratings. For example, teachers may have more readily rated youngsters in negative ways, such as rating them as aggressive. This explanation does fit our data, as the teacher mean was higher, though not at a significant level, than the research associate mean on the rating scale.

A third reason for the modest correlation may have been the different settings where teachers and research associates observed students. Specifically, teachers observed youngsters in a limited number of settings—usually in homerooms and in one class. The research associates on the other hand spent sustained amounts of time observing students in many different contexts across the school year. They observed students in the halls, the cafeteria, and at free time. The cafeteria was particularly important for the research associates as this unstructured setting was characterized by relatively high social density and relatively low levels of teacher supervision, both of which support peer aggression (Craig & Pepler, 1997; Craig et al., 2000; Smith & Connolly, 1980). Relatedly, the contexts in which teachers and research associates spent time with children may have elicited specific behavior unique to those settings. Differences between raters (e.g., parents and teachers) of youngsters' problem behavior are often attributed to the different demands of the situations in which each spends time with the youngster (e.g., Achenbach, 1985).

High-Stakes Assessments

These results have important implications for school policy. If teacher rating scales are to be used in "high-stakes" assessments (e.g., to place students in special classes), then we suggest that raters spend substantial and sustained periods of time observing youngsters across a variety of settings. This is a rather simple sampling issue. Reliable and valid sampling is a result of repeated observations in settings where children are relatively free to interact with each other. Additionally, these results suggest that places where large groups of youngsters congregate with minimal supervision, like the cafeteria, may support aggression. Vigilant supervision of such places by adults and peers tends to lower incidents of aggression (Olweus, 1993).

Information from teachers generally correlates well with information collected from peers among older primary school and middle school children, possibly reflecting extensive and varied experiences among the raters and nominators (Caspi, 1998). Teacher ratings and peer nominations also tend to converge when they are both rating "public" phenomena, such as public aggression displays (Cairns & Cairns, 1986). From our perspective, youngsters' public aggression may be used as a dominance display for peers. This sort of public display is especially evident during early adolescence, a time when social status is in a state of flux, probably due to rapid body changes and changes in social groups. Under these circumstances, individuals use physically coercive strategies to establish or maintain status when they are entering new peer groups, such as new schools (Pellegrini & Long, 2002).

Age-Related Concerns

In contrast to the above, using peer nominations with preschool children can present problems of reliability and, consequently, validity. For example, we have known for many years that preschoolers' responses are highly susceptible to administration variations and that peer nominations of aggressive peers do not always correspond with other methods of assessment (Archer, 2004). By contrast, direct observational methods, unlike informant sources, can provide relatively unbiased accounts of focal subjects' actions and reactions in specific circumstances, regardless of comparisons with others (Cairns & Cairns, 1986). Minimizing bias with direct observations depends upon an extensive corpus of data, however—for example, observational measures tend *not* to correlate well across time (Caspi, 1998), possibly because of situational specificity and limited samples of observations (Pellegrini, 2004). This problem can be minimized by sampling behavior in a variety of settings, across long periods of time. We also recommend that researchers employ longitudinal methods of data analysis when using observational data, the combination of which provides a more complete account of the dynamism of this developmental period (Long & Pellegrini, 2003).

Ethical Concerns

The inherent distress and harm associated with bullying and victimization raise important ethical concerns about any effort to study these phenomena. These concerns are especially important when observing naturally occurring behavior, where bullying demands that observers must weigh the importance of unbiased data against the moral imperative of helping someone in harm's way. Following Pellegrini (1998), there are at least three relevant concerns:

1. Issues of informed consent
2. The duty to warn or report dangerous behavior
3. Limits imposed on communicating results

The informed consent of children's parent or guardian is required for most university-based and federally funded research. Consent is typically obtained through a written consent form explaining both the risks and benefits associated with participation. A youngster's guardian must sign the form, but, importantly, the participant him/herself has the right to withdraw, even if consent was granted. In some states, adolescent participants are allowed to participate in research even when their parents or guardians do not give consent (Fisher, 1993), the assumption being that by the time youngsters are adolescents, they probably have the cognitive capacity to evaluate the risks and benefits associated with their participation in a research project.

A second ethical issue concerns warning individuals of risks or potentially dangerous behavior (Pepler & Craig, 1995). As recommended by Pepler and Craig, researchers should develop guidelines with school personnel as to when a warning is appropriate. Especially with bullying and victimization, a thin line divides social responsibility and objective, unobtrusive observation.

A third issue relates to communication and confidentiality. A general rule is that children's identities should remain confidential in any discussions of findings. As Pepler and Craig (1995) note, this is particularly important when using videotapes. Videotapes should be used only for research purposes, and they should not be viewed by school personnel for diagnostic or surveillance purposes.

Importantly, practitioners must also recognize that different ages of children are differentially susceptible to the ethical concerns listed above (Thompson, 1990). For example, younger, compared to older, children are more susceptible to socioemotional disorganization accompanying stress. And, in contrast, older children, compared to younger, are more susceptible to threats to their self-concept. In the specific case of working with primary and middle school youngsters, care should be taken when interviewing them about their status as a victim. For example, practitioners may use debriefing procedures as an opportunity to inform these children about ways to prevent others from victimizing them.

Building on the ethical concerns outlined above, it is also true that direct observations cannot be conducted in all settings (Pepler & Craig, 1995). For example, participants cannot be directly observed in locker rooms or lavatories, venues where bullying sometimes occurs. As mentioned previously, indirect observational methods provide a viable alternative (Pellegrini, 2004). With this technique participants record their behavior at predetermined intervals, that is, interval contingent responses, on standardized forms. Similar methods have been used in the child and educational psychology literature. For example, Bloch (1989) sampled children's play behavior at home and in the community by calling their homes and asking the caregiver where and with whom children were playing. Csikzentmihalyi (1990) provided participants with pagers that were programmed to "beep" across the day, at which point participants recorded their behavior. Diaries have also been used extensively with primary school children to record relevant behaviors and participants at specified daily intervals (e.g., Pellegrini, Galda, Shockley, & Stahl, 1995).The reliability and validity of indirect methods is maximized when participants are given specific sampling intervals in which to record behavior and a specific vocabulary or categories to use to record behavior (Pellegrini, 2004).

Illustrative Research on Assessment of Bully–Victim Problems

In our own work, we have used direct observations with preschoolers and compared these to more easily obtained teacher ratings. For early adolescents, we have used indirect observations that involved sampling participants' behavior using diary methodology for 1 school day/month across a whole school year for early adolescents and compared these to other methods, including direct observation, self-reports, and peer nomination. Disadvantages of indirect observations methods include social desirability biases and shared methods variance. However, these are minimized when indirect observational data are related to other data sources, such as peer nominations. We used this kind of mixed-method design as part of our analyses of bullying among early adolescents, and, as you will see below, the associations between the various instruments provide useful information about the extent to which individual instruments could be used to identify bullies and victims. However, before these comparisons, we first describe our data sources for the preschool and adolescent samples. Given the methodological focus of this chapter, a relatively detailed description of our methods is important.

Data Sources
Preschoolers

We studied 65 children (ranging in age from 3.2 to 5.2 years) across a school year (for more detail, see Pellegrini, Roseth et al., 2007). Children's social behavior was directly observed by a team of observers and teachers who rated children's social behavior, including bullying. For preschoolers, we limited our comparisons to direct observations and teacher ratings. These two methods represent extremes in efficiency, with direct observations probably the most valid type of data but also the most "expensive," especially in terms of time for training and actual data collection. Teacher ratings, by contrast, are relatively "cheap" to the extent that they are completed once per year by one person. Practically, then, if teachers' ratings of children's behaviors are significantly correlated with the more expensive and more valid behavioral observations, then it becomes practical to use measures that are "useable" (i.e., less expensive) but also valid.

Procedurally, children were observed following scan and event sampling procedures and instantaneous and continuous recording rules (Pellegrini, 2004), respectively. Researchers conducted the observations after a training regimen of about 4 weeks that entailed videotape viewing and discussions, followed by live recording and discussion. Children were observed during their free play time in their classrooms, on the playground, and in the gymnasium.

In terms of the scan sample/instantaneous recording procedures, observers entered a classroom each day with a predetermined, randomized list of children to observe. A variety of behaviors were instantaneously recorded, but for the purposes of this chapter we report only children's cooperative behavior. Cooperative behavior was defined as instances where individuals were in immediate physical proximity (next to each other or in the same social group) and where there was reciprocal social exchange involving mutual gaze, verbal interaction, or physical exchanges (e.g., pats on the back, passing and receiving a toy).

Interrater agreement was established by comparing the coding of two simultaneous coders, between all observers, every 8 weeks across the 9-month school year. In total, 485 scan sessions were recorded across the school year, resulting in a total of 778 instantaneous scan samples across all children and, on average, 24.18 ($SD = 6.03$) scans per child.

Event sampling with continuous recording rules occurred when an observer saw an aggressive competitive bout, such as two children competing over a toy, a treat, place in a queue, or a peer's attention. Children's behavior was recorded for the duration of the aggressive bout and for 4 minutes after the aggressive behavior terminated. For aggressive bouts, observers recorded the following information: the identity of the child who initiated the bout and the identity of the target of the aggression, the nature of the aggression (e.g., physical, verbal, and social aggression, including both direct and indirect forms such as shunning and spreading rumors, snatching an object, or displacing a peer in line or at an activity), and the context of the aggression; that is, was it over an object, person, place in line, etc. Aggression was scored both in terms of relative frequency (Aggression/Number of times a child was scanned) and in terms of a "win" index (Total aggressive bouts – Losses). A total of 173 aggressive events were observed across the school year.

In the late fall/early winter and in the spring of the school year, classroom teachers completed a rating scale of children's aggression and social dominance as part of a more general measure of social competence, based on Dodge and Coie's (1987) Teacher Checklist. Teachers rated children's proactive aggression (e.g., starts fights, get others to gang up on peer), and their social dominance (e.g., dominates classmates, tells others what to do, stands up for self).

Early Adolescents

Early adolescent participants were part of a study of aggression in middle school. In total, there were 367 students in their first year at two rural middle schools (grades 6–8). In the course of the school year (which began in mid-August) children were observed directly at least once per week for each of the 9 months of the school year. Morning observations took place in the hallways between classes and in the cafeteria, where youngsters waited before entering their homerooms. Afternoon observations took place in the hallways between classes and in the cafeteria during lunch (approximately 20 minutes), and during a free time (20–30 minutes) held once per week. The free time observations took place in the halls, classrooms, and occasionally outdoors.

In terms of the direct observations, focal child sampling/continuous recording rules were utilized (Pellegrini, 2004). Following a counterbalanced list of 17–20 focal participants, research assistants observed focal children for 3-minute sampling intervals, continuously recording the behavior of the focal child on a check sheet. Both the type of aggression and the target of aggression (victims) were coded, as part of a larger observation schedule (including cooperative, solitary, parallel, rough play, tease, and submissive behaviors).

Research associates were given a different cohort of focal youngsters every 10 weeks to minimize their becoming too familiar with each other. Thus, by the end of the school year, each research associate had observed all subjects in the school, and each focal child being observed at least one time per week with a minimum of 40 observations per focal child. Behavioral measures were derived using relative scores, thus equating differing numbers of observations per participant.

For indirect observations, youngsters were asked to keep a diary once per month for the whole school year (October through June). The aim of the diary was to collect information on children's experiences during the day which would be difficult for us to observe directly. Youngsters were asked to recount experiences in the last 24 hours, answering general questions about whom they spent time with and more specific questions about being an aggressor (i.e., Did you tease or hit anyone? Who?) and being a target of aggression (i.e., Did anyone hit or tease you? Who?). Youngsters were also asked how this was done, and they were provided with a list of standardized responses from which to choose (e.g., slapped, kicked, pushed, called a name). Aggression scores were derived by summing the positive responses to questions about being an aggressor, then dividing these sums by the numbers of diaries collected. Only data from the school day were utilized in this report.

For peer nominations and self-report measures, trained research associates administered these measures to those subjects that they had *not* previously observed, thus minimizing possible tester bias. For one peer nomination measure, youngsters were assembled in groups in early spring of the school year and given rosters of individuals in their homerooms. Research associates asked youngsters questions aimed at nominating three aggressive youngsters and three youngsters who were targets of aggression, or victims (Schwartz, Dodge, & Coie, 1993). The aggressive youngster questions included: who starts fights, who says mean things, and who gets mad easily? Aggression-bully scores were derived by summing the number of nominations received in each category and averaging scores within home rooms.

The self-report measure was Olweus' (1989; see also Olweus, 1993) widely used Senior Bully/Victim Questionnaire. This measure has a Likert-like scoring format and was administered in the winter of the school year. It is a widely used measure that yields factors for bullying (e.g., "Do you think it's fun to make trouble for other students?").

Some Empirical Comparisons
Preschoolers

The correlations presented in Table 7.1 support our view of preschool bullying as an aspect of proactive aggression used for social dominance. These findings also support the use of teacher ratings for this age group as a valid substitute for more costly behavioral observations. For example, the teacher rating of bullying correlated positively and significantly with the behavioral measure of social dominance ("wins") and with teachers' ratings of both social dominance and proactive aggression.

Table 7.1

Intercorrelations among Measures for Preschoolers

	Teacher Ratings		Directly Observed Behavior	
	2	3	4	5
1. Proactive aggression	.53**	.34**	.51**	.38**
2. Teacher-rated social dominance		.61**	.29*	.22
3. Teacher-rated bullying			.43**	.33**
4. Observed wins				.31*
5. Observed cooperation				

Note. Measures 1–3 are teacher ratings (1–7 Likert-type scale), and measures 5 and 6 are direct observations. *$p < .05$; **$p < .01$.

That being said, however, we note that the magnitude of the mixed-method correlations are moderate, accounting for about 25% of the variations in children's aggression and bullying. The magnitude of the correlations, and consequently the validity of the construct, bullying, can be maximized if multiple measures are used. So, for example, if we are trying to predict or identify bullies in a classroom, using teacher ratings alone would predict at one level, in this case $r = .43$. However, we would increase the magnitude of the correlations by aggregating teacher ratings with other measures of bullying, such as peer nominations and self-reports (Cronbach, 1971; Rushton, Brainerd, & Pressley, 1983). It is a psychometric truth that aggregating across measures minimizes error variance, which, in turn, maximizes the magnitude of the correlation coefficient (Rushton et al., 1983).

Additionally, by taking assessments from different perspectives, such as peers, teachers, and children themselves, we are then able to tap the knowledge of individuals in a variety of settings and from a variety of perspectives, again with the result of maximizing the validity of our construct. This type of multimeasurement strategy is especially important with young children because, as noted above, their behaviors and perceptions can be unreliable. The more data points that we have and the more these data are taken from different perspectives, the more likely that our conclusions will be valid.

Maximizing construct validity is also important for educators and clinicians who design programs to minimize bullying. Our results show that bullies are rather sophisticated in terms of their social cognitive skills, suggesting that bullying interventions should not be framed solely in terms of teaching these children alternative social skills and behaviors (see also Rodkin & Hodges,

2003). Some bullies already have these skills, suggesting that a more fruitful intervention might involve minimizing the rewards that children accrue from using aggression toward instrumental ends.

Our research with preschool children (e.g., Pellegrini, Roseth et al., 2007; Roseth et al., 2007) and also with middle school students (e.g., Pellegrini & Long, 2003) has shown that social cohesion among students may contribute to a reduction in the frequency of bullying throughout the school year. When there is greater social cohesion among students, the frequency of bullying decreases. Schools with relatively stable populations are likely to see a reduction in bullying across the school year because students are able to maintain social cohesion. With fewer new students being added to the group there are fewer disruptions to the social hierarchy and consequently fewer incidences of aggression and bullying. Teachers and administrators should therefore pay particular attention to potential bullying when new students are added to the school environment or following any event that may cause a disruption in social cohesion (e.g., Pellegrini & Long, 2002; Roseth et al., 2007).

Social cohesion can also be maximized by keeping students in stable cohorts across an extended period of time. For example, some middle schools in Minneapolis place youngsters in a cohort of students when they enter school in the 5th grade and the youngsters stay in that cohort for their entire 3-year middle school experience. In this model, group cohesion is sustained across time, and children not only form close relationships with peers, in the form of friendships, but also with teachers. These close relationships may minimize bullying by providing support and by providing an environment where children feel safe and secure in enlisting teachers' and peers' help if they are bullied. This environment is valuable because an important barrier to minimizing bullying in schools is children's reluctance to tell their teachers that they are being bullied (Eslea & Smith, 1998).

Early Adolescents

Compared to preschoolers, assessing bullying among early adolescents is in many ways easier because self-reports and peer nominations are more reliable. Thus, the correlations presented in Table 7.2 show that each form of observation, despite lack of direct correspondence with each other, did relate to specific, and predicted, sources of information. Specifically, the diary, or indirect observational measure of aggression/bullying and victimization related significantly to the other "private" measure of bullying/aggression, the self-report measure. Additionally, the indirect measures of bullying/

Table 7.2
Intercorrelations among Measures for Adolescents

	2	3	4	5
1. Peer nominations	.47**	.23*	.34**	.28**
2. Self-reported bullying		.03	.20*	.24**
3. Observed aggression			.01	.18**
4. Diary-reported aggression				.08
5. Teacher-rated aggression				

$*p < .05; **p < .01.$

aggression related positively and significantly to peer measures of aggression/bullying and victimization, but not to the teachers' ratings of aggression, arguably a stronger indicator of public displays of aggression. The direct observation measures of aggression/bullying related to the peer nominations measure and to the teacher rating of aggression by teachers.

That the diaries were systematic correlates of self-report and peer, but not adult, measures in this age group suggests that the aggression and victimization are phenomena more readily accessible to insiders than to outsiders. It is probably the case that much aggression and victimization takes place when adults, be they observers or teachers, are not present (Craig et al., 2000; Craig & Pepler, 1997; Olweus, 1993). Students, however, may witness these acts. It is plausible that bullies deliberately victimize peers in the presence of other students as a way in which to display their physical prowess and, consequently, boost their status with certain peers (Pellegrini, 2002). The use of aggression to get things done, generally (Crick & Werner, 1998), and specifically to establish and maintain social dominance among peers is characteristic of the early adolescent period (Pellegrini, 2002).

Also interesting was the finding that indirect (i.e., diary), but not direct, observations were significantly correlated with self-report measures of bullying. This may reflect the fact that some instances of victimization are brief and done in a very clandestine and deliberate manner (Craig & Pepler, 1997). As noted above, peers were also privy to this information, as indicated by the correlation between diaries and peer nominations. The sampling rules followed in our direct observations (i. e., focal child sampling) may have missed these infrequently occurring behaviors. Future research should address this problem by utilizing a sampling technique (i.e., event/behavior sampling) that is more sensitive to rare events (Pellegrini, 2004).

These results have several important implications. Regarding research, our indirect observation results show that diaries are valid indicators of aggression as seen through the eyes of other students, and especially as seen through the eyes of bullies themselves. Using a structured diary approach where we specified the sampling (i.e., behavior was sampled on a specific day and for specific sorts of events) and recording rules (i.e., a specific vocabulary list was provided to answers questions) may have been especially important (Pellegrini, 2004). A less structured approach may have sampled less diverse behaviors and recorded them in a more idiosyncratic fashion, thus attenuating correlations with other measures of aggression. In short, indirect observations should be added to those of external raters, observers, and teachers. Indeed, results suggest that the diary data account for variance in the identification of bullies not available through direct observation.

The different sources of student data may also have implications for identifying risk factors associated with bullying. Specifically, self-reports, compared to peer reports, of victimization are related to dysfunctional intrapsychological consequences (Graham & Juvonen, 1998). More work needs to be done to explore the extent to which diary and self-report measures differentially predict dysfunction.

Instrument Utility for Interventions

The sensitivity of different instruments in identifying aggression and victimization at relatively low levels of severity is a particularly important test of its utility in school settings. Specifically, it is probably more difficult for an instrument to identify less severe than more severe problems of aggression and victimization, simply because the less severe forms are less visible and less persistent. Instruments that can be used with relative ease to identify problems at this level of severity should be used as a quick and easy first step in identifying and remediating problems before they become more extreme. Our analyses indicate that all forms of peer and self-report measures were associated in their identification of aggressive youngsters/bullies. Thus, because of their association, educators could utilize any of the three formats in their classrooms with relative ease as a first level of assessment. We stress here that the use of any one of these measures is just a first step in more thorough assessment. As our results have shown, different data sources are complementary; thus, subsequent assessment, using peer, self-, and observational measures should be used as a follow up to identify specific problems.

Our analyses indicated that while there was significant overlap between teachers' and research associates' ratings of aggressive youngsters, the magnitude of the correlation was modest. We argued that this may have been due to the differences in bias and between the contexts in which raters observed youngsters. Future research should address this problem more directly by examining the degree to which opportunities to observe in a variety of specific venues influences observers' ratings. Further, personal biases of raters could be examined by comparing their ratings of youngsters observed in the same contexts.

We defined accuracy of rating in terms of measures approximating students' perceptions of bullying and victimization. This choice, while subjective, seems reasonable for two reasons. First, bullying and victimization often are hidden from adults' view but the perpetrators, victims, and sometimes peers are direct witnesses to these problems. Second, combining self-assessment with peers' assessments provides information on youngsters' dispositions on phenomena that are both private *and* public. Self-assessment alone provides information on the private feelings of being aggressive and victimized, but it does not provide more normative information on being aggressive and victimized. By combining both dimensions, we capture both normative and ipsative referential standards (Cairns & Cairns, 1986). In this same way the validity of aggression/bullying constructs can be maximized when peer and adult measures are aggregated with observational measures (Patterson & Bank, 1989; Rushton et al., 1983).

These findings also have implications for educators confronting problems of bullying. We have demonstrated that different measures provide different perspectives on the problem of antisocial behavior in school. "Objective," direct observations of youngsters' behavior were consistently correlated with youngsters' and adults' perceptions of aggression/bullying and victimization. Given the extraordinary expense of observational measures, this means that ratings and nominations completed by teachers and peers seem to provide a useful alternative.

By way of caution, however, we emphasize guarding against using a limited battery of measures when conducting "high stakes" assessments. In such instances, we suggest a multimethod approach, where direct observations, as well as different forms of informant scales, are used. Further, when observations and outside raters are used as part of such a battery, they should observe students in a wide variety of settings across a number of months. Less extensive samples of experience with youngsters will yield less reliable and valid data.

Implications for Practice

Given the ubiquity of bullying and the damage it causes to its victims, it is easy to see why it remains a topic of concern for anyone concerned with protecting children and optimizing their school experience. In this chapter we have shown ways in which different types of data collection procedures complement each other in assessing bullying among preschool children and early adolescents. Our aim was to recommend reliable, valid, and useful techniques for researchers, clinicians, and educators.

As part of this effort we also outlined our view that, at root, bullying is a social phenomenon that cannot be understood solely in terms of particular individuals or particular behaviors. Instead, bullying and victimization represent ecological phenomena, products of the complex interplay between inter- and intraindividual variables (Espelage & Swearer, 2004). Such complexity makes it all the more important to recognize the strengths and limitations of any given method of gauging the nature and frequency of bullying, as solely relying on any one method risks overlooking the variety of ways that bullying and victimization may be propagated.

Related to this last point, this chapter also made the argument that some bullies—whether preschoolers or early adolescents—use aggression to achieve and maintain social dominance. This perspective contrasts with more traditional views characterizing bullies as socially inept and disconnected from mainstream peer ecologies. While some bullies are rejected or hang out with deviant peers, others have high social status and enjoy a variety of relationships. Practitioners and researchers who focus exclusively on rejected bullies risk leaving unaddressed the more socially skilled bullies whose victimization of peers is supported by the larger peer group. Moreover, failing to intervene with these high-status bullies risks sending the message to other children that bullying and victimization mean different things when perpetrated by high- and low-status peers. At worst, these high-status bullies may influence a school's social norms.

For practitioners, recognizing that bullies and victims represent heterogeneous groups has important methodological and intervention implications. First and foremost, practitioners should determine whether the bully is a member of a group and, if so, whether the bully is a leader or a "wannabe" (Farmer, 2000). Relatedly, Rodkin and Hodges (2003) emphasize that children's peer groups must be reliably identified, as there is some suspicion that teachers and other adults may underestimate the degree to which high-status boys and girls contribute to the bullying dynamic, either as leaders or as bystanders.

Comparing methods used to study bullying in preschoolers and early adolescents highlights several important points. First, researchers and practitioners alike must consider the way development and methodology interact. In this chapter we saw that preschoolers' peer nominations are much more susceptible to extraneous influences, thus increasing the importance of using observational methods in combination with teacher ratings to maximize construct validity. We also saw that, for early adolescents, there are important differences between public and private measures of bullying. Results showed that even while teacher ratings and peer nominations may be considered valid measures of early adolescents' bullying and victimization, the former corresponds more closely with direct (or public) observational data, and the latter with indirect (or private) observational data. Once again, the implication is that maximizing construct validity requires multiple sources of information.

A second point of emphasis is that developmental differences must be taken into account when considering the form, frequency, and function of bullying behaviors. For example, relative to earlier periods in development, aggression is viewed less negatively by peers during early adolescence (Bukowski, Sippola, & Newcomb, 2000; Graham & Juvonen, 1998; Moffitt, 1993; Pellegrini et al., 1999). This view may reflect young adolescents' casual associations with bullies because they represent challenges to adult roles and values (Moffitt, 1993). Less negative views of aggression may also be shaped by the series of abrupt changes in early adolescents' social lives. For example, adolescence is characterized by rapid body changes, including increased body size and the onset of sexual maturity. Such rapid change in body size leads to the reorganization of youngsters', but especially boys' social dominance hierarchies (Pellegrini & Bartini, 2001), with bigger and stronger being associated with higher dominance status and, in turn, greater attractiveness (Pellegrini & Bartini, 2001).

A second abrupt change during this period involves the move from typically small, personal primary schools with well-established social groups into larger, less supportive middle schools. This transition requires the re-establishment of social relationships during a time when peer relations are particularly important (Eccles, Wigfield, & Schiefele, 1998). During such transitions, aggression is often used in the service of establishing status with peers. Our longitudinal study (i.e., Pellegrini & Long, 2002) of youngsters making the transition from one school to another certainly supports this view. In this study, bullying increased from 5th to 6th grade, and then decreased from 6th to 7th grade. These results are consistent with the view that aggression will increase as youngsters move into a new school and thus try to establish social dominance relationships. Once social dominance relationships are established, however, levels of aggression decrease as this form of bullying is no longer used to maintain dominance status.

The finding that bullying increases at the transition to middle school stands in contrast to the more general context of age-related decline of bullying (Smith, Madsen, & Moody, 1999). Specifically, a large body of research suggests that there is a monotonic decrease in bullying, victimization, and aggression with age (see Pellegrini, 2002 for a review). By this we mean that rates of bullying and victimization generally decrease as youngsters get older. These decreases have been reported in a series of large-scale investigations, often with nationally representative samples from countries in western Europe and North America (again, see Pellegrini, 2002 for a review). These monotonic decreases during early adolescence, however, are evident only when youngsters do not change schools. When same-age youth do change schools, there is an initial increase at this transition point, followed by a decrease. In our view, the decrease reflects re-established dominance relationships, as dominance hierarchies, once stabilized, serve the important function of reducing in-group aggression (Dunbar, 1988; Vaughn, 1999).

Our studies of preschoolers show that similar phenomena characterize young children's aggression and bullying (e.g., Pellegrini, Roseth et al., 2007; Roseth et al., 2007). Specifically, our research shows that preschoolers' social ominance relationships serve to minimize aggressive bouts over the school year, and that physical and verbal aggression follow distinct longitudinal trajectories. These findings are especially relevant to teachers' intervention strategies, as the results suggest that preschoolers' aggression may also serve a negotiating function between peers. Simply put, the frequency of aggressive behavior should not be considered the sole indicator of social problems in the preschool years. A more precise indicator of social competence (or, conversely, social problems) may be the *combination* of *(a)* the effectiveness with which a preschooler uses aggression to secure resources (e.g., win-rate), and *(b)* the extent to which the form and frequency of the child's aggression changes across the school year. Applied research in early intervention and prevention programs should carefully consider these variables as they debate whether preschoolers should be allowed to "work things out" among themselves. For example, intervention strategies may need to change across the school year, perhaps allowing children greater opportunity to work things out among themselves, especially early in the school year.

References

Achenbach, T. M. (1985). *Assessment and taxonomy of child and adolescent psychopathology.* Newbury Park, CA: Sage.

Archer, J. (2004). Sex differences in aggression in real-word settings: A meta-analytic review. *Review of General Psychology, 8,* 291–198.

Bloch, M. (1989). Young boys' and young girls' play at home and in the community. In M. Bloch & A. D. Pellegrini (Eds.), *The ecological context of children's play* (pp. 20–154). Norwood, NJ: Ablex.

Boulton, M. J., & Smith, P. K. (1994). Bully/victim problems in middle school children: Stability, self-perceived competence, peer perceptions, and peer acceptance. *British Journal of Developmental Psychology, 12,* 315–329.

Bukowski, W. M., Sippola, L. A., & Newcomb, A. F. (2000). Variations in patterns of attraction to same- and other-sex peers during early adolescence. *Developmental Psychology, 36,* 147–154.

Cairns, R. B., & Cairns, B. D. (1986). The developmental-interactional view of social behavior: Four issues of adolescent aggression. In D. Olweus, J. Block, & M. Radke-Yarrow (Eds.), *Development of antisocial and prosocial behavior* (pp. 315–342). New York: Academic Press.

Caspi, A. (1998). Personality development across the life course. In N. Eisenberg (Ed.), *Handbook of child psychology: Social, emotional, and personality development* (pp. 311–388). New York: John Wiley & Sons, Inc.

Coie, J. D., Dodge, K. A., & Coppotelli, H. (1982). Dimensions and types of social status: A cross-age perspective. *Developmental Psychology, 18,* 557–570.

Craig, W. M., & Pepler, D. J. (1997). Observations of bullying and victimization in the schoolyard. *Canadian Journal of School Psychology, 13,* 41–59.

Craig, W. M., Pepler, D. J., & Atlas, R. (2000). Observations of bullying in the playground and in the classroom. *School Psychology International, 21,* 22–36.

Crick, N. R., & Dodge, K. A. (1994). A review and reformulation of social information-processing mechanisms in children's social adjustment. *Psychological Bulletin, 115,* 74–101.

Crick, N. R., & Grotpeter, J. K. (1995). Relational aggression, gender, and social–psychological adjustment. *Child Development, 66,* 710–722

Crick, N. R., & Werner, N. E. (1998). Response decision processes in relational and overt aggression. *Child Development, 69,* 710–727.

Cronbach, L. J. (1971). Validity. In R. L. Thorndike (Ed.), *Educational measurement* (pp. 443–507). Washington, DC: American Council on Education.

Csikszentmihalyi, M. (1990). *Flow: The psychology of optimal experience.* New York: Harper and Row.

Dodge, K. A., & Coie, J. D. (1987). Social information processing factors in reactive and proactive aggression in children's peer groups. *Journal of Personality and Social Psychology, 53,* 1146–1158.

Dodge, K. A., & Coie, J. D. (1998). Aggression and antisocial behavior. In N. Eisenberg (Ed.), *Handbook of child psychology, Vol. 3* (pp. 779–862). New York: John Wiley & Sons, Inc.

Dunbar, R. I. M. (1988). *Primate social systems.* Ithaca, NY: Cornell University Press.

Eccles, J. S., Wigfield, A., & Schiefele, U. (1998). Motivation to succeed. In N. Eisenberg (Ed.), *Handbook of child psychology, Vol. 3* (pp. 1017–1096). New York: John Wiley & Sons, Inc.

Eslea, M., & Smith, P. K. (1998). The long-term effectiveness of anti-bullying work in primary schools. *Educational Research, 40*, 203–218.

Espelage, D. L., Bosworth, K., & Simon, T. R. (2000). Examining the social context of bullying behaviors in early adolescence. *Journal of Counseling & Development, 78*, 326–333.

Espelage, D. L., Holt, M. K., & Henkel, R. R. (2003). Examination of peer group contextual effects on aggressive behavior during early adolescence. *Child Development, 74*, 205–220.

Espelage, D. L., & Swearer, S. M. (2004). *Bullying in American schools: A social-ecological perspective on prevention and intervention.* Mahwah, NJ: Erlbaum.

Farmer, T. W. (2000). The social dynamics of aggressive and disruptive behavior in school: Implications for behavior consultation. *Journal of Educational & Psychological Consultation, 11*, 299–321.

Farmer, T. W., Leung, M., Pearl, R., Rodkin, P. C., Cadwallader, T. W., & Van Acker, R. (2002). Deviant or diverse peer groups? The peer affiliations of aggressive elementary students. *Journal of Educational Psychology, 94*, 611–620.

Fisher, C. B. (1993). Integrating science and ethic in research with high-risk children and youth. *Society for Research in Child Development Social Policy Report, 7(4)*, 1–27.

Graham, S., & Juvonen, J. (1998). A social cognitive perspective on peer aggression and victimization. In R. Vasta (Ed.), *Annals of child development* (pp. 23–70). London: Jessica Kingsley Publishers.

Hawley, P. H., Little, T. D., & Rodkin, P. C. (Eds.). (2007). *Aggression and adaptation: The bright side to bad behavior.* Mahwah, NJ: Erlbaum.

Humphreys, A. P., & Smith, P. K. (1987). Rough and tumble, friendship, and dominance in schoolchildren: Evidence for continuity and change with age. *Child Development, 58*, 201–212.

Juvonen, J. & Graham, S. (eds.) (2001). *Peer harassment in school: The plight of the vulnerable and victimized.* New York: Guilford Publications.

Long, J. D., & Pellegrini, A. D. (2003). Studying change in dominance and bullying with linear mixed models. *School Psychology Review, 32*, 401–417.

Moffitt, T. E. (1993). Adolescent-limited and life-course-persistent anti-social behavior: A developmental taxonomy. *Psychological Review, 100*, 674–701.

Morita, Y., Smith, P. K., Junger-Tas, J., Olweus, D., Catalano, R. & Slee, P. (Eds.) (1999). *Sekai no ijime.* Tokyo: Kaneko Shobou.

Olweus, D. (1993). *Bullying at school.* Cambridge, MA: Blackwell.

Patterson, G. R., & Bank, L. (1989). Some amplifying mechanisms for pathologic processes in families. In M. Gunnar & E. Thelen (Eds.), *The Minnesota symposium on child psychology, Vol. 22* (pp. 167–209). Hillsdale, NJ: Erlbaum.

Pellegrini, A. D. (1988). Elementary school children's rough-and-tumble play and social competence. *Developmental Psychology, 24*, 802–806.

Pellegrini, A. D. (1998). Bullies and victims in school: A review of and call for research. *Journal of Applied Developmental Psychology, 19*, 165–176.

Pellegrini, A. D. (2002). Bullying, victimization, and sexual harassment during the transition to middle school. *Educational Psychologist, 37*, 151–163.

Pellegrini, A. D. (2004). *Observing children in their natural worlds* (2nd ed.). Mahwah, NJ: Erlbaum.

Pellegrini, A. D., & Bartini, M. (2000). A longitudinal study of bullying, victimization, and peer affiliation during the transition from primary school to middle school. *American Educational Research Journal, 37*, 699–725.

ellegrini, A. D., & Bartini, M. (2001). Dominance in early adolescent boys: Aggressive and affiliative dimensions and possible functioning. *Merrill-Palmer Quarterly, 47*, 142–163.

Pellegrini, A. D., Bartini, M., & Brooks, F. (1999). School bullies, victims, and aggressive victims: Factors relating to group affiliation and victimization in early adolescence. *Journal of Educational Psychology, 91*, 216–224.

Pellegrini, A. D., Galda, L., Shockley, B., & Stahl, S. (1995). The nexus of social and literacy experiences at home and at school: Implications for primary school oral language and literacy. *British Journal of Educational Psychology, 65*, 273–285.

Pellegrini, A. D., & Long, J. D. (2002). A longitudinal study of bullying, dominance, and victimization during the transition from primary through secondary school. *British Journal of Developmental Psychology, 20*, 259–280.

Pellegrini, A. D., & Long, J. D. (2003). A sexual selection theory longitudinal analysis of sexual segregation and integration in early adolescence. *Journal of Experimental Child Psychology, 85*, 257–278.

Pellegrini, A. D., Long, J. D., Roseth, C. J., Bohn, C. M., & Van Ryzin, M. (2007). A short-term longitudinal study of preschoolers' (*Homo sapiens*) sex segregation: The role of physical activity, sex, and time. *Journal of Comparative Psychology, 121*, 282–289.

Pellegrini, A. D., Roseth, C. J., Mliner, S., Bohn, C. M., Van Ryzin, M., Vance, N., et al. (2007). Social dominance in preschool classrooms. *Journal of Comparative Psychology, 121*, 54–64.

Pepler, D. J. & Craig, W. M. (1995). A peek behind the fence: Naturalistic observations of aggressive children with remote audiovisual recording. *Developmental Psychology, 31*, 548–553.

Perry, D. G., Kusel, S. J., & Perry, L. C. (1988). Victims of peer aggression. *Developmental Psychology, 24*, 807–814.

Rodkin, P. C., Farmer, T. W., Pearl, R., & Van Acker, R. (2000). Heterogeneity of popular boys: Antisocial and prosocial configurations. *Developmental Psychology, 36*, 14–24.

Rodkin, P. C., & Hodges, E. V. E. (2003). Bullies and victims in the peer ecology: Four questions for psychologists and school professionals. *School Psychology Review, 32*, 384–400.

Roseth, C. J., Pellegrini, A. D., Bohn, C. M., Van Ryzin, M., & Vance, N. (2007). Preschoolers' aggression, affiliation, and social dominance relationships: An observational, longitudinal study. *Journal of School Psychology, 45*, 479–497.

Rubin, K. H., Bukowski, W., & Parker, J. G. (2006). Peer interactions, relationships, and groups. In N. Eisenberg (Ed.), *Handbook of child psychology: Vol 3. Social, emotional, and personality development* (6th ed.) (pp. 571–645). New York: Wiley.

Rushton, J., Brainerd, C., & Pressley, M. (1983). Behavioral development and construct validity: The principle of aggregation. *Psychological Bulletin, 94*, 18–38.

Salmivalli, C., Huttunen, A., & Lagerspetz, K. (1997). Peer networks and bullying in schools. *Scandinavian Journal of Psychology, 38*, 305–312.

Salmivalli, C., Lagerspetz, K., Bjorkqvist, K., Osterman, K., & Kaukiainen, A. (1996). Bullying as a group process: Participant roles and their relations to social status within the group. *Aggressive Behavior, 22*, 1–15.

Schwartz, D., Dodge, K. A., & Coie, J. D. (1993). The emergence of chronic peer victimization. *Child Development, 64*, 1755–1772.

Schwartz, D., Pettit, G. S., Dodge, K. A., & Bates, J. E. (1997). The early socialization and adjustment of aggressive victims of bullying. *Child Development, 68*, 665–675.

Smith, P. K., & Connolly, K. (1980). *The ecology of preschool behavior.* London: Cambridge University Press.

Smith, P. K., Madsen, K. C., & Moody, J. C. (1999). What causes the age decline in reports of being bullied at school? Towards a developmental analysis of risks of being bullied. *Educational Research, 41*, 267–285.

Smith, P.K, Morita, Y., Junger-Tas, J., Olweus, D., Catalano, R., & Slee, P. (Eds.) (1999). *The nature of school bullying: A cross-national perspective.* Florence, KY: Taylor & Frances/Routledge.

Smith, P. K., & Sharp, S. (1994). The problem of school bullying. In P. K. Smith & S. Sharp (Eds.), *School bullying* (pp. 1–19). London: Routledge.

Sutton, J., Smith, P. K., & Swettenham, J. (1999a). Bullying and "Theory of Mind": A critique of the "Social Skills Deficit" view of anti-social behavior. *Social Development, 8*, 117–127.

Sutton, J., Smith, P. K., & Swettenham, J. (1999b). Social cognition and bullying: Social inadequacy or skilled manipulation? *British Journal of Developmental Psychology, 17*, 435–450.

Thompson, R. A. (1990). Vulnerability in research: A developmental perspective on research risk. *Child Development, 61*, 1–16.

Vaughn, B. E. (1999). Power is knowledge (and vice versa): A commentary on "On winning some and losing some: a social relations approach to social dominance in toddlers." *Merrill-Palmer Quarterly, 45*, 215–225.

8

Selected Group Interventions for Children Who Exhibit Significant Involvement in Bullying

Kelly S. Flanagan and Kendra B. Battaglia

Bullying represents a major concern for schools, parents, and youth in the United States and internationally (Kasen, Berenson, Cohen, & Johnson, 2004; Pepler, 2006). Despite the development of prevention and intervention programs, the effectiveness of these programs has generally been modest (Smith, Pepler, & Rigby, 2004). Bullying remains an ongoing school crisis with the involvement of an alarmingly large number of youth (Kasen et al., 2004; Nansel et al., 2001; Smith et al., 2004; Whitted & Dupper, 2005). The goal of the current chapter is to describe the extant selected group interventions for youth who are significantly involved in bullying as either bullies or victims. Because there are few empirically evaluated group interventions conducted with youth involved in bullying, we also identify related interventions (e.g., those that target children and adolescents who are aggressive or socially awkward, more generally) that provide good examples of the types of approaches that could be applied to address bullying and victimization. Various individual counseling approaches that have been used with bullies and/or victims will not be discussed (Nation, 2007; see also Chapter 6), nor the components of school-wide programs (see Chapter 10).

Compatible with a substantial amount of research regarding the dynamics involved in bullying, a social-ecological view has been endorsed with interventions developed according to this view (Hazler & Carney, 2006; Swearer & Espelage, 2004; see also Chapter 2). Thus, although anti-bullying programs vary greatly, since the first empirically evaluated bullying program, interventionists have tended to target the school context as a first and essential step. As an important adjunct to systemic levels of intervention, it has been argued that individual-level interventions also be conducted (Olweus, 1993; see also Chapters 6 and 9).

Thus far specific interventions targeting the individual (i.e., those youth who are chronically involved in bullying either as bullies or victims) are scarce and rarely empirically evaluated. Most research is conducted to determine the effectiveness of school-wide programs (Fox & Boulton, 2003a; Nation, 2007). For example, the Sheffield Anti-bullying Project, a school-wide intervention, includes individual strategies for working with students involved in bullying such as group assertiveness training for victims (Sharp & Cowie, 1994). Overall, the intervention resulted in reduced bullying and increased student self-esteem; yet the contribution of the individual treatment components was not separately evaluated (Eslea & Smith, 1998).

Although the focus on reducing the amount of bullying in a school is crucial, improvement in the functioning and the adjustment of those who frequently engage in bullying behavior and those who have experienced frequent and chronic victimization is also needed (Nation, 2007). In tandem with school-wide interventions, a concurrent focus on individuals involved in bullying is crucial, as some youth may not benefit from systemic changes; for example, some students may not develop the social skills necessary for competence within the peer group from involvement in a school-wide program alone (Orpinas & Horne, 2006). Further, without evaluation of selected interventions with bullies and victims, those working in multiple contexts will be unable to respond effectively to either further eradicate bullying or improve the lives of victims.

Recently, Pepler (2006) has suggested that a developmental-systemic view of bullying might lead to two organizing principles for an integrative intervention, including "social architecture" (i.e., the systemic approaches utilized thus far by interventionists) and "scaffolding," which focuses on the individual youth involved in bullying. Pepler argues that interventions should not be conducted in such a way that the problems of the individual youth who is either bullying or being bullied are not addressed; rather, more comprehensive interventions to address both the context as well as the individual difficulties of bullies and victims should be developed. It is our contention that the systemic-level interventions are of utmost importance to our ability to decrease the rates of bullying in our schools. Yet we cannot ignore the plight of those who are victimized or avoid attempts to alter the behavior of those who bully.

Group interventions may be a particularly advantageous individual-level treatment for youth involved in bullying for several reasons (Card, Isaacs, & Hodges, 2007; DeRosier & Marcus, 2005; Gresham, 1997). First, meeting with same-age peers allows for peer modeling and the opportunity to practice interpersonal skills under adult supervision within a safe, structured environment. Constructive feedback from peers may initiate needed changes in behavior, reinforce interpersonal skills, and provide new ways of viewing bullying as well as counter any dysfunctional cognitive processes. For example, the structured and supportive environment of groups might ensure that positive behaviors are rewarded and negative behaviors such as aggression become viewed as undesirable for social interactions. Also, the heterogeneity of experiences and personalities inherent in groups may promote increased understanding of and compassion for others. Further, groups that meet in important contexts (i.e., schools, youth groups outside of school) may promote the development of friendships and positive peer interactions. For example, we have seen group participants sit together and stick up for each other in the lunchroom, indicating that friendship developed out of the group intervention that could buffer youth against bullying. Finally, group interventions may also increase youths' motivation to change bullying situations or their own behavior and may make them feel less alone in their experiences with bullying.

Existing Group Interventions for Bullies and/or Victims

The two existing group interventions that have empirical support focus specifically on the interpersonal dynamics that contribute to bullying. Specifically, these interventions emphasize a social skills training approach.

Social Skills Training Programme
Objectives

Based on research indicating that targets of bullying exhibit behaviors that might contribute to their victimization (Hodges & Perry, 1999), Fox and Boulton developed and evaluated a program involving social skills training for victimized youth (Fox & Boulton, 2003a, 2003b). The aim of program sessions was to teach both verbal and nonverbal strategies to help victims deal with the bully by reducing behaviors that might make the victim an easy target and that reinforce the bully such as looking scared, crying, and submission (Fox & Boulton, 2003a). The program also sought to build prosocial skills that encourage the formation and maintenance of friendships, as friendships can help protect victims from bullying (e.g., Fox & Boulton, 2003a; Hodges, Boivin, Vitaro, & Bukowski, 1999).

Treatment included mixed-gender groups of 5 to 10 students ages 9 to 11 years who were identified through peer report as victims with poor social skills. Groups met weekly for 8 sessions that were 1 hour long and covered the following topics: friendship (i.e., listening and having conversations, asking to join in); body language; assertiveness; and dealing with bullies. Progressive muscle relaxation, social problem-solving skills, and games to enhance self-esteem were also included in session material. Sessions were led by two adults who used modeling, role play, feedback, and reinforcement techniques and assigned homework to encourage generalization of session content. This intervention has limited evaluation but promising preliminary data.

Social Skills Group Intervention Program
Objectives

Based on the need to address the negative effects of poor peer relationships, DeRosier (2004) developed social skills group intervention (S.S.GRIN), a school-based group intervention for children with social difficulties, including peer rejection, peer victimization, and social anxiety. Its offers a combination of empirically validated skills and techniques derived from social learning and cognitive-behavioral theories (e.g., communication, initiation, anger management and impulse control, cognitive restructuring, positive assertion) that address skill problems displayed by many bullies and victims. By addressing a diverse set of peer problems, the intervention was designed for applicability in real-world settings (DeRosier, 2007). The overarching goals were threefold: (1) to build social skills, (2) to enforce prosocial attitudes and behaviors, and (3) to improve children's coping strategies in dealing with social problems such as teasing (DeRosier, 2004).

Components and Evidence

This intervention was designed for elementary school–aged children. Group participants were selected based on elevated levels of at least one of the following: peer rejection, peer victimization (determined through sociometric methodology), or self-reported social anxiety. Groups of six to eight children met once a week for about 1 hour over 8 consecutive weeks. Each week was designed as a building block for subsequent sessions (DeRosier, 2004). To address intervention goals, each session of this manualized group treatment included didactic instruction through scripts, modeling, and role plays to promote prosocial communication skills, initiation, negotiation, cooperation, and compromise (DeRosier & Marcus, 2005). Also, the groups were structured to reduce negative behaviors through instruction on how to control impulses, manage emotions, and explore assumptions (DeRosier & Marcus, 2005). Thus, this intervention could address the heterogeneity in levels of aggression seen among victims (Haynie et al., 2001; Schwartz, 2000; Unnever, 2005). Specifically, it might be useful with aggressive or provocative victims ("bully victims") who are more reactive and dysregulated in their behavior and affect, and less likely to be withdrawn or to display nonassertive/submissive behavior as compared to nonaggressive victims. The S.S. GRIN intervention has shown both immediate and long-term efficacy (i.e., 1-year follow-up) for participating children regardless of their social problems (DeRosier, 2004, 2007; DeRosier & Marcus, 2005). Notably, positive effects included increased social acceptance, decreased use of aggressive behaviors, and fewer instances of peer victimization, as compared to the no-treatment control group.

Summary

These two promising interventions have shown some efficacy in addressing the difficulties of victims, suggesting that social skills training may be a useful approach. In addition, S.S.GRIN has demonstrated positive effects with a heterogeneous group of children, including those with social difficulties who are also aggressive. However, neither intervention specifically targeted bullies or youth older than elementary age. Further, they represent one type of approach to treatment (addressing behavioral deficits and coping skills) that should be compared with other approaches. Yet these interventions represent a solid foundation for efforts to develop group interventions at the individual level.

Potential Group Interventions

We argue that the continued development of effective group interventions must be informed by the characteristics of those involved in bullying (Orpinas & Horne, 2006). In offering suggestions for interventions, we will focus specifically on the intra- and interpersonal characteristics of victims and bullies.

Victims

As recently reviewed by Card and colleagues (2007), a large body of cross-sectional and longitudinal research has shown that victims display behaviors and socioemotional problems that result from as well as provoke or encourage bullying. Interventions should address both interpersonal skill deficits and emotional difficulties to decrease the likelihood of being bullied and increase quality of life. We highlight below the general practice of social skills training and specific interventions targeting internalizing problems that are ideally suited for victims.

Addressing Interpersonal Skills

Social skills training (SST) is a broad entity that comprises decades of research on the nature of, and particular methods that might impact, youths' social competence. It has generally targeted youth with peer relationship problems (La Greca, 1993). Social skills training assumes that social competence can be improved through the development of necessary behavioral skills required for successful social interaction, based on a "social-skills deficit model" (Beelmann, Pfingsten, & Losel, 1994; La Greca, 1993).

Social skills training approaches demonstrate efficacy in improving targeted skills particularly for withdrawn or socially isolated youth (Beelmann, Pfingsten, & Lösel, 1994; Bierman & Erath, 2006; La Greca, 1993; Moote, Smythe, & Woodarski, 1999). Thus, SST with victimized youth represents a potentially potent and flexible group intervention approach, as victims are generally characterized as timid, socially withdrawn, and isolated (Card et al., 2007; Coleman & Byrd, 2003).

Victims of bullying exhibit a broad range of social skill difficulties such as misinterpreting social signals, poor prosocial skills (e.g., joining in groups, cooperativeness, assertiveness, friendliness) and conflict management skills, and poor emotional control and aggressiveness (Card et al., 2007; Coleman & Byrd, 2003; Fox & Boulton, 2005; Perry, Willard, & Perry, 1990). Thus, both basic and complex skills involved in successful social interactions should be targeted (Spence, 2003). For example, conversational skills include knowledge and appropriate use of eye contact, facial expression, and volume of speech, as well as more complex skills such as selection of appropriate topics of conversation. Commonly targeted skills in SST relevant to youth who are bullied include verbal and nonverbal communication and conversation skills, assertiveness, problem solving, emotion regulation, perspective taking, conflict resolution, and dealing with difficult peer situations (Bierman & Erath, 2006; La Greca, 1993; Spence, 2003).

It may be particularly useful to expand SST to include a specific focus on coping skills when working with victims. Qualitative research suggests that youth tend to handle bullying through seeking revenge or ignoring the situation, neither of which is effective at reducing bullying (Varjas et al., 2006). Indeed, among elementary-age children endorsement of revenge-seeking coping strategies in response to hypothetical vignettes was related to increases in victimization across a school year, whereas endorsement of conflict-resolution coping strategies was related to decreases in victimization (Kochenderfer-Ladd, 2004). Unfortunately, there are few studies evaluating the actual use of coping strategies in response to bullying, though this might contribute to or prevent further victimization experiences and adjustment.

Relevant to the potential of SST for the treatment of victims, Moote and colleagues (1999) reviewed 25 empirical studies of school-based SST that involved training in prosocial skills, relaxation, problem solving, and assertiveness, and concluded that SST can lead to skill development for participants in educational settings. In implementation, group leaders should use the following techniques: instruction and coaching, modeling, structured opportunities to practice skills (i.e., rehearsal, role play), and performance feedback and reinforcement of skills (Bierman & Erath, 2006; Spence, 2003). Results from extensive reviews and meta-analytic studies indicate that SST is related to moderate positive effects on specific skills; however, it is less clear whether skill acquisition generalizes to change in children's peer relationships (Beelman et al., 1994; Erwin, 1994; La Greca, 1993). Enhancement of the beneficial effects of SST with victims may be gained by inclusion of socially competent peers to establish and reinforce improved social abilities and overcome existing peer dynamics.

Social skills training may not be appropriate or sufficient for all youth, and thus we suggest the evaluation of the strengths and weaknesses of targeted youth (Fox & Boulton, 2003a; Pepler, 2006). A distinction has been made between social skill acquisition deficits versus performance deficits (Spence, 2003). This distinction may be particularly crucial in the treatment of victims because some bullied youth may possess adequate social skills but be unable to adequately perform them due to emotional arousal or contextual constraints (Perry, Hodges, & Egan, 2001). In our groups, we have found it useful to assess participants' social skills and emotional functioning prior to selecting session material. Understanding the type of deficit will better inform treatment selection and most likely increase the effectiveness of the chosen SST components. Finally, consideration of the developmental level of targeted youth is recommended; reviews indicate that younger children may benefit more from behavioral than cognitive approaches to social skills training (Spence, 2003).

Addressing Internalizing Problems

Victims of bullying also experience higher rates of depression, and generalized and social anxiety as well as lower self-concept when compared with their nonvictimized peers (Card et al., 2007; Hawker & Boulton, 2000). Research also indicates that bullying is associated with depression and loneliness (Swearer, Grills, Haye, & Cary, 2004). One bully-victim we have treated experienced sadness about his home situation and felt disconnected from peers. Once these feelings were identified and understood, it was easier for him to engage in skills training to address the behaviors (including aggression) that contributed to his victimization by peers.

Research on the treatment of anxiety and depression among children and adolescents has found substantial support for the use of group cognitive-behavioral therapy (Albano, Marten, Holt, Heimberg, & Barlow, 1995; Barrett & Shortt, 2003; Clarke, Rhode, Lewinsohn, Hops, & Seeley, 1999; Stark et al., 2006). Similar to SST, the group format provides opportunities for modeling and reinforcement of skills, and the normalization of experiences through group processes and leader facilitation (Shortt, Barrett, & Fox, 2001; Stark et al., 2006). These group treatments may address the internalizing difficulties of victims of bullying. Further, the empirically validated treatments reviewed below also promote friendships and social support and the development of appropriate social skills.

In the treatment of anxious youth, the FRIENDS program (Barrett, Lowry-Webster, & Turner, 2000a, 2000b) is an excellent example of a group-based program that could be used to target victims' anxious arousal, negative attributions, and unassertiveness. Selection of this program is indicated if youth report concurrent anxiety or depression. The rationale for the FRIENDS program rests on the conceptual model that anxiety has physiological, cognitive, and emotional components and the recognition that youths' contexts affect their behavior. Crucial to the treatment of victims, the FRIENDS program encourages and teaches youth how to build social support networks and to utilize friendships when in difficult situations as well as to solve problems for situations that are worrisome or difficult (Barrett & Shortt, 2003). The group format allows youth, particularly those who are withdrawn or shy, to interact with peers in a safe setting and facilitate new social skills, both of which are important for many victims (Barrett & Shortt, 2003). Two different manuals are available to address the developmental needs of children between the ages of 7–11 and 12–16. Detailed leaders' manuals allow for flexible implementation to address specific groups' needs. Group sessions meet weekly for approximately 1 hour for 10 weeks followed by two booster sessions. The program also includes a family skills component administered in a group format to help parents learn how to better support and reinforce their children, which may address parenting characteristics associated with victimization (e.g., overprotectiveness, intense closeness, coercive parenting) (Bowers, Smith, & Binney, 1994; Card et al., 2007). The FRIENDS program has shown efficacy for clinically anxious youth and normative youth in a universal school-based prevention program format (Barrett & Turner, 2001; Farrell, Barrett, & Claassens, 2005; Shortt et al., 2001).

In addition to the FRIENDS program, two group-based comprehensive social skills training programs have been specifically developed for anxious youth. First, social effectiveness therapy for children (SET-C; Beidel, Turner, & Morris, 2000) involves both a group SST component and an individual training session once per week over 12 weeks. The recruitment of "peer helpers" from the community provides peer modeling, opportunities for positive peer experiences, and practice of skills with peers. Although developed for children ages 8 through 12 with social phobia, the format of the intervention could serve as a model for working with victims of bullying. Specific skill deficits of each child can be targeted in individual sessions, group sessions can focus on the practice and natural reinforcement of these behavioral skills, and peer generalization activities can promote the generalization of skills beyond the therapy setting.

Second, the cognitive behavioral group treatment for adolescents (CBGT-A; Albano et al., 1995) was developed specifically for adolescents ages 13 to 17. Group sessions consist of psychoeducation, exposure-based activities, and skills building through social skills training, social problem solving, and cognitive restructuring. Based on the proven efficacy among anxious youth, SET-C and CBGT-A are two potential programs to be chosen if goals include improved social skills, increased peer interaction, and/or reduced social anxiety and depression (Albano et al., 1995; Beidel et al., 2000).

A third group program that is applicable to the treatment of victimized youth is the adolescent coping with depression course (CWD-A; Clarke et al., 1999). Session material targets mood monitoring, engagement in pleasant activities, relaxation training, identification of negative-irrational thoughts and cognitive restructuring, and skills training (e.g., problem solving, communication and conflict resolution skills). Mixed-gender groups of up to

10 adolescents meet for sixteen 2-hour sessions. Research indicates that adolescents participating in this group intervention have higher recovery rates from depression and greater reduction in depressive symptoms than waitlist control groups at 2-year follow-up (Clarke et al., 1999). Notably, CWD-A has also demonstrated some efficacy and effectiveness with the more severe population of adolescents referred from a juvenile justice setting (Rhode, Clarke, Mace, Jorgensen, & Seeley, 2004). In this treatment, the course was used flexibly (e.g., repetition of critical treatment concepts across sessions, "make-up" sessions, rewards for participation and attendance, assistance with reading and writing, and shortened writing assignments), suggesting that modifications can be made while still resulting in positive treatment effects. Thus, the intervention may be useful in school settings in which flexibility is necessary.

Summary

Although social skills training programs and the reviewed treatment programs for anxiety and depression differ somewhat in their underlying models, the general goals are to improve youths' coping skills, social and problem-solving skills, interpersonal functioning, and emotion regulation. These goals are compatible when working with victims of bullying in order to address their intra- and interpersonal functioning.

In general, several recommendations for working with victims of bullying derived from our experiences and found in the literature should be emphasized (Whitted & Dupper, 2005). First, interventions should offer support and protection for victims, helping them to feel less alone and more supported by other peers and adults. Victims of bullying value social support more highly than their nonvictimized peers, and they feel that they receive little support (Demaray & Malecki, 2003). Groups provide the unique opportunity to alter potentially negative histories, but this goal needs to be achieved within a structured, controlled environment. For instance, group facilitators who are not aware of the interpersonal histories of youth within groups they conduct may actually prevent feelings of safety. We have found it necessary to individually explore group members' experiences of victimization to ensure our awareness of any previous instances of bullying between group members. We are then able to create a safe setting in which the victim can express his or her hurt and facilitate understanding between the group members. Second, interventionists should strive to assist victims to solve the problem of bullying without making them feel "at fault" for the bullying. Skills training can focus on helping victims recognize factors that place them at risk for bullying and modify that which is in their power to change. However, whether and which skill deficits might exist among youth must be assessed, and skills training components chosen accordingly. Finally, the strengthening of peer relationships through either the involvement of nonvictimized peers in groups or the facilitation of groups in naturalistic contexts (e.g., the classroom) may reduce the bullying that victims experience and improve their social functioning (Pellegrini, Bartini, & Brooks, 1999).

Bullies

Although there does exist a "pure" bullying group that does not experience peer victimization themselves, there is significant overlap among children who engage in bullying and who are the recipients of bullying. Bullies are treated here as a distinct group from victims in order to most clearly refer to the associated characteristics that should be addressed. However, interventionists should not forget that there is significant heterogeneity among bullies. Some bullies may choose to initiate aggression to gain personal rewards such as lunch money (proactive aggression), whereas others may misinterpret social cues and react defensively to what they perceive as a threatening situation (reactive aggression) (Griffin & Gross, 2004; Unnever, 2005). Further, some bullies may be quite popular or socially competent, with a good understanding of others, and thus capable of dominating their peers and gaining social power through their proactive aggressive behavior (Pellegrini et al., 1999; Schwartz, 2000). Indeed, there is growing support for the argument that some youth effectively utilize aggression in order to control resources and gain social prominence with fewer negative consequences than those who are more reactively (and ineffectively) aggressive (Bukowski, 2003; Hawley, Little, & Card, 2007; Little, Brauner, Jones, Nock, & Hawley, 2003). The following interventions may be most suitable for bullies who demonstrate difficulties with emotion regulation, social skills, and social-cognitive processes.

Addressing Aggression, Anger, and Social Skill Deficits

There are clear and useful parallels between bullying interventions and youth violence prevention programming. Although aggression and bullying are distinct constructs, anger, aggression, and general misconduct problems are characteristics of bullies and may be targeted via programs developed to treat these problems (Bosworth, Espelage, & Simon, 1999; Card et al., 2007; Haynie et al., 2001). Bullies have been found to be aggressive, dominant, and easily angered (Olweus, 1993; Unnever, 2005). In fact, anger has emerged as a powerful predictor of bullying behavior (Bosworth et al., 1999; Espelage, Bosworth, & Simon, 2001). Research indicates that treatment involving training in social skills, problem solving, and anger management successfully reduces youth behavior problems (Lochman & Wells, 2004; Webster-Stratton, Reid, & Hammond, 2004). We will review four group interventions designed with aggression as their central focus that may be applied in the remediation of bullying behavior. Attention to the type and severity of problems and the age of group members should inform the selection of a particular program.

First, the Anger Coping and the Coping Power programs developed by Lochman and colleagues (Lochman & Wells, 2004) target deficits in children's social competence and social-cognitive skills. Bullies tend to use and view retaliation as the most effective means of handling conflict (Camodeca & Goossens, 2005). Further, bullying is associated with a positive outlook on the use of violence to solve problems and a lack of confidence in the use of nonviolent interpersonal strategies (Bosworth et al., 1999; Espelage et al., 2001; Griffin & Gross, 2004; Pellegrini et al., 1999). Bullies display difficulties with conflict resolution, cooperation, problem solving, and communication skills (Haynie et al., 2001; Rigby, Cox, & Black, 1997; Schwartz, 2000).

The Anger Coping Program consists of 18 group sessions of five to seven school-age children who meet weekly for 60 to 90 minutes. Relevant to the characteristics of bullies, session material addresses anger management, emotional awareness, relaxation training, perspective taking, social problem solving, and social skills enhancement (Lochman, Barry & Pardini, 2003). As an extension of the Anger Coping Program, the Coping Power Program consists of a greater number of group sessions (33 sessions), individual sessions, and a parent component (Lochman & Wells, 2004). The additional group sessions focus on further building social skills and advanced emotional awareness and positive social and personal goals, which could increase bullies' empathy for peers as well as their choice of less aggressive means to reach goals.

These programs have been evaluated through various experimental designs, including comparison of different versions of the program, and a quasi-experimental design evaluating different treatment lengths (see Lochman et al., 2003). In comparison to children in control conditions, participating children showed reductions in aggressive and acting-out behavior, and increases in classroom on-task behavior, self-regulation, social competence, and self-esteem. Lower levels of substance use and delinquent behavior among participants were also found (Lochman, 1992; Lochman & Wells, 2004). Important to the selection of group participants, children who benefited the most from this program were those who exhibited poor problem-solving skills, peer problems (i.e, rejection by the peer group), internalizing difficulties, an internalized attributional style, and lower perceived hostility (Lochman et al., 2003). Efficacy may be optimized when participants set their own behavioral goals and attend at least 18 sessions (Lochman, Whidby, & Fitzgerald, 2000).

Second, a more specific intervention, the Brain Power program consists of 12 sessions designed to change children's cognitive attributions in order to lessen their anger and reduce their aggressive reactions to perceived provocation (Hudley & Graham, 1993; Hudley & Friday, 1996). One-hour sessions were held twice a week for 6 weeks with 3rd through 6th grade aggressive, rejected ethnic minority boys. Groups also included nonaggressive peer models to provide positive socialization experiences and to counteract negative attitudes and behaviors toward aggressive children. This strategy could potentially change peer dynamics through overcoming reputational biases by providing bullies with the opportunity to change their behavior and be positively received by their peers. The curriculum has three specific goals: (1) to strengthen children's ability to make accurate attributions of others' intentions, (2) to increase the likelihood of making nonhostile attributions to ambiguous social interactions, and (3) to generate decision rules for how to respond to ambiguous situations (Hudley & Graham, 1993). Videotapes, hypothetical vignettes, role plays, and group discussions of personal experiences are used to promote learning and practice of social cognitive skills. In comparison to active and waitlist controls, this program has demonstrated immediate and long-term efficacy in reducing hostile attributions and reactive aggression (Hudley & Graham, 1993; Hudley et al., 1998).

With its exclusive focus on attributions, the Brain Power program most likely needs to be accompanied by other treatment components to address nonattributional causes of aggression (Hudley & Friday, 1996). The Anger Coping and the Brain Power programs have the potential to effectively address maladaptive social cognitions of bullies, particularly those who display reactive aggression. Its effectiveness with aggressive girls or youth who are primarily relationally aggressive may be limited.

A third intervention program, the Dinosaur Child Training Curriculum of the empirically supported Incredible Years intervention targets the behaviors of preschool to early elementary age children with aggressive, disruptive problems (Webster-Stratton & Reid, 2003; Webster-Stratton, Reid, & Hammond, 2001). Relevant to bullies, the Dinosaur Social, Emotional, and Problem Solving Child Program targets deficits in social skills and problem solving, loneliness and negative attributions, limited empathy or perspective taking, and limited use of emotion language (Webster-Stratton et al., 2001). Thus, session content includes training in interpersonal problem solving and conflict resolution, communication and friendship skills, emotional understanding and expression, and anger management. Small groups of five to six children ages 4 to 8 meet for 2-hour sessions for 18–22 weeks. Videotaped vignettes provide opportunities to view models of children coping with stressful situations and engaging in problem solving, and they initiate discussion and role plays of hypothetical situations and common interpersonal difficulties. Further, session content is provided in other developmentally appropriate methods (i.e., use of child-size puppets, cartoons, coloring books, prizes, fantasy play; Webster-Stratton & Reid, 2003). Generalization is promoted through group activities, homework assignments, and encouraged involvement of teachers and parents to reinforce skills. Detailed group leader manuals are designed to be used across settings by mental-health providers.

There is a substantial evidence base for this group intervention. Children participating in the child training program demonstrated significantly greater decreases in behavior problems at home and school, increases in positive affect at home and prosocial behavior with peers, and improved problem-solving skills, compared to children in a waitlist control group (Webster-Stratton & Hammond, 1997; Webster-Stratton et al., 2001; Webster-Stratton, Reid, & Hammond, 2004). Children participating in this program also demonstrated greater improvements over time in observed peer interactions and problem-solving skills in comparison to a parent training-only treatment condition (Webster-Stratton & Hammond, 1997; Webster-Stratton et al., 2004). The parent training component could be combined with the child curriculum in the treatment of some bullies, particularly bully victims (Webster-Stratton & Reid, 2003). This multimodal approach may be crucial because bullying has been associated with family factors such as coercive parenting, parental hostility, low parental warmth and involvement, marital conflict, and exposure to violence in the home (Bowers et al., 1994; Haynie et al., 2001; Olweus, 1993).

Finally, for older youth, the Aggression Replacement Training (ART) program, developed initially for violence prevention and intervention with high-risk adolescents, involves three components that each are facilitated for at least 10 weeks with small groups of six to eight youth (Glick & Goldstein, 1987; Goldstein, Glick, & Gibbs, 1998). The first two components, "skill streaming" and anger control training, are similar to the previously mentioned programs and address anger management and deficits in prosocial behavior typical of aggressive youth (e.g., communication, problem solving, conflict resolution, coping skills for stressful situations). The third component, moral reasoning training, is unique to ART and is designed to raise youths' awareness of justice, fairness, and concern for others' rights and needs. This component utilizes moral dilemmas to engage and push youth to a higher level of "mature" moral reasoning (Goldstein et al., 1998). Weekly group sessions utilize coaching and instruction, role plays, reinforcement and feedback, and "transfer training," which encourages generalization of learned skills to real-world settings.

Empirical evaluation with highly aggressive adolescent boys has found that youth who participated in ART displayed significantly greater acquisition of taught skills, increases in moral reasoning, and decreases in acting-out behavior, anger, and impulsiveness than did comparison groups (i.e., no treatment, and a brief instruction control group) (Glick & Goldstein, 1987; Goldstein & Glick, 1994). The developers of this program provide reviews of the use of ART in diverse settings that include community and educational settings (e.g., whole school districts and alternative schools) (Goldstein et al., 1998).

The ART program provides an approach that might be particularly useful with bullies, including the socially skilled bullies (Hawley et al., 2007), due to its core focus on moral reasoning. The development of moral reasoning and empathy has been suggested by interventionists and even included in some bullying and violence prevention programs (e.g., Frey, Hirschstein, & Guzzo, 2000; Hazler & Carney, 2006; Orpinas & Horne, 2006). Yet we are unaware of any explicit empirical evaluation of this specific intervention component with bullies. A focus on moral reasoning and empathy may be effective in emphasizing the inappropriateness of aggression and motivating aggressive youth to utilize prosocial approaches to achieve social goals, particularly as bullies may view aggression as a legitimate interpersonal strategy (Unnever, 2005). Further, the ability to understand and appropriately respond to others' feelings and to share in their emotional state (i.e., empathy) is positively related to prosocial behavior and negatively associated with aggression (Miller & Eisenberg, 1988). Thus, training in empathy and moral reasoning could increase emotional understanding of self and other, as well as perspective-taking skills and prosocial behavior. Indeed, the universal prevention program Second Step, which includes empathy training, has resulted in significant improvements in perspective-taking abilities and prosocial behavior, and decreases in physical aggression (Frey et al., 2000). Based on limited research, more empathic concern for others is associated with more negative views of bullying and thus less bullying behavior (Espelage & Swearer, 2003). Understanding of others' experiences and feelings may be crucial to effective group interventions that target the reduction of aggression and bullying (Hazler & Carney, 2006).

The behavior of bullies should first be addressed with general redirection, rules, and consequences for their actions. If these strategies are ineffective, we recommend that behavior management approaches and skills training (e.g., anger management, perspective taking, development of empathy) be implemented (Smith et al., 2004). In order to ensure that group processes are as effective and noniatrogenic as possible, it is important for group sessions to be clearly focused on the development of skills and involve behavior management, or to be conducted with a mix of nonaggressive and aggressive youth to decrease chances for escalation of aggression or reinforcement of bullying behavior. We have witnessed the consequences of a group that lacked explicit behavioral guidelines and contingencies; this set-up permitted a dominant, socially skilled group member to spur on other participants to gang up against a less assertive group member. Group facilitators should ensure that aggressive strategies displayed within the group are not effective in gaining instrumental goals or dominance over peers.

In choosing one of the reviewed programs or their components, assessment of group participants' social competence should be conducted because bullies vary widely in their particular strengths and difficulties. For example, a bully may display difficulties with social skills, empathy, emotional and behavioral regulation abilities, problem-solving and conflict resolution skills, or any combination of the above. Given bullies' positive attitudes toward aggression and the impact these attitudes may have on program effectiveness, group leaders should assess *(1)* bullies' recognition that their behavior is problematic, and *(2)* their level of motivation to change their behavior (Lochman et al., 2003). Overall, the reviewed group interventions suggest that bullies with problem profiles that include aggression and concurrent social skill deficits can be treated effectively.

Future Directions

As the research base on bullying has become more detailed, it is apparent that youth involved in bullying are not easily characterized. The heterogeneity among bullies and victims necessitates more targeted group interventions that consider their individual characteristics (Griffin & Gross, 2004; Pepler, 2006; Salmivalli, Karhunen, & Lagerspetz, 1996). For example, social skills training might be useful with youth who have difficulties with reactive aggression and anger management, yet ineffective with others who might possess well-developed social skills and social leverage or power within the peer group (Hawley et al., 2007; Pellegrini et al., 1999). Until we have a clearer understanding of what interventions work for whom, broad-based group interventions may currently be the most promising given the heterogeneity of children with social problems (e.g., DeRosier, 2007).

Given the few developed and empirically evaluated individual-level treatments, it is also imperative that we understand why this level of intervention has generally been neglected. Our review of the literature suggests several possibilities. First, it may be that the heterogeneity among bullies and victims makes it difficult for interventionists to adequately assess bullying, correctly identify youth who need help, or develop comprehensive approaches that address individual differences. Second, it may also be that difficulties of some of these youth are overlooked due to the internalizing nature of their problems. We should take care to recognize the potential problems of youth who may be struggling but who are not "behavior problems" in the classroom or other settings. Third, it may be that adults are generally biased to like effective bullies and blame provocative or "bully victims." Adults may also underestimate the frequency of bullying or view bullying as a normal part of child development (Espelage & Swearer, 2003). Education about bullying to overcome these biases or perceptual errors is necessary to effectively engage adults in the treatment of bullies and victims, particularly as the active participation of key individuals in youths' environment (i.e., peers, teachers, parents) should be encouraged (Limber, 2004). Finally, it might be that financial, staffing, and time resources to implement group interventions are not readily available; Vernberg and Gamm's (2003) review of reasons for resistance to the implementation of school violence prevention programs suggests that a shared vision and "buy in" of all involved in selected interventions is necessary.

In summary, there exists a large body of research to guide the development of group interventions for youth who are involved in bullying. Two existing interventions have effectively utilized this research to treat the interpersonal difficulties of victims. Relevant intervention programs also exist to improve the emotional and social functioning of victims and bullies and alter peer dynamics. We are hopeful that in the future greater attention will be given to the development and evaluation of individual-level interventions, and specifically group interventions, to achieve these critical goals with bullies and victims.

Practice Implications for Group Interventions with Youth Involved in Bullying

Assessment

Consider the following factors when assessing whether a child or adolescent could benefit from a group intervention for involvement in bullying.

- Recognize overlap among bullies and victims
- Recognize individual differences among bullies, victims, and bully victims
- Assess individual youths' social, emotional, and behavioral competencies
- Identify interpersonal skill versus performance deficits
- Assess for emotional functioning, particularly internalizing difficulties
- Evaluate dynamics of bullying and maintaining factors (e.g., youth motivation, success of bullying behavior, reinforcement by peer group)

Content

Consider participants' needs when determining what skills to teach. Utilize evidence-based approaches for teaching those skills. See Table 8.1 for a listing of interventions reviewed in this chapter and their targeted ages and skill areas.

- Social skills training has been used effectively to address social difficulties
- Competence areas include communication and assertiveness skills, problem solving and conflict resolution skills, anger management, emotion understanding and regulation, moral reasoning and empathy, coping with difficult peer situations
- Additional targets: anxious arousal, depressive symptoms, attributional biases, building and utilizing social support networks and friendships
- Effective group strategies include instruction and coaching, modeling, structured opportunities to practice skills, performance feedback and reinforcement, generalization strategies

Facilitation

Keep the following in mind while running group sessions to make them a safe place for youth and to help them learn and apply new skills.

- Encourage supportive environment that normalizes experiences
- Watch for opportunities to make the skills "real" by applying them to real-life situations

Table 8.1
Resources for Group Interventions

Name of Program	Age / Grade Range	Targeted Populations	Targeted Areas	More Information
Adolescent Coping with Depression (CWD-A)	13–17	Victimized youth with depression	Mood monitoring Social skills Relaxation training Cognitive restructuring Problem solving Conflict resolution	A free manual is available for mental health professionals at: http://www.kpchr.org/public/acwd/acwd.html
Aggression Replacement Training (ART)	12–17	Aggressive/violent adolescents with anger management difficulties	Prosocial behavior Anger reduction Moral reasoning	For more information or to purchase a manual: http://www.researchpress.com/product/item/5004/
Anger Coping/Coping Power	9–12	Aggressive and disruptive youth with anger management difficulties	*Anger Coping* Anger reduction Social problem solving Social skills Emotional awareness *Coping Power* Also includes: Individual treatment Parent training	Larson, J. & Lochman, J. E. (2002). *Helping school children cope with anger: A cognitive behavioral intervention.* New York: Guilford.

(continued)

Table 8.1
(Continued)

Name of Program	Age / Grade Range	Targeted Populations	Targeted Areas	More Information
Brain Power	3rd–6th grade	Aggressive and socially rejected children	Social information processing Anger reduction	For more information or to purchase a manual: http://www. brainpowerprogram.com/
Cognitive Behavioral Group Treatment for Adolescents (CBGT-A)	13–17	Socially anxious youth	Social skills Social problem solving Cognitive restructuring Also includes: Psychoeducation Exposure activities	Albano, A., & DiBartolo, P. (2007). Cognitive-behavioral therapy for social phobia in adolescents: Stand up, speak out. New York: Oxford University Press. (therapist guide and workbook) http://www. oup.com
Social Effectiveness Therapy for Children (SET-C)	8–12	Socially anxious youth	Social skills Also includes: Peer generalization Exposure activities	For more information or to purchase a manual, visit the Multi-Health Systems, Inc. website: http://www.mhs.com

Program	Age	Target population	Skills	More information
Dinosaur Child Training Curriculum	4–8	Aggressive children with disruptive behavior problems	Problem-solving Conflict resolution Communication Friendship Emotion understanding Anger management	For more information or to purchase a manual, visit The Incredible Years Training Series (Webster-Stratton) website: http://www.incredibleyears.com/program/child.asp
FRIENDS	7–11 or 12–16	Youth with anxiety and/or depression	Social support development Problem solving Emotion understanding and expression Anger reduction	For more information or to purchase a manual, visit the FRIENDS website: http://www.friendsinfo.net/
Social Skills Group Intervention (S.S. GRIN)	Elementary school-aged children	Youth with poor peer relations and/or social anxiety	Social skills Communication skills Emotion regulation	For more information or to purchase a manual, visit the 3-C Institute for Social Development website: http://www.3cisd.com/
Social Skills Training (SST)	9–11	Victimized youth with poorly developed social skills	Friendship development Understanding body language Progressive muscle relaxation Social problem solving Self-esteem Assertiveness	To obtain more information, please contact: Dr. Claire Fox School of Psychology University of Keele Staffordshire e-mail: c.fox@psy.keele.ac.uk

- Address interpersonal dynamics (e.g., homework, involvement of peers, build friendships, facilitation in naturalistic settings)
- Be aware of dynamics of group and interpersonal histories of participating youth
- Provide a safe, structured, controlled environment that does not blame participants
- Ensure that aggressive strategies are not effective or reinforced in group setting
- Involve important adults in youths' contexts in the treatment if possible

References

Albano, A. M., Marten, P. A., Holt, C. S., Heimberg, R. G., & Barlow, D. (1995). Cognitive-behavioral group treatment for social phobia in adolescents: A preliminary study. *Journal of Nervous and Mental Disease, 183*, 649–656.

Barrett, P. M., Lowry-Webster, H., & Turner, C. (2000a). *FRIENDS program for children: Group leaders manual*. Brisbane: Australian Academic Press.

Barrett, P. M., Lowry-Webster, H., & Turner, C. (2000b). *FRIENDS program for youth: Group leaders manual*. Brisbane: Australian Academic Press.

Barrett, P. M., & Shortt, A. L. (2003). Parental involvement in the treatment of anxious children. In A. E. Kazdin & J. R. Weisz (Eds.), *Evidence-based psychotherapies for children and adolescents* (pp. 101–119). New York: Guilford.

Barrett, P. M., & Turner, C. (2001). Prevention of anxiety symptoms in primary school children: Preliminary results from a universal school based trial. *British Journal of Clinical Psychiatry, 40*, 399–410.

Beelmann, A., Pfingsten, U., & Lösel, F. (1994). Effects of training social competence in children: A meta-analysis of recent evaluation studies. *Journal of Clinical Child Psychology, 23*, 260–271.

Beidel, D. C., Turner, S. M., & Morris, T. L. (2000). Behavioral treatment of childhood social phobia. *Journal of Consulting and Clinical Psychology, 68*, 1072–1080.

Bierman, K. L., & Erath, S. A. (2006). Promoting social competence in early childhood: Classroom curricula and social skills coaching programs. In K. McCartney & D. Phillips (Eds.), *Blackwell handbook of early childhood development* (pp. 595–615). Malden, MA: Blackwell.

Bosworth, K., Espelage, D. L., & Simon, T. R. (1999). Factors associated with bullying behavior in middle school students. *Journal of Early Adolescence, 19*, 341–362.

Bowers, L., Smith, P. K., & Binney, V. (1994). Perceived family relationships of bullies, victims and bully/victims in middle childhood. *Journal of Social and Personal Relationships, 11*, 215–232.

Bukowski, W. M. (2003). What does it mean to say that aggressive children are competent or incompetent? *Merrill-Palmer Quarterly, 49*, 390–400.

Camodeca, M., & Goosens, F. A. (2005). Children's opinions on effective strategies to cope with bullying: The importance of bullying role and perspective. *Educational Research, 47*, 93–105.

Card, N. A., Isaacs, J., & Hodges, E. V. (2007). Correlates of school victimization: Implications for prevention and intervention. In J. E. Zins, M. J. Elias, & C. A. Maher (Eds.), *Bullying, victimization, and peer harassment: A handbook of prevention and intervention* (pp. 339–365). New York: Hawthorn Press.

Clarke, G. N., Rhode, P., Lewinsohn, P. M., Hops, H., & Seeley, J. R. (1999). Cognitive-behavioral treatment of adolescent depression: Efficacy of acute group treatment and booster sessions. *Journal of American Academy of Child and Adolescent Psychiatry, 38*, 272–279.

Coleman, P. K., & Byrd, C. P. (2003). Interpersonal correlates of peer victimization among young adolescence. *Journal of Youth and Adolescence, 32*, 301–314.

Demaray, M. K., & Malecki, C. K. (2003). Perceptions of the frequency and importance of social support by students classified as victims, bullies, and bully/victims in an urban middle school. *School Psychology Review, 32*, 471–489.

DeRosier, M. E. (2004). Building relationships and combating bullying: Effectiveness of a school-based social skills group intervention. *Journal of Clinical Child and Adolescent Psychology, 33*, 196–201.

DeRosier, M. E. (2007). Peer-rejected and bullied children: A safe schools initiative for elementary school students. In J. E. Zins, M. J. Elias, & C. A. Maher (Eds.), *Bullying, victimization, and peer harassment: A handbook of prevention and intervention* (pp. 257–267). New York: Hawthorn Press.

DeRosier, M. E., & Marcus, S. R. (2005). Building friendships and combating bullying: Effectiveness of S.S.GRIN at one-year follow-up. *Journal of Clinical Child and Adolescent Psychology, 34*, 140–150.

Erwin, P. G. (1994). Effectiveness of social skills training with children: A meta-analytic study. *Counseling Psychology Quarterly, 7*, 305–310.

Eslea, M., & Smith, P. K. (1998). The long-term effectiveness of anti-bullying work in primary schools. *Educational Research, 40*, 203–218.

Espelage, D. L., Bosworth, K., & Simon, T. (2001). Short-term stability and change of bullying in middle school students: An examination of demographic, psychosocial, and environmental correlates. *Violence and Victims, 16*, 411–426.

Espelage, D. L., & Swearer, S. M. (2003). Research on school bullying and victimization: What have we learned and where do we go from here? *School Psychology Review, 32*, 365–383.

Farrell, L., Barrett, P., & Claassens, S. (2005). Community trial of an evidence-based anxiety intervention for children and adolescents (the FRIENDS program): A pilot study. *Behaviour Change, 22*(4), 236–248.

Fox, C. L., & Boulton, M. J. (2003a). A social skills training (SST) programme for victims of bullying. *Pastoral Care in Education, 21*, 19–26.

Fox, C. L., & Boulton, M. J. (2003b). Evaluating the effectiveness of a social skills training (SST) programme for victims of bullying. *Educational Research, 45*, 231–247.

Fox, C. L., & Boulton, M. J. (2005). The social skills problems of victims of bullying: Self, peer and teacher perceptions. *British Journal of Educational Psychology, 75*, 313–328.

Frey, K. S., Hirschstein, M. K., & Guzzo, B. A. (2000). Second Step: Preventing aggression by promoting social competence. *Journal of Emotional and Behavioral Disorders, 8*, 102–112.

Glick, B., & Goldstein, A. P. (1987). Aggression replacement therapy. *Journal of Counseling and Development, 65*, 356–362.

Goldstein, A. P., & Glick, B. (1994). Aggression replacement training: Curriculum and evaluation. *Simulation and Gaming, 25*, 9–26.

Goldstein, A. P., Glick, B., & Gibbs, J. C. (1998). *Aggression replacement training: A comprehensive intervention for aggressive youth.* Champaign, IL: Research Press.

Gresham, F. M. (1997). Social competence and students with behavior disorders: Where we've been, where we are, and where we should go. *Education and Treatment of Children, 20*, 233–249.

Griffin, R. S., & Gross, A. M. (2004). Childhood bullying: Current empirical findings and future direction for research. *Aggression and Violent Behavior, 9*, 379–400.

Hawker, D. S. J., & Boulton, M. J. (2000). Twenty years' research on peer victimization and psychosocial maladjustment: A meta-analytic review of cross-sectional studies. *Journal of Child Psychology and Psychiatry, 41*, 441–455.

Hawley, P. H., Little, T. D., & Card, N. A. (2007). The allure of a mean friend: Relationship quality and processes of aggressive adolescents with prosocial skills. *International Journal of Behavioral Development, 31*, 170–180.

Haynie, D. L., Nansel, T., Eitel, P., Crump, A. D., Saylor, K., Yu, K., et al. (2001). Bullies, victims, and bully/victims: Distinct groups of at-risk youth. *Journal of Early Adolescence, 21*, 29–39.

Hazler, R., & Carney, J. (2006). *Critical characteristics of effective bullying prevention programs.* Mahwah, NJ: Erlbaum.

Hodges, E., Boivin, M., Vitaro, F., & Bukowski, W. M. (1999). The power of friendship: Friendship as a factor in the cycle of victimization and maladjustment. *Developmental Psychology, 35*, 94–101.

Hodges, E. & Perry, D. (1999). Personal and interpersonal antecedents and consequences of victimization by peers. *Journal of Personality and Social Psychology, 76*, 677–685.

Hudley, C., Britsch, B., Wakefield, W. D., Smith, T., Demorat, M., & Cho, S-J. (1998). An attribution retraining program to reduce aggression in elementary school students. *Psychology in the Schools, 35*, 271–282.

Hudley, C., & Friday, J. (1996). Attributional bias and reactive aggression. *American Journal of Preventive Medicine, 12*, 75–81.

Hudley, C., Graham, S. (1993). An attributional intervention to reduce peer-directed aggression among African American boys. *Child Development, 64,* 124–138.

Kasen, S., Berenson, K., Cohen, P., & Johnson, J. (2004). *The effects of school climate on changes in aggressive and other behaviors related to bullying.* Mahwah, NJ: Erlbaum.

Kochenderfer-Ladd, B. (2004). Peer victimization: The role of emotions in adaptive and maladaptive coping. *Social Development, 13,* 329–349.

La Greca, A. M. (1993). Social skills training with children: Where do we go from here? *Journal of Clinical Child Psychology, 22,* 288–298.

Limber, S. (2004). Implementation of the Olweus Bullying Prevention Program in American schools: Lessons learned from the field. In D. L. Espelage & S. M. Swearer (Eds.), *Bullying in American schools: A social-ecological perspective on prevention and intervention* (pp. 351–363). Mahwah, NJ: Erlbaum.

Little, T. D., Brauner, J., Jones, S. M., Nock, M. K., & Hawley, P. H. (2003). Rethinking aggression: A typological examination of the functions of aggression. *Merrill-Palmer Quarterly, 49,* 343–369.

Lochman, J. E. (1992). Cognitive-behavioral intervention with aggressive boys: Three-year follow-up and preventive effects. *Journal of Consulting and Clinical Psychology, 60* (3), 426–432.

Lochman, J. E., Barry, T., & Pardini, D. (2003). *Anger control training for aggressive youth.* New York: Guilford.

Lochman, J. E., & Wells, K. C. (2004). The Coping Power Program for preadolescent aggressive boys and their parents: Outcome effects at the 1-year follow-up. *Journal of Consulting and Clinical Psychology, 72,* 571–578.

Lochman, J. E., Whidby, J. M., & Fitzgerald, D. P. (2000). Cognitive-behavioral assessment and treatment with aggressive children. In P. C. Kendall (Ed.), *Child and adolescent therapy* (2nd ed., pp. 31–87). New York: Guilford.

Miller, P., & Eisenberg, N. (1988). The relation of empathy to aggressive and externalizing/ antisocial behavior. *Psychological Bulletin, 103,* 324–344.

Moote, G. T., Smyth, N. J., & Woodarski, J. S. (1999). Social skills training with youth in school settings: A review. *Research on Social Work Practice, 9,* 427–465.

Nansel, T. R., Overbeck, M., Pilla, R. S., Ruan, W. J., Simon-Morton, B., & Scheidt, P. (2001). Bullying behaviors among US youth: Prevalence and association with psychosocial adjustment. *Journal of the American Medical Association, 285,* 2094–2100.

Nation, M. (2007). Empowering the victim: Interventions for children victimized by bullies. In J. E. Zins, M. J. Elias, C. A. Maher (Eds.), *Bullying, victimization, and peer harassment: A handbook of prevention and intervention* (pp. 239–255). New York: Hawthorn Press.

Olweus, D. (1993). *Bullying at school: What we know and what we can do.* Malden, MA: Blackwell.

Orpinas, P. & Horne, A. M. (2006). *Bullying prevention: Creating a positive school climate and developing social competence.* Washington, DC: American Psychological Association.

Pellegrini, A. D., Bartini, M., & Brooks, F. (1999). School bullies, victims and aggressive victims: Factors relating top group affiliation and victimization in early adolescence. *Journal of Educational Psychology, 91,* 216–224.

Pepler, D. J. (2006). Bullying interventions: A binocular perspective. *Journal of Canadian Academy of Child and Adolescent Psychiatry, 15,* 16–20.

Perry, D. G., Hodges, E., & Egan, S. (2001). Determinants of chronic victimization by peers: A review and new model of family influence. In J. Juvonen & S. Graham (Eds.), *Determinants of chronic victimization by peers: A review and new model of family influence* (pp. 73–104). New York: Guilford.

Perry, D. G., Willard, J., & Perry, L. (1990). Peers' perceptions of consequences that victimized children provide aggressors. *Child Development, 61,* 1289–1309.

Rigby, K., Cox, I., & Black, G. (1997). Cooperativeness and bully/victim problems among Australian schoolchildren. *Journal of Social Psychology, 137,* 357–368.

Rohde, P., Clarke, G. N., Mace, D. E., Jorgensen, J. S., & Seeley, J. R. (2004). An efficacy/effectiveness study of cognitive-behavioral treatment for adolescents with comorbid major depression and conduct disorder. *Journal of American Academy of Child and Adolescent Psychiatry, 43,* 660–668.

Salmivalli, C., Karhunen, J., & Lagerspetz, K. M. J. (1996). How do the victims respond to bullying? *Aggressive Behavior, 22,* 99–109.

Schwartz, D. (2000). Subtypes of victims and aggressors in children's peer groups. *Journal of Abnormal Child Psychiatry, 28,* 181–192.

Sharp, S., & Cowie, H. (1994). Empowering students to take positive action against bullying. In P. K. Smith & S. Sharp (Eds.), *School bullying: Insights and perspectives.* London: Routledge.

Shortt, A. L., Barrett, P. M., & Fox, T. (2001). Evaluating the FRIENDS program: A cognitive behavioral group treatment for anxious children and their parents. *Journal of Clinical Child Psychology, 30,* 525–535.

Smith, P., Pepler, D., & Rigby, K. (2004). *Bullying in schools: How successful can interventions be?* New York: Cambridge University Press.

Spence, S. H. (2003). Social skills training with children and young people: Theory, evidence and practice. *Child and Adolescent Mental Health, 8,* 84–96.

Stark, K. D., Sander, J., Hauser, M., Simpson, J., Schnoebelen, S., Glenn, R., & Molnar, J. (2006). Depressive disorders during childhood and adolescence. In E. J. Mash & R. A. Barkley (Eds.), *Treatment of childhood disorders* (3rd ed., pp. 336–407). New York: Guilford.

Swearer, S. M., & Espelage, D. L. (2004). Introduction: A social-ecological framework of bullying among youth. In D. L. Espelage & S. M. Swearer (Eds.), *Bullying in*

American schools: A social-ecological perspective on prevention and intervention (pp. 1–12). Mahwah, NJ: Erlbaum.

Swearer, S. M., Grills, A. E., Haye, K. M., & Cary, P. T. (2004). Internalizing problems in students involved in bullying and victimization: Implications for intervention. In D. L. Espelage & S. M. Swearer (Eds.), *Bullying in American schools: A social-ecological perspective on prevention and intervention* (pp. 63–83). Mahwah, NJ: Erlbaum.

Unnever, J. D. (2005). Bullies, aggressive victims, and victims: Are they distinct groups? *Aggressive Behavior, 31*, 153–171.

Varjas, K., Meyers, J., Henrich, C. C., Graybill, E. C., Dew, B. J., Marshall, M. L. et al. (2006). Using a participatory culture-specific intervention model to develop a peer victimization intervention. *Journal of Applied School Psychology, 22*, 35–57.

Vernberg, E. M., & Gamm, B. K. (2003). Resistance to violence prevention interventions in schools: Barriers and solutions. *Journal of Applied Psychoanalytic Studies, 5*(2), 125–138.

Webster-Stratton, C., & Hammond, M. (1997). Treating children with early-onset conduct problems: A comparison of child and parent training interventions. *Journal of Consulting and Clinical Psychology, 65*, 93–109.

Webster-Stratton, C., & Reid, J. (2003). The Incredible Years parents, teachers, and children training series. In A. E. Kazdin & J. R. Wesiz (Eds.), *Evidence-based psychotherapies for children and adolescents* (pp. 224–240). New York: Guilford.

Webster-Stratton, C., Reid, J., & Hammond, M. (2001). Social skills and problem-solving training for children with early-onset conduct problems: Who benefits? *Journal of Child Psychology and Psychiatry and Allied Disciplines, 42*, 943–952.

Webster-Stratton, C., Reid, M. J., & Hammond, M. (2004). Treating children with early-onset conduct problems: Intervention outcomes for parent, child and teacher training. *Journal of Clinical Child and Adolescent Psychology, 33*, 105–124.

Whitted, K. S., & Dupper, D. R. (2005). Best practices for preventing or reducing bullying in schools. *Children & Schools, 27*, 167–175.

9

What Works in Bullying Prevention?

Wendy M. Craig, Debra J. Pepler, Ashley Murphy, and Heather McCuaig-Edge

Bullying is a relationship problem and is based on a power differential: children who bully are in a position of power relative to the children who are being victimized.* The power advantage of the children who bully can arise from many aspects of the relationship: a differential in size, strength, age, or social status; or from recognition of the other's vulnerabilities. Recent research is highlighting the issue of power dynamics in bullying. Some children who bully are popular, have high status within their peer groups, and have significant social control within their groups (Xie, Cairns, & Cairns, 2004). As bullying unfolds over time, the power differential between the children who bully and those who are being victimized increases and consolidates. As bullying continues and the power differential consolidates, victimized children may become increasingly vigilant and sensitive to subtle bullying behaviors. Consequently, it becomes more and more difficult for victimized children to extract themselves from a bullying relationship because they lack the power to shift the dynamics in the relationship and to put a stop to this form of abuse. Children involved in either bullying or victimization require intervention because this combination of power and aggression underlies many problems related to interpersonal violence. There is a concern that the lessons learned in bullying within peer relationships at school will carry over to other relationships as children move through adolescence and into adulthood.

Bullying can be best understood as a relationship problem that requires relationship solutions (Pepler, Jiang, Craig, & Connolly, 2008). Because bullying is a dynamic interaction that unfolds and consolidates over time, interventions are required to disrupt the processes that maintain the interactions and to enable

---

*We avoid using labels such as "bully," "victim," and "bully/victim." Through our research, we have come to recognize that bullying unfolds within the context of relationships, in part, as a function of group dynamics, rather than arising solely from an individual's personal characteristics or stable traits.

individual children to move out of this destructive relationship. Children who bully require interventions to develop understanding and reduce their tendencies to use power aggressively. They require formative, rather than punitive, consequences—interventions that not only provide a clear message that bullying is unacceptable but also build awareness, skills, empathy, and insights, and provide youth with alternatives to bullying. Children who are victimized require interventions to protect them from peer abuse and to enable them to establish positive relationships within their peer groups. Interventions that address the relationship problems of children who bully and those who are victimized are necessary, but not sufficient. To promote positive relationships, all children involved in bullying incidents, perpetrators, victimized youth, as well as bystanders, must be included in bullying interventions. The relationship solutions need to extend beyond the students, themselves, to include relationships with teachers, within the family, and in the community. In this chapter, we review the prevention programs to identify what works in preventing and intervening in bullying and to determine the characteristics of successful programs.

Theoretical and Research Framework for Bullying Interventions

Interventions to address bullying must be grounded in a strong theoretical and research framework. As emerging research in the field of bullying reveals the complexity of the problem, the theoretical framework reflects a focus on developmental and systemic perspectives. The underlying causes of bullying and victimization must be considered from a developmental perspective that takes into account the individual characteristics of children, problems within the family, dynamics within the peer group, problems within the classroom and school, and problems in the broader community.

A Developmental Perspective

Through a developmental perspective, we recognize age-related changes in the salient issues and challenges that children and adolescents face, and in the relationships of importance to them. Both the individual child's behaviors, as well as the ways in which others react to the child, become consolidated and increasingly resistant to change with development. In choosing interventions for bullying, therefore, it is important that they be designed to meet the specific needs of girls and boys at different developmental stages.

A developmental perspective also highlights the need for early intervention: the earlier a problem is identified and addressed, the more likely that behaviors can be changed. The call for early intervention is particularly relevant for bullying and victimization. Without support, children who bully appear to learn how to use power and aggression to dominate others as they diversify in adolescence to use sexual harassment and dating aggression (Connolly, Pepler, Craig, & Taradash, 2000; McMaster, Connolly, Pepler, & Craig, 2002; Pepler, Madsen, Webster, & Levene, 2004). Children's experiences of being systematically victimized and stereotyped seldom consolidate or stabilize before ages 8 to 9 years (Goldbaum, Craig, Pepler, & Connolly, 2003). Therefore, intervention programs that focus on children in the early elementary grades may be able to prevent vulnerable children from developing social interactional patterns of bullying or from falling into a stable victim role from which it may be difficult to escape. Although early intervention is recommended, it is not sufficient: children need support for bullying problems throughout their school careers. There appears to be stronger positive effects on bullying problems among elementary school students compared with high school students. With age, interventions to reduce bullying become increasingly challenging for a number of developmental reasons:

- Younger children are generally more accepting of adults' authority, curriculum activities, and school policies.
- Younger students are generally more willing to talk to teachers and parents about bullying.
- Younger students are more trusting and confident that adults will be able to assist with bullying problems.
- Older students—especially those involved in bullying and other antisocial activities—may explicitly reject teacher influence and values advocated by the school. In some ways, therefore, it may be more difficult, but just as necessary, to intervene with older students.
- Students' empathy for and attitudes about victimized peers become somewhat more negative in adolescence, particularly among boys (Olweus & Endresen, 1998).

Given the developmental changes in childhood, interventions in elementary school cannot be expected to inoculate students for problems that arise in senior public and high schools. Therefore, support for children's relationship capacity is essential throughout the school years so that new bullying problems can be addressed as they emerge, rather than when they have become established behavior patterns, reputations, or roles. A developmental perspective of changes with age informs interventions in several ways:

- Early interventions prevent problems.
- The nature of bullying changes with age; consequently, how we intervene changes.
- Students rely on adults less with increasing age, as they develop skills and have an increased capacity to lead interventions (i.e., peer mediation in high school).

Boys' and Girls' Bullying

When considering interventions for bullying, it is important to understand the gender differences in the forms and contexts of aggression and bullying. Boys' aggressive behaviors often involve direct physical aggression, yelling, and assertion, with goals of establishing status and dominance (Cairns & Cairns, 1994). In contrast, girls tend to use indirect aggression that involves hostile acts which unfold in the context of social relationships—for example, gossiping and manipulating others to exclude a victim (Crick & Grotpeter, 1995; Underwood, 2003).

Data from Canadian students in the Health Behaviors in School Children Survey reflect these patterns of gender differences in victimization. According to the children who reported being bullied by others, significantly more girls than boys reported being teased (79% versus 67%) and having rumours spread about them (72% and 63%, respectively). The prevalence of these forms of victimization did not significantly decrease with age. In contrast, significantly more boys (approximately 45%) were likely to report physical victimization compared to girls (approximately 21%). In general, boys and girls report being victimized at relatively similar rates, suggesting that gender may not be a risk factor for victimization (Craig & Harel, 2004). In designing and implementing programs to address bullying, it is important to recognize the differences in the forms and dynamics of boys' and girls' bullying. For example, girls' social bullying such as gossip and exclusion is difficult to detect. Girls tend to have more favorable attitudes about victimized peers. Girls have prosocial orientations and are more willing to take a role in defending victimized children.

An understanding of the general age and gender patterns in social interactions in general and in bullying, in particular, informs choices about the nature and timing of general interventions. There are, however, substantial differences among children in their involvement in bullying problems. It is essential, therefore, to consider individual children's needs when developing and implementing an intervention for bullying problems.

Matching Level of Risk to the Intensity of Interventions

In terms of bullying and victimization, children vary in their risk for involvement. Through our research and that of others, we have identified three groups of children who are either bullied or victimized, or both, and require varying intensities of intervention (Fig. 9.1). The first includes children who are relatively uninvolved in bullying or victimization (approximately 75%–80%). These children may be negatively influenced when they form the peer group that watches bullying. The second group includes children who are occasionally involved in bullying or victimization (approximately 10%–15% of children). The third group consists of children who are frequently involved in bullying or victimization (more than twice a week) or have a stable involvement over time (approximately 5%–10% of children). These children experience the most serious problem behaviors, and these problems are relatively stable over time.

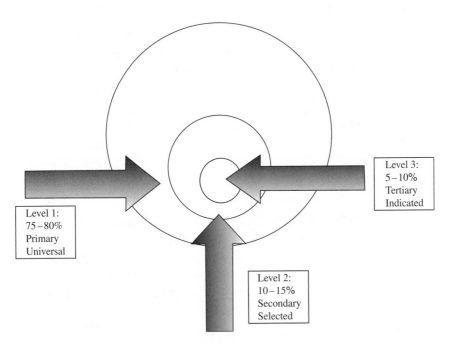

Figure 9.1 Matching intensity of intervention to the level of risk for bullying and victimization.

Some of these children may be especially at risk if they both bully others and are victimized themselves.

These three groups of children require different levels of intervention to address their problems. These levels of risk provide direction for the nature and intensity of interventions for bullying and victimization. The outside circle in Figure 9.1 represents those children who are not involved in bullying and victimization—the group with the lowest risk for associated problems. For the majority of peers who are uninvolved in bullying, a primary prevention or universal program directed at developing awareness of bullying and empowering children to intervene on behalf of victims will likely be sufficient.

The intermediate circle represents those children who have transient involvement and who experience problems at the times when they are involved in bullying or victimization. Children involved in bullying infrequently or in a transitory way will benefit from a secondary prevention or selected program specifically designed to address and prevent the developmental continuity of these peer relationship problems. These children may exhibit early warning signs that indicate risk for future involvement in bullying and/or victimization. Teachers or parents of children involved in bullying and/or victimization problems may recognize some warning signs. Individual and social relationship difficulties may signal an increased risk for becoming involved in bullying or victimization, as well as risk for experiencing chronic and stable bullying or victimization. For example, high rates of sexual harassment perpetration and victimization by peers are warning signs that students may later begin to perpetrate bullying (Pepler et al., 2006). Internalizing problems, such as depression and anxiety, are warning signs that students may become victimized at a later point in time (Goldbaum et al., 2003). Victimized students often have friendships that lack affection and emotional support. Therefore, interventions that build friendships and peer support would increase the likelihood of peer intervention in bullying.

Children in the innermost circle of Figure 9.1 experience the highest rates of bullying and victimization as well as associated emotional, behavioral, and social problems. When children engage in bullying others, they report high levels of aggression, externalizing problems, and delinquency (Goldbaum et al., 2003). When children are being victimized, they also report high levels of internalizing problems, such as anxiety and somatization problems, as well as problematic relationships (Goldbaum et al., 2003). For these troubled children, an intensive tertiary or indicated intervention is required that focuses not only on the serious emotional, psychological, physical, educational, and social adjustment difficulties that these children experience but also on their relationship problems within significant social systems, such as the family, peer group, school, and community.

A thorough assessment is the first step in determining how to tailor interventions for students who are seriously at risk due to bullying and/or victimization. The interventions to support these children can be drawn from empirically validated programs that address these specific problems. In addition, and perhaps more important, it is the moment-to-moment interactions that at-risk children have with their teachers, fellow students, parents, and others that help them develop skills for positive relationships. In the course of a day, there are many teachable moments when problems appear to be developing or when they arise. A few moments of support at critical teachable moments may enable children to develop skills and understanding so that they can move beyond their involvement in bullying and/or victimization. The small group of high-risk children often have needs that require more support and more intensive interventions than a school can provide. For these children, it is critical to join with parents and link with community agencies that provide mental-health services to children and their families.

Systemic Perspective

Bullying problems extend beyond the children who bully and who are victimized. The systemic perspective highlights the need for changes in awareness and behavior strategies not only for those children who are directly involved but also for their peers, their teachers, their parents, and beyond in the broader community. Since the first efforts in Norway, interventions for bullying problems have focused broadly on systemic change.

Peers

The systemic perspective focuses on the social dynamics surrounding bullying. Research has highlighted the central role of peers in bullying: they serve both to reinforce and perpetuate bullying problems and to defend victimized students (Hawkins, Pepler, & Craig, 2001; O'Connell, Pepler, & Craig, 1999). Therefore, interventions must occur within the classroom and be broad in scope to promote positive interactions and social experiences of all children. Interventions to counter the peer processes that exacerbate bullying focus on supporting positive interactions, discouraging bullying, promoting empathy for victimized children, and encouraging children to intervene in bullying. These efforts to promote positive interactions must extend to areas outside of the classroom where bullying is likely to occur, such as the playground, halls, washrooms, and the lunchroom. The systemic perspective not only highlights the need to reshape the behaviors and attitudes of peers but also sheds light on the need for change among adults, such as teachers and parents, who are essential in supporting children involved in bullying and/or victimization.

School Staff

Teachers are the critical agents of social change in bullying programs. They have an essential role in creating a collaborative and respectful classroom climate, in managing their classrooms effectively, in promoting open communication about bullying issues, and in responding in a sensitive and supportive manner to the children involved in bullying. An education or teacher training opportunity will promote awareness of bullying problems and the importance of positive relationships for learning. With training, teachers are able to recognize the problems of bullying more readily and to intervene early to make a difference in bullying problems before they become part of the classroom fabric.

Together, principals and teachers are key to achieving success in school-based interventions for bullying. These adults are responsible for creating a school climate that discourages bullying and encourages students to support and include vulnerable children. The important roles of teachers and principals are highlighted in intervention research:

- Principals' commitment to allocate time and resources to bullying-related activities appears to be associated with improvements (Olweus, 2004).
- Teachers are the key agents of change with regard to adoption and implementation of the Olweus Bullying Prevention Program in school (Olweus, 2004).
- Teachers who participate in a bullying prevention program feel more confident about handling bullying problems, have more supportive attitudes about victims, and feel more positively about working with parents regarding bullying problems (Alsaker, 2004).
- The extent to which a school-based program is taken up and implemented is related to the degree of improvement in bullying indicators (Salmivalli, Kaukiainen, Voeten, & Sinisammai, 2004).

The majority of bullying interventions begin with a whole-school policy that defines the problem and the roles and responsibilities of all those in the school community. Bullying interventions that involve the whole school focus not only on reducing bullying problems but also promote caring and respectful relationships in a positive school climate. The organization of elementary and high schools influences the extent to which the recommended interventions components pertaining to the teachers' and principal's involvement can be effectively implemented. In terms of the whole-school approach and the focus on enhancing relationships among all members of the school community, there are advantages in the smaller context of elementary schools compared to high schools as follows:

- The organizational structure of large middle and secondary schools creates distance between the principal and students.
- The rotational system for classes makes it difficult for teachers to be familiar with the strengths and challenges of individual students.
- Unless students have a trusting relationship with an adult at school (e.g., teacher, counselor), they will be reticent to come forward to report their own or others' experiences of bullying.
- Without the opportunity to observe and interact with the same students throughout the school day, it is more difficult for teachers to detect and intervene in bullying problems.
- Large schools tend to be organized by grade groupings rather than by class, making whole-school processes more difficult to promote effectively (Arora, 1994).

Family

A systemic perspective also focuses on the family as a primary context in children's lives. In developing school-based interventions for bullying, parents are essential partners. Parents of victimized children are often aware of their children's distressing experiences long before the school recognizes the problem. Parents can raise their concerns with teachers and participate in finding ways to support their children in social interactions. Parents of children who bully are also important in the interventions; however, they may not be as easy to engage. Talks with the parents of children who bully have been an essential element of the Norwegian programs (Olweus, 1993), as well as other interventions.

Although bullying problems occur most frequently at school, bullying is not just a school problem. Bullying can unfold in any context where children and youth come together. To enhance the potential for change, connections with the community can be established to extend an understanding of bullying and to promote consistent responses to bullying problems throughout the broader community. Community partners and resources can also be drawn in to support schools in meeting the needs of its most vulnerable students.

In summary, the systemic perspective provides direction for the design and implementation of programs to address bullying. It highlights the importance of involving all contexts where students interact with others:

- Peers, who play a central role in bullying
- Teachers and principals, whose commitment is essential for a successful program
- All members of a school because caring and respectful relationships within school are critical to preventing bullying
- Communities and parents because partnerships beyond the school reinforce the goals of a school-based bullying intervention program

Building on Past Research

Rigby (2002) conducted a meta-analysis of the only 13 published studies evaluating the effectiveness of bullying programs. Rigby's review highlighted the limited data on the effectiveness of bullying programs, especially in the younger age groups where bullying is more prevalent. Only one of the studies he reviewed included a sample of kindergarten students, and only four focused on primary students. The majority of evaluation studies indicated a significant decrease in bullying, and a few indicated substantial reductions in bullying behavior following the implementation of a bullying program. The most substantial decreases were reported by Olweus in Bergen, Norway, where there was a 50% reduction in bullying (Olweus, 1991). In contrast, other researchers have provided evidence of little or no positive change, as in the Toronto study by Pepler, Craig, Ziegler, and Charach (1994) or even negative change, as in the evaluation conducted by Roland (1989) in the Rogaland area of Norway. In Rigby's review, he noted that most intervention studies had a reduction in bullying that was considerably lower than Olweus's benchmark of 50%.

The primary outcome for most studies was a general measure of bullying rather than measures that addressed specific types of bullying. An exception is the Alsaker's study in Bern with kindergarten children where outcome measures included physical and verbal aggression. With this early intervention, physical forms of bullying decreased more readily than verbal forms. Rigby (2002) noted that programs were more effective for younger children compared to older children (secondary school). The meta-analysis revealed inconsistent results when comparing outcomes for boys and girls. Rigby (2002) suggested that the inconsistency may reflect the possibility that long-term outcomes differ for boys and girls.

At this point in time, there is fairly consistent evidence from evaluations conducted in many countries that bullying problems can be reduced significantly by well-planned, comprehensive, school-wide intervention programs. Reductions in bullying, however, tend to be relatively modest. Furthermore, effects may be specific, as in the Bernese kindergarten study where physical bullying was lowered but levels of verbal bullying did not change.

Research on effective bullying, aggression, and violence programs reveals a trend for multilevel interventions. They included complementary components directed at different levels: the school community, the classroom, and intensive interventions for individual students involved in incidents of bullying. Rigby identified key elements in successful interventions, including the following:

- Education and training to increase awareness of the problem
- A "whole-school approach" whereby the resources of the whole school community, including parents, teachers, and students, are coordinated in a systematic manner
- A school curriculum with lessons and activities to help children develop knowledge, attitudes, and skills to deal more effectively with issues of bullying
- Providing students with social skills, such as conflict resolution, to enhance the likelihood they will help others
- Developing strategies and skills to deal effectively with individuals involved in bully–victim problems
- Working cooperatively with parents

Despite the similarity in the content of the programs reviewed by Rigby, he identified the important factor of commitment to program implementation as a key factor related to positive outcomes. For example, Eslea and Smith (1998) reported a substantial correlation between rated staff involvement in applying the program and the reduction of bullying.

A Review of Bullying Prevention Programs

A primary goal for this chapter was to review the current literature on bullying programs to identify key components of successful programs. To this end, we systematically evaluated bully intervention programs reported in outcome studies based on "model program" criteria as suggested by the Center for the Study and Prevention of Violence (2004). The highest standard that prevention programs can reach is that of the "model program." According to the Center for the Study and Prevention of Violence's Blueprints website, model programs are evidence-based prevention programs. They are developed on an *experimental or scientific basis* and must include *evidence of a deterrent effect.* Blueprints also require proof of *sustained effects, multiple site replication, analyses of mediating factors, and proof of cost-effectiveness.* A slightly different set of criteria was suggested by Roberts and Hinton-Nelson (1996). According to these researchers, the first common characteristic of a good model program is being founded upon *a theoretical framework,* as well as providing *theoretical evidence about how the program should improve the problem.* Model programs are *systemic* in nature; they include *collaboration with a variety of specialized services,* which reduce barriers to access for children and adolescents at risk. Finally, model programs provide *detailed information about program monitoring and outcome data so that replication is possible* and assistance is available.

Method

As a first step, we conducted a search of empirical studies, review articles, books, and book chapters through PsycInfo, the Queen's University library catalogue system, cross-references, and Google. We used keywords such as *bullying, intervention, prevention,* and *school.* Results from these searches were reduced by sources that did not specifically address an intervention or prevention program for bullying (e.g., programs for generally aggressive behavior or violence without any mention of bullying). This research search identified 48 programs aimed at reducing bullying. These programs are described in Table A.1 of the Appendices.

Following a compilation and description of the intervention programs, we developed summary tables to display key information on the scientific merit, program content, and program implementation for each prevention or intervention program. These data are presented in Tables A.2, A.3, and A.4 for bullying. The information identified for each of the summary tables was based on the criteria for model programs. In an effort to operationalize and delineate the common characteristics of model programs, we created a list of criteria and had colleagues review these criteria. Each of the interventions was given a rank for its scientific merit (Table A.2), program content (Table A.3), and a separate rating for implementation (Table A.4). The overall score for scientific merit was based on the sum of the following scores: multisite interventions, a control group, a follow-up, multiple informants, random assignment, sample size, measurement, systemic outcomes, tailoring the intervention, and a lack of experimenter bias. The overall score for program implementation was based on the sum of the following scores: manual, training, and who delivered the program. The scoring system is fully described in the Appendices.

Results

The present review of bullying intervention programs included 48 documented evaluated interventions, substantially more than Rigby's 2002 review. The larger number reflects two trends: there has been a proliferation of interest in interventions to address bullying; and we have cast a wider net, with less stringent criteria than Rigby, in order to be comprehensive in our review. In interpreting the data, we try to differentiate between those programs that had rigorous scientific evaluations and those that did not have a rigorous methodology. Another challenge in conducting this review was the lack of critical information in the reports of intervention evaluations. To overcome the missing data, we based our percentage calculation on the data that were available by including only those programs that identified an element. We caution the reader that there may be an undetectable bias in the reporting: missing information may be essential in differentiating the successful and unsuccessful programs.

Of the 48 studies, 23 (48%) reported only positive results reducing bullying and victimization; 2 (4%) reported only negative results; 12 (25%) reported mixed results (e.g., some positive effects and some negative effects; 7 (15%) reported no change; and 4 studies (8%) did not include specific data about reductions in bullying and victimization. Thus, the majority of programs are successful at reducing bullying and victimization at school. Across all 48 interventions, 35 (73%) programs had some positive results; 23 (48%) showed a reduction in bullying (8 no data); 16 (33%) showed a positive outcome for victimization (13 no data); 12 (25%) showed a positive result on school climate (15 no data). There are several conclusions that can be drawn from these results. First, it is better to have a bullying prevention program than not to have one. Consequently, all schools need a program to address bullying and victimization. Some programs can have unintended effects; for example, they can make the problem worse. To ensure programs are having the desired positive impacts, programs need to be evaluated.

In the next sections, we describe the features of the 48 programs and compare successful programs with those programs that were unsuccessful with respect to a developmental and systemic perspective, matching individual needs to the intervention, program implementation, and scientific merit. We believe that both successful and unsuccessful programs provide opportunities to identify what works in bullying prevention programs. Much can be learned about intervention failures as well as from intervention successes. It is often difficult to ascertain the full spectrum of intervention successes and failures from the published research because when programs have no effect or a negative effect, there is a tendency to not publish the negative or null results. Several of the studies that showed negative results for this chapter were published in a recent book that provided an overview of the major anti-bullying interventions in 11 countries (Smith, Pepler, & Rigby, 2004). Within these chapters, authors were encouraged to reflect on both successes and failures in programs designed to reduce bullying. We can learn from these reflections. Table 9.1 summarizes features of the intervention programs, including the grade level that the program was directed to, the type of intervention, the components of the intervention, the aspects of the systemic perspective that were addressed, the implementation, and the scientific merit of the research on the program. These features are shown for all programs: successful programs, unsuccessful programs, the top six programs (in terms of measured outcomes), and promising programs (those ranked 7–10 in measured outcomes).

Scientific Merit

We present the data on scientific merit first because we believe it provides a necessary frame to interpret the results presented in Table 9.1. From the mean scientific score, it is evident that the most successful programs (those in the top five) had the highest scores on scientific merit. The top 10 programs scored higher on scientific merit compared to the average of all programs. These results support the notion that evaluating programs in a rigorous empirical manner adds strength to the intervention and provides the data needed to highlight the success of the program. Evaluation of programs can support the sustainability of the programs, through highlighting their successes. More

Table 9.1
Summary of 48 Bullying Prevention Programs

	All Interventions (48)	Successful (25)	Unsuccessful (2)	Top Six Programs	Promising Programs (Ranked 7–10)
Developmental Level					
Elementary	66.7%*	68%	100%	100%	100%
Intermediate	40%*	36%	N/A	83%	25%
High school	31%*	20%	N/A	50%*	25%
Scope of Intervention					
Universal	88%	84%	100%	100%	75%
Secondary or tertiary	21%	16%	N/A	0%	25%
Individual Support					
Cognitive	65%	80%	50%	83%	100%
Social	81%	80%	50%	83%	100%
Emotional-behavioral	65%	64%	100%	100%	50%
Systemic Perspective					
Peers/classroom	83%	72%	100%	100%	75%
Teacher training	65%	68%	50%	100%	50%

(continued)

Table 9.1
(Continued)

	All Interventions (48)	Successful (25)	Unsuccessful (2)	Top Six Programs	Promising Programs (Ranked 7–10)
Parent involvement	33%	28%	50%	50%	25%
Community involvement	15%	8%	50%	50%	50%
Implementation					
Length	1.5 hours–ongoing (10-year project)	1.5 hours–ongoing	18 months–3 years	12 weeks–ongoing (10-year project)	14 weeks–18 months
Delivered by educators	67%	72%	100%	83%	100%
Training for facilitators	81%	84%	100%	100%	100%
Manual	42%	48%	50%	83%	25%
Assessment integral	48%	48%	50%	83%	100%
Maintenance plan	31%	24%	0%	67%	25%
Mean scientific merit score	8.11	8.28	**	13.33	10.25

Note: Five programs were designed to target two out of three levels.

* Seven programs were designed for all three levels.

** Missing data represent only two programs; therefore, this may not be representative of all unsuccessful programs. N/A, not applicable.

importantly, it enables consumers and professionals implementing the program to know what works and what does not work, despite perhaps good intentions. This review clearly indicates that programs can have positive as well as negative effects. If we are to implement a program in schools it is essential to know that it works. It is not enough to have a program; we need to have effective programs. Furthermore, many programs reported reducing problems, but they lacked scientific rigor. Consequently, the results from some of the reviewed programs may not have strong validity. Nonetheless, in designing evaluations, some organizations may require a new partnership with researchers that can provide expertise in program evaluation and design. By evaluating programs before they are implemented, at the end of the program, and at regular intervals we can ensure the program effects are maintained over time.

Developmental Processes

The majority of programs were designed to be implemented in elementary schools. Intermediate and high schools are underrepresented regarding programs for bullying and victimization. Traditionally, researchers and educators have not examined bullying beyond the elementary school years. Given the mounting evidence that suggests that bullying is a problem for students of all ages, there is a need to develop more programs for older students. Of those elementary programs that reported results, 17 (35%) had positive results, 2 (4%) had negative results, 6 (13%) had mixed results, and 4 (8%) had no change. Among the programs aimed at intermediate students, 8 (17%) were successful at reducing bullying and victimization and 0 (0%) had negative effects (5 [10%] had mixed effects and 4 [8%] had no change). Among the high school programs, 5 (10%) were successful, 0 (0%) have negative results, and 6 (13%) reported no change (2 [4%] had mixed results, but these were programs aimed at all levels). Interestingly, while the majority of programs were aimed at the elementary school–aged students, programs in the intermediate level were more successful. Similarly, elementary school–based programs were more likely to report negative effects. High school programs were the most likely to report no change, perhaps indicating that by high school the problems are stable and may require more intensive interventions. In addition, many of the high school programs were based on peer interventions or were led by the peer group. While this type of intervention is developmentally appropriate, bullying is fundamentally about a power differential. Hence, it is essential for adults to intervene and potentially lead (or guide) interventions in order to address this power differential. That is, even peer-led interventions require adult support and leadership. Finally, some of the programs implemented interventions through all the grades. In some cases there were positive effects in the younger grades and negative effects in the older grades (e.g., Stevens, De Bourdeauhuij, & Van Oost, 2000; Peterson & Rigby, 1999), highlighting the need for developmentally sensitive evaluations.

Gender Perspective

In our review, we did not find any program that was gender specific (i.e., boys and girls received the same intervention). In addition, three studies reported results that varied by gender. Eslea and Smith (1998) reported negative results for girls. On the other hand, Olweus and Endresen (1998) found more substantial reductions in girls' rather than boys' bullying. Similarly, Rahey and Craig (2002) found more positive effects of the bullying prevention program for girls. With the exception of these three studies, these results indicate that the underlying processes involved in bullying and victimization are similar for boys and girls. The research, however, indicates that the form and the content of the bullying may differ by gender. Consequently, while there is not a need for gender-specific bullying prevention programs, the educational content of bullying programs must address all forms of bullying to increase awareness of both boys' and girls' bullying.

Systemic Perspective

The vast majority of programs had a comprehensive model that involved individuals, peers, teachers, and classrooms. A systemic approach to intervention ensures that students, peers, parents, and educators have the same understanding and approach to intervention. On the school yard, on the bus, in the hallways, and in the bathrooms, bullying is responded to in the same way. As a consequence, the effect of the program is felt on many different levels and systems in which the student interacts. Interestingly, our review indicates that the majority of both the successful and unsuccessful programs have many of the elements that are recommended as key features based on the developmental-systemic perspectives. In fact, there appear to be few differences in the components of the programs with evaluations published or posted on websites. In some respects, it is reassuring to find such consistency in the bullying prevention programs being implemented around the world. There were however, two notable differences.

One of the differences between our top 10 successful and the unsuccessful programs was the involvement of parents. Four of our top 10 programs included a parent component in their programs compared to only 50% of the unsuccessful programs. Parents are an integral part of preventing bullying and the first step is to provide education on several key points.

The first is recognizing that bullying is a significant problem for children. Adults' attitudes may mitigate against interventions. When adults assume that "bullying is just a normal part of growing up" or that "bullying isn't serious— it's just kids being kids," then they are less likely to intervene. The second involves the subtlety and power differential in bullying. It is often difficult to detect and address. Sometimes adults are not able to determine whether a behavior is "unwelcomed" in children's and adolescents' interactions. A third is information on the ways in which children obtain power. Adults often fail to recognize the ways in which children have acquired power over others. Children who have power and choose to use it aggressively usually recognize that adults do not approve of aggressive behavior and develop a diverse repertoire of behaviors to avoid detection. A bully–victim relationship develops over time: each time a bully is successful in causing distress to the victimized individual, the bully gains in relative power and the victim loses power in the relationship. When bullying has unfolded over weeks or months, the aggressive individual need only gesture subtly to communicate that the other should be fearful of what might ensue. Adults seldom recognize these subtle gestures as aggressive behaviors. It is important, therefore, that adults observe and listen carefully to children when they express concerns about bullying.

Fourth, parents must recognize and respond to the dynamics of bullying in order to support the children who are victimized. The power differential that is consolidated through multiple repeated bullying episodes eventually renders victims powerless to defend themselves. Children who are bullied respond in the best way that they can each time they are victimized (e.g., they ignore, walk away, state their annoyance, use humor, seek others to play with, etc.). If these responses are successful, the bullying generally stops. For some children in some situations, none of the strategies they try is adequate to deter the aggressor, who gains power and often excitement from the repeated bullying attacks. When children are totally defeated and frustrated by the ongoing bullying, they may finally reach out to an adult for help. If that adult dismisses the report (e.g., "Your glasses are fine," "You are not fat or stupid") and tells the child to solve the problem him or herself (e.g., "Tell them to leave you alone," "Just ignore them"), the adult has failed to provide the essential protection and support for the child's safety. Finally, parents need to know how to advocate for their children in addressing bullying problems.

A second difference between the successful and unsuccessful programs was the involvement of communities. Over a third of the successful programs included a community component, whereas none of the unsuccessful programs reported any form of community involvement. Furthermore, our top 10 programs had the highest percentages of community involvement. We have argued that bullying is not only a school problem but a community issue. The importance of community involvement reflects Roberts and Hinton-Nelson's (1996) contention that model programs should include *collaboration with a variety of specialized services*, which reduce barriers to access for children and adolescents at risk. The potential for influence in the school–community connection is bi-directional. As recommended by Roberts and Hinton-Nelson, the community agencies that serve children and their families may have offered essential support to the schools in their efforts to reduce the problems of bullying and victimization. Thus, because the successful bullying prevention programs were more likely to have community involvement, they likely were more able to connect with community agents to provide extra support for the at-risk kids. In addition or alternatively, the schools may have successfully reached out to the community and sought to raise awareness and consistency in responses to bullying in the broader neighborhood.

Matching Level of Risk to the Intensity of Intervention

Eighty-eight percent of all bullying prevention programs were universal, that is, they targeted all children in the school. Of the universal programs, many had components that also worked with the high-risk children (e.g., Conduct Problems Prevention Research Group, 2002; Olweus & Endresen, 1998; Rahey & Craig, 2002). However, there was limited information on the nature of interventions with individual children experiencing bullying or victimization problems. As indicated in Figure 9.1, not all children require the same level of intensity. Of the tertiary interventions, 67% of them were successful at reducing bullying or victimization in the target population and 33% had mixed results. None of the unsuccessful programs targeted the individual children who regularly experience bullying and victimization. Thus, the unsuccessful program did not include program components that matched the level of risk to the intensity of intervention. Children who are regularly involved in bullying and victimization need more support, protection, and training in relationship skill building. Without intervention the problems of these students will likely increase over time. Currently, there are limited mechanisms in schools to enhance their relationship capacities. The current mechanisms to address the issues of at-risk children who bully are not based on developing relationship skills; instead, schools use suspensions to punish these children, which further isolates them from their peers.

The majority of all changes involved addressing social behavior. The successful programs, however, were more likely to include cognitive, social and emotional components (80%, 80%, and 64%, respectively) than unsuccessful programs (50%, 50%, and 100%). Interestingly, 7 out of the top 10 ranked programs included cognitive, social, and emotional-behavioral components, while 9 out of the top 10 programs included at least two of cognitive, social, and emotional-behavioral components. In other treatment research, cognitive-behavioral therapy is the most effective form of intervention (Quinsey, Skilling, Lalumière, & Craig, 2004). Changes in the way children think about bullying experiences may be needed in order to facilitate behavioral changes. These results suggest that preventing bullying involves addressing how students think, how they interact with others, and developing the behavioral and emotional skills that promote building relationship capacity and competencies.

Implementation

There are several key aspects to implementing a program. In order for others to replicate a bullying prevention program, it is essential to provide information about the program and how it is implemented. We coded several aspects of implementation: who delivers the program, training, manual, assessment, and maintenance plans. The majority of the programs were implemented by educators. Leadership from educators is important because it will ensure the longevity, continuity, and maintenance of the program over many school years. The majority of programs were more likely to have training for the facilitators versus unsuccessful, 84% and 100%, respectively. Training is essential in order to ensure that there is consistency in program delivery. Five out of the top 6 programs were more likely than the unsuccessful programs to have a manual that outlined the program. A manualized program will also ensure the integrity and consistency of the intervention. However, having a manualized treatment is necessary but not sufficient. The manual may provide guidance, lesson plans, and suggested activities, but successful bullying prevention programs need to go beyond the box. The lessons learned in the manual provide a foundation upon which educators can create a safe and caring classroom through their moment-to-moment interactions with students. Five out of the top 6 bullying prevention were more likely to include an assessment as integral to the implementation. Through an assessment it is possible to identify particular areas of concern regarding the intervention. Consequently, the intervention can be tailored to address problematic issues. Finally, there were significant differences between the successful and unsuccessful programs on the development of maintenance plans (24% vs. 0%, respectively). Maintenance plans are critical to ensuring the longevity of the program over time.

One of the observations from this review is that there was limited information concerning the process of implementation to determine how it is implemented and how thoroughly and consistently it was implemented. If we are to replicate successful programs, obtaining this data is critical. In addition to these data, we also were unable to code the motivation and understanding of educators. There is research to suggest that educators play a significant role in the effectiveness of bullying prevention programs. It may be that variables such as the motivation of educators may explain some of the differences between successful and unsuccessful programs. In a recent chapter, Olweus (2004) provides a careful analysis of factors affecting the implementation of his bullying program. He found the following five factors contributed to classroom intervention measures: perceived staff importance, teachers having read program information, teachers' perceptions of level of bullying in the class, teachers' own victimization during childhood, and effective teacher involvement in the program.

According to Olweus, "Teachers who saw themselves, their colleagues, and the schools as important agents of change for counteracting bully/victim problems among their students were more likely to involve themselves in anti-bullying efforts" (p. 26). He noted that this teacher characteristic also may reflect teachers' motivations and beliefs in their responsibility and their potential to reduce bullying problems through a systematic intervention. Teachers' concern and empathy for victimized children may also play a role in their efforts to address these problems.

In addition, Olweus (2004) reported on school-level predictors of intervention measures undertaken. He found three factors to be related: openness in communication among the teachers, school attention to bullying problems, and teacher–teacher collaboration (negatively associated). Although the patterns of effects were complex, Olweus made the interpretation that "Schools characterized by openness in communication among staff and a generally positive attitude to change were particularly likely to implement the program"

(p. 30). The negative influence of teacher–teacher collaboration was cautiously interpreted as perhaps a collective unwillingness to change school practices.

These requirements of educators are significant and consequently we need to ensure that educators are adequately trained to implement bully prevention programs. There is a pressing need for this type of education and training to occur during preservice teacher training in college education programs; such training cannot be left to the chance that a principal or school system will see fit to implement a program. Preservice teacher-training programs can inform teachers of the complex social dynamics in children's peer relations and create awareness of the social, emotional, and educational advantages of addressing these problems.

Implications for Schools

In this chapter we have presented a review of the current efforts to prevent and intervene in bullying at school. There are clear recommendations for schools from this review, including the following:

1. All schools need a program to address bullying and victimization.
2. Implementing school-based programs to reduce bullying and victimization is an effective strategy. Having a program is better than not having a bullying prevention program.
3. Programs need to be evaluated (because some have negative effects).
4. Evaluations are essential—before a program is implemented (for baseline), at the end of the program (for outcomes), and at regular intervals to ensure outcomes are maintained.
5. Bullying prevention programs need to be developmentally appropriate and implemented at all levels: primary, junior, intermediate, and high school.
6. Student leadership and involvement are critical in high school interventions, but adult guidance is also necessary.
7. Bullying prevention programs need an educational component that highlights the different form and content of bullying for students, staff, parents, and all adults.
8. Assessments of bullying and victimization should include all the ways in which boys and girls bully (physical, verbal, social, sexual harassment, dating aggression, Internet).
9. Effective bullying prevention programs comprise three levels of intervention: universal programs for the entire school population,

indicated programs for students in the early stages of involvement in bullying or victimization, and selected programs for those who have serious problems with bullying and/or victimization.

10. Prevention of bullying involves addressing how students think, how they interact with others, and developing the emotional and behavioral skills that promote relationship capacity and competencies.

11. The field needs a component and person-oriented analysis of bullying prevention programs to increase our understanding of what works for whom.

12. Parents are essential partners in bullying prevention programs. They are key advocates for their children; home-school communication strengthens the understanding and responses to bullying.

13. Collaboration with the community supports bullying prevention programs in schools.

14. Educators who implement bullying prevention programs require a manual, training, and ongoing support to promote healthy relationships among students.

15. Assessments provide critical information for tailoring programs to meet a school's needs.

16. Effective bullying programs last a minimum of 2 years. Promoting healthy relationships and reducing the use of power and aggression within a school is an ongoing process that depends on plans to maintain the program over time.

Conclusions

Bullying is a relationship problem that requires relationship solutions. Being safe in relationships is a fundamental human right. Every child and youth has the right to be safe and free from involvement in bullying. Understanding bullying as a destructive relationship problem provides important direction for interventions. Children and youth need help understanding that bullying is wrong, developing respect and empathy for others, and learning how to get along with and support others. Effective bullying prevention and intervention activities for children and youth enable them to develop the skills essential for healthy relationships. Promoting the development of healthy relationships for children and youth will, in turn, reduce the significant societal costs associated with bullying. These social costs of bullying extend beyond the individual and also impact society as a whole. Health problems due to bullying cause increased use of the health-care system; low school attainment raises educational costs; and criminality associated with bullying increases costs for the police and the justice and corrections systems (Pepler et al., 2008; Rigby, 2003). These costs are preventable and avoidable by reducing and mitigating the effects of the negative use of power and aggression in children's relationships. The patterns of using power and aggression through bullying, established in childhood, can have long-term impacts through adolescence and into adulthood. It is essential to identify children at risk for bullying and/or victimization and to provide support for their development and relationships.

Promoting relationships is everybody's responsibility because bullying occurs in all contexts where individuals come together to work and play. As the primary institution and a major socialization force in children's lives, schools play a leadership role in addressing bullying problems. In efforts to reduce bullying, however, schools need the supportive attitudes and responses of all systems in which children live: at home, in sports, in recreation centers, and in the neighborhood. By providing consistency across systems in the messages, responses, and supports to address bullying problems, we can promote healthy relationships for all children and youth.

References

Alsaker, F. D. (2004). Bernese programme against victimization in kindergarten and elementary school. In P. K. Smith, D. Pepler, & K. Rigby (Eds.), *Bullying in schools: How successful can interventions be?* (pp. 289–306). Cambridge, England: Cambridge University Press.

Arora, C. M. J. (1994). Is there any point in trying to reduce bullying in secondary schools? A two year follow-up of a whole-school anti-bullying policy in one school. *Association of Educational Psychologists Journal, 10,* 155–162.

Cairns, R. B., & Cairns, B. D. (1994). *Lifelines and risks: Pathways of youth in our time.* New York: Cambridge University Press.

Center for the Study and Prevention of Violence. (2004). *Blueprints model programs selection criteria.* Retrieved November 14, 2004, from the Center for the Study and Prevention of Violence website: http://www.colorado.edu/cspv/blueprints

Conduct Problems Prevention Research Group. (2002). The implementation of the Fast Track program: An example of large-scale prevention science efficacy trial. *Journal of Abnormal Child Psychology, 30,* 1–18.

Craig, W. M., & Harel, Y. (2004). Bullying, physical fighting and victimization. In C. Currie, C. Roberts, A. Morgan, R. Smith, W. Settertobulte, O. Samdal, et al. (Eds.), *Young people's health in context: International report from the HBSC 2001/02 survey.*

WHO Policy Series: Health policy for children and adolescents (Issue 4, pp. 133–144). Copenhagen, Denmark: WHO Regional Office for Europe.

Crick, N. R., & Grotpeter, J. K. (1995). Relational aggression, gender, and social-psychological adjustment. *Child Development, 66,* 710–722.

Connolly, J., Pepler, D., Craig, W., & Taradash, A. (2000). Dating experiences of bullies in early adolescence. *Child Maltreatment: Journal of the American Professional Society on the Abuse of Children, 5,* 299–310.

Eslea, M., & Smith, P. K. (1998). The long-term effectiveness of anti-bullying work in primary schools. *Educational Research, 40,* 203–218.

Goldbaum, S., Craig, W. M., Pepler, D., & Connolly, J. (2003). Developmental trajectories of victimization: Identifying risk and protective factors. *Journal of Applied School Psychology, 19,* 139–156.

Hawkins, D. L., Pepler, D. J., & Craig, W. M. (2001). Naturalistic observations of peer interventions in bullying. *Social Development, 10,* 512–527.

McMaster, L. E., Connolly, J., Pepler, D., & Craig, W. M. (2002). Peer to peer sexual harassment in early adolescence: A developmental perspective. *Development & Psychopathology, 14,* 91–105.

O'Connell, P., Pepler, D., & Craig, W. (1999). Peer involvement in bullying: Insights and challenges for intervention. *Journal of Adolescence, 22,* 437–452.

Olweus, D. (1991). Bully/victim problems among schoolchildren: Basic facts and effects of a school based intervention program. In D. J. Pepler, & K. H. Rubin (Eds.), *The development and treatment of childhood aggression* (pp. 411–448). Mahwah, NJ: Erlbaum.

Olweus, D. (1993). *Bullying at school: What we know and what we can do.* Malden, MA: Blackwell.

Olweus, D. (2004). The Olweus Bullying Prevention Programme: Design and implementation issues and a new national initiative in Norway. In P. K. Smith, D. Pepler, & K. Rigby (Eds.), *Bullying in schools: How successful can interventions be?* (pp. 13–36). Cambridge, England: Cambridge University Press.

Olweus, D., & Endresen, I. M. (1998). The importance of sex-of-stimulus object: Age trends and sex differences in empathic responsiveness. *Social Development, 7,* 370–388.

Pepler, D., Craig, W. M., Connolly, J. A., Yuile, A., McMaster, L., & Jiang, D. (2006). A developmental perspective on bullying. *Aggressive Behavior, 32,* 376–384.

Pepler, D. J., Craig, W. M., Ziegler, S., & Charach, A. (1994). An evaluation of an anti-bullying intervention in Toronto schools. *Canadian Journal of Community Mental Health, 13,* 95–110.

Pepler, D., Jiang, D., Craig, W., & Connolly, J. (2008). Developmental trajectories of bullying and associated factors. *Child Development, 79,* 325–338.

Pepler, D., Madsen, K., Webster, C., & Levene, K. (Eds.) (2004). *Development and treatment of girlhood aggression.* Mahwah, NJ: Erlbaum.

Peterson, L., & Rigby, K. (1999). Countering bullying at an Australian secondary school with students as helpers. *Journal of Adolescence, 22,* 481–492.

Quinsey, V. L., Skilling, T. A., Lalumière, M. L., & Craig, W. M. (2004). *Juvenile delinquency: Understanding the origins of individual differences.* Washington, DC: American Psychological Association.

Rahey, L., & Craig, W. M. (2002). Evaluation of an ecological program to reduce bullying in schools. *Canadian Journal of Counseling, 36,* 281–296.

Rigby, K. (2002) *A meta-evaluation of methods and approaches to reducing bullying in preschools and in early primary school in Australia.* Canberra, Australia: Commonwealth Attorney-General's Department.

Rigby, K. (2003). Consequences of bullying in schools. *Canadian Journal of Psychiatry, 48,* 583–590.

Roberts, M. C., & Hinton-Nelson, M. (1996). Models for service delivery in child and family mental health. In M. C. Roberts (Ed.), *Model programs in child and family mental health* (pp. 1–21). Mahwah, MJ: Erlbaum.

Roland, E. (1989) Bullying: the Scandinavian tradition. In D. P. Tattum & D. A. Lane (Eds.), *Bullying in schools* (pp. 21–32). Stoke-on Trent, England: Trentham Books.

Salmivalli, C., Kaukiainen, A., Voeten, M., & Sinisammai, M. (2004). Bullying in schools—How successful can interventions be? In P. K. Smith., D. Pepler, & K. Rigby. *Bullying in schools: How successful can interventions be?* (pp. 251–273). New York: Cambridge University Press.

Smith, P. K., Pepler, D., & Rigby K. (Eds.) (2004). *Bullying in schools: How successful can interventions be?* Cambridge, England: Cambridge University Press.

Stevens, V., De Bourdeaudhuij, I., & Van Oost, P. (2000). Bullying in Flemish schools: An evaluation of anti-bullying intervention in primary and secondary schools. *British Journal of Educational Psychology, 70,* 195–210.

Underwood, M. K. (2003). *Social aggression among girls.* New York: Guilford.

Xie, H., Cairns, B. D., & Cairns, R. B. (2004). The development of aggressive behaviors among girls: Measurement issues, social functions, and differential trajectories. In D. Pepler, K. Madsen, C. Webster, & K. Levene (Eds.), *Development and treatment of girlhood aggression* (pp. 103–134). Mahwah, NJ: Erlbaum.

PART III

STRATEGIES FOR IMPLEMENTING BEST PRACTICES

10

Empowering Schools to Prevent Bullying: A Holistic Approach

Anneliese A. Singh, Pamela Orpinas, and Arthur M. Horne

Reducing bullying in schools takes courage and vision—courage to initiate dialogues within schools about universal values of moral and character development, and vision to imagine that schools may be free of bullying behaviors. Bullying is defined as repeated and intentional acts of aggression within a context where the bully holds more power than the victim (Hoover & Oliver, 2007; Newman, Horne, & Bartolomucci, 2000; Olweus, 1993). Thus, we invite readers to recognize the complexity of school bullying and violence prevention. It is often tempting to address bullying as an individual problem and seek simple solutions: isolate the bullies, treat them, and expect that the school will improve as a whole. A commitment to reducing bullying across an entire school inherently translates into a comprehensive examination of school climate in a holistic manner, considering the roles students, staff, parents, and other community members have in reducing bullying.

The goal of this chapter is to discuss the role of empowerment in the process of preventing bullying, and to examine the difficult questions that researchers, policy makers, and administrators must ask about the whole school environment. This chapter is organized into five sections. The first section discusses the components of building a positive school climate and the role of school values in bullying prevention. The second section explores assessment issues in prevention of school bullying. The third section examines school violence prevention programs, including selection and implementation issues. The fourth section explores how models of youth empowerment may inform bullying reduction efforts in schools. The final section discusses future directions in facilitating positive school climates. Throughout the chapter, we will identify key questions that educators may ask when addressing school bullying through whole-school interventions as a way to empower key stakeholders within a school (e.g., students, families, teachers, administrators).

Positive School Climate

Best practices in bullying prevention do not merely seek to target individual students or solely focus on "nationally tested" program implementation, but rather aim to transform a school's climate and culture (Whitted & Dupper, 2005). A positive school climate "refers to the characteristics of the school—the quality of interactions among the members of the school community and the influence of the physical and aesthetic of the school community of the school building and its surroundings—that enhance learning and nurture an individual's best qualities" (Orpinas & Horne, 2006, p. 80). Therefore, it becomes important to ask the questions: Are there strong and meaningful relationships and connections among people in the school across statuses (e.g., student, teacher, administrator)? Is the school building an inviting structure? Do the school surroundings appear welcoming? Do school members enjoy being at school? Do students and educators feel motivated to excel in their learning and teaching activities?

As the previous definition of a positive school climate implies, the school climate is composed of several factors. Orpinas and Horne (2006), based on an extensive examination of theory, research, and practice, proposed the School Social Competence Development and Bullying Prevention Model (Fig. 10.1). This model has two components: the school climate and the students. The first component, a positive school climate, is composed of eight elements: excellence in teaching, school values that support respect for all, awareness of strengths and of problems, clear policies for bullying prevention and accountability of offenders, an environment that shows caring and respect, positive expectation for student learning, support for teachers, and a safe and inviting physical environment. The second component, students' social competence, is organized into six areas: awareness of bullying, handling of emotions, cognitive skills to manage conflict, character education that promotes positive values, other general social and academic skills, and support for mental health and learning abilities. Because school bullying prevention can feel overwhelming to address, schools may be tempted to view these negative behaviors solely on an individual level. This model's importance rests in its multiple components and inclusion of social competence—skills and behaviors that assist school community members in performing at their best in their interactions with others. Because bullying is a complex phenomenon, schools must evaluate what aspects of the school climate and of the students' behaviors are most relevant to how bullying manifests at their school. For instance, one school may have high levels of relational bullying among girls, while another school may

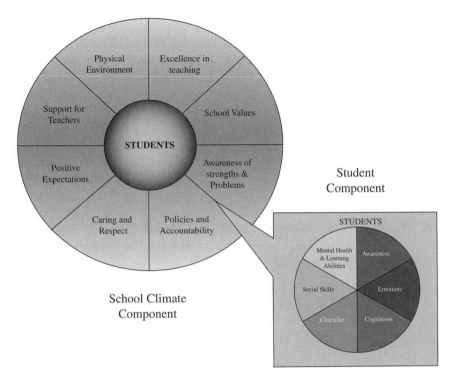

Figure 10.1 School social competence development and bullying prevention model.

have high levels of physical aggression as a consequence of gang rivalry. The model is a helpful reminder to understand and prevent bullying at a systemic level and at an individual level.

From this model, we will highlight two aspects that are first steps in creating this positive environment: examining the school values and its mission statement. These two components are particularly relevant for empowerment. When school members are empowered to identify a set of values guiding interpersonal relationships within a school and then establish a mission statement that reflects these shared school values, school-wide bullying interventions will become more effective. We discuss these important two components further below.

School Bullying: The Role of Universal Values

When building a positive school climate, administrators must pay specific attention to the role of school values. Violence prevention curricula are naturally designed to reduce bullying. However, they often are remiss in asking, What are the values that school community members (e.g., students, teachers, administrators, parents) hold as important? This is a critical question, yet many bullying prevention programs come from a top-down perspective, prescribing a "solution" for bullying without searching for the root causes of negative school behaviors. A program that focuses on empowerment takes a different approach, reflecting a value orientation of inclusion of all community members in prevention efforts. We use Zimmerman's (2000) definition of empowerment as he applies it to the *process* of community empowerment: "empowerment processes are ones in which attempts to gain control, obtain needed resources, and critically understand one's social environment are important" (p. 45).

From an empowerment perspective, the school community members first must examine the universal principles that may (or may not) be present or held by *all* of those within the school (e.g., students, families, teachers, administrators). Distinguishing between personal values and universal principles will help this process. There is a real difference between the personal values individuals hold (e.g., being a vegetarian versus being a meat eater) and universal principles (e.g., being honest is better than cheating) a school chooses to endorse. To exemplify this difference, a male parent of a middle school child who was skeptical and disdainful of the bullying prevention efforts said, "This is a dog-eat-dog world, and I want my son to be a dog-eater, not the one eaten." This statement demonstrates the tension that may exist between individual values ("I want my son to win") and collective school principles ("We want our school to be a safe for all children"). It also reminds us it may not be realistic to assume that *all* school and community members ascribe to the same beliefs due to differences in cultures and socialization processes. However, this same parent may be more likely to embrace the school value of collective safety if the parent is involved in the process of defining the school values or if the parent receives a clear explanation of how the school values pertain to his son. Ultimately, any initiative designed to empower school members to define a shared set of values will involve tension between competing sets of values.

Despite this tension, values shape our lives. Values are the guiding principles that govern our thoughts, emotions, and behaviors when no one else is looking (Sukiennik, Bendat, & Raufman, 2006). Values serve as monitors of accountability. Therefore, values are *the* place to begin when engaging in whole-school interventions with school bullying. We suggest three values that should be common to every school: *(1)* all children can learn, *(2)* all people deserve to be treated with dignity and respect, and *(3)* violence does not have a place in the school setting (Horne, Orpinas, Newman-Carlson, & Bartolomucci, 2004; Orpinas & Horne, 2006). School community members

Table 10.1
Questions That Guide the Identification of School Values

1. What values do we hold in this school?
2. Which values do we model?
3. If we had visitors for a day at this school, what values would they notice in practice? What values would they not see in practice?
4. What are our challenges, or growing edges, as a school?
5. When our youth leave school, what are the values we would like them to remember?

should engage in meaningful dialogues about what values they would like the school to embrace. Table 10.1 provides examples of questions to guide school community members to identify and develop their value system. These simple questions are often difficult to answer because of their large scope. Having this complex discussion and identification of values with key stakeholders within the school setting (e.g., students, parents, teachers, administrators, counselors) is a necessary and important first step to identify bullying behaviors. This system of values will pave the way for creating the school mission statement and, then, for developing a meaningful school bullying intervention.

School Mission Statements: Declaration of Values

Ideally, once the school members identify their values, the school community can declare its values in the form of a mission statement that sets the standard for a positive school environment (Sullivan, 2000). In actuality, schools' mission statements do not always assert the importance of a positive school environment. Ideally, the mission should emerge from school and community dialogues of shared universal values that they would like to promote. For example, Chimacum Middle School (Chimacum, Washington) developed the following mission statement:

> Chimacum Middle School is committed to high academic
> achievement and life skills development in a safe environment. We
> promote students' investment in realizing their potential by providing
> a variety of learning and teaching strategies, as well as assessment
> opportunities. Our school is a diverse family of learners, which
> provides a transitional bridge between elementary and high school.

Chimacum's mission statement accomplishes two critical goals that bullying prevention research has identified as important. First, it links students' school achievement and social skills development to a safe environment. Research has long noted the inverse relation between bullying and school achievement, that is, youth who feel safe at school will perform better academically (Barnes, Belsky, Broomfield, & Melhuish, 2006; Espelage & Swearer, 2003; Hahn et al., 2007; Orpinas & Horne, 2006; Whitted & Dupper, 2005). Second, the Chimacum Middle School's mission statement acknowledges the importance of celebrating diversity within the school "family." This recognition paves the way for the school to also acknowledge how the lack of understanding and embracement of diverse community members may be linked to school bullying (Hoover & Oliver, 2007). In achieving these two goals, the mission statement reflects the universal values of the school: values of school achievement, social skills development, safety, and diversity. However, Chimacum Middle School does not merely stop at its mission statement in identifying its goals. The school goes further to link this belief system to the importance of establishing a positive school climate:

> "Education is power" is our school-wide belief, and we work together on strengthening school climate! We offer all students a wonderful advisory program known as Eagle Time to help strengthen our school climate.

"Eagle Time" at Chimacum Middle School refers to an advisory program intended to build a positive school climate. In this program, an advocate is paired with individual students to track their academic progress, as well as to give them a "voice and choice" within the school setting, which empowers students. We will return to an exploration of youth empowerment later in the chapter, specifically in its relation to the reduction of bullying. The next section discusses the importance of assessing bullying behaviors, as well as the characteristics of the school climate that promote or hinder these behaviors.

Assessment: A Critical Step in Bullying Prevention

Because bullying is a complex set of behaviors and bullying characteristics may vary from school to school, taking a "one-size-fits-all" approach to prevention efforts is unlikely to work (Orpinas & Horne, 2006; Whitted & Dupper, 2005). The assessment of the types, characteristics, and consequences of bullying behaviors is necessary to develop meaningful solutions. Using multiple evaluation methods will more accurately help identify the types and levels of problem behaviors, as well as the individual and environmental factors that maintain those behaviors. Results of the evaluation can also help create awareness of the problem among some members of the community who may not see bullying as a "problem" in a school, but rather as a normal part of youth development (Bullock, 2002). In addition, school staff may not be aware of the extent of bullying within their schools, as much of these behaviors occur outside of adult supervision in hallways or bathrooms (Glover, Gough, Johnson, & Cartwright, 2000).

A comprehensive assessment of bullying perpetration and victimization will help define the magnitude of the problem, identify the characteristics of the problem, provide a baseline for evaluating the impact of interventions, and create an opportunity for empowerment, as it should include the many voices of stakeholders within the school. Additionally, information about the local context in which the school resides can provide valuable insights about ways that the local community is (or is not) addressing these types of negative social behaviors. For instance, the local community may have mental-health resources or organizations that address specific types of bullying (e.g., bullying related to sexual orientation).

In addition to being a critical component of the needs assessment, evaluation provides guidelines to ensure the success of school-wide programs designed to reduce school bullying. We should distinguish two types of evaluations: formative and summative. Formative evaluation is conducted during the development of an intervention or campaign to improve the efficacy and cultural relevance of its components. For instance, examine whether the program is reaching all members of the school (e.g., gender, race/ethnicity). Results from a formative assessment will help refine the program by strengthening its weaker aspects. Summative evaluation provides information about the efficacy of an anti-bullying program. For instance, a summative evaluation may encompass surveying students and teachers before and after a program is implemented to examine changes in bullying behavior, as well as focus groups conducted at the end of a program to assess participants' perception of its level of success.

Most assessments of school climate are quantitative in nature, using surveys to gather data on types and levels of bullying within a school (Cole, Cornell, & Sheras, 2006). Surveys have a number of benefits: students and other members of the community can complete the survey anonymously, and thus increase trustworthiness of responses; they can provide a voice to everyone; several surveys are available; and schools can easily evaluate the impact of their program. As with all evaluation methods, surveys do have some challenges: some surveys are not free, schools may not be able to set aside specific time within the academic schedule to conduct the survey, and schools may not have the resources to analyze the survey results.

A thorough compilation of available scales can be found in *Measuring Violence-Related Attitudes, Behaviors, and Influences among Youths: A Compendium of Assessment Tools* (Dahlberg, Toal, Swahn, & Behrens, 2005), a free document available at the website of the National Center for Injury Prevention and Control, Centers for Disease Control and Prevention (http://www.cdc.gov/ncipc). Researchers caution those using assessment scales to carefully examine whether the measures are appropriate to their local school culture (e.g., gender, race/ethnicity, sexual orientation, socioeconomic status) (Hoover & Oliver, 2007; Orpinas & Horne, 2006). They also advise using many different assessment tools to gather data on the diverse perspectives of students, teachers, and parents on school bullying.

Qualitative methods of data collection, such as focus groups or interviews, can provide the meaning and nuances of numbers. Focus groups can also provide a voice to students and, as such, increase a sense of connectedness to one another and to demonstrate that their voices are valued (Fetterman, 2001; Orpinas & Horne, 2006). In our research, students have consistently shared how important the focus groups were for them, as a way to share their thoughts and feelings about bullying. In addition, students have asked us for more time in the future where they may share their thoughts and feelings about their experiences in school. These experiences have led us to trust that youth need more spaces where they may connect with one another and with adults outside of a typical classroom or social setting. Table 10.2 provides sample questions to ask in evaluation focus groups.

An Empowerment Approach to Evaluation of Bullying Prevention Efforts

The ways evaluation could create empowering spaces for school community members, especially youth, has received little attention. Regardless of the methods

Table 10.2
Focus Group Questions That Create Empowerment

1. Are the key subgroups of our school represented in this focus group? If not, whose voices are missing and why?
2. What aspects of the bullying prevention efforts have been most effective?
3. What aspects of the bullying prevention efforts should be different or should be added?
4. How do the school and students support the role of an active bystander to interrupt bullying behaviors? What else can administrators, teachers, and students do?
5. What should the next steps in bullying prevention be in this school?

of evaluation, evaluation approaches that have an empowerment focus must support the self-determination of all school community members. Fetterman, who from a community psychology perspective coined the term "empowerment evaluation" (Fetterman, 1994, 2001; Fetterman & Haertel, 1990), defined self-determination of community members as:

> numerous interconnected capabilities, such as the ability to identify and express needs; establish goals or expectations and a plan of action to achieve them; to identify resources; to make rational choices from various alternative courses of action; to take appropriate steps to pursue objectives; to evaluate short- and long-term results, including reassessing plans and expectations and taking necessary detours and to persist in the pursuit of those goals. (Fetterman, 2001, p. 13)

Fetterman's description of empowerment evaluation highlights the importance of community participation; obtaining useful, meaningful data; and working with an external evaluator, who will facilitate the process. The external evaluator works in collaboration with a school to ensure all stakeholders in the school are included in the evaluation process, avoiding "group think" that may be holding schools back in their prevention efforts (e.g., "We know what works best for this school" or "Bullying will never go away in our school"). Most importantly, the external evaluator may help schools link their recent progress and/or challenges in bullying prevention efforts with long-term goals of building a positive school climate. Fetterman's empowerment evaluation process is not that different from what we have proposed in this chapter: (1) developing a mission statement that reflects the group's values; (2) listing, rating, and prioritizing problems (this rating will represent the baseline evaluation), as well as strategies or activities that should be accomplished; and (3) establishing plans for the future. The process continues with interim measures or feedback loops (similar to formative evaluation) and a second data point (similar to summative evaluation). Probably one of the strongest empowerment aspects of this process is the community participation in all steps in defining the problem and actions to solve it.

Violence Prevention Programs

The selection—and then implementation—of bullying prevention policies, programs, and strategies follow as natural steps after the school climate assessment. Most schools have a school discipline plan that creates guidelines and consequences for school violence (Hyman & Perone, 1998; Sugai &

Table 10.3
Assessing School Discipline Plans for a Bullying Prevention Focus

1. Does the school have policies for handling bullying? Does the policy include relational and verbal bullying?
2. Is the policy fairly applied to all students regardless of differences of societal status (e.g., race/ethnicity, gender)?
3. How are the voices of students, teachers, and families incorporated into the school discipline plan (e.g., student dialogues, teacher–family meetings, written feedback)?
4. What rules and consequences stated in the school discipline plan clearly display a value for a prevention focus (e.g., "What could have prevented this bullying behavior?")?
5. How can students communicate bullying behaviors in a safe, discreet way?
6. Does the administration take seriously all acts of bullying? Are students aware of it?

Horner, 2002). These plans, however, often focus on physical bullying (Hoover & Oliver, 2007), without specific attention to nonphysical acts, such as name-calling, intimidation, and newer forms of bullying such as cyber-bullying. Some schools, frequently mandated by state laws, have adopted "zero-tolerance policies" for violence-related behaviors, in hopes that instituting more severe consequences will reduce the targeted behaviors. These policies often have good intentions, but they may be problematic because they are a reaction to the problem rather than a method of prevention (Orpinas & Horne, 2006). Zero-tolerance policies have also been criticized for being applied unfairly across students, lacking data on their success, and limiting teachers' and administrators' ability to use their judgment when deciding on consequences (Orpinas & Horne, 2006; Skiba, 2000). Table 10.3 provides a list of questions regarding the school discipline plan to help assess the extent to which a school is building a school bullying prevention model into its disciplinary practices. We do endorse zero-tolerance policies for bullying; we do not endorse a one-size-fits-all system of consequences. Clear policies that support respectful school environments—and thus do not support bullying—are an important component in creating safe schools.

Implementation of Prevention Programs

A review of implementation research identified that the research on program implementation is not as strong as studies examining and identifying successful programs (Fixsen, Naoom, Blase, Friedman, & Wallace, 2005). A major reason for this gap in research is that rigorous implementation research can only be conducted once programs have been long established (Forgatch, 2003).

Therefore, although effective programs have been identified, information on how exactly these programs are successfully executed is lacking. In our experience researching whole-school programs that are successful, the school administration has made a commitment to prioritize prevention programs by ensuring that time and resources are invested into the program's implementation. For instance, rather than handing out teacher manuals on a prevention program, teachers should receive specific training where they could learn about the program's components. In this type of training, teachers could also be empowered to be active contributors to commenting on program components and effectiveness.

To increase the investment of school community members in program implementation, a focus on empowerment is important. This empowerment refers to the valuing of the key people who will be implementing a program through intentionally structuring time and opportunities to gather input and information on program implementation from them. Some view an empowerment approach to implementation as setting up obstacles to program implementation, as this type of approach requires an allotment of resources and time that schools may feel they cannot afford. In our experience, the opposite is true. Scheduling regular opportunities for program review during the implementation phase of a prevention program and taking the time to hear from the voices of those involved in implementing a program serve as a critical step to strengthening program effectiveness. In addition, such measures reveal where a school's values and priorities stand with regard to building a positive school climate and bullying prevention. Essentially, program selection and implementation is a *process* that does not happen overnight or with a simple manualized solution. Rather, effective bullying prevention programs happen over time with the commitment and investment of the people within the school.

Violence Prevention Programs

Research has demonstrated the value and effectiveness of whole-school prevention and intervention programs on school bullying (Hahn et al., 2007). Numerous violence prevention programs are available, but not all are efficacious, and many have differing levels of demonstrated efficacy. As stated previously, selection of a violence prevention program should follow a thorough qualitative and quantitative assessment of school bullying and should include the voices of as many of the key school community stakeholders as possible (e.g., students, families, teachers, administrators). Examples of violence prevention programs that focus on the entire school as a site of change are as follows:

- The Bully Busters Program has three different components, one for elementary schools (Horne, Bartolomucci, & Newman-Carlson, 2003), one for middle schools (Newman et al., 2000), and one for families (Horne, Stoddard, & Bell, 2008). The school manuals provide class exercises that teachers can use to increase their own as well as their students' knowledge and awareness of bullying, methods for students to use to address bullying and victimization in the classroom and school setting, and activities that increase teachers' skills and abilities to intervene effectively in issues of school bullying. The parent's manual (Horne et al., 2008) parallels the school program for parents to gain greater understanding of the problem of bullying as well as approaches for reducing it.
- The Bullying Prevention Program (Olweus, 1993) includes students, teachers, and families in its program to reduce bullying behaviors in grades K through 12. The program is intended to modify the whole school, using prevention activities at the school, class, and individual levels.
- The Target Bullying Program (Espelage & Swearer, 2004) engages students, families, teachers, and administrators in grades 5 through 9 in bullying reduction efforts. The program emphasizes the use of needs assessment data to develop intervention strategies, uses an ecological model for prevention, and encourages the participation of all school community members.
- The Peaceful Schools Project focuses on the school as a whole to reduce bullying in grades K through 5. The program uses manuals to organize a school-wide bullying prevention program, but it also builds in opportunities for a school to tailor the program philosophy to its specific needs. The project uses a Back Off Bully Program curriculum (e.g., manual, video) to train teachers, students, and parents to become active bystanders in bullying prevention (Twemlow et al., 2001).

Youth Empowerment: The Role of Students in Reducing Bullying

School bullying often goes unnoticed by teachers and administrators in school (Espelage & Swearer, 2003; Orpinas & Horne, 2006; Varjas et al., 2007; Whitted & Dupper, 2005). The other side of this story is that students are those who witness most school bullying (Cornell, Sheras, & Cole, 2006). It makes sense, then, that if school bullying reduction programs are to be effective, they must give a voice to students. This section explores models of youth empowerment in bullying prevention. Of course, in exploring youth empowerment models of school bullying, the most appropriate place to begin is with a story of intervention led by youth themselves:

> David Shepherd and Travis Price were both in their final year at Central Kings Rural High School in Canada when they heard the story of a ninth grade boy who was verbally and physically threatened for wearing a pink shirt on his first day of school. David and Travis also learned that six to ten older students surrounded the victim and called him anti-gay epithets. They decided to take action about bullying in their school, and bought 75 pink shirts for male students to wear and pink headbands to distribute to supporters. Using the Internet, the seniors rallied male and female students alike, asking them to wear the color pink the next day in school as a show of solidarity with the student who had been bullied. David and Travis called this call for solidarity the "Sea of Pink."
>
> On the following day at Central Kings Rural High School, half of the approximately 830 students wore pink, sending a clear message to bullies that targeting students in this manner at their school was unacceptable. After the Sea of Pink took over their school that day, David and Travis reported that the bullies were initially angry but haven't bullied others since their activism. They shared that standing up for the ninth-grade student was the "right" thing to do, and that the boy had been happy to see the school's show of support. David also indicated that it was easier for them to take on the bullies with the community's support saying, "If you can get more people against them . . . to show that we're not going to put up with it and support each other, then they're not as big as a group as they think they are." (CBS News, 2007)

The Sea of Pink story demonstrates the critical role that youth may play in bullying prevention, especially in terms of using bystander status, technology, creativity, and activism. The role that bystanders (e.g., students, teachers) play in reducing bullying has been widely noted (Espelage & Swearer, 2003; Orpinas & Horne, 2006; Whitted & Dupper, 2005), and although Shepherd and Price did not directly witness the school bullying of a 9th grade student, they adopted an active bystander role. Using the Internet allowed the students to gain quick access to Web-based social networks (e.g., http://www.myspace.

com and http://www.facebook.com) that their peers were already widely using. Interestingly, Shepherd and Price used creativity and an innovative method in targeting bullying, as they reframed the very thing that the bullies used to bully: the pink shirt. Finally, the Sea of Pink provides a story of youth who felt empowered enough to take action against bullying, and in doing served as a "tipping point" to ignite activism against bullying in their peer group.

Components of Youth Empowerment Interventions

The philosophy of youth empowerment is grounded in a wellness construct that focuses on youth participation, supporting youth "voice and choice" (self-determination), and developing skill sets, attitudes, and competence (self-efficacy) for youth to act as agents of change in their environment (Prilleltensky, Nelson, & Peirson, 2001). Interestingly, youth empowerment interventions have been recently identified as a best practice in the field of tobacco prevention (Evans, Ulasevich, & Balhut, 2004).

Of course, adults play an important role in youth empowerment interventions. The following six guidelines have been identified as best practices for adult roles in programs with a youth empowerment focus (Hilfinger Messias, Fore, McLoughlin, & Parra-Medina, 2005). First, adults must put youth first as a priority, valuing youth perspectives and acknowledging their ability to learn and grow from their strengths and challenges. Second, adults should set the bar high for youth performance. Similar to the idea of scaffolding (Vygotsky, 1962), adults should provide youth with high expectations and opportunities to develop leadership skills. Third, adults can provide the structure for youth empowerment to happen, from functioning in an administrative role and managing a program's details to assessing how much a program is a supportive and fun environment for youth. Fourth, adults should be in active relationships with youth, giving emotional support and critical feedback as youth engage in leadership as change agents. Fifth, adults have the opportunity to influence, model, and use their authority status to set healthy boundaries, discipline, appreciation for diversity, and expand the potential that youth have in leadership roles. Finally, adults should ensure that youth are connected with a larger community in order to access needed resources for making change in peer groups.

Specific youth empowerment interventions have been surprisingly rare in the field of school bullying prevention. Several successful interventions have been designed to reduce school bullying by creating a positive school climate, and in this process they frequently empower students. These interventions have in common that they are process oriented, that is, they provide a step-by-step process to reduce bullying but are not prescriptive in terms of which strategies to use (Bosworth, Orpinas, & Hein, 2009). For example, BreakAway is a youth involvement/empowerment model for school change that has been used since the late 1970s (Lofquist, 1983; Lynn & Lofquist, 2002). In the BreakAway process, youth are not the passive recipients of services, but active partners in identifying problems and solutions. Another example is the Caring School Community program (http://www.devstu.com), an elementary school program that focuses on increasing commitment and bonding to school, with specific strategies for student participation (Battistich, Solomon, Watson, & Schaps, 1997; Solomon, Battistich, Watson, Schaps, & Lewis, 2000).

Future Directions in Facilitating Positive School Climate

The landscape of bullying prevention continues to shift as a reflection of societal changes. This section identifies three emerging bullying prevention areas that often become thorny issues within the school: bullying toward sexual minority youth, bullying toward obese youth, and cyber-bullying.

Bullying toward Lesbian, Gay, Bisexual, Transgender, and Queer Youth

Bullying toward lesbian, gay, bisexual, transgender, and queer (LGBTQ) students has always been a challenge in schools; however, the problem has been gaining more attention recently (Espelage & Swearer, 2003; Varjas et al., 2007). A 2005 National School Climate Survey conducted by GLSEN (Gay, Lesbian, and Straight Education Network, 2005) identified that 75.4% of students heard anti-gay epithets, such as "faggot" or "dyke." Over half of the students had experienced physical harassment due to their sexual orientation or gender expression, with almost 30% of youth in the survey reporting being physically assaulted due to the same reason. The survey also found that LGBTQ youth were five times more likely to skip school due to bullying. For those in the survey experiencing the highest levels of bullying, the students demonstrated lower grade point averages in high school and were two times more likely to not attend college.

In our experience with bullying prevention programs in schools, administrators and teachers often overlook bullying toward LGBTQ youth. When speaking with teachers about the lack of intervention on LGTBQ bullying, common responses range from "There aren't gay students in our school" to "The kids are just saying what they hear at home." Therefore, LGBTQ bullying is the result of socially accepted norms of heterosexism, homophobia, and transphobia that diminish the worth of LGBTQ people in general society. Because of the extent of discrimination toward LGBTQ people and the high rates of LGBTQ bullying, we recommend that whole-school bullying prevention programs specifically include sexual orientation and gender identity. Although evaluation of specific LGBTQ bullying programs is lacking (Varjas et al., 2007), in schools where steps have been taken to include LGBTQ issues within the school curriculum (e.g., LGBTQ history, LGBTQ models), LGBTQ students have reported feeling a greater sense of safety and support, in addition to reporting fewer instances of LGBTQ bullying (Blake et al., 2001; O'Shaughnessy, Russell, Heck, Calhoun, & Laub, 2004; Szalacha, 2003).

Bullying toward Obese Youth

Obesity in children and adolescents is a growing public health concern (Georgetown University Institute for Healthcare Research and Policy, 2002; Levin, Lowry, Brown, & Dietz, 2003). As this public health concern grows, so does school bullying toward obese youth (Rimm & Rimm, 2004). In this area, significant gender differences must be acknowledged. Research has shown that obese boys experience higher rates of overt bullying (e.g., name-calling, aggression) than obese girls (Pearce, Boergers, & Prinstein, 2002), whereas obese girls experience more bullying that is relational (e.g., exclusion from social networks) in nature than obese boys (see also Chapter 5).

Teachers may overlook bullying of obese students as an uncomfortable, but normal part of life for obese youth (Robinson, 2006). Continued bullying of obese youth may lead to increased absence from school, and it often results in reporting somatic complaints to not attend school where the victimization is occurring (Raskauskas & Stolz, 2004; Robinson, 2006). In the needs assessment, school personnel should examine absenteeism patterns of obese youth, evaluate whether school personnel's attitude toward obese youth may be limiting interventions (e.g., believing that obesity is a result of lack of self-control or weakness), and determine whether the food choices in the school cafeteria may be adding to the problem of obesity. Youth obesity is a serious public health concern, and bullying of these children adds a new layer of problems.

Cyber-bullying

A new challenge to bullying prevention programs is cyber-bullying, or bullying using interactive technology (e.g., text-messaging devices, instant messages, cell phones, eomails, Internet chatrooms, or "meeting spaces" such as http://www.myspace.com). Cyber-bullying behaviors may include sending direct negative messages, as well using cyber-bashing websites to post hateful messages, posting negative messages on the child's webpage, or sending thousands of messages to the child's cell phone, which can result in a very expensive phone bill. Students can also steal the password and ID of a peer, which is then used to impersonate that peer. Cyber-bullying is particularly difficult for schools, as it frequently occurs outside of school hours, but it affects students in the school. In our experience, counselors and teachers often mention that they must manage the effects of cyber-bullying from the "night before" in the classroom and that they struggle on how to handle these attacks, given the lack of clear policies.

The literature on cyber-bullying is slowly but steadily increasing. Williams and Guerra (2007) conducted a study in elementary, middle, and high schools comparing the difference of physical and verbal bullying with Internet bullying. Researchers found that verbal bullying was the most prevalent type of bullying, followed by physical and Internet bullying. The three types of bullying were all significantly linked to attitudes that normalized bullying, negative school climate, and lack of peer support. Because all types of bullying shared these risk factors, school-wide prevention efforts to build a positive school climate and change accepted norms of bullying behaviors are likely to also reduce cyber-bullying. However, prevention efforts should specifically educate students about the legal and emotional consequences of cyber-bullying and the school should have clear policies specific to cyber-bullying. In addition, teachers and other school personnel should receive adequate training on the types and characteristics of cyber-bullying. A number of Internet resources provide more information on what cyber-bullying is and how to stop it (National Crime Prevention Council: http://www.stopcyberbullying.org; Center for Safe and Responsible Internet Use: http://cyberbully.org).

Practice Implications

There are several practice implications for empowering schools to use a holistic approach to address bullying and violence. The following list is a summary of these implications:

1. Use an empowerment philosophy to guide all stages of bullying prevention (e.g., assessment, implementation, evaluation) to ensure voices of all community members are involved in prevention efforts.

2. Invest time and resources into bullying prevention programs. Successful prevention and intervention efforts happen over a period of time. Do not aim for a short-term fix.
3. Define and identify the specific behaviors of school bullying, in addition to the way these behaviors may be endorsed by discrimination and prejudice toward certain groups (e.g., gender, race/ethnicity, sexual orientation).
4. Assessing bullying and school climate factors are precursors to effective prevention. Use quantitative and qualitative methods to carefully gather data on the bullying specific to a school.
5. Use assessment results to guide the selection of appropriate prevention policies, programs, and strategies.
6. Create spaces for youth to empower themselves to generate programs and campaigns that they feel will be effective in their schools.
7. Consult with other schools and bullying prevention specialists to learn and share strengths and challenges in reducing bullying. Stay current on the best practices for bullying prevention. Always ask what areas of bullying prevention are working and which aspects need improvement.
8. Use evaluation results to strengthen the program and measure effectiveness. Evaluation methods (e.g., surveys, focus groups) should be an ongoing aspect of prevention.

References

Barnes, J., Belsky, J., Broomfield, K. A., & Melhuish, E. (2006). Neighbourhood deprivation, school disorder, and academic achievement in primary schools in deprived communities in England. *International Journal of Behavioural Development, 30*, 127–136.

Battistich, V., Solomon, D., Watson, M., & Schaps, E. (1997). Caring school communities. *Educational Psychologist, 32*, 137–151.

Blake, S. M., Ledsky, R., Lehman, T., Goodenow, C., Sawyer, R., & Tack, T. (2001). Preventing sexual risk behaviors among gay, lesbian, and bisexual adolescents: The benefits of gay-sensitive HIV instruction in schools. *American Journal of Public Health, 91*, 940–946.

Bosworth, K., Orpinas, P., & Hein, K. (2009). Development of a positive school climate. In M. E. Kenny, A. M. Horne, P. Orpinas, & L. E. Reese (Eds.), *Realizing social justice: The challenge of preventive interventions* (pp. 229–248). Washington, DC: American Psychological Association.

Bullock, J. (2002). Bullying among children. *Childhood Education, 78*, 130–133.

CBS News. (2007). *Bullied student tickled pink by schoolmates' T-shirt campaign.* Retrieved December 26, 2007, from http://www.cbc.ca/canada/nova-scotia/story/2007/09/18/pink-tshirts-students.html?ref=rss

Cole, J. C. M., Cornell, D. G., & Sheras, P. (2006). Identification of school bullies by survey methods. *Professional School Counseling, 9*(4), 305–314.

Cornell, D. G., Sheras, P. L., & Cole, J. C. M. (2006). Assessment of bullying. In S. R. Jimerson and M. Furlong (Eds.), *Handbook of school violence and school safety: From research to practice* (pp. 191–209). Mahwah, NJ: Erlbaum.

Dahlberg, L. L., Toal, S. B., Swahn, M., & Behrens, C. B. (2005). *Measuring violence-related attitudes, behaviors, and influences among youths: A compendium of assessment tools* (2nd ed.). Atlanta, GA: Centers for Disease Control and Prevention, National Center for Injury Prevention and Control.

Espelage, D. L., & Swearer, S. M. (2003). Research on school bullying and victimization: What have we learned and where do we go from here? *School Psychology Review, 32* (3), 365–383.

Espelage, D. L., & Swearer, S. M. (Eds.). (2004). *Bullying in American schools: A social-ecological perspective on prevention and intervention.* Mahwah, NJ: Erlbaum.

Evans, W. D., Ulasevich, A., & Balhut, S. (2004). Adult and group influences on participation in youth empowerment programs. *Health Education and Behavior, 31*(5), 564–576.

Fetterman, D. M. (1994). Steps of empowerment evaluation: From California to Cape Town. *Evaluation and Program Planning, 17*(3), 305–313.

Fetterman, D. M. (2001). *Foundations of empowerment evaluation.* Thousand Oaks, CA: Sage Publications.

Fetterman, D. M., & Haertel, E. H. (1990). *A school-based evaluation model for accelerating the education of students at-risk.* Clearinghouse on Urban Education. (ERIC Document Reproduction Service No. ED313495). Retrieved on November 23, 2009, from http://www.eric.gov

Fixsen, D. L., Naoom, S. F., Blase, K. A., Friedman, R. M., & Wallace, F. (2005). *Implementation research: A synthesis of the literature.* Tampa: University of South Florida, Louis de la Parte Florida Mental Health Institute, The National Implementation Research Network (FMHI Publication #231). Retrieved on September 8, 2009 from http://www.fpg.unc.edu/~nirn/resources/publications/Monograph/.

Forgatch, M. S. (2003). Implementation as a second stage in prevention research. *Prevention and Treatment, 6,* Article 24 pre 0060024c. Retrieved September 8, 2009, from http://www.journals/apa.org/prevention/volume6/pre0060024c.html

Gay, Lesbian, and Straight Education Network [GLSEN]. (2005). *From teasing to torment: School climate in America. A survey of students and teachers.* Retrieved February 14, 2008, from http://glsen.org

Georgetown University Institute for Healthcare Research and Policy (2002). *Childhood obesity: A lifelong threat to health.* Retrieved December 30, 2007, from http://www.ihcrp.georgetown.edu/agingsociety/phtml/obesity/obesity/html

Glover, D., Gough, G., Johnson, M., & Cartwright, N. (2000). Bullying in 25 secondary schools: Incidence, impact, and intervention. *Educational Research, 42,* 141–156.

Hahn, R., Fuqua-Whitley, D., Wethington, H., Lowy, J., Crosby, A., Fullilove, M., et al. (2007). Effectiveness of universal school-based programs to prevent violent and aggressive behavior. *American Journal of Preventive Medicine, 33*, 2, 114–129.

Hilfinger Messias, D. K., Fore, E. M., McLoughlin, K., & Parra-Medina, D. (2005). Adult roles in community-based youth empowerment programs: Implications for best practices. *Family Community Health, 28*, 4, 320–337.

Hoover, J. H., & Oliver, J. H. (2007). *The bullying prevention handbook: A guide for principals, teachers, and counselors* (2nd ed.). Bloomington, IN: Solution Tree.

Horne, A. M., Bartolomucci, C. L., & Newman-Carlson, D. (2003). *Bully Busters: A teacher's manual for helping bullies, victims, and bystanders (Grades K-5).* Champaign, IL: Research Press.

Horne, A. M., Orpinas, P., Newman-Carlson, D., & Bartolomucci, C. L. (2004). Elementary school Bully Busters program: Understanding why children bully and what to do about it. In D. L. Espelage & S. M. Swearer (Eds.), *Bullying in American schools: A social-ecological perspective on prevention and intervention* (pp. 297–325). Mahwah, NJ: Erlbaum.

Horne, A. M., Stoddard, J. L., & Bell, C. D. (2008). *A parent's guide to understanding and responding to bullying: The Bully Busters approach.* Champaign, IL: Research Press.

Hyman, I. A., & Perone, D. C. (1998). The other side of school violence: Educator policies and practices that may contribute to student misbehavior. *Journal of School Psychology, 36*, 7–27.

Levin, S., Lowry, R., Brown, D. R., & Dietz, W. H. (2003). Physical activity and body mass index among U.S. adolescents. *Archives of Pediatrics and Adolescent Medicine, 157*, 816–820.

Lofquist, W. A. (1983). *Discovering the meaning of prevention: A practical approach to positive change.* Tucson, AZ: Associates for Youth Development.

Lynn, D. D. & Lofquist, W. A. (2002). *Breakaway: A framework for creating positive school communities. A leadership team workbook.* Tucson, AZ: Development Publications.

Newman, D. A., Horne, A. M., & Bartolomucci, C. L. (2000). *Bully Busters: A teacher's manual for reducing bullying behavior in middle school students.* Champagne, IL: Research Press.

Olweus, D. (1993). *Bullying at school: What we know and what we can do.* Cambridge, MA: Blackwell.

Orpinas, P., & Horne, A. M. (2006). *Bullying prevention: Creating a positive school climate and developing social competence.* Washington, DC: American Psychological Association.

O'Shaughnessy, M., Russell, S., Heck, K., Calhoun, C., & Laub, C. (2004). *Safe place to learn: Consequences of harassment based on actual or perceived sexual orientation and gender non-conformity and steps for making schools safer.* San Francisco: California Safe Schools Coalition and 4-H Center for Youth Development.

Pearce, M. J., Boergers, J., & Prinstein, M. J. (2002). Adolescent obesity, overt and relational peer victimization, and romantic relationships. *Obesity Research, 10*, 386–393.

Prilleltensky, L., Nelson, G., & Peirson, L. (2001). The role of power and control in children's lives: An ecological analysis of pathways toward wellness, resilience, and problems. *Journal of Community and Applied Social Psychology, 11*, 143–158.

Raskauskas, J., & Stolz, A. D. (2004). Identifying and intervening in relational aggression. *Journal of School Nursing, 20*, 209–215.

Rimm, S., & Rimm, E. (2004). *Rescuing the emotional lives of overweight children*. Emmaus, PA: Rodale.

Robinson, S. (2006). Victimization of obese adolescents. *The Journal of School Nursing, 22, 4*, 201–206.

Skiba, R. J. (2000). *Zero-tolerance, zero evidence: An analysis of school disciplinary practices*. Bloomington: Indiana Education Policy Center.

Solomon, D., Battistich, V., Watson, M., Schaps, E., & Lewis, C. (2000). A six-district study of educational change: Direct and mediating effects of the Child Development Project. *Social Psychology of Education, 4*, 3–51.

Sugai, G., & Horner, R. (2002). The evolution of discipline practices: School-wide positive behavior supports. *Child and Family Behavior Therapy, 24*, 23–50.

Sukiennik, D., Bendat, W., & Raufman, L. (2006). *The career fitness program: Exercising your options* (8th ed.). Upper Saddle River, NJ: Prentice Hall.

Sullivan, K. (2000). *The anti-bullying handbook*. Auckland, New Zealand: Oxford University Press.

Szalacha, L. A. (2003). Safer diversity climates: Lessons learned from an evaluation of Massachusetts safe schools program for gay and lesbian students. *American Journal of Education, 110*, 58–88.

Twemlow, S. W., Fonagy, P., Sacco, F. C., Gies, M. L., Evans, R., & Ewbank, R. (2001). Creating a peaceful school learning environment: A controlled study of an elementary school intervention to reduce violence. *American Journal of Psychiatry, 158*, 808–810.

Varjas, K., Graybill, E., Mahan, W., Meyers, J., Dew, B. J., Marshall, M., et al. (2007). School and community providers' perspectives on gay, lesbian, and questioning bullying. *Journal of LGBT Issues in Counseling, 2*, 45–66.

Vygotsky, L. S. (1962). *Thought and language*. Cambridge, MA: MIT Press.

Whitted, K. S., & Dupper, D. R. (2005). Best practices for preventing or reducing bullying in schools. *National Association of Social Workers, 27, 3*, 167–175.

Williams, K. R., & Guerra, N. G. (2007). Prevalence and predictors of Internet bullying. *Journal of Adolescent Health, 41*(6), 14–21.

Zimmerman, M. A. (2000). Empowerment theory: Psychological, organizational, and community levels of analysis. In J. Rappaport and E. Seldman (Eds.), *Handbook of community psychology* (pp. 2–45). New York: Plenum.

11

Incorporating Bully–Victim Interventions into Clinic-Based Mental-Health Service

Fred Frankel

"Bullying" has received widespread attention in the media. It has been poorly defined by journalists, parents, and researchers alike. Thus, when parents call a practitioner to seek help for their child who they say is being "bullied," specific questions need to be asked to determine the type of victimization the child is experiencing. There are three different categories of victimization that can be helped through social skills training: teasing, physical aggression, and bullying. A practitioner must evaluate the type of victimization in order to provide the most effective course of action.

The first step in incorporating bully–victim interventions into clinic-based practice is becoming familiar with the skill deficits associated with peer victimization and the type of skill assets that promote healthier peer relationships. Knowing the types of aversive exchanges children experience and the types of responses that lead to successful versus unsuccessful outcomes is important for determining which skills to teach in an intervention. In the first section of this chapter, I review the types of victimization to which children are commonly subjected, the types of reactions that are likely to lead to negative outcomes, and the responses associated with greater social success. I also review the determinants of children becoming perpetrators. Next, I present evidence for how social skills interventions may help and what the key features of successful interventions appear to be. We have developed and tested Parent-Assisted Children's Friendship Training (CFT; Frankel & Myatt, 2003), a 12-week manualized outpatient group treatment that addresses peer relationship problems. We have recently adapted this model to teens with social problems (Laugeson, Frankel, Mogil, & Dillon, 2009). I will present details of these interventions as a guide to how social skills interventions may help in the treatment of frequently victimized children and teens. I conclude with guidance for implementing social skills groups in clinical settings, using our CFT intervention as an example.

Involvement in Aversive Peer Exchanges: Rationale for Social Skills Interventions
General Findings for Victimization

Two findings in regard to victimization bear on how children's social skills groups can help. The first finding is that the magnitude of children's victimization scores is negatively correlated with peer liking, and positively correlated with peer disliking (Schwartz, Dodge, Pettit, & Bates, 1997). In studies of victimization among 4th and 5th graders, rejected children had victimization scores about four times greater than popular and average accepted children (Perry, Kusel, & Perry, 1988; Ray, Cohen, Secrist, & Duncan, 1997). Hodges, Boivin, Vitaro, and Bukowski (1999) have demonstrated that having a best friend protects against victimization. Kochenderfer and Ladd (1997) found the strategy of "having a friend help" was associated with reduced victimization, whereas "fighting back" was related to stable victimization. Thus, interventions that increase peer liking and promote best friendships may protect against victimization. In more practical terms, it is hard for a bully to victimize a child who is usually surrounded by friends. If bullying persists in this context, the potential victim is a more difficult target and the reputation of the bully may be diminished by the peer support.

The second finding is that it is important to help children select their associates. Rejected boys were found to victimize their mutual friends more than any other combination of sex and sociometric status (Ray et al., 1997). Thus, interventions that help children select for others who do not victimize may protect against victimization.

In general, social skills training with the following components may help decrease victimization and/or bullying:

- Increasing peer liking
- Promotion of best friendships
- Helping children select their associates from among others who are liked by peers and are less likely to victimize others

Teasing

Most victimization involves teasing. Research suggests teasing is common in elementary school with some teasers and teased pupils in every classroom. The predominant motivation reported by perpetrators of teasing is their pleasure at the discomfort of the victim (Warm, 1997). Teasing may be humorous, but the humor is at the expense of the victim. Younger children tease primarily by name-calling, while older children tease by disparaging statements about the victim or the victim's family (Frankel, 1996). Teasing is frequently done in front of onlookers.

Shapiro, Baumeister, and Kessler (1991) found that among 3rd and 5th graders the most common content of teasing was about appearance (39%), especially being overweight (13%). Thus, overweight children are especially at risk. Wilfley et al. (unpublished data) collected preliminary data on the extent of teasing in overweight children. Among a group of 21 overweight boys and girls with ages ranging from 5 to 17, 90.4% reported being teased (9.5%), criticized (47.6%), or both (33%), with overweight girls being especially vulnerable.

Fear of being teased may discourage overweight children from trying new physical activities, joining other peers engaged in such activities, or persisting with new activities. Success in handling teasing promotes more risk taking in terms of beginning and maintaining a more physically active lifestyle. In children without weight problems, effective responses to teasing may increase self-esteem and improve reputation among peers.

A Note on Informational Feedback, Often Confused with Teasing

> Ten-year-old Mark wants to be included in all basketball games regardless of the skill level of the other children. While playing with some boys who were much better at basketball than he was, he allowed the ball to be stolen from him while dribbling and missed three shots to the basket, which were recovered by boys on the opposing team. This distressed the other members of his team. Finally, one boy from his team said to him, "Mark, you stink!"

This was not teasing, where the primary intent was to get Mark upset for the entertainment of the teaser. It was just a tactless way to tell Mark that he had considerably less skill at basketball than the others. A healthy response here was for Mark to play with other boys closer to his skill level in the future so that everyone would have a better time. Other examples of negative feedback are statements about poor hygiene or disgusting personal habits. Dealing with it as teasing would not solve the problem. The better approach is to employ behavior programs to modify hygiene and personal habits.

In summary:

- Teasing is the most common form of victimization.
- Overweight children are especial vulnerable.
- Onlookers are frequently present during teasing episodes so that responses to teasing may impact peer liking.
- Teasing should not be confused with negative feedback about poor performance, poor hygiene, or disgusting personal habits.

Ineffective and Effective Ways of Handling Teasing

Children who tend to get angry, upset, or physically aggressive when teased tend to be rejected by peers (Shantz, 1987). This reaction probably motivates the perpetrator to continue, even if the victim uses physical aggression (Shantz, 1987). In contrast, employing humor or assertion in response to being teased is more effective and is associated with improved peer liking (Perry, Williard, & Perry, 1990). Scambler, Harris, and Milich (1998) had children between 8 and 11 years old view videotaped interactions of one child being teased by two other children. They saw the victim respond either with humor, by ignoring, or with hostility. Subjects rated the humorous response as the most effective, followed by ignoring, and the hostile response as least effective. Furthermore, the victim's response to teasing significantly affected the rater's perceptions of the friendliness and popularity of the teasers and victim. Thus, responses to being teased may be an important avenue to impact a child's reputation. It is of prime importance that social skill groups train children in effective ways of handling teasing that do not involve teasing back.

The evidence base is good that children and teens can be taught to decrease this form of victimization on their own without the immediate help of adults. The instructional techniques and target response are very similar across children and teens. A module on informational feedback has been very helpful with teens to get them to change offensive personal habits (Laugeson et al., 2009). In summary:

- Appropriate responses to being teased may enhance a child's reputation.
- Using humorous comebacks that do not involve teasing back may gain the respect of onlookers and thwart the perpetrator.
- Teens can be taught to modify personal hygiene and offensive personal habits to reduce negative feedback from their peers.

Frequent Fighters

Frankel (1996) distinguished between frequent fighters, who are nonselective in their targets and generally aggressive (Patterson, 1986), and bullies, who are very selective in targets and not generally aggressive (Olweus, 1993). Frequent fighting is associated with peer rejection (Newcomb, Bukowski, & Pattee, 1993). Approximately 30%–50% of rejected boys are also frequent fighters (Cillesson, Van Ijzendoorn, Van Lieshout, & Hartup, 1992; Coie, Christopoulos, Terry, Dodge, & Lochman, 1989). According to Schwartz et al. (1997), rejected-aggressive 3rd grade boys escalate their aggression if resisted and continue to fight until the victim submits. Aggressive-nonrejected boys do not tend to persist. Aggressive-rejected boys are twice as likely to form relationships with other high-conflict children as nonaggressive-rejected boys, with each boy disliking the other.

> ... as boys grow older, they begin to recognize when it makes sense to let some negative exchanges pass without comments or overt reaction. Rejected boys do not seem to keep pace with these changing norms for aggressive behavior. They continue to use direct aggression as a way of getting what they want ... While, on the surface of things, they may seem to be getting away with this inappropriate behavior, to the extent that other boys fail to reciprocate, they also pay a serious price for this social deviance. Other boys dislike them and increasingly avoid interacting with them ... they become limited in their choice of relationships to boys who are much like themselves. (Schwartz et al., 1997, p. 233)

Patterson, DeBaryshe, and Ramsey (1989) followed a cohort of aggressive boys, documenting the contribution of poor parental monitoring and inadequate child disciplinary skills in early childhood, and peer rejection and school failure in middle childhood. Such children, if left to associate with other highly aggressive children, have a high risk for delinquency by their teen years. In summary, we know the following about frequent fighting:

- It is strongly associated with peer rejection and lack of best friends.
- Some frequent fighters escalate their aggression if resisted. Thus, fighting back may be ineffective.
- Some frequent fighters are more likely to associate with others who are rejected and aggressive. These friendships are problematic and should be discouraged.

Fighting back is the most common approach advocated by parents in response to their child being picked on by a frequent fighter. Under very narrow circumstances this may be effective (the victim is stronger than the perpetrator, the perpetrator is a nonrejected aggressive child, and the victim is neither rejected nor generally aggressive). However, there are many negative side effects for this approach:

- It gives the message that fighting can be acceptable and it is the nonaggressive victim who is at fault.
- It encourages aggression by children who are at times the instigator.
- A victim fighting back may himself get into trouble for fighting.
- Fighting back may intensify the aggression from some perpetrators.

Since frequent fighters are nonselective with regard to victims (i.e., whoever gets in their way), they can be more easily observed by adult supervisors. Effective strategies to employ on the school yard by victims of frequent fighters may involve the following: *(1)* avoid playing with a frequent fighter, *(2)* play in a group of friends, and *(3)* play near adult supervisors. In this way, the potential victim makes a more difficult target and makes detection of fighting easier for adult supervisors. This partially hinges upon schools providing adequate supervision on the playground. Studies have not systematically tested this approach with victims.

Treatment Approaches for Frequent Fighters

Generally, we have found that frequent fighting is associated with either a comorbid disorder, most commonly attention-deficit/hyperactivity disorder (ADHD), and/or chronic parent inaction regarding the child's fighting. If the comorbid condition is ADHD, stimulant medication may be necessary but not sufficient to address frequent fighting. On a parent-intervention level, the effectiveness varies with parent motivation and socioeconomic disadvantage (Patterson & Chamberlain, 2006; Wahler & Dumas, 1989). Parent training in behavior management techniques is effective with motivated parents at higher socioeconomic levels (see below). Younger children, with less severe aggression and motivated parents, can be treated in outpatient social skills groups. An important rule to enforce is to prohibit group members from mingling socially after sessions and to discourage children with aggressive histories from becoming friends after the last group session.

On a school level (not involving parents in a central way), frequent fighters are relatively easy for adults to spot and several approaches may be effective.

Social skills training programs have been effective with children with higher rates of fighting (Bierman & Conduct Problems Prevention Research Group, 1997).

Moving children out of the rejected category and promoting association with friends who do not have antisocial interests (and whom they may like better) can decrease frequent fighting and may have a great impact on the eventual outcome of frequent fighters. However, older and more highly aggressive children cannot easily be maintained in outpatient social skill programs. They may constantly challenge the group leader and attempt to recruit others to their way of thinking. Furthermore, their inclusion in such groups may discourage others in the group from continuing.

In summary, effective approaches to treating frequent fighters include the following:

- Parent training in behavior management techniques can be effective when parents are motivated and have adequate resources.
- School-based social skills programs can be effective for frequent fighters if parents are unmotivated to address their child's aggression.
- School-based interventions should involve adequate playground supervision and consequences for fighting.
- Outpatient social skills programs can be effective with children who are less aggressive and have poor friendship skills.
- Outpatient social skills programs should screen out highly aggressive children and teens and refer to parent interventions.

Bullying

Bullying is defined as repeated (once per week or more) attempts to inflict unprovoked injury or discomfort at one and the same victim by one or more specific other peers (Olweus, 1993). Olweus recommends severing ties between the bully and his bullying group. Social skills groups may be helpful for those who have difficulty making new friends.

Victims of bullying among 8- to 9-year-olds were more likely to play alone rather than participating in larger groups (Boulton, 1999). Thus, victims of bullying can also be helped in developing new friendships (but not in the same intervention group as the former perpetrator).

In our practice, running social skills group for teens with autism spectrum disorders (ASD), we noticed two patterns in this population. First, a higher proportion of teens with ASD were being bullied than typically developing teens, because they often have few defenses and make easy targets. It is common for at least one patient to report being moderately to severely bullied in our groups for teens with ASD. Second, there is sometimes a pattern of unknowing provocation from these teens. They attempt to fit in with a crowd that does not want to accept them (e.g., "jocks" when they are "computer nerds"), they fail to perceive the subtle forms of rejection they get in these attempts (or in at least one case the parent was encouraging the girl to persist), so they keep on trying. Eventually, more poorly behaved members of the crowd will start to physically intimidate the teen. The intimidation may last beyond the point at which the teen stops attempting to join the crowd.

In summary:

- Victims of bullying as well as perpetrators can be helped through developing new friendships.
- Teens with ASD may be victims of bullying after trying to fit in with the wrong crowd.

Social skills training, to the extent that it can promote friendships, can help protect children against bullying. However, once bullying has begun, victims cannot resolve it successfully by themselves. Social skills groups for teens with ASD require several modules to prevent bullying. These modules need to teach the teen to do the following:

- Identify the crowd that the teen would best fit into (with the help of parents)
- Learn how to approach members of this crowd
- Learn when their friendship overtures have been turned down
- Learn graceful ways to extricate themselves if their approach was not accepted (Laugeson et al., 2009)

Potential Benefits of Social Skills Training

Research evidence suggests that socials skills training groups can have substantial impact on teasing, frequent fighting, and bullying. It can train effective responses to teasing. It can improve peer acceptance of children. Improving peer acceptance can also protect children against frequent fighters and bullies.

Most community-based social skills treatment takes the form of small groups of children meeting within a school setting, without the involvement of their parents (Beelman, Pfingsten, & Lösel, 1994; Erwin, 1993) and usually without any formal syllabus. Beelman et al. (1994) reported that parent and teacher measures showed little improvement from this type of group.

Meta-analysis confirms that the degree of generalization of treatment gains to children's actual environment from these groups has been small (Quinn, Kavale, Mathur, Rutherford, & Forness, 1999). Perhaps due to the difficulty in implementing treatment in moderate-sized groups or the findings of limited generalization, clinicians and researchers have sought alternative treatments. The next two sections briefly review these alternatives.

Alternative 1: Individual Treatment to Enhance Friendships

Malik and Furman (1993, p. 1316), in commenting on group versus individual approaches to social skills enhancement concluded, "Although inclusion of peers makes this approach much less practical for individual practitioners, we have found little evidence that training sessions with adults will generalize to interactions with peers." In partial support of this contention, Bierman and Furman (1984) found that small group training of conversational skills was more effective in changing peer ratings than individual coaching. Many friendless children prefer the company of adults rather than other children. Thus, it is difficult to see how individual treatment with an adult therapist would make a friendless child more skilled with other children.

Alternative 2: Peer Pairing

Peer pairing is another technique used to improve the social status of rejected children. Pairing unpopular children with more popular peers alone was not as effective as peer pairing with concomitant social skills training (Bierman, 1986a). For example, developmentally disabled children were paired with more popular nondisabled children without concomitant social skills instruction. Once the pairing stopped, the benefits disappeared (Chennault, 1967; Lilly, 1971; Rucker & Vincenzo, 1970).

Two studies used socially competent peers both as instructors in sessions and as prompters within the classroom situation. Middleton and Cartledge (1995) used two or three socially competent peers as models during instruction with each of five highly aggressive 1st and 2nd grade boys. The peers also gave prompts to each target child in the classroom. Hitting and arguing was reduced to 16.8% of baseline, but there were no effects upon acceptance by other peers. Prinz, Blechman, and Dumas (1994) conducted small treatment groups of children usually composed of four aggressive children and four socially competent children (total n's were 48 aggressive and 52 competent children) during a median of twenty-two 50-minute sessions. Each session employed role playing, in which the socially competent child first demonstrated the correct example. Aggressive behavior decreased in comparison with a control group, but their low peer acceptance was unchanged.

Peer pairing has been proposed as an effective alternative on several grounds. First, it may make a friendless child more comfortable around peers. Second, socially competent peers can model appropriate behavior in a way that is more salient to the friendless child. These assertions seem reasonable in the light of the results obtained. In contrast, other assertions have not been supported. There is little evidence that the friendless child will become friends with the peer tutor or that the peer tutor might facilitate friendships within his friendship circle in any lasting way. Anecdotal accounts suggest that the tutor rarely will mix socially with his pupil outside of the tutoring situation.

Rationale for Parent Participation in Social Skills Interventions

According to Ladd, LeSieur, and Profilet (1993), parents may directly influence young children's peer relations in the following ways:

- Parents may integrate their child into social environments outside the home.
- Parents may help their child select playmates.
- Parents may arrange play dates and supervise interactions with peers.
- Parents may help their child solve interpersonal problems.

It is also reasonable to expect that parental involvement would enhance treatment generalization (Frankel, 1996; Ladd, Profilet, & Hart, 1992; Lollis & Ross, 1987, cited in Ladd, 1992). Despite the major roles that parents may play in their child's friendships, parents have been notably absent from participating in social skills training programs (Budd, 1985; Ladd & Asher, 1985; La Greca, 1993; Sheridan, Dee, Morgan, McCormick, & Walker, 1996). Some researchers have begun to integrate parents into training programs in two ways: teaching parents either to better manage their child's behavioral problems or to better manage their child's friendships.

Teaching Parents to Manage Better Their Child's Behavior Problems

Parent training in behavior management is an approach that comes from a research tradition that focuses upon the reduction of frequent fighting. The rationale for application of this approach to friendship problems is that rejected children are usually aggressive (Dishion, 1990) and their aggression is a key cause of peer rejection. However, Bierman and Smoot (1991), using a standard method of classifying rejected children, found that only about one-third of boys with poor peer relations fit this model. Other authors (Bierman, 1986b; French, 1988) found about half of all rejected children exhibit behavior problems at school. Thus, for many victimized children, parent management training may not address key issues in establishing friendships (Powell, Salberg, Rule, Levy, & Itzkowitz, 1983), although it may be effective for treating the frequent fighter (Barth, 1979 for a review; Kazdin, Esveldt-Dawson, French, & Unis, 1987).

Teaching Parents to Manage Better Their Child's Friendships

As reviewed above, parents may play four different important roles in their child's acquisition of social competence. Some parents may need guidance to fulfill these roles. Parents of rejected children may fail to teach their child conflict management skills and rules of behavior (Kennedy, 1992), but they also may unwittingly allow their child to maintain coercive control of play (Ladd, 1992). Mothers of rejected children were less likely to appropriately monitor play experiences (Ladd et al., 1992; Pettit, Bates, Dodge & Meece, 1999) than mothers of popular children and had less social competence themselves (Prinstein & LaGreca, 1999).

Several researchers have found behaviors of mothers of rejected children that parallel the social errors of their children. Dodge, Schlundt, Schocken, and Delugach (1983) found that mothers of rejected children were more likely to dominate a group of children at play and ignore ongoing activity than mothers of popular children. Russell and Finnie (1990) found that mothers of rejected preschool children would coerce an ongoing play group to integrate their child rather than help their child observe ways to fit in. Thus, an additional justification for including parents is to correct the behaviors of some parents that teach inadequate friendship skills.

Perhaps the view that parents may lack social skills themselves and are thus less able to teach them to their children has inhibited development of social skills programs involving parents (Budd, 1985). Three studies refute the contention that parents of friendless children are unable to help in delivery of treatment components to their children. Cousins and Weiss (1993) combined training children in social skills with training parents in management skills relevant to peer relationships. They advocated teaching parents to organize the child's social agenda and having the parents debrief the child after social contacts. Pfiffner and McBurnett (1997) demonstrated that when parents were trained to promote generalization, social skills training benefits readily generalized to the home. Sheridan et al. (1996) taught parents supportive listening skills, helping their child solve social problems, setting social goals, and helping their child transfer skills to the home environment. Parent and teacher reports suggested improvement for most boys.

Parent-Assisted Children's Friendship Training

Children's friendship training (CFT) has been shown to be effective for children with ASDs (Frankel & Myatt, 2007), ADHD (Frankel, 2005; Frankel, Myatt, & Cantwell, 1995), oppositional defiant disorder (Frankel, Myatt, Cantwell, & Feinberg, 1997), and children with fetal alcohol spectrum disorders (Frankel, Paley, Marquardt, & O'Connor, 2006; O'Connor et al., 2006). A recent modification for teens with ASD has also been demonstrated to be effective (Laugeson et al., 2009). Elements of CFT have been incorporated into weight maintenance programs, which have been successful as long as 2 years after weight reduction treatment (Frankel, Sinton & Wilfley, 2007; Wilfley et al., 2007).

Unique features of CFT are as follows:

- Incorporating parents as an integral part of the intervention
- Including homework assignments as part of the treatment sessions
- Teaching socially valid skills
- Structuring play dates to be maximally effective in promoting best friendships

A comprehensive description of this manualized intervention can be found in Frankel and Myatt (2003). We briefly review how each of the above features are incorporated into CFT.

Incorporating Parents as an Integral Part of the Intervention

Children and parents attend separate but concurrent sessions that are 60 minutes in length and meet weekly for 12 weeks. Parents are assigned homework to do with their child and are fully informed about the purpose and goals of the homework. The parent's role in each homework assignment is clearly delineated and described in handouts.

Focusing on Homework Compliance

Five features of the intervention facilitate the performance of the homework: (1) The date, time, and other party to the assignment are prearranged with parent and child before they leave the session. *(2)* The assignments are easier at first and gradually become more difficult. *(3)* High compliance for the easier assignments, together with pressure from the group, sets an expectation for homework compliance. *(4)* Discussion of potential barriers to implementation is encouraged when the homework is presented. *(5)* Homework assigned in the previous session is first on the agenda for the next session, again focusing upon how the homework was accomplished and problem solving with parents over any additional barriers to implementation.

Teaching Socially Valid Skills

Socially valid skills are defined as those that discriminate socially successful from unsuccessful children. Teaching these skills facilitates generalization by helping children to attend to key situations in their social world and helping them notice that when they perform these skills they are more successful. Critical child and parent behaviors that have been shown to discriminate accepted children from rejected children include the following:

- *Informational exchange with peers, which leads to common-ground activities* (Black & Hazen, 1990; Coie & Kupersmidt, 1983; Dodge, 1983; Garvey, 1984). Socially successful children are able to find others who have interests similar to theirs. They do this through their initial conversations with peers, during which they discuss likes and dislikes.
- *Peer entry into a group of children already at play* (Gelb & Jacobson, 1988). Entry into a group of children already at play is one of the most common and easiest means that young children make new friends. The initial stage is very important as it involves observing the other children at play and judging whether they are nice children who may be fun to play with and who are at the same skill level as the child thinking about joining them. It is just as important for the child to walk away from peers who do not fit these criteria as to join those who do.
- *Responses to teasing that employ humor or assertion* (Kochenderfer & Ladd, 1997; Perry et al., 1990). In teaching effective responses to teasing, it is important for the child to differentiate teasing from tactless informational feedback. Parents must help the child deal with these types of statements, by helping the child practice humorous comebacks to being teased, remediate poor personal hygiene, or select peers at the same competence level.

Structuring Play Dates

Avoiding conflict with best friends discriminates children with more versus fewer best friends (Fonzi, Schneider, Tani, & Tomada, 1997; Rose & Asher, 1999). Parents are integral to implementing this skill (Frankel, 1996). Immediately before the time of the play date, the parents should remind the child of the rules of a good host and to limit media viewing (watching television, playing electronic games, and computers). At the time of the play date, the parents monitor the play date from afar (Ladd & Golter, 1988) to ensure that playmates have been selected well and that conflict is minimized on the play date itself. Parents should not be a formal part of the play date, but they should intervene in conflicts (Lollis & Ross, 1987, cited in Ladd, 1992).

Other Important Characteristics

Other important characteristics of effective social skills groups for children are as follows:

- A syllabus composed of evidence-based modules for parents and children
- Homework assignments and detailed review of homework attempts
- Prohibition of social contact between group members
- Focus upon play date supervision and friend selection by the parent

The teen intervention (Laugeson et al., 2009) contains all of these features. We have previously discussed the following enhancements:

- Identification of appropriate crowds for the teen to attempt to join
- Gracefully exiting unsuccessful conversations
- Distinguishing between teasing and embarrassing feedback

Other enhancements we have found necessary for teen groups are as follows:

- Having parents and teens work together to expand the teen's social network through the participation of extra-curricular activities
- Teaching rules for electronic communication, including phone etiquette, rules of text messaging, instant messaging, and e-mailing, and online safety
- Teaching ways to expedite changing a bad reputation (i.e., laying low, following the crowd, changing one's "look," and "owning up" to a previously bad reputation)

Forming Treatment Groups: Practical Advice

It is clear that there has been no effective substitute for manualized group training of children's social skills. One reason why such groups are not more widespread is the formidable obstacles to formation of these groups in outpatient settings, especially the first few groups. The next paragraphs will suggest some tricks of the trade that we have learned in implementing CFT in an outpatient setting over the last 18 years, with over 140 groups.

Screening

In order to conduct groups that are maximally beneficial to the children needing friendship training, it is necessary to screen children who would benefit from the skills being taught and group children together who will be comfortable in being together in the same class. Effective screening, beginning with the initial phone call, ensures that the eventual group experience will be compatible with the child's problems and the parent's expectations. The initial phone call can establish whether the child meets more obvious criteria and inform the parent about the program and how to present the initial visit to the child. Parents of children who do not meet obvious criteria can be referred to other resources.

Frankel and Myatt (2003) discuss telephone screening in more detail. Mothers are usually the most reliable informants, since they are most likely to supervise the play dates, that is, if play dates are being supervised by either parent. It is strongly suggested that the telephone intake be done with the mother in order to engage her in treatment. Entries into the database (see below) are made during the initial call from the parent. In addition to the demographic information, a running log of contacts and appointment cancellations is kept in the comments text field. Parents who have several previous cancellations are given a low priority for entry into any group.

Prior to the intake appointment, parents are advised to tell their child or teen that there is a class that teaches children how to make and keep friends and that they will be talking to someone about this class. It is counterproductive to get a child or teen to admit that they have peer problems. Discussion about how much the child or teen needs this class is also discouraged.

Some children and teens appear unwilling to take the class. We find that if the parent is solidly behind them coming and perhaps offer some small reward, that usually by about the third treatment session, children are fully engaged in treatment. On the other hand, it is necessary for a teen to make the choice to take the class without being coerced by the parent. Teens who do not want to be in the class may offer insurmountable problems in treatment compliance.

The final and most important component of screening is the mental status exam with the child. This is a rough assessment of the social cognitive abilities of the child, serving as a confirmation of the parent reports thus far. Occasionally parents distort the capabilities of their child in the short-sighted hope of getting the child into the group. In one case, a mother grossly exaggerated the abilities of her child during telephone screening, making him seem as though he was a typically developing child. When we saw him for the mental status exam, it was clear that his language abilities and social interests were substantially delayed and the group would not meet his needs. Table 11.1 presents the structured mental status exam checklist we have used for this purpose.

Table 11.1
Child Mental Status Exam

Child Name_____

1. Did your parents tell you why you're here today?
   ☐ gave correct answer   ☐didn't know, incorrect
2. We have a class that teaches kids how to make and keep friends. Is that something you might be interested in?
   ☐yes   ☐no   ☐don't know
3. I'd like to find out about the things you like to play. Do they have a time at your school when you are free to pick whatever you want to play?
   ☐yes   ☐no (skip to question #10)
4. What do you usually do at recess?
   ☐play with other kids   ☐alone
5. Are there kids that you usually hang around with?
   ☐yes   ☐no (skip to question#10)
6. What are their first names?
   ☐provides up to 5 first names
   ☐provides no first names or tries to name everyone in class
7. Are they the same age, older, or younger than you?
   ☐same age   ☐not same age
8. How do you meet at recess?
   ☐We decide together   ☐I find where they are
9. What kind of games do you usually play?
   ☐just talk/sit & watch others   ☐outdoor sport, specify_____
10. What kinds of games do you like to play outside your house?
    ☐Skate/ride bike or scooter   ☐climbing\chasing\hide & seek   ☐ sport, specify_____

Table 11.1
(Continued)

11. Have you been on any teams (have child specify which teams)?
   ☐no ☐yes, specify_____

12. What kinds of games do you like to play inside your house (don't accept arts/crafts, reading, or TV)?
   ☐electronic games ☐board games

13. What board games do you have in your house that you like to play?
   ☐Board games named by child ☐none

14. Is there anyone who comes over to your house just to play with you?
   ☐yes ☐no (end interview)

15. When was the last time someone was over?
   Within last ☐week ☐month ☐longer than 1 month

16. What was the child's name?
   ☐gave name, specify_____ ☐couldn't remember (end interview)

17. What did you do together (prompt for complete answer)?
   ☐mixed different activities ☐exclusively electronic games and/or TV

18. Reported interest in a class that teaches kids how to make and keep friends:
   ☐Not interested, has plenty of friends
   ☐Showed interest by asking questions about the class
   ☐Stated interest in the class

Global Impressions:
Oriented x 3? ☐Yes ☐No
Mood and affect appropriate to the situation ☐Yes ☐No
Established rapport with the examiner? ☐readily ☐eventually ☐never
Cognitive abilities: ☐below average ☐average ☐above average
Social maturity: ☐1–2 years below age level ☐age level ☐above age level
Characteristics of Note: _____

Source: Reprinted by permission of the UCLA Children's Friendship Program, Los Angeles, California.

Setting up Infrastructure to Handle Short-Term Group Treatment

Setting up an ongoing but time-limited group treatment poses numerous logistical problems. In order to maintain two groups of 10 children each running at any time, there are typically as many as 50 children in the pipeline. The modal delay for our groups from when a parent initially calls to when they and their child begin group treatment is about 6 weeks. Even though parents are asking for group treatment, in many cases their expectations for individualized attention from therapists prior to beginning treatment are the same as for obtaining individual treatment. These expectations can be modified once they come for the intake appointment, but not easily within the phone contacts.

In order to provide more individualized attention, it is essential to set up an infrastructure for tracking the many potential patients through the process. A database is indispensable in this regard. The advantages are that no one gets lost (e.g., forgetting to call the parent when the treatment group is about to start) and parent questions about the status of their admission to the program can be answered quickly. After doing this for awhile, we can project when enough children will be gathered to start a group and we are able to give potential participants a tentative start date. Figure 11.1 is a partial screen shot of

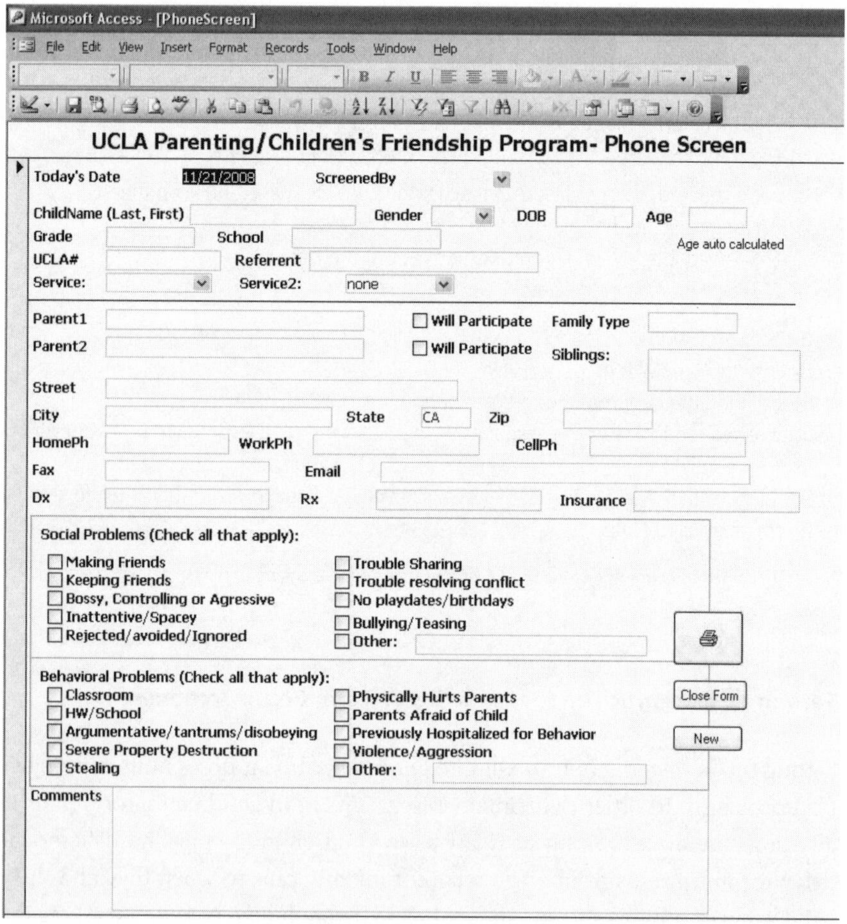
Microsoft Access - [PhoneScreen]
File Edit View Insert Format Records Tools Window Help

UCLA Parenting/Children's Friendship Program- Phone Screen

Today's Date 11/21/2008 ScreenedBy
ChildName (Last, First) Gender DOB Age
Grade School Age auto calculated
UCLA# Referrent
Service: Service2: none

Parent1 Will Participate Family Type
Parent2 Will Participate Siblings:
Street
City State CA Zip
HomePh WorkPh CellPh
Fax Email
Dx Rx Insurance

Social Problems (Check all that apply):
- Making Friends
- Keeping Friends
- Bossy, Controlling or Agressive
- Inattentive/Spacey
- Rejected/avoided/Ignored
- Trouble Sharing
- Trouble resolving conflict
- No playdates/birthdays
- Bullying/Teasing
- Other:

Behavioral Problems (Check all that apply):
- Classroom
- HW/School
- Argumentative/tantrums/disobeying
- Severe Property Destruction
- Stealing
- Physically Hurts Parents
- Parents Afraid of Child
- Previously Hospitalized for Behavior
- Violence/Aggression
- Other:

Close Form
New

Comments

Figure 11.1 Telephone screening page. (Reprinted by permission of the UCLA Children's Friendhsip Program, Los Angeles, California.)

Child N	Service	Grade	Gender	Dx	Age	Packet Out	Packet In
	CFT 147***	3	F	Adjustment NOS	8	4/16/2008	4/28/2008
	CFT 147***	2	M	Asperger's	7	9/5/2008	9/12/2008
	CFT 147***	3	M	ADHD-PI	8	9/3/2008	9/9/2008
	CFT 147***	6	F	Asperger's	11	7/28/2008	8/21/2008
	CFT 147***	2	M	Adjustment NOS	7	8/11/2008	8/20/2008
	CFT 147***	2	F	r/o Asperger's	7	6/6/2008	6/13/2008
	CFT 147***	3	M	Asperger's	8	1/30/2008	2/6/2008
	CFT 147***	2	M	Asperger's	7	7/16/2008	7/23/2008
	CFT 147***	2	M	ADHD-C	7	8/12/2008	8/21/2008
	CFT 148***	5	F	Adjustment NOS	10	6/10/2008	6/20/2008
	CFT 148***	5	M	ADHD-C	10	8/11/2008	8/20/2008
	CFT 148***	5	M	Adjustment NOS	10	7/9/2008	8/6/2008
	CFT 148***	5	M	ADHD-C, Dysthymia	10	3/31/2008	4/11/2008
	CFT 148***	4	F	r/o ADHD-PI	9	6/22/2008	9/4/2008
	CFT 148***	6	M	Asperger's	11	5/16/2008	6/20/2008
	CFT 148***	6	M	ADHD-C	12	6/18/2008	7/7/2008
	CFT 148***	6	M	PDD NOS	11	4/7/2008	5/8/2008
	CFT 148***	4	M	ADHD-C	9	7/31/2008	8/4/2008
	CFT 149	2	M	none	7	7/31/2008	
	CFT 149	2	M	none	8	6/14/2008	
	CFT 149	2	M	none	7	7/30/2008	
	CFT 149	3	F	none	8	9/25/2008	
	CFT 149	2	M	high funct autism	7	7/21/2008	
	CFT 149	3	M	ADHD, fetal alc exp	8	6/9/2008	
	CFT 149	2	M	ADHD	8	1/29/2008	
	CFT 149	3	M	ADHD	8	7/31/2008	
	CFT 149	1	M	none	7	11/3/2008	
	CFT 149	2	F	none	7	11/10/2008	
	CFT 149*	3	M	r/o ADHD	8	5/21/2008	6/6/2008
	CFT 149*	2	M	none	7	6/12/2008	7/17/2008
	CFT 149*	2	M	high funct autism	8	7/28/2008	8/12/2008
	CFT 149**	2	M	Anxiety, ADHD	7	11/4/2008	8/12/2008
	CFT 149**	3	M	ADHD, ODD	8	9/25/2008	10/3/2008
	CFT 149**	2	M	none	8	8/29/2008	10/29/2008
	CFT 149***	3	M	ADHD-C, r/o Autism	7	3/26/2008	4/8/2008
	CFT 149***	2	F	ODD	7	12/21/2007	1/17/2008
	CFT 149***	2	F	ADHD-PI	7	3/27/2008	4/10/2008
	CFT 149***	2	F	Adjustment w/dep	8	3/13/2008	4/28/2008
	CFT 149***	2	M	ADHD-C	7	4/30/2008	8/26/2008
	CFT 149*Hold	3	M	ASD	9	4/28/2008	4/28/2008

Figure 11.2 Children's friendship program database. (Reprinted by permission of the UCLA Children's Friendship Program, Los Angeles, California.)

Child N	Service	Grade	Gender	Dx	Age	Packet Out	Packet In
	CFT 149*Hold	4	F	none	9	5/13/2008	6/13/2008
	CFT 150	2	F	r/o ADHD	7	9/4/2008	
	CFT 150	5	M	ADHD, PDD	10	10/28/2008	
	CFT 150	5	F	none	11	10/8/2008	
	CFT 150	4	M	Tics, r/o ADHD	9	9/8/2008	
	CFT 150	5	M	none	11	10/16/2008	

Figure 11.2 (Continued)

our telephone screening data entry page, and Figure 11.2 is an example of a database created from the telephone contact entries. Some information has been altered and the child name (left-hand column), date of birth, and school have been deleted for purposes of this presentation.

We number each group sequentially. CFT147 and 148 are currently running (three stars means that all intake and screening procedures are done), while we are screening for groups CFT149 and 150. We list diagnosis, as we like to mix no more than four children with ASD in any group. For group CFT 149, we have 23 potential patients at various stages. Five have been accepted into the group, three (having two stars) have been scheduled for intakes, and three have just returned completed packets (baseline measures and outpatient required forms). We accept a maximum of 10, so that we have one more with returned packets than we have room. The last one to return a packet of forms is placed on the waiting list in case anyone ahead of him or her does not work out. Notice in addition to the 13 potential patients who have returned packets, there are 10 listed under CFT 149 and 5 under CFT 150 that have called for information, had a packet mailed to them, and have not yet returned the packet. Some have had packets mailed to them over 10 months before. It is fairly typical that about half who call for information and packets never follow through in mailing packets back. Our clinic coordinator will call to remind them up to three times to see if they are still interested (and document each call in the comments section of the telephone screen page). If they state they are interested, then they are kept active. If they do not respond after the third call, they are deleted from the database. We list the school name so that we can alert potential subjects in the rare event that another potential subject is from the same school (and the child may possibly breach confidentiality as to group membership). We ascertain, without divulging the identity of the other potential patient, if this is acceptable to both parties

Group Composition

Each specific class of children needs to be limited in their range of socio-developmental level. It is better to keep each group of children within one grade of each other for small total group size (less than 8 children) or within two grade levels for a group of 10 children. There are two reasons to limit the range of sociodevelopmental levels within each group: (1) Children will have difficulty interacting with each other within the sessions and may show more resistance to interacting with group members who are at substantially lower levels than they are. It is appropriate for children to be selective in this regard. (2) Parents may be uncomfortable about this divergence, fearing that the intake professional felt their child was more severely disabled than they can accept. Parents may also worry that their child may learn deviant behaviors from group members who are at significantly lower developmental levels (however, with tightly run groups where leaders maintain strict discipline, this is not an issue).

Gender issues are problematic, as referral rates for boys are about three times greater than for girls. Many elementary school girls would not be comfortable if they were the only girl in a group with nine boys. This is less an issue for groups for teens with ASD. Since same-sex friendships among elementary-aged children are encouraged, three girls within one grade of each other is an ideal minimum (we have rarely had more in one group). If only two girls are available for a group, then it is wise to consult with the parents of both girls to see if they are willing to risk having their girl be alone with the boys for a session if the other girl is absent. If a girl is comfortable playing with boys, then parents generally do not mind.

The First Few Groups

The most difficult part of the process is the formation of the first few groups. Referral sources have not been alerted to the groups or what they can provide and no "track record" has been established (either in the capacity to form adequate groups or the benefits to children). In order to start a group, parents of children with comparable characteristics must be enrolled within about a 3-month period of each other. Any longer than this and parents will usually not want to wait or will lose confidence that the professional can provide the intervention that has been described to them. The professional should not compromise on the range of ages or sociodevelopmental levels of potential group members in order to get the initial groups under way. It is best to get at least six in a group. This is the "critical mass" or the minimum number of participants that feels like a "group" to both participants and group leaders. Seven or eight participants is a safer number to start, as absences will be less likely to take the group below critical mass. Recommended maximum group size is 10 for 1-hour sessions, as this allows parents adequate time for discussion. If the session length is 90 minutes, then 12 may be a comfortable maximum size.

Physical Parameters

There are three locations to secure before beginning the class: separate indoor locations for parent and child classes and an outdoor location (play deck) for some of the child/teen games. Parent and child rooms and the outside play area should be as close as possible to each other for quick transport during each session. The parent room should have a large table and enough space for all parents to be seated together at the same time. It is helpful to create a classroom atmosphere for the child/teen and parent sessions. The child/teen room should have a blackboard or marker board, and tables and chairs for children to sit in. There must be "floor room" for sessions focusing on play dates for child sessions or as an alternative area during periods of inclement weather. The outside play area used to teach skills for outside games should resemble a playground as much as possible. It should have sports equipment such as a basketball hoop, soccer goal net, and tetherball pole and should be fully fenced in for safety.

Session Structure

The next sections describe the session structure of CFT. The child and teen versions have only a few structural differences, which are elucidated where needed.

Parent Sessions

The mission of the parent session is to teach skills, correct parent errors, and help effect the solution of specific impediments to homework compliance. The standard session agenda facilitates staying on track. Each parent session is broken down into four segments: *(1) Initial gathering (5 minutes)*: Parents and children/teens gather and the group leaders inspect the toys/activities that the children/teens have brought in from home before the start of their session. The children/teens then go to their session room. *(2) Homework review (25 minutes)*:

Each parent reports the results of the previously assigned homework. Putting the homework review here emphasizes the importance of homework completion. *(3) Parent handout/homework assignment (20 minutes)*: A handout is presented and reviewed. *(4) End of session reunification (10 minutes)*: The parent and child/teen are reunited. The date, time, and other party to the homework assignment are negotiated between each parent and child/teen before they leave the session.

Child/Teen Sessions

The child/teen session begins as they are led out of the parent room and into the child/teen room. Coaches and group leaders act as consultants rather than playmates, watching and dispensing verbal reinforcement and tokens (only for some child sessions), and providing consequences for misbehavior (Ladd & Golter, 1988). They avoid playing and conversing with children/teens. Each child/teen session (except for the first and last) is broken down into three segments. *(1) Homework review (10 minutes)*: Participants report on the results of the homework assignment given in the previous session. Motivation for participants to do the homework comes from parent involvement in it, combined with hearing the other participants' successes and getting a star on the blackboard for attempting it. *(2) Didactic (20 minutes)*: The didactic presentation may help participants to attend to key situations in their social world and lay the groundwork for subsequent practice in session and at home. *(3) Real play (20 minutes)*: This is the segment of the session the participants like the most.

Homework review and didactic segments mimic a classroom setting. The group leaders only recognize participants who raise their hand. Participants' responses during these segments require specific feedback so that they can identify things they do correctly and eliminate counterproductive behaviors. Correcting errors might make a participant uncomfortable at the moment but will make clear to the participant and the other group members that the response was incorrect. It is advisable to keep the homework review and didactic segments as brief as possible (covering all of the material in the session plan) so that the real-play segment will last as long as possible.

Verbal instruction can be effective in orienting participants to the skill being taught, especially if a Socratic method is used. However, participants consolidate knowledge more readily through coaching in the real-play segment. Remember, however, that most of the important practice will be done during the homework assignments.

Every session has parent handouts and/or homework assignment sheets that are distributed to parents to take home as reminders. These handouts are simple and are given out only one at a time (not the whole set at once) so that parents will be more apt to look at them when they need to be reminded.

At the time of writing, we have conducted 143 groups of CFT (children) and 13 groups for teens. The mean group size of children completing treatment was 8.6. Thus over 18 years we have seen over 1200 children in CFT and in the past 4 years, 100 in the teen intervention. It took us about 2 years to build up our child referral base so that we rarely have a gap between groups of more than 2 weeks. On the other hand, services are lacking for teens, and it took less than 6 months to build up our referral base for the teen intervention. The potential for parent-assisted social skills treatment to help both perpetrators and their victims is great, both in the impact of treatment and the large numbers of children who can be treated.

Summary

The major points of this chapter are:

- Socials skills programs can promote the development of close friendships, which is a general protective factor against bullying.
- Parents should be an integral part of the social skill treatment of their child.
- Social skills groups can effectively teach children and their parents to discriminate teasing from tactless feedback and act accordingly to diminish victimization.
- Victimization by nonselective physical aggression (frequent fighting) can also be dealt with in social skills groups by teaching children to avoid the frequent fighter.

References

Barth, R. (1979). Home-based reinforcement of social behavior: A review and analysis. *Review of Educational Research, 49,* 436–458.

Beelman, A., Pfingsten, U., & Lösel, F. (1994). Effects of training social competence in children: A meta-analysis of recent evaluation studies. *Journal of Clinical Child Psychology, 23,* 260–271.

Bierman, K. L. (1986a). Process of change during social skills training with preadolescents and its relation to treatment outcome. *Child Development, 57,* 230–240.

Bierman, K. L. (1986b). The relationship between social aggression and peer rejection in middle childhood. In R. Prinz (Ed.), *Advances in behavioral assessment of children and families* (Vol. 2., pp. 151–178). Greenwich, CT: JAI Press.

Bierman, K. L., & Conduct Problems Prevention Research Group. (1997). Implementing a comprehensive program for the prevention of conduct problems in rural communities: The Fast Track experience. *American Journal of Community Psychology, 25*, 493–514.

Bierman, K. L., & Furman, W. (1984). The effects of social skills training and peer involvement in the social adjustment of preadolescents. *Child Development, 55*, 151–162.

Bierman, K. L., & Smoot, D. L. (1991). Linking family characteristics with poor peer relations: The mediating role of conduct problems. *Journal of Abnormal Child Psychology, 19*, 341–356.

Black, B., & Hazen, N. L. (1990). Social status and patterns of communication in acquainted and unacquainted preschool children. *Developmental Psychology, 26*, 379–387.

Boulton, M. J. (1999). Concurrent and longitudinal relations between children's playground behavior and social preference, victimization, and bullying. *Child Development, 70*, 944–954.

Budd, K. S. (1985). Parents as mediators in the social skills training of children. In L. L'Abate & M. A. Milan (Eds.), *Handbook of social skills training and research* (pp. 245–262). New York: Wiley.

Chennault, M. (1967). Improving the social acceptance of unpopular educable mentally retarded pupils in special classes. *American Journal of Mental Deficiency, 72*, 455–458.

Cillesson, A. H., Van Ijzendoorn, H. W., Van Lieshout, C. F., & Hartup, W. W. (1992). Heterogeneity among peer rejected boys: Subtypes and stabilities. *Child Development, 63*, 893–905.

Coie, J. D., Christopoulos, C., Terry, R., Dodge, K. A., & Lochman, J. E. (1989). Types of aggressive relationships, peer rejection, and developmental consequences. In B. H. Schneider, G. Attili, J. Nadel, & R. P. Weissberg (Eds.), *Social competence in developmental perspective* (pp. 223–237). Boston: Kluwer Academic Publishers.

Coie, J. D., & Kupersmidt, J. B. (1983). A behavioral analysis of emerging social status. *Child Development, 54*, 1400–1416.

Cousins, L. S., & Weiss, G. (1993). Parent training and social skills training for children with attention-deficit hyperactivity disorder: How can they be combined for greater effectiveness? *Canadian Journal of Psychiatry, 38*, 449–457.

Dishion, T. J. (1990). The family ecology of boys' peer relations in middle childhood. *Child Development, 61*, 874–892.

Dodge, K. A. (1983). Behavioral antecedents of peer social rejection and isolation. *Child Development, 54*, 1386–1399.

Dodge, K. A., Schlundt, D. C., Schocken, I., & Delugach, J. D. (1983). Social competence and children's sociometric status: The role of peer group entry strategies. *Merrill-Palmer Quarterly, 29*, 309–336.

Erwin, P. (1993). *Friendships and peer relations in children.* New York: Wiley.

Fonzi, A., Schneider, B. H., Tani, F., & Tomada, G. (1997). Predicting children's friendship status from their dyadic interaction in structured situations of potential conflict. *Child Development, 68*, 496–506.

Frankel, F. (1996). *Good friends are hard to find: Help your child find, make, and keep friends*. Los Angeles: Perspective Publishing.

Frankel, F. (2005). Parent-assisted children's friendship training. In E. D. Hibbs & P. S. Jensen (Eds.), *Psychosocial treatments for child and adolescent disorders: Empirically based approaches* (2nd ed., pp. 693–715). Washington, DC: American Psychological Association.

Frankel, F., & Myatt, R. (2003). *Children's friendship training*. New York: Brunner-Routledge Publishers.

Frankel, F., & Myatt, R. (2007). Parent-assisted friendship training for children with autism spectrum disorders: Effects associated with psychotropic medication. *Child Psychiatry and Human Development, 37*, 337–346.

Frankel, F., Myatt, R., & Cantwell, D. P. (1995). Training outpatient boys to conform with the social ecology of popular peers: Effects on parent and teacher ratings. *Journal of Clinical Child Psychology, 24*, 300–310.

Frankel, F., Myatt, R., Cantwell, D. P., & Feinberg, D. T. (1997). Parent assisted children's social skills training: Effects on children with and without attention-deficit hyperactivity disorder. *Journal of the Academy of Child and Adolescent Psychiatry, 36*, 1056–1064.

Frankel, F., Paley, B., Marquart, R., & O'Connor, M. J. (2006). Stimulants, neuroleptics and children's friendship training in children with fetal alcohol spectrum disorders. *Journal of Child and Adolescent Psychopharmacology, 16*, 777–789.

Frankel, F., Sinton, M., & Wilfley, D. (2007). Social skills training and the treatment of pediatric overweight. In W. O'Donohue, B. Moore, & W. B. Scott (Eds.), *The handbook of pediatric and adolescent obesity treatment* (pp. 105–115). New York: Taylor & Francis.

French, D. C. (1988). Heterogeneity of peer-rejected boys: Aggressive and non aggressive subtypes. *Child Development, 59*, 976–985.

Garvey, C. (1984). *Children's talk*. Cambridge, MA: Harvard University Press.

Gelb, R., & Jacobson, J. L. (1988). Popular and unpopular children's interactions during cooperative and competitive peer group activities. *Journal of Abnormal Child Psychology, 16*, 247–261.

Hodges, E. V. E., Boivin, M., Vitaro, F., & Bukowski, W. M. (1999). The power of friendship: Protection against an escalating cycle of peer victimization. *Developmental Psychology, 35*, 94–101.

Kazdin, A. E., Esveldt-Dawson, K., French, N. H., & Unis, A. S. (1987). Problem-solving skills training and relationship therapy in the treatment of antisocial child behavior. *Journal of Consulting & Clinical Psychology, 55*, 76–85.

Kennedy, J. (1992). Relationship of maternal beliefs and childrearing strategies to social competence in preschool children. *Child Study Journal, 22*, 39–55.

Kochenderfer, B. J., & Ladd, G. W. (1997). Victimized children's responses to peers' aggression: Behaviors associated with reduced versus continued victimization. *Development and Psychopathology, 9*, 59–73.

Ladd, G. W. (1992). Themes and theories: Perspectives on processes in family-peer relationships. In R. D. Parke & G. W. Ladd (Eds.), *Family-peer relationships: Modes of linkages* (pp. 3–34). Hillsdale, NJ: Erlbaum.

Ladd G. W., & Asher, S. R. (1985). Social skill training and children's peer relations. In L. L'Abate & M. A. Milan (Eds.), *Handbook of social skills training and research* (pp. 219–244). New York: Wiley.

Ladd, G. W., & Golter, B. S. (1988). Parents' management of preschoolers peer relations: Is it related to children's social competence? *Developmental Psychology, 24,* 109–117.

Ladd, G. W., LeSieur, K., & Profilet, S. (1993). Direct parental influences on young children's peer relations. In S. W. Duck (Ed.), *Understanding relationship processes 2: Learning about relationships* (pp. 152–183). London: Sage.

Ladd, G. W., Profilet, S. M., & Hart, C. H. (1992). Parents' management of children's peer relations: Facilitating and supervising children's activities in the peer culture. In R. D. Parke & G. W. Ladd (Eds.), *Family-peer relationships: Modes of linkages* (pp. 215–253). Hillsdale, NJ: Erlbaum.

La Greca, A. M. (1993). Social skills training with children: Where do we go from here? *Journal of Clinical Child Psychology, 22,* 288–298.

Laugeson, E. A., Frankel, F., Mogil, C., & Dillon, A. R. (2009). Parent-assisted social skills training to improve friendships in teens with autism spectrum disorders. *Journal of Autism and Developmental Disabilities, 39,* 596–606.

Lilly, M. S. (1971). Improving social acceptance of low sociometric status, low achieving students. *Exceptional Children, 37,* 341–347.

Malik, N. M., & Furman, W. (1993). Practitioner review: Problems in children's peer relations: What can the clinician do? *Journal of Child Psychology & Psychiatry, 34,* 1303–1326.

Middleton, M. B., & Cartledge, G. (1995). The effects of social skills instruction and parental involvement on the aggressive behaviors of African American males. *Behavior Modification, 19,* 192–210.

Newcomb, A. F., Bukowski, W. M., & Pattee, L. (1993). Children's peer relations: A meta-analytic review of popular, rejected, neglected, controversial, and average sociometric status. *Psychological Bulletin, 113,* 99–128.

O'Connor, M. J., Frankel, F., Paley, B., Schonfeld, A. M., Carpenter, E. M., Laugeson, E. A., et al. (2006). A controlled social skills training for children with fetal alcohol spectrum disorders. *Journal of Consulting and Clinical Psychology, 74,* 639–648.

Olweus, D. (1993). Bullies on the playground: The role of victimization. In C. H. Hart (Ed.), *Children on playgrounds* (pp. 45–128). Albany: State University of New York Press.

Patterson, G. R. (1986). Performance models for antisocial boys. *American Psychologist, 41,* 432–444.

Patterson, G. R., & Chamberlain, P. (2006). A functional analysis of resistance during parent training therapy. *Clinical Psychology: Science and Practice, 1,* 53–70.

Patterson, G. R., DeBaryshe, B. D., & Ramsey, E. (1989). A developmental perspective on antisocial behavior. *American Psychologist, 44,* 329–335.

Perry, D. G., Kusel, S. J., & Perry, L. C. (1988). Victims of peer aggression. *Developmental Psychology, 24,* 807–814.

Perry, D. G., Williard, J. C., & Perry, L. C. (1990). Peer perceptions of the consequences that victimized children provide aggressors. *Child Development, 61,* 1310–1325.

Pettit, G. S., Bates, J. E., Dodge, K. A., & Meece, D. W. (1999). The impact of after-school peer contact on early adolescent externalizing problems is moderated by parental monitoring, perceived neighborhood safety, and prior adjustment. *Child Development, 70,* 768–778.

Pfiffner, L. J., & McBurnett, K. (1997). Social skills training with parent generalization: Treatment effects for children with attention deficit disorder. *Journal of Consulting & Clinical Psychology, 65,* 749–757.

Powell, T. H., Salzberg, C. L., Rule, S., Levy, S., & Itzkowitz, J. S. (1983). Teaching mentally retarded children to play with their siblings using parents as trainers. *Education and Treatment of Children, 6,* 343–362.

Prinstein, M. J., & La Greca, A. M. (1999). Links between mothers' and children's social competence and associations with maternal adjustment. *Journal of Clinical Child Psychology, 28,* 197–210.

Prinz, R. J., Blechman, E., & Dumas, J. E. (1994). An evaluation of peer coping-skills training for childhood aggression. *Journal of Clinical Child Psychology, 23,* 193–203.

Quinn, M. M., Kavale, K. A., Mathur, S. R., Rutherford, R. B., Jr., & Forness, S. R. (1999). A meta-analysis of social skill interventions for students with emotional or behavioral disorders. *Journal of Emotional and Behavioral Disorders, 7,* 54–64.

Ray, G. E., Cohen, R., Secrist, M. E., & Duncan, M. K. (1997). Relating aggressive and victimization behaviors to children's sociometric status and friendships. *Journal of Social & Personal Relationships, 14,* 95–108.

Rose, A. J., & Asher, S. R. (1999). Children's goals and strategies in response to conflicts within a friendship. *Developmental Psychology, 35,* 69–79.

Russell, A., & Finnie, V. (1990). Preschool children's social status and maternal instructions to assist group entry. *Developmental Psychology, 26,* 603–611.

Rucker, C. N., & Vincenzo, F. M. (1970). Maintaining social acceptance gains made by mentally retarded children. *Exceptional Children, 36,* 679–680.

Scambler, D. J., Harris, M. J., & Milich, R. (1998). Sticks and stones: Evaluations of responses to childhood teasing. *Social Development, 7,* 234–249.

Schwartz, D., Dodge, K. A., Pettit, G. S., & Bates, J. E. (1997). The early socialization of aggressive victims of bullying. *Child Development, 68,* 665–675.

Shantz, C. U. (1987). Conflicts between children. *Child Development, 58,* 283–305.

Shapiro, J. P., Baumeister, R. E., & Kessler, J. W. (1991). A three-component model of children's teasing: Aggression, humor, and ambiguity. *Journal of Social & Clinical Psychology, 10,* 459–472.

Sheridan, S. M., Dee, C. C., Morgan, J. C., McCormick, M. E., & Walker, D. (1996). A multimethod intervention for social skills deficits in children with ADHD and their parents. *School Psychology Review, 25,* 57–76

Wahler, R. G., & Dumas, J. E. (1989). Attentional problems in dysfunctional mother-child interactions: An interbehavioral model. *Psychological Bulletin, 105,* 116–130.

Warm, T. R. (1997). The role of teasing in development and vice versa. *Journal of Developmental & Behavioral Pediatrics, 18,* 97–101.

Wilfley, D. E., Stein, R. I., Saelens, B. E., Mockus, D. S., Matt, G. E., Hayden-Wade, H. A., et al. (2007). Efficacy of maintenance treatment approaches for childhood overweight: A randomized controlled trial. *Journal of the American Medical Association, 298,* 1661–1673.

12

Creating and Administering Successful Policy Strategies for School Anti-Bullying Programs

Stuart W. Twemlow and Frank C. Sacco

P olicy makers set the tone for a school district's priorities and level of activity concerning anti-bullying efforts. Many of the chapters in this book focus on the evidence-based content and procedures that have been found to be effective in various programs. This chapter emphasizes the diligent policy maker's role in promoting the positive awareness and sustained effort needed to reduce bullying and create peaceful school learning environments. This requires that a series of framework issues need to be considered by the policy maker. Oversimplification of these complex issues and especially a lack of attention to power dynamics and school climate will erode the effectiveness of even the best of programs (Twemlow & Sacco, 2008).

Our perspective has been shaped from working with a number of school systems across the United States as well as internationally in countries such as Jamaica, Australia, New Zealand, Hungary, and Paraguay. This cross-national viewpoint is one that is both grounded in empirical scientific exploration of the topic of bullying and victimization as well as considerable field research into the application of violence prevention. This work has highlighted the need to adapt programs to the school rather than the school to the program.

We have also been influenced by our work with the FBI's Critical Incident Response Group in trying to understand the recent spate of U.S. school shootings and how school environments can become very hostile and humiliating places to be (e.g., Twemlow, Fonagy, Sacco, O'Toole, & Vernberg, 2002). When studying school shootings, it is clear that the eruption of violence in these settings is often revenge–retaliation style. Young students are exposed to long-term shame and their revenge is sometimes a planned targeted attack to symbolically express their frustration with feeling socially humiliated and disconnected from their peer groups and families (Twemlow, Fonagy, Sacco, &

Vernberg, 2008). Social aggression in these suburban settings can be lethal, leading to suicide attempts and occasionally attempts at homicide (Klomek, Marrocco, Kleinman, Schonfield, & Gould, 2007). Although both suicide and homicide are relatively rare, chronic failure of children to achieve at their potential even in affluent suburban schools is a chronic and serious problem.

We have worked with a continuum of school systems that ranges on the one hand from highly resourced and achievement-oriented private and public school environments to the most impoverished schools in the United States and in evolving nations. In our experience, critical framework issues related to power dynamics and school climate are played out in some form in all school systems we have studied irrespective of affluence and geography (Twemlow & Sacco, 2008). Policy makers need to understand the dynamics of each school's climate. What types of violence patterns are being expressed? Take time to walk the corridors and see for yourself. Is the school in control? Are there unrepaired physical facilities, broken windows, or graffiti? Are there alienated youth? Do social cliques exclude students? Are there any active groups working on improving climate? Are teachers happy and in control of their classrooms? Are natural leaders being used to help build a positive climate?

Understanding Power Dynamics and Bullying

We have worked in a number of countries to help build peaceful schools. In so doing we have realized the value of using a deeper understanding of the power dynamics in a social system, especially schools. Power is a universal human motivation that can be acted out differently from culture to culture and in many different forms within each culture.

Peaceful and creative learning environments require that the climate be free of targeted aggression either in direct confrontational or indirect psychological forms. We feel that the fundamental theoretical understanding of how programs operate depends on whether they can target the patterns of actions acted out through a process we call the bully-victim-bystander power dynamic (Twemlow, Sacco, & Williams, 1996). The social system in which schools operate is seen as a multilayered structure of stakeholders (Twemlow, Fonagy, & Sacco, 2005a). When power dynamics in any of these layers become imbalanced, it becomes possible for bullying to emerge. For example, a teacher or building administrator may develop a bullying role with peers or students, as may individual students within a specific classroom (Twemlow & Fonagy, 2005). It is important to understand in this theoretical perspective that bullying is seen as a reflection of what each layer of this complex social system allows. The idea is that bullies will always accomplish what bystanders allow. Strong leadership that is active, involved, and seemingly ever-present allows for less chance for pathological power dynamics to build up within that school. If key school administrators have a "hands off, hide in the office" style, pathological power dynamics have plenty of time to gather in various pockets within the social system and undermine the development of a positive school learning environment.

A school policy maker thus needs to assess the power dynamics that exist between and within all elements in the school, including teachers, students, support staff, parents, administrators, volunteers, and even the surrounding community before selecting and implementing a program intended to create a positive learning environment. It is important to reiterate that this discussion is aimed at assisting policy makers and senior school administrators in understanding the problems that are occurring before they take reflective action. Developing a theoretical understanding of how the social system operates is one way to begin to create metaphors that will assist in evaluating and designing programs to reduce bullying within the overall school system.

Understanding School Climate

A school's climate is hard to see or measure with great precision. However, it is often apparent at an intuitive level when one walks into a school. Some schools are alive with positive activity and echo with the sounds of children engaged in high-interest learning. In other schools frustrated and angry teachers can be heard ranting and other students are bouncing off one and another in disruptive chaos. These are the rather obvious signs of climate. Perceptions of the school's psychological climate may be shaped by its physical presence. In some cases, schools are extraordinary well maintained and have a high level of physical resources. In many schools the physical structures are tolerable and are sufficient to allow teaching to occur. These physical characteristics are often beyond the control of most policy makers. There is little need to argue that educational policy makers and school administrators are always fighting for additional resources to build physical structures, keep equipment modern, and stay with the pace of proper salaries for all educational staff. It is important to recognize, however, that within tolerable limits how well a school is maintained is little related to its psychological climate (see also Chapter 13).

The psychological climate of the school can be influenced with little invest-ment of dollars, but positive change requires that the power dynamics within the system be understood and managed. Unhealthy power dynamics entrenched within pockets of the school system must be recognized and addressed, yet these entrenched patterns may be among the most difficult to acknowledge. Shame and humiliation can occur often within limited cliques or social groups of children, especially directed toward children who do not excel on highly valued attributes (Twemlow, Fonagy, & Sacco, 2003). Highly achievement-oriented schools may create a competitiveness based on that dynamic. Similarly, a school focused on sports prowess will similarly overvalue such efforts at the expense of other needs. For example, in one prominent high school we visited, everyone entering the school was confronted by 6-foot-high photographs of a school basketball team and their trophies. On the second floor of the same school in a back corridor were photographs of award-winning forensics and debate teams that had far less priority within the school. This school system had spent millions of dollars on a new athletic stadium, while a public bond referendum failed to provide the money necessary to air-condition the school.

The policy maker needs to realize that many of the power dynamics are quite unconscious, or, are so much a part of the way a school operates that nobody sees them as pathological or even present. For example, if the school is entirely focused on winning everything, then the negative impact on the children who have to do the winning will not be seen very clearly. Similarly, a less involved child lost in a crowd of other children driven by coaches and adult mentors and models has little voice in bringing these issues out as critically important.

A positive school climate is one that promotes a sense of connectedness and a reflective mindset in all of the groups involved (Twemlow, Fonagy, & Sacco, 2005b). Such schools have a singular interest in searching for ways to improve the school climate by attending to interpersonal and communication issues rather than an endless and relatively exclusive emphasis on academic achievement or athletic skills. A truly integrated school community gives equal value to all its members.

Common Myths and Fallacies about Bullying

Through our efforts in trying to help schools change, we have repeatedly encountered certain mistaken beliefs that create barriers to creating and sustaining change in schools (Table 12.1). These false assumptions surface

Table 12.1
Myths and Realities

Myth	Reality
This school is too good or too bad.	Schools reflect the value communities place on them. Schools are as good or bad as a community allows. High-achieving schools can have rampant social aggression.
School violence is someone else's problem.	Everyone is connected in creating peaceful schools, from community leaders to the custodial staff.
Zero tolerance works.	Zero tolerance creates adversarial school relationships and blocks critical student communication about risk and threat.
School size matters.	Social climate is what counts, not school size.
Today's kids are the same as "when we were young."	Today's kids have a unique struggle due to hyper-connectivity from cellular phones and the Internet.
Eliminating the bully solves the problem.	Eliminating the bully does not address the climate that fostered the bully role.
	Someone else will quickly fill that role. Expulsion leads to more expulsion.
More money means safer schools.	Safety cannot be bought. When money is not an issue, social status is and vicious social or relational aggression infects the school climate with lethal consequences.
Bullying is just a kid thing.	Bullying is a *human* thing. Frequent humiliating communications entrap victims.
Focus on problem kids will improve climate.	Change the school climate and problem kids will be easier to help.

regardless of the economic status of the school and create unsuccessful, frustrating, and potentially dangerous processes that hinder serious attempts to address bullying in schools, whether physical or psychological. The following fallacies we have collected over time represent how social systems consistently avoid reflecting on their own collective selves in assuming responsibility for a social problem.

This School Is Too Good or Too Bad

Many schools have a vision about their own situation, which is often dominated by perceptions of physical safety or danger. If a school is impoverished and in a violent neighborhood, people may assume (often justifiably) that the school is unsafe. Struggling schools often lose hope and communities frequently abandon their schools when they are considered beyond repair, unconsciously allowing them to become breeding grounds for future violence.

On the other hand, a school that is neat, clean, and high achieving with students who seldom engage in physical fights has no guarantee that students and teachers are free from nonphysical types of social aggression. Good schools that strive for perfection and indulge students and teachers with resources can still be very unhealthy and unhappy environments for students (McMahon & Luthar, 2006). Columbine High School, for instance, was an example of a great school, and everyone in Jefferson County, Colorado, thought so. As we now know, this fantasy ended tragically because of two unhappy boys in a climate which unconsciously tolerated the humiliation of students by other students. Having spent time with many of the teachers and principals who have had shootings in their schools, we definitely believe there is a potential school shooter in every suburban school. When social aggression is allowed to continue unchecked, the social climate becomes infected by humiliation. When an *injustice collector* (someone who blames problems on others and resentfully feels like the victim of social injustice) begins to break away from adult and peer connections, the likelihood of such an individual becoming an avenging victim increases dramatically (Twemlow et al., 2008). The Columbine High School shooters were known to have been targets of social aggression from their peers. Their lethal acts became their final way of communicating their despair with a system that considered itself "too good" to be harboring this degree of unhappiness.

The invisible force at work in seemingly safe schools like Columbine can be considered a silent killer. It has notably few outward symptoms, which can easily slip below the radar and remain there until unexplained explosions of violence, high rates of addiction, suicide, and sudden academic failures become visible. The school in question may not have many open fights. There may be no weapons at all inside the building because the weapon of choice in social aggression is the spoken word and its subsequent echoes over the Internet. Some students may be particularly at risk for victimization or for assuming the victimizer's role. Bystanders are everywhere, and it is up to schools to look deeper into the larger group climate in order to recognize the signs of this type of violence (Twemlow, Fonagy, & Sacco, 2004). Simply patrolling and insuring that there are no guns or knives in a school are clearly not sufficient. Furthermore, bullying shifts from predominantly physical intimidation in middle school to a more social form of bullying in high school, based primarily on social inclusion and exclusion.

School Violence Is Somebody Else's Problem

This fallacy is very common in a staggering number of schools. In a private school, parents may be paying big money for their children's education. Their expectation may also be that they are paying for the right not to have to parent while the children are at school. Public school parents are often busy working or struggling in poverty, and they also believe that the school should handle its own problems. Parents may see their responsibility ending when their children go out the front door. If the school calls the parents about their child's misbehavior, the modern response appears to begin and end with a finger-pointing process. The days of administrators, educators, and parents being automatically on the same page about their children's school behavior are all but gone. Regardless of whether a school is private or public, parents are letting their children's schools do much of the parenting, and guiltily criticizing school personnel.

Our experience has shown us time and again that successfully resolving school problems must be a community priority. When a school stands alone in the community, it becomes isolated and loses its ability to be enriched by its environment. Instead, this sort of school devours its own energy internally until something tragic occurs and causes the school to implode. We must remember that the school represents a critical social context that actively promotes the development of a community's future. Public schools are funded by local, state, and federal taxes, with property taxes often providing a high percentage of funding. Thus, affluent families have access to more affluent schools. When a family has a child in school, they tend to pay more attention to the allocation of funds, but they still may not become heavily involved with ensuring their children's safety and well-being.

Unfortunately, parents are transferring more responsibilities to the school for a variety of understandable reasons. Urban schools in the United States are populated by an increasing number of children from dysfunctional homes with absent or abusive fathers and overwhelmed or traumatized mothers, and increasing numbers of children living in foster homes. Many of these children suffer from environmentally induced behaviors that are both self-destructive and disruptive (Gilligan, 1996). In U.S. suburbs, parents are working harder than ever before. There are more two-parent working families who send their children to school, leaving them to fend for themselves or to spend their time in after-school programs until their exhausted parents finish work and come to collect them.

The net result of these different pressures is that parents are more likely to point their fingers at the school, demanding service and dealing out blame after their child underperforms or gets into trouble. The idea that the education of children is purely a school job stems from different sources, but it quickly becomes a convenient way to avoid accepting collective responsibility for the creation of peaceful schools. For instance, some members of the community are not yet parents or have already raised children who have graduated and moved away. When the school asks for a budget increase, these citizens may feel less connected to their community's schools, and again, the school is considered an isolated institution continually in need. When the school fails, the community resorts to blame, further isolating the school.

Zero Tolerance Reduces Destructive Decisions

It is can be comforting to fantasize that simply forbidding something can be sufficient to solve a problem like bullying at school. It is, of course, common sense to reason that bullying should not be tolerated, but this is a gross oversimplification of the work that needs to be done in order to eliminate bullying. The spirit of zero tolerance is punitive and results in expulsions, conflict, denial, and favoritism (see also Chapter 10). At the other end of the continuum is the implementation of dismissive social contexts. In this scenario, the school turns a blind eye to bullying and dismisses the value of reporting bullying or of taking steps to intervene.

Zero tolerance also leads to prejudice in how situations in a school are handled. When a collective mindset engages in nonreflective, overly simple reactions to very complicated problems, the thinking becomes stereotypical and narrow minded. The fact remains that students are children who are still growing up in a wide range of family constellations and community and economic circumstances. Mandating punishment for bullying drives it underground and avoids dealing with the more complex reasons why coercive energy exists in the system. Zero tolerance may be applied harshly or inappropriately and can result in very destructive effects on children and their families.

The practical disadvantage of the zero-tolerance approach to bullying is that it closes out potentially valuable field intelligence gathered by the other students (Twemlow et al., 2002, 2008). If the peer group at any age thinks that "telling" an authority figure about bullying might result in harsh punishment, they will be less likely to report that someone is being humiliated, has made a threat, or has a drug problem. This becomes a critical issue, especially for middle and high school students. When the FBI and Secret Service studied school shooters, both agreed that most shooters gave plenty of advance warning, especially to their friends. Teen suicide has a very similar pattern.

These tragedies occur when desperate young people act in extreme ways to relieve the unending burdens and intense emotional pain they experience while we all deny the seriousness of the messages they give.

School Size Matters

Every school has unique climate zones. Simply being small or exclusive does not guarantee a peaceful school. Columbine was large, whereas Pearl, Mississippi, was small. Yet both had shootings. The size of a school in and of itself defines only a small part of the formula for understanding what is needed to create a more positive school climate.

We have worked with one high school that breaks all the rules about size. It has 4000 students who are very high achieving for a public high school. The grade point average for the senior class is 3.6. However, this is not the secret to their success. They have managed to create a peaceful and functioning school. This school invests 25 minutes each day to discuss with students problems and successes experienced at the school. The school is large, but it created a way for the students and the faculty to make one-on-one connections. The school metaphorically shrunk itself by increasing student and teacher time focused on relationships rather than just academics (Twemlow et al., 2005b).

This high school is still struggling to manage the Problem of Excellence; that is, how can students manage their parents' pressure to be the best of the best? It invested tremendous amounts of time to organize meetings to bring together groups interested in improving the learning environment. They were not afraid to discuss the undiscussables. They talked about problems of excellence and the potential to lose track of alienated kids left out of the academic achievement frenzy. Here we have an example of a very large school that creates closeness by focusing on human connection and facilitating communication. It was not the size of this school that mattered.

Today's Kids Are No Different Than When We Were Young

Parents and teachers have long commented about how different new generations seem from "when *we* were young." Nowhere is this generation gap more obvious than in schools. Every generation reflects changing cultures, and history is full of examples of this inevitable process. Just as the 1960s represented a rebellion against traditional values, in the twenty-first century, a new generation has had to cope with a set of challenges unknown to their own parents.

The arrival of the digital era has created a culture that is more connected by a number of devices than at any other time in history. The Internet has created a connected world: digital phones provide new ways to stay in touch; e-mails can be received on phones that are also mini-computers; cellular phones can take pictures and send them to computers and to other phones. Technology shapes how children live from an increasingly younger and younger age. Maintaining a sense of self in the face of such easily dispersed images and information is a challenge this generation faces.

With regard to bullying and violence, we must consider technology as a factor with two sides. On the positive side, being tremendously connected offers unlimited opportunities for the sharing of positive feelings, information, images, and resources. Families can stay connected "in real time" with distant relatives. Pictures and e-mails can keep people together and involved in each other's life. Children who are trapped in poverty can reach out to the world and create hope for themselves. Shy people can meet other shy or trapped people and create virtual realities that help them cope with their lives in more positive ways. Communication is facilitated with virtually every task once done on paper now being completed "online." In our own research, we have used the Internet to connect U.S. and Jamaican schools, and we hope to expand this concept to include a worldwide network of students, parents, and teachers interacting about ways to improve school climates.

The negatives, however, involve the misuse of the Internet's connection power to exploit others sexually, financially, and emotionally (Twemlow & Sacco, 2008). It is not surprising that child predators and hate groups thrive online. This virtual world allows for the faster evolution of deviant interests Access to information can also lead to exposure to hate and deviance online. Many of the recent American school shooters used the Internet to explore resources and to develop plans for murder as an act revenge for being bullied. An alienated child who sits at home and types "hate" into a search engine will be connected to an unimaginable number of active and technologically savvy hatemongers. These virtual connections espousing hate often masquerade as understanding male figures offering to help "set things right." The Internet has also broken down the barriers between the social world of the school and the home. Social aggression that begins at school is carried through the Internet to the home through techniques such as instant messaging. Groups and cliques form online and can be used to create mean-spirited dialogues, which in turn are continued when the participants are back in school.

Eliminating the Bully Solves the Problem

It is impossible to dispute the periodic need to identify disturbed children and refer them for treatment. Certainly, when a child hurts someone, carries a weapon to school, or in other ways seriously threatens him- or herself or the school at large, a school suspension is warranted. This, however, does not solve the problem if the social context continues to allow bullying to occur.

We have observed this phenomenon at work in the war on drugs as well. As soon as one street corner dealer is arrested, another takes his place. Nothing in the neighborhood changes, so nothing will prevent another drug dealer from claiming the momentarily vacant spot. Bullies act the same way in schools. Schools that target and suspend bullies are missing the point. When a bully is suspended, plenty of "bully bystanders" are simply waiting to be activated as soon as a bullying role opens. Eliminating one person playing a role does not solve the problem of how a bully gains power using cruelly coercive tactics.

If finding and suspending bullies from their schools worked, then school violence would be a very easy problem to solve. The problem would instead become a matter of who is bullying "too much," since everybody bullies a little at one time or another. While the finer points about just how much is too much for one student compared to another are debated, the social role of bully still is allowed to achieve a measure of social status for the individual who inhabits it. In other words, the goal of bullying is to gain social status.

More Money Leads to More Peaceful Schools

There are undeniably many elements of education that require money to operate more effectively. Science is taught better when students have access to expensive laboratories with new equipment and cutting-edge technology. Computers are needed in order to teach successful computer science courses. Peaceful learning environments, on the other hand, do not cost a lot of money and creating one does not require as much funding as a new roof, a set of computers, or a new gymnasium. Having a peaceful learning environment requires some allocation of time and sustained effort directed toward changing attitudes and patterns of behavior. It does not cost more to have a peaceful school than it does to have a troubled one. Having an abundance of resources is no guarantee that there will be a peaceful school.

Some of the schools we visited and worked with had very little funding at all. One school in Jamaica had so few resources that students shared desks, pencils, and had no reliable transportation to and from school. This school jumped at the chance to work on a project to redirect some of the nonpeaceful energy. Using a craft project, the school created a reason for older kids to be nicer to teachers and the younger students. Being included in the craft class was a sign of social status. The price of admission was being helpful to others. This project was begun with very few donated dollars, but it ultimately proved extremely successful at ridding the school of nonpeaceful energy (Twemlow, Fonagy, Sacco, & Vernberg, 2009).

Some social systems are corrupt by nature. Our work in Jamaica taught us very early on that if you bring resources in through the top, they may get sucked dry before they hit the bottom (Twemlow & Sacco, 1996). This is also true in many U.S. cities, where law enforcement is continually investigating and prosecuting corrupt officials. Evolving nations provide many examples of how desperately poor nations' funds are skimmed by corrupt leaders. Unfortunately, corruption often eats up the resources that are designed to help the human infrastructure and the larger social context. When the poor get angry or do not improve their quality of life, the victims get blamed for their situations. Some cities pay upward of $10,000 to educate a child in war zone schools that are desperate and run down. It costs more money to run corrupt systems, and the corrupt system ensures that circumstances will not change.

The reality of corruption often creates a sense of despair in schools. Municipal workers also share this feeling of being underappreciated and mistreated; everybody gives up. Some individuals, however, disconnect from the reality of corruption and unfairness. They define their classrooms or their municipal duties as a reflection of their own characters. We have seen many examples of dedicated, underappreciated teachers inspiring their students in school systems known for failure. We watched the Jamaican teachers growing hoarse while teaching packed rooms of children, combating open classrooms, oppressive heat, low pay, and uncertain futures (Sacco & Twemlow, 1997). They stood tall and took pride in teaching math or helping their students learn to read and write. These classrooms were pure and immune from corruption. The "raw teacher" response is a personality trait that wants to teach, wants to see children grow and learn, and needs to be respected by the community for these noble efforts. Money is not the necessary ingredient that guarantees peaceful schools.

When visiting private boarding schools in Australia, we learned again that it was not the fancy quarters or prestigious history that made the school what it was; it was the staff. The elite nature of the school, in fact, adds a burden to these teachers. They are working under close scrutiny and always are walking a delicate line. Teachers often serve as house-parents to children. We thought we would see spoiled and entitled teachers not open to our ideas of bully-victim-bystander power dynamics. To our surprise, the most elite school we visited had the most focused and open-minded counselors and teachers. It was not the money or prestige; it was the kids who motivated the staff. These teachers were the most hungry for new ways to improve their learning environments.

Bullying Is Just a Kid Thing

For many people the word *bullying* evokes a normal part of childhood, a familiar childhood scene on a playground. It is very common for adults to minimize or dismiss bullying as a "kid thing," and even to mock those parents who complain about the nonphysical bullying. Bullying often entails the frequent use of small and humiliating communications. Kids today may use the Internet and texting to entrap their victims in an almost inescapable social web of shame and humiliation. This sequence of activity is virtually untraceable unless a parent can obtain printed versions of these interactions, video phone images, and can disprove the "my friend used my computer defense." Again, while none of this activity is physically aggressive, its impact can be far more lethal than a punch, a shove, or a kick.

Focusing on Problem Kids Will Improve the School Climate

There is no doubt that some students in a school will require special services in order to deal with medical issues and psychiatric disorders such as attention-deficit/hyperactivity disorder, bipolar disorder, and disruptive behavior disorders. They become easy prey or targets in a school that allows coercive roles to thrive unchecked. It is not the psychiatric disorder that causes the school dynamic, but the school climate that fans the flames and allows children with emotional conditions to be bullied or targeted for social aggression (Luis, 2004; see also Chapter 5). Simply noticing, referring, and treating these students will not solve the problem of a socially aggressive school climate. These problem children often come from homes that are emotionally toxic, lack basic nurturance, and they may already suffer from seriously dysfunctional family dynamics.

When there are fewer visible "problem kids," then, the school climate may be the place where problems develop because of the opportunities allowed within a school. Many suburban and private schools fantasize that they have successfully screened out potential problem kids. Parents are recruited and attracted by the mistaken belief that their child's school will not have problem kids. This illusion leads to the denial of a problem with social aggression and to a subsequent lack of commitment to creating and maintaining peaceful schools. Social aggression feeds off of achievement-driven adults. The competition to succeed academically or athletically may be unwittingly condoning socially aggressive behavior on the part of the more successful students and their parents. Teachers and coaches are easily pulled into the competition game, which leads to a lack of focus on the marginalized students who then become the problem kids. These problems follow them home and are further inflamed by the pressures of human development.

Critical Steps for Creating a Model School Bullying Prevention Approach

Creating a successful school anti-bullying program is a highly individual task that varies from school to school. Even within the same school district, each school has its own climate and this in great part is a reflection of how the overall district and state are structured. Despite their similar policies and procedures, the needs of each school should be assessed independently in a coherent, simple, and high-priority process to establish ways to improve the school climate for both students' and teachers' security and growth (Table 12.2).

Table 12.2
Policy Questions for Creating Successful School Anti-Bullying Programs

What is the plan to foster *buy in?*
Who does and does not support the need to address bully–victim problems?
How does the program create a sense of safety?
Do you understand the power dynamics of your schools?
Are any school leaders *abdicating bystanders?*
Who are the *natural leaders* in your school?
Are there any groups already thinking about peaceful schools?
Does your school climate support mentalizing?
What are the undiscussables in your school? Is adult bullying ever discussed?
How are your programs evaluated? Have the students been asked about their experiences at school?

Create Buy In

Arguably the most critical step of all, *buy in* is not a commonly used term outside of the United States. It refers to two main issues. First, it demonstrates the degree to which all the staff and students involved with schools prioritize the need to make an anti-bullying program successful (Biggs, Vernberg, Twemlow, & Fonagy, 2008). An institution with a high level of buy in has a group of concerned and engaged individuals who consider the program essential and necessary to follow. The factors that render the buy in as high rather than low are variable, but a high buy in cannot be mandated from the "top down" alone.

Many times, a high level of concern about bullying in an individual school is a result of a crisis involving violent acts. We observed this tendency during our first experience with a small elementary school. This particular school had the highest out-of-school suspension rate and the poorest academic performance in the school district when a 2nd grade girl was sexually assaulted by several 2nd grade boys, and as a result, we observed a group of concerned individuals who were extremely eager to buy in or support an anti-violence program in their school (Twemlow, Fonagy, & Sacco, 2001). This school is still a model for others, not only quiet, orderly, and altruistic, but with higher academic performance levels for African American students. Is there another way to enhance "buy in" before waiting to react to a tragic or critical incident? We believe there is, and part of that process entails ensuring the program will work for individual situations, regardless of the opinions of the expert consultants.

The second main issue included in the concept of buy in is that an anti-bullying program also requires institutional support and must be compatible with the institution's mission and culture. Creating a framework designed by teachers and students working together to change their particular school will lead to noticeably higher levels of "buy in," and a relatively smooth development and implementation process, as we observed during the pilot phase of our research and work. In the aforementioned school where the project was devised, for instance, the teachers actually did the project. They compiled their ideas, and worked together creatively to set up the criteria to measure change, and, with assistance, devised and selected the use of instruments to measure change. They administered the instruments, and teachers even volunteered to score them. Although this process initially developed because we simply did not have a lot of funding for a research evaluation, we inadvertently created a very smooth data collection process, method of evaluation, and a program that fit seamlessly into that particular school, causing virtually no problem (Twemlow, Fonagy, Sacco, Gies, et al., 2001). Why did the program in this case seem so easy to implement?

It was easy because the school in essence designed and instituted it—their "buy-in" level of acceptance and dedication to it was high.

Help Students and Staff Feel Safe

This basic step is critical to any organizational system. A program's internal functioning depends on whether the individuals in it feel safe. What does it mean to "feel safe?" Obviously, physical safety is a crucial part of feeling safe, and that is the area we unfortunately are compelled to focus on most in schools, with the use of metal detectors, security guards, and other visible methods. In New York City, all schools in the Bronx have school security guards who have been elevated to the level of police officer and are responsible for matters of discipline. Little if any disciplining is done by teachers. Schools like these resemble war zones or prisons, places where each day begins with metal detector screenings before first period. Can these schools also function as learning environments? Generally not. It takes a huge amount of work to make sure an environment is safe enough so that individuals can thrive and relax enough to absorb new knowledge.

One solution we have tried to improve students' sense of safety is to incorporate defensive martial arts training into physical education classes (Twemlow, Biggs, et al., 2008). This "Gentle Warrior" training provides non-aggressive skills for self-defense. The training also gives an opportunity to teach relaxation skills and helpful bystander behaviors.

Address Power Issues

When choosing a program, every school needs to consider whether the power differential between the various roles and positions of authority within the school are reasonably balanced (Twemlow et al., 2005a). Failing to understand and acknowledge this issue will undermine the chances a program has for success. It should be noted that Columbine High School had an anti-bullying program prior to the shootings in 1999, but it was completely ineffective due largely to the unresolved power differential between the athletically inclined "white cap" students and the intellectuals or "trench coat mafia." Many types of power issues exist in everyday life and people continue to experience power struggles long after they have left the school environment.

In a nutshell, the circle of power in power dynamics has everything to do with the co-created nature of the following interchangeable roles: victim, victimizer, and bystander (Twemlow et al., 2004). These are not medical diagnoses, mainly because we are all capable of playing all three; these roles are part of our normal everyday "psychopathology." They are co-created; one cannot exist without the other and the roles are generally fluid in most people. If they become fixed, however, the victim may turn into an avenging victim, who then focuses total attention on revenge, as we learned from studying the tragic events. We must remember that patterns, when fixed, tend to repeat themselves.

Address Bystanding

An anti-bullying program ideally stresses character development and positive valuing of all members of a school. Thus, it is important for the whole school to participate. The "whole school" includes not just students and teachers but also volunteers, parents, the administrative staff, the superintendent, the school board, and even the surrounding community.

In many situations, "abdicating" bystanders gather together after the fact and wonder what can be done about school violence (Twemlow et al., 2004). They tend to place blame on those in work roles, such as poorly functioning teachers and security guards. School staff may then feel overly pressured to solve problems that they cannot solve without the participation of the school community as a whole. Take time to look carefully at the extent to which bystanders are avoiding taking part in the essential role of changing the structure of the school's climate. Teaching the importance of honesty, for example, as an element of character structure will not work well in an environment with high rates of pathological bystanding. For the school climate to change with regard to bully–victim problems, change in bystanding attitudes and behavior must be broadly supported.

Utilize Natural Leaders

As an anti-bullying program begins to be implemented, natural leaders play a major in how much that program succeeds or fail. Natural leaders do not organize a group using Robert's Rule of Order, but instead function more like group facilitators. In our work with elementary schools we have described these natural leaders as "helpful bystanders" (Fonagy et al., 2009). These are bystanders in the positive sense, as opposed to "abdicating bystanders," and they display a number of qualities that render them excellent individuals to engage with or involve in the elements of the specific anti-bullying program chosen by a school.

The critical element that distinguishes the natural leader from the charismatic leader is that natural leaders, who often do not think of themselves as leaders, are nonetheless persons motivated to act for the good of the group as a whole. They may not volunteer like charismatic leaders tend to, but they feel the need to show people and to lead by example. Natural leaders tend to promote creativity, to reach benevolently out for help, and always to provide for their successors a natural flow of their non-self-centered leadership style. In other words, this style models altruism to others and encourages them to become natural leaders as well. Any school that wants a program to succeed should consciously make its natural leaders (or helpful bystanders) key people in planning, selected, and instituting the program.

Address Hidden Problems: The Undiscussables

However well a program focuses on the needs of a school, there is no way it can be successful if it does not address some of the more hidden or difficult elements of the problem. For example, in some areas where bussing is used, community schools have become a thing of the past. Children are often not brought up in the neighborhoods surrounding the school; they instead come to school from a great distance. We often encounter factors like this one that will fragment a school and yet do not appear in the average day-to-day discussion of what program will work best in schools. In this instance, it may be critical to acknowledge and discuss this issue, then work to create a greater sense of common purpose and connectedness for the school community.

Another undiscussable is the problem of school staff who bully students or other members of the school community (Twemlow & Fonagy, 2005; Twemlow, Fonagy, Sacco, & Brethour, 2006). We have also become very aware of students who bully their teachers, especially in high school, as well as parents who bully teachers, and administrators who bully teachers. In one school we reviewed, teachers were so scared of students that every teacher in the break room was asleep from stress and exhaustion.

Are these variations of traditional bullying situations easy to address? No, they are certainly not. Teachers' associations in the United States have functioned more like labor unions than professional associations and are understandably defensive about how their teachers work. We have been able to carry out our work only because we have a record of years of altruistic action aimed at helping schools, and the teacher's unions in each situation were subsequently positive and supportive about our efforts.

Evaluate and Communicate

Measuring and evaluating the impact of an antiviolence intervention seems like common sense. People do not like to do it, however, because it smacks of research, although often the necessary instruments are quite painless, and the procedures themselves are brief. This step is very helpful as a way to evaluate an entire school district or group of schools in an anonymous way using a variety of instruments. For example, a school principal who knows quite well that his or her school needs an anti-bullying approach could convince school leadership with other agendas to promote and financially support the purchase of such a program, provided the necessary data are available and compelling. This may include information on the connection between bullying and academic achievement (Fonagy, Twemlow, Vernberg, Sacco, & Little, 2005).

Bringing together people, including students and administrators, who take account of and monitor of all these steps is essential. We recommend that data be collected for school districts as a whole, rather than focusing on individual classes. Grade-by-grade analyses with anonymous questionnaires often provide useful data in a relatively nonthreatening way.

Focus on People

Creating change in a social system is all about people; it does not really depend upon specialized programs or unusual levels of expertise. People who are on the same page move in the same direction and will, if allowed, create a peaceful school learning environment. We offer a few basic steps to mobilize this change process. First, identify natural leaders among students and staff who share the sense of altruism needed to bring about positive changes. Second, gather stakeholders together and establish a process that defines similarities, acknowledges differences, and creates a safe outlet for negative emotions. This group of people must be able and willing to discuss "undiscussables" and to stimulate and humanize each other. Third, set boundaries, agree on a common language, define the problem, and establish a long-term plan that resists quick fixes. Fourth, create collaborative work groups that give feedback, monitor, and establish interdisciplinary communication. Fifth, train future trainers in the particulars of small group dynamics. The goal is to facilitate action within the group by following these rules in order to establish a highly mentalizing climate of critical self-reflection (Twemlow & Sacco, 2008).

Educational leaders must ask themselves the question: How important is a positive school climate? As one way to gain perspective, measure this against the time, money, and energy already spent on any one athletic activity, even the least popular. Then, try to find the "go to" person responsible for school climate. Most administrators and teachers will tell you there simply is not enough time. Try to see how much community involvement there is at any school and why.

We advise that leaders look at the operational level for answers. Administrators often know the least about climate. Are there big undiscussables? Are schools relying on oversimplified approaches? Does the answer fit with your "gut" feeling after visiting a school? Are there coercive adults in the schools? Is there a creative solution for adults with problems that create coercion in a school? Can you understand the power dynamics in any one school? Are they clear or hard to read? Ask these basic questions and apply this structural framework to guide actions. Insist on open and reflective dialogue about problems relating to coercion within the schools. A community can be judged by the quality of its schools. Creative and safe schools are a reflection of educational leaders that take the time to commit to improving school learning environments.

References

Biggs, B. K., Vernberg, E. M., Twemlow, S. W., & Fonagy, P. (2008). Teacher adherence and its relation to teacher attitudes and student outcomes in an elementary school-based violence prevention program. *School Psychology Review, 37,* 533–549.

Fonagy, P., Twemlow, S. W., Vernberg, E. M., Nelson, J. M., Dill, E. J., Little, T. D., & Sargent, J. A. (2009). A cluster randomized controlled trial of child-focused psychiatric consultation and a school systems-focused intervention to reduce aggression. *Journal of Child Psychology and Psychiatry, 50,* 607–616.

Fonagy, P., Twemlow, S. W., Vernberg, E. M., Sacco, F. C., & Little, T. D. (2005). Creating a Peaceful School Learning Environment: The impact of an antibullying program on educational attainment in elementary schools. *Medical Science Monitor, 11,* 317–325.

Gilligan, J. (1996). *Violence: Our deadly epidemic and its causes.* New York: Putnam.

Klomek, A. B., Marrocco, F., Kleinman, M., Schonfield, I. S., & Gould, M. S. (2007). Bullying, depression, and suicidality in adolescents, *Journal of the American Academy of Child Psychiatry, 46,* 40–49.

Luis, N. B. San. (2004). Bullying: Concealed by behavioral and somatic symptoms, *Journal of Developmental & Behavioral Pediatrics, 25,* 348–349.

McMahon, T. J., & Luthar, S. S. (2006). Patterns and correlates of substance use among affluent, suburban high school students. *Journal of Clinical Child and Adolescent Psychology, 35,* 72–89.

Sacco, F. C., & Twemlow, S. W. (1997). School violence reduction: A model Jamaican secondary school program. *Community Mental Health Journal, 33,* 229–234.

Twemlow, S. W., Biggs, B. K., Nelson, T. D., Vernberg, E. M., & Fonagy, P., & Twemlow, S. W. (2008). Effects of participation in a martial arts-based antibullying program in elementary schools. *Psychology in the Schools, 45,* 947–959.

Twemlow, S. W., & Fonagy, P. (2005). The prevalence of teachers who bully students in schools with differing levels of behavioral problems. *American Journal of Psychiatry, 162,* 2387–2389.

Twemlow, S. W., Fonagy, P., & Sacco, F. C. (2001). An innovative psychodynamically influenced intervention to reduce school violence. *Journal of the American Academy of Child and Adolescent Psychiatry; 40,* 377–379.

Twemlow, S. W., Fonagy, P., & Sacco, F. C. (2003). Modifying social aggression in schools. *Journal of Applied Psychoanalytic Studies, 5,* 211–222.

Twemlow, S. W., Fonagy, P., & Sacco, F. C. (2004). The role of the bystander in the social architecture of bullying and violence in schools and communities. *Annals of the New York Academy of Sciences, 1036,* 215–232.

Twemlow, S. W., Fonagy, P., & Sacco, F. C. (2005a). A developmental approach to mentalizing communities: I. A model for social change. *Bulletin of the Menninger Clinic, 69,* 265–281.

Twemlow, S. W., Fonagy, P., & Sacco, F. C. (2005b). A developmental approach to mentalizing communities: II. The Peaceful Schools experiment. *Bulletin of the Menninger Clinic, 69,* 282–304.

Twemlow, S. W., Fonagy, P., Sacco, F., & Brotheur, J. (2006). Teachers who bully students: A hidden trauma. *International Journal of Social Psychiatry, 52,*187–198.

Twemlow, S. W., Fonagy, P., Sacco, F. C., Gies, M., Evans, R., & Ewbank, R. (2001). Creating a peaceful school learning environment: A controlled study of an elementary school intervention to reduce violence. *American Journal of Psychiatry, 158,* 808–810.

Twemlow, S. W., Fonagy, P., Sacco, F. C., O'Toole, M. E., & Vernberg, E. M. (2002). Premeditated mass shootings in schools: Threat assessment. *Journal of the American Academy of Child and Adolescent Psychiatry, 41,* 475–477.

Twemlow, S. W., Fonagy, P., & Sacco, F. C., & Vernberg, E. (2008). Assessing adolescents who threaten homicide in schools. *Clinical Social Work Journal, 36,* 131–142.

Twemlow, S. W., Fonagy, P., Sacco, F., & Vernberg, E. M. (2009) *Young guns: Approaching extremely violent and prejudiced children in a Jamaican school.* Manuscript submitted for publication.

Twemlow, S. W., & Sacco, F. C. (1996). Peacekeeping and peacemaking: The conceptual foundations of a plan to reduce violence and improve the quality of life in a midsized community in Jamaica. *Psychiatry: Interpersonal and Biological Processes, 59*, 156–174.

Twemlow, S. W., & Sacco, F. C. (2008). *Why school anti-bullying programs don't work.* Lanham, MD: Rowman & Littlefield.

Twemlow, S. W., Sacco, F. C., & Williams, P. (1996). A clinical and interactionist perspective on the bully/victim/bystander relationship. *Bulletin of the Menninger Clinic, 60*, 296–313.

13

Implementing Bullying Prevention in Diverse Settings: Geographic, Economic, and Cultural Influences

Nancy G. Guerra and Kirk R. Williams

S ince the mid-1990s, bullying prevention has been at the forefront of school and community agendas for youth in the United States and internationally. In some cases, bullying prevention programs such as Bully Busters (Horne, Orpinas, Newman-Carlson, & Bartolomucci, 2004) and the Olweus Bullying Prevention Program (Limber, 2004; Olweus, 1993) have replaced other aggression prevention efforts such as conflict resolution training, peer mediation, and mentoring, which had all gained prominence in the 1980s (Guerra, Tolan, & Hammond, 1994). In other cases, anti-bullying programs have been incorporated into broader aggression and violence prevention programming or implemented alongside these programs (Knoff, 2007; Nation, 2007).

However, it is not clear whether bullying deserves special attention as a unique form of childhood aggression that requires specific and focused programming or whether it is similar to other types of aggression and youth violence. On the one hand, research studies have shown that bullying and aggression go hand in hand— bullies are more likely to be aggressive and aggressive children are more likely to bully (Craig, 1998; Espelage & Swearer, 2003; Kokkinos & Panayiotou, 2004). Like some forms of aggression and violence (often called *instrumental* or *proactive*), bullying is *intentional* and involves a *power imbalance* between the bully and the victim to achieve some *end goal* (Pellegrini, 2002; Sveinsson & Morris, 2007). On the other hand, unlike bullying, aggression in conflict situations is often *reactive* in response to provocation. Furthermore, much serious aggression and youth violence occurs between people who do not know each other or who have minimal contact, for example, armed robbery and carjacking. In contrast, bullying can only occur in settings where people have ongoing and regular social interactions such as schools.

A logical question to follow is whether bullying and more serious forms of childhood aggression and youth violence have similar predictors or causes. This is important because bullying prevention and intervention programs will be most effective if they are closely tied to the specific causes of bullying (particularly if the causes of bullying are more limited or are different from the causes of other types of aggression and violence). As an example, there is a long history of research suggesting that serious aggression and violence are more likely for youth living in disadvantaged urban communities with high rates of poverty and marginalization often linked to ethnic minority status (Fingerhut, Ingram, & Feldman, 1998; Guerra & Phillips-Smith, 2005; McCord & Ensminger, 1997; Kramer, 2000; Sampson & Lauritsen, 1994; Snyder & Sickmund, 2006). This is particularly apparent when looking at arrests for serious violent crimes, including homicide; however, these patterns are less obvious when looking at information from self-reports (U.S. Department of Health and Human Services, 2001).

Unfortunately, very few studies have looked at whether bullying in schools is highest in poor, urban areas or whether other cultural characteristics support bullying. The research that has been done generally has found that bullying occurs at similar frequencies across socioeconomic class and ethnic groups (Bosworth, Espelage, & Simon, 1999; Junger, 1990). Still, with some exceptions (Bosworth et al., 1999), much of this research has been conducted in Scandinavia and Europe, where there is much less ethnic and economic variation than in the United States. It is unclear whether bullying in the United States is shaped by broader social, economic, and cultural forces related to exclusion and marginalization where children growing up and attending schools in poor, urban communities are more likely to engage in bullying behavior than children in communities with more resources.

Given the diversity in U.S. schools and their surrounding communities, it is important for bullying prevention to understand how demographic and cultural characteristics are related to the prevalence of bullying over time. This information can be useful for identifying schools that are most vulnerable and most in need of targeted bully prevention programming. These characteristics may also impact the feasibility of program implementation and the likelihood of preventing or reducing bullying behavior within a given setting. In other words, it may be that bullying behavior does not vary by demographic or cultural conditions, but that these conditions make it more difficult to implement programs and change bullying. For example, in a large-scale preventive intervention study conducted in inner-city and urban schools, preventive effects were only noted for programs in moderate- versus low-resource schools

(Metropolitan Area Child Study Research Group, 2002). Presumably, schools in the most distressed inner-city settings were overwhelmed by the day-to-day challenges in a climate of scarce resources and were unable to generate necessary levels of collaborative effort to prevent aggressive behavior.

It may also be that it is not poverty, ethnicity, or urban scarcity per se that promotes bullying, but the normative climate or culture that develops as children learn to cope with the challenges of a particular setting (Guerra, Huesmann, Tolan, Van Acker, & Eron, 1995). Although normative support (in other words, approval) of aggression and related behaviors such as bullying may be higher in schools and communities where they help children negotiate the stressors of daily life in disadvantaged inner-city communities, it is also possible that other dynamics influence the normative climate, particularly in settings characterized by ongoing and regular social interactions. For example, variations in the transition from elementary to middle school (for instance, whether students change schools between elementary and middle school) can influence the acceptability of bullying behavior and its normative status (Pellegrini & Long, 2004). Therefore, it is important to examine whether variation in rates of bullying is linked to variations in normative support within a given setting. This is consistent with bullying prevention efforts such as the Olweus program that focus on changing classroom and school climate to reduce support for bullying.

In this chapter, we examine how bullying is related to demographic and cultural characteristics, including the ethnic composition of a school, percentage of poor students, geographic location (urban vs. rural), and normative support (approval) of bullying among students. We also look at whether these demographic and cultural characteristics and bullying are related to negative bystander behaviors, such as gathering in a large group and cheering for bullies, that can exacerbate the problem (Salmivalli, 2001). We address three specific questions, followed by a discussion of the practical implications of this information and how it can be applied to bullying prevention efforts. The three questions are as follows:

- Do bullying and negative bystander behavior cut across geographic, ethnic, and economic lines?
- Is there more bullying in schools where children approve of the behavior (normative support) and bystanders reinforce it (negative bystander behavior)?
- Do demographic characteristics and approval of bullying make it more difficult to change this behavior over the school year regardless of what program is implemented?

We rely on findings from a large study evaluating a statewide initiative in Colorado, the Bullying Prevention Initiative (BPI). The BPI is a 3-year

$8.6 million initiative designed to strengthen the skills and willingness of youth and adults to intervene in bullying situations. It was funded by a private grant-making foundation in Denver, The Colorado Trust. The larger BPI evaluation will help us better understand bullying and bystander behavior among students, including an increased awareness of this behavior, social cognitive processes involved in the prevention of bullying, the social context surrounding bullying incidents, the involvement of adults and youth in preventing such incidents, and factors that enhance program implementation and sustainability. The larger study includes quantitative surveys given over 3 years and a supplemental qualitative study of adults and youth participating in the interventions.

Methods

The data for the analyses presented in this chapter are part of the larger evaluation described above. Although the grantees funded by this initiative include school districts, individual schools, and community-based organizations, we limit our focus in this chapter to programs in 66 schools across 40 of Colorado's 64 counties, evenly split between rural and urban areas of the state. A major component of this empirical evaluation involves collecting pre-post survey data from youth in the fall and the spring of three academic years (Year 1, 2005–06; Year 2, 2006–07; and Year 3, 2007–08). This design allows the assessment of single-year changes in individual youth (from pre-test to post-test within a given year) and contextual (school-level) changes over the full 3 years of the BPI (using different informants each year over the course of 3 years). In this chapter, we report on whether the incidence of bullying depended on school demographic and cultural characteristics and whether changes in bullying from one year to the next depended on these characteristics. School-level data drawn from the pre-test of Year 1 and the pre-test of Year 2 are analyzed, with the results reported below. All instruments developed to collect data from youth were piloted in the summer of 2005 before full implementation of bullying prevention programs in the fall of that year, with all indices having acceptable reliabilities (alpha coefficients beyond .70).

Participants in the Present Study

During the first year of the BPI evaluation, 3339 youth completed questionnaires in 66 schools during the fall of 2005, and another 3798 youth in a different sample participated in the pre-test survey in the fall of 2006. Data were collected in 5th, 8th, and 11th grades, representing transition years in elementary, middle, and high schools. Because of missing data on some indicators and/or grades and relatively minor changes in the sample of schools between years, the final sample for the analysis is comprised of 61 schools having data on all indicators included in the analysis. The data collection was conducted in compliance with the protocol approved by the human subjects review board, including acquiring active parental consent and youth assent.

Procedures

Data were collected using two different electronic methods, with the choice of methods negotiated with schools in terms of what was deemed best for their students. However, paper questionnaires were used by a small percentage (4.4%) of youth absent the day data collection was scheduled. First, data collectors used an LCD projector to present questionnaire items in classrooms of approximately 30 students or less (used by 57.7% of the students). After the data collectors read each question aloud, youth used a wireless response pad to enter their answers, which were automatically recorded in an electronic database and linked to the student identification code. The questionnaire was administered in English or Spanish as needed, using standard back-translation methods. Second, the questionnaire was adapted to a Web-based format linked to the electronic database (37.9% of students). The youth Web-based questionnaire was administered in school computer labs. Data collectors assisted youth in logging on to the password-protected questionnaire and were available for assistance as youth answered questions at their own pace. No evidence was found that these different data collection procedures influenced responding.

Measures

Bullying and Negative Bystander Behavior

Items bearing on the perpetration (not victimization) of different types of bullying were adapted from Espelage, Holt, and Henkel (2003). Youth were asked to respond to the following four items: I pushed, shoved, tripped, or picked fights with students I know are weaker than me; I teased or said mean things to certain students; I spread rumors about some students; and I told lies about some students through the Internet (e.g., e-mail, instant messaging, cell phone text messaging, websites). Youth were also asked whether they engaged in five other forms of negative bystander behavior, specifically, whether they encouraged students to push, shove, or trip weaker students; cheered when someone was beating up another student; joined in when students were teasing and being mean to certain students; joined in when students told lies about other students; or stood by and watched other students getting hit, pushed, shove, or tripped. Numeric coding (in parentheses) and response options for all nine items included *(1)* never, *(2)* one or two times, *(3)* several times, and *(4)* a lot. *An average index* was calculated by summing scores on each of the nine items and dividing by nine. This procedure generated reliable summary indices of bullying and negative bystander behavior (coefficient alpha = .90 in Year 1 and .84 in Year 2). These indices were aggregated to the school level by calculating an overall average of the individual summary index scores of students within each school.

School Demographic Characteristics

Geographic, ethnic, and economic characteristics of schools were coded as follows. Geographic location was indicated by whether a school was situated in an urban or rural area of the state. Ethnic composition was indicated by the percent of students identified as African American, Latino, or non-Latino white. These were the dominant ethnic groups in the sample, constituting approximately 95% of the sample in Year 1. The other 5% was Asian American, Native American, or other ethnic groups, with the representation being too small for reliable school-level indicators. To ensure that a school had substantial representation of a particular ethnic group, the percentage distribution for each of the three ethnic groups was subdivided into quintiles, and schools in the upper quintile (upper 20% of the distribution for each ethnic group) were compared to each other and to those in the lower four quintiles (lower 80% of the distribution for each ethnic group) in terms of the average incidence of bullying. The overall economic status of students in schools was measured by the percent of students receiving free or reduced lunch. Similar to ethnic composition, this percentage distribution was also subdivided into quintiles, with the upper quintile compared to the lower four quintiles in terms of the average incidence of bullying.

School Culture

This characteristic was measured by the normative climate of schools, specifically, the normative disapproval of bullying and normative disapproval of negative bystander behavior by students in each school. Normative disapproval of bullying perpetration and bystander involvement in bullying situations was assessed by asking students to evaluate seven different items on a 4-point Likert-type scale ranging from "really wrong" to "perfectly ok." These items were taken from the *Normative Beliefs about Aggression Scale* (Huesmann & Guerra, 1997) and were modified slightly to refer to bullying instead of aggression. The items included bullying perpetration (four items) and negative bystander involvement (three items). These seven items were averaged by summing the individual scores and dividing by seven (coefficient alpha = .88). They were then aggregated to the school level by calculating an average of the individual student summary scores within each school. High scores indicate schools where students generally disapprove of bullying and negative bystander behavior, and low scores indicate schools where students perceive such behavior as generally "ok." This measure and procedure for aggregation are appropriate for capturing the normative orientation of students about bullying and bystander behavior overall, not individual normative beliefs.

Results

We present results to help answer each of the three questions posed earlier. Although the findings are reported with some technical language, we try also to explain the meaning of these findings and their relevance for bullying prevention efforts in each section and in the discussion that follows.

Question 1: Do Bullying and Negative Bystander Behavior Cut across Geographic, Ethnic, and Economic Lines?

To answer this question, schools in rural areas of the state were compared to those in urban areas, schools with substantial representation of African American, Latino, and non-Latino whites (upper quintile of the respective ethnic group distribution) were compared with each other and with those with a more diverse ethnic composition, and schools with substantial representation of students on reduced and free lunch (upper quintile of the distribution) were compared with those having a lower percentage of students on reduced and free lunch. The results of these analyses are presented in Figures 13.1–13.3.

These three bar graphs convey a common message: the incidence of bullying and negative bystander behavior is similar across schools regardless of geographic location, ethnic composition, and economic status. In other words:

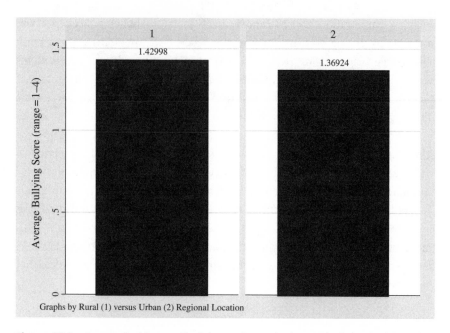

Figure 13.1 Average incidence of bullying and negative bystander behavior by rural or urban geographic location.

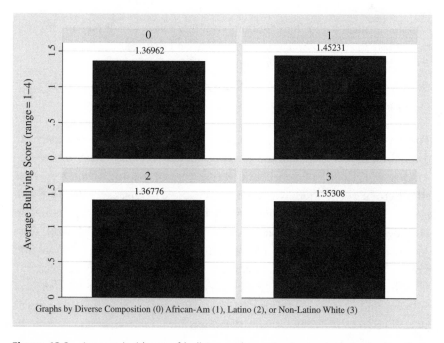

Figure 13.2 Average incidence of bullying and negative bystander behavior by ethnic composition of students in schools.

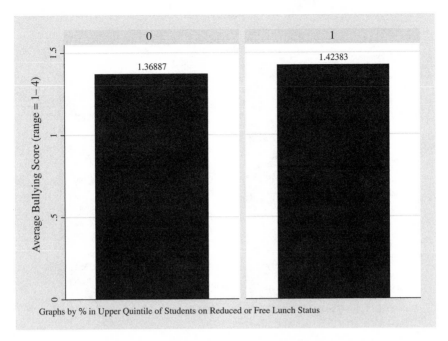

Figure 13.3 Average incidence of bullying and negative bystander behavior by students on free or reduced lunch.

- Rural schools have about the same average incidence of bullying and negative bystander behavior as urban schools.
- Schools with a substantial representation of a particular ethnic group (African American, Latino, Non-Latino white) have about the same average incidence of such behavior and as more ethnically diverse schools.
- Schools with a substantial representation of students receiving reduced and free lunch have about the same average incidence as those with a lower percentage of such students.

Question 2: Is There More Bullying in Schools Where Children Approve of the Behavior (Normative Support) and Bystanders Reinforce It (Negative Bystander Behavior)?

Figure 13.4 shows how the average incidence varies by schools scoring high (upper quintile of the distribution) on normative disapproval and those scoring lower on this cultural index. Year 2 data on the average incidence of bullying and negative bystander behavior are used in this graph because the referent period for the self-reported items on such behavior in Year 1 is the

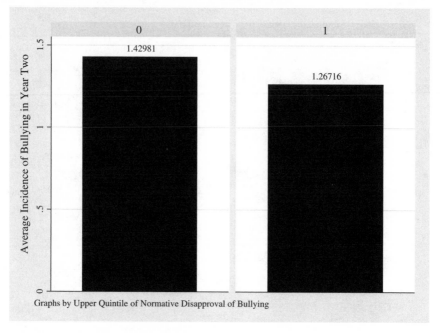

Graphs by Upper Quintile of Normative Disapproval of Bullying

Figure 13.4 Average incidence of bullying and negative bystander behavior by normative disapproval of such behavior.

preceding 12 months; however, normative disapproval data are collected with respect to perceptions at the present (in other words at the time of data collection). By using Year 2 information on bullying and negative bystander behavior, behavior from Year 1 to Year 2 is linked to normative beliefs at Year 1.

Unlike the comparisons in Figures 13.1–13.3, this bar graph shows that, indeed, normative disapproval differentiates schools having a higher versus a lower average incidence of the combined bullying/negative bystander behavior index, with the difference being statistically significant (t-value = 2.90, p = .005).

A more rigorous method of further documenting the patterns shown in Figures 13.1–13.4 is to estimate the independent effects of geographic location, ethnicity, economic status, and the disapproval of bullying and negative bystander behavior on the average incidence of this behavior. This estimation was done by conducting a multivariate hierarchical regression analysis (using an OLS estimation procedure) in which school demographic characteristics were incorporated into the regression equation initially (step one), with the school culture index (normative disapproval) incorporated subsequently (step two). The results of the OLS estimation procedure are shown in Table 13.1.

Table 13.1
Hierarchical Regression Estimates of the Effects of School Demographics and Normative Disapproval of Bullying on the Average Incidence of Bullying in Schools

Step 1				Step 2		
Independent Variables	Beta	b	t-value	Beta	b	t-value
Regional location	−.251	−.084	−1.78	−.165	−.005	−1.35
Reduced/free lunch %	.123	.001	.77	.001	.001	.01
African American representation	.26	.108	1.77	.220	.091	1.73
Latino representation	−.004	−.001	−.03	−.059	−.025	−.44
Non-Latino white representation	−.034	−.014	−.25	.034	.014	.28
Normative disapproval				−.532	−.004	−4.44*
Constant	1.459			1.628		
R^2	.107			.349		

$N = 61$ (schools).
*$p \leq .01$ (two-tailed test).

It is important to note that none of the estimated coefficients for geo-graphic location, percent of students receiving reduced or free lunch, or the ethnicity groupings are statistically significant in the initial step of the analysis. Those estimated coefficients remain statistically insignificant in the subsequent step of the analysis, but notice that in this step, the estimated effect of normative disapproval is both statistically significant and substantial in mag-nitude (Beta = −.532, t-value = −4.44, $p < .01$). These multivariate results corroborate the comparisons shown in Figures 13.1–13.4, again suggesting that bullying and negative bystander behavior vary little across these demo-graphic characteristics of schools, but school culture as indicated by normative disapproval of bullying appears to be associated with a lower average incidence of bullying and negative bystander behavior.

Question 3: Do Demographic Characteristics and Approval of Bullying Make It More Difficult to Change This Behavior over the School Year Regardless of What Program Is Implemented?

In addition to demonstrating whether the above characteristics distinguished between schools having a higher compared to a lower average incidence of bullying and negative bystander behavior, we were interested in whether they would impact the outcome of interventions. Addressing this question requires a measure of behavioral change, and residualized change scores were calculated for this purpose. The attractive feature of residualized change scores is that they adjust for the starting point, meaning change is measured relative to the initial score on the average bullying and negative bystander index as of the fall of 2005. This adjustment eliminates the problem of schools experiencing a high incidence of such behavior having a greater chance of change (moving downward) than those having a low (or no) incidence of bullying as of Year 1. Stated simply, residualized change scores allow for the measurement of change across all schools in the sample regardless of where they fall in the initial distribution of bullying and negative bystander behavior in the fall of 2005 (Year 1).

A similar analytic procedure was used as in the multivariate analysis of the average incidence of this behavior at a single point in time (Year 1, as in Table 13.1). Specifically, hierarchical regression was conducted in which the school demographic characteristics were initially included in the multivariate regression equation, and a subsequent equation was estimated (again using an OLS estimation procedure) that included these characteristics along with normative disapproval.

The difference here, compared to the previous multivariate analysis (see Table 13.1), is that the estimated effects of these independent variables are on change from Year 1 to Year 2 in the average incidence of bullying and negative bystander behavior. Moreover, a measure of change in normative disapproval is also used in this analysis. The reason is that unlike geographic location, ethnic composition, or economic status, this cultural characteristic is more dynamic, meaning it is more amenable and likely to change over time. As with measuring change in normative disapproval, change in bullying and negative bystander behavior was measured using residualized change scores (calculated as described above).

The results of the hierarchical regression analysis are presented in Table 13.2. The estimated effects of the demographic characteristics are statistically insignificant in both steps of the analysis, similar to the results shown in Table 13.1. Moreover, the estimated effect of change in normative disapproval on change in bullying and negative bystander behavior from Year 1 to Year 2 is both statistically significant and substantial in magnitude (Beta = $-.569$, t-value = -3.81, $p < .01$).

What this means is that change in bullying over 1 year (regardless of specific type of intervention) did not depend on school geographic location, ethnic composition, or poverty. However, in schools where

Table 13.2

Hierarchical Regression Estimates of the Effects of School Demographics and Change in Normative Disapproval of Bullying on Change in Bullying Behavior from Year 1 to Year 2

Step 1				Step 2		
Independent Variables	Beta	b	t-value	Beta	b	t-value
Regional location	−.115	−.036	−.80	−.068	−.022	−.49
Reduced/free lunch %	.049	.001	.30	.165	.001	1.06
African American representation	.216	.083	1.43	.016	.007	.11
Latino representation	.019	.008	.12	−.204	−.089	−1.33
Non-Latino white representation	−.013	−.005	−.09	−.133	−.051	−.95
Normative disapproval				−.569	−.007	−3.81*
Constant	.008			−.003		
R^2	.052			.287		

$N = 61$ (schools).
*$p < .01$ (two-tailed test).

normative climate improved (reflecting less support for bullying), bullying and negative bystander behavior were likely to be reduced.

Discussion and Implications for Practice

At the beginning of this chapter, we suggested that it is important to consider whether the causes of bullying during childhood and adolescence are similar to the causes of more serious aggression and youth violence. To the extent that there are similar causes, it is likely that programs to prevent aggression and violence will be equally effective in preventing bullying.

However, in this chapter we report findings showing that bullying, unlike more serious forms of aggression and youth violence, appears to cut across social class, ethnic, and geographic lines. In addition, changes in bullying and negative bystander behavior were not related to these demographic characteristics.

In other words, the stressors associated with urban living, economic disadvantage, and ethnic minority status did not appear to play a significant role in predicting higher levels of bullying at the school level or in limiting (or helping) the impact of interventions. The finding that bullying is an "equal opportunity" problem affecting a broad range of schools and communities suggests that bullying prevention programs should not be focused on a specific geographic and/or demographic setting, but should be implemented more broadly. In other words, no school is immune from bullying and all schools should carefully assess their bullying problem and whether it requires focused and specific attention. This also suggests that bullying may, indeed, be a distinct form of aggression (particularly in settings where low levels of bullying are relatively commonplace) that should benefit from focused interventions directed at the specific dynamics of bullying within a given setting.

Of course, these results are relevant for understanding between-school differences at the aggregate level rather than within-school differences at the individual level. It is important to keep in mind that there may be variation in bullying and victimization within schools that is not captured in the research reported in this chapter. For example, to the extent that victims are targeted because they are different or less powerful, it may be that ethnic minority and economically disadvantaged students are more likely to be targeted as victims in settings characterized by greater majority/minority distinctions (Graham & Juvonen, 2002; Hanish & Guerra, 2000).

Bullying was linked more closely to normative support for bullying (as measured by student approval of bullying and negative bystander behavior). Stated otherwise, bullying was more likely to occur in schools where students viewed bullying and peer support for bullying (negative bystander behavior) as acceptable and was less likely to occur in schools where students did not approve of these behaviors. Reductions in bullying were also related to reductions in normative support within a particular school. This finding is consistent with the literature on children's aggressive behavior, whereby aggression is related to the normative status of aggression within a social group such as the classroom (Henry, Guerra, Tolan, & Huesmann, 2000) and is often a primary focus of bullying prevention programs.

Although we did not examine differences in bullying by age or school level, previous research suggests that this behavior escalates during middle school and is particularly linked to the elementary/middle school transition and the reshuffling of dominance hierarchies (Pellegrini & Long, 2004). The qualitative work we have been conducting as part of the BPI Initiative evaluation in Colorado supports and extends this finding. In addition to the recalibration of peer status in a new context, middle school involves learning the boundaries of the peer culture—what is considered normative or "cool" and what is considered unacceptable within a specific clique or for youth more generally. For some youth in some settings, bullying may represent a convenient currency for establishing these boundaries, particularly if it is accepted and unlikely to lead to informal or formal sanctions. As one 7th grade student observed, "You can be bullied for being too bad or too good, anything out of the ordinary, class clown or teacher's pet." We also have reported elsewhere that the prevalence of bullying increases from elementary to middle school and remains at elevated levels through high school for Internet and verbal bullying, although physical bullying declines in high school (Williams & Guerra, 2007).

The need to establish and find one's place in a normative fold that incorporates dominance hierarchies, in-group/out-group distinctions, and opportunities for status within a specific peer culture can be understood as a developmental task of early adolescence that paves the way for identity development (Erikson, 1968). Negotiating this task in settings where there is ongoing social interaction (such as schools) can be quite problematic, and bullying appears to be one strategy that provides some currency toward this end. From this perspective, it is not surprising that bullying perpetration did not vary by geographic location, economic disadvantage, or ethnic minority status because it is grounded more in the challenges of development for youth, particularly during early adolescence, than in the challenges of larger social structural issues.

Still, it is noteworthy that there is considerable variation between schools in the acceptability of bullying and negative bystander behavior as legitimate venues for peer social interaction, and this normative culture does predict corresponding rates in the incidence of bullying and changes over 1 year. Although the current chapter did not focus directly on explaining variations in normative support, research has highlighted the importance of clear and consistent messages, adult engagement in bullying prevention, a warm and trusting social climate, and clear consequences for bullying (Limber, 2004). In our qualitative work with BPI, middle school and high school students we spoke with also underscored the importance of starting in the early elementary school years, when attitudes and beliefs are beginning to crystallize (e.g., Huesmann & Guerra, 1997), so that children encode this behavior as unacceptable from an early age. This sets the stage for what "not to do" but does not address how best to help children negotiate their emerging peer relationships during the difficult adolescent years. An important lesson learned is that bullying prevention programs must also consider the adaptive functions of this behavior for a particular age group and provide alternative venues for navigating the challenges of development. Unfortunately, most of the evidence-based programs such as the Olweus bullying prevention program and other similar efforts have largely been confined to elementary school–aged children. Relatively little is known about how best to change normative culture at the middle school or high school level. Again, our findings suggest that it is more important to consider these age and school context differences in understanding the dynamics of bullying, linked to developmental shifts, than environmental factors such as poverty or geographic location more typically associated with serious aggression and violence.

In sum, looking holistically at the findings reported in this chapter, research on child and adolescent development, and studies of aggression and youth violence, there are several implications for bullying prevention efforts. These include the following:

- In contrast to causes and correlates of serious aggression and youth violence, bullying behavior in children and adolescents is not linked to larger community and contextual influences such as economic disadvantage, ethnic minority status, or living in urban communities. Bullying cuts across class, ethnic, and geographic lines—programs to prevent bullying are needed in all settings for all youth. Further, the effectiveness of prevention programs does not seem to vary by these demographic characteristics.
- Normative culture that supports bullying is strongly associated with incidence of bullying in schools. Furthermore, changes in this normative culture predict changes in bullying behavior. This suggests that prevention programs should carefully consider the sources of normative support within a specific context and how best to effect change.
- Bullying can become a convenient currency for negotiating social relations, particularly when children learn that it is an acceptable and normative behavior. Because these normative beliefs crystallize early in development, prevention programs to establish clear anti-bullying standards must begin during the early elementary school years and must be infused in the peer, adult, and community culture (as much as possible).
- Bullying behavior appears to emerge, in part, as a strategy for negotiating the developmental challenges of adolescence; prevention programs must also provide alternative support to help youth navigate the increasingly salient demands of their peer culture.

References

Bosworth, K., Espelage, D. L., & Simon, T. R. (1999). Factors associated with bullying behavior in middle school students. *Journal of Early Adolescence, 19,* 341–362.

Craig, W. (1998). The relationship among bullying, victimization, depression, anxiety, and aggression in elementary school children. *Personality and Individual Differences, 24,* 123–130.

Erikson, E. (1968). *Identity, youth, and crisis.* New York: Norton.

Espelage, D. L., Holt, M., & Henkel, R. R. (2003). Examination of peer group contextual effects on aggression during early adolescence. *Child Development, 74,* 205–220.

Espelage, D. L., & Swearer, S. (2003). Research on school bullying and victimization: What have we learned and where do we go from here? *School Psychology Review, 23,* 365–383.

Fingerhut, L., Ingram, D., & Feldman, J. (1998). Homicide rates among U.S. teenagers and young adults: Differences by mechanism, level of urbanization, race and sex, 1967 through 1995. *Journal of the American Medical Association, 280,* 423–427.

Graham, S., & Juvonen, J. (2002). Ethnicity, peer harassment, and adjustment in middle school: An exploratory study. *Journal of Early Adolescence, 22,* 173–199.

Guerra, N. G., Huesmann, L. R., Tolan, P. H., Van Acker, R., & Eron, L. D. (1995). Stressful events and individual beliefs as correlates of economic disadvantage and aggression among urban children. *Journal of Consulting and Clinical Psychology, 63,* 518–528.

Guerra, N. G., & Phillips-Smith, E. (Eds.). (2005). *Preventing youth violence in a multicultural society.* Washington, DC: American Psychological Association.

Guerra, N. G., Tolan, P. H., & Hammond, W. R. (1994). Prevention and treatment of adolescent violence. In L. D. Eron, J. H. Gentry, & P. Schlegel (Eds.), *Reasons to hope: A psychological perspective on violence and youth* (pp. 383–404). Washington, DC: American Psychological Association.

Hanish, L. D., & Guerra, N. G. (2000). The roles of ethnicity and school context in predicting children's victimization by peers. *American Journal of Community Psychology, 55,* 201–223.

Henry, D., Guerra, N. G., Tolan, P. H., & Huesmann, L. R. (2000). Classroom norms and children's aggressive behavior. *American Journal of Community Psychology, 28,* 59–81.

Horne, A. M., Orpinas, P., Newman-Carlson, D., & Bartolomucci, C. L. (2004). Elementary school Bully Busters Program: Understanding why children bully and what to do about it. In D. L. Espelage & S. M. Swearer (Eds.), *Bullying in American schools* (pp. 297–325). Mahwah, NJ: Erlbaum.

Huesmann, L. R., & Guerra, N. G. (1997). Social norms and children's aggressive behavior. *Journal of Personality and Social Psychology, 72,* 408–419.

Junger, M. (1990). Intergroup bullying and racial harassment in the Netherlands. *Sociology and Social Research, 74,* 65–72.

Knoff, H. M. (2007). Teasing, taunting, bullying, harassment, and aggression: A schoolwide approach to prevention, strategic intervention, and crisis management. In J. E. Zins, M. J. Elias, & C. A. Maher (Eds.), *Bullying, victimization, and peer harassment* (pp. 389–412). New York: Haworth Press.

Kokkinos, C. M., & Panayiotou, G. (2004). Predicting bullying and victimization among early adolescents: Associations with disruptive behavior disorders. *Aggressive Behavior, 30,* 520–533.

Kramer, R. C. (2000). Poverty, inequality, and youth violence. *ANNALS of the American Academy of Political and Social Science, 567,* 123–139.

Limber, S. P. (2004). Implementation of the Olweus Bullying Prevention Program in American schools. In D. L. Espelage & S. M. Swearer (Eds.), *Bullying in American schools* (pp. 351–363). Mahwah, NJ: Erlbaum.

McCord, J., & Ensminger, M. E. (1997). Multiple risks and comorbidity in an African-American population. *Criminal Behaviour and Mental Health, 7*, 339–352.

Metropolitan Area Child Study Research Group. (2002). A cognitive-ecological approach to preventing aggression in urban settings: Initial outcomes for high-risk children. *Journal of Consulting and Clinical Psychology, 70*, 179–194.

Nation, M. (2007). Empowering the victim: Interventions for children victimized by bullies. In J. E. Zins, M. J. Elias, & C. A. Maher (Eds.), *Bullying, victimization, and peer harassment* (pp. 239–255). New York: Haworth Press.

Olweus, D. (1993). *Bullying at school: What we know and what we can do.* New York: Blackwell.

Pellegrini, A. D. (2002). Bullying, victimization, and sexual harassment during the transition to middle school. *Educational Psychologist, 37*, 151–163.

Pellegrini, A. D., & Long, J. D. (2004). Part of the solution and part of the problem: The role of peers in bullying, dominance, and victimization during the transition from primary school to secondary school. In D. L. Espelage & S. M. Swearer (Eds.), *Bullying in American schools* (pp. 107–117). Mahwah, NJ: Erlbaum.

Salmivalli, C. (2001). Peer-led intervention campaign against school bullying: Who considered it useful, who benefited? *Educational Research, 43*, 263–278.

Sampson, R. & Lauritsen, J. (1994). Violent victimization and offending: Individual, situational, and community-level risk factors. In A. J. Reiss & J. A. Roth (Eds.), *Understanding and preventing violence* (Vol. 3, pp. 451–481). Washington, DC: National Academy Press.

Snyder, H. N. & Sickmund, M. (2006). *Juvenile offenders and victims: 2006 national report.* Washington, DC: National Center for Juvenile Justice, Office of Juvenile Justice and Delinquency Prevention, Office of Justice Programs, United States Department of Justice.

Sveinsson, A. V., & Morris, R. J. (2007). Conceptual and methodological issues in assessment and intervention with school bullies. In J. E. Zins, M. J. Elias, & C. A. Maher (Eds.), *Bullying, victimization, and peer harassment* (pp. 9–26). New York: Haworth Press.

U.S. Department of Health and Human Services. (2001). *Youth violence: A report of the Surgeon General.* Washington, DC: U.S. Department of Health and Human Services.

Williams, K. R., & Guerra, N. G. (2007). Prevalence and predictors of internet bullying. *Journal of Adolescent Health, 41*, S14–S21.

14

Preventing and Treating Bullying and Victimization: Best Practices and Future Directions

Bridget K. Biggs and Eric M. Vernberg

G rowing worldwide concern about bullying and victimization and its effects on children and adolescents has generated much activity among scholars who are trying to understand the extent of the problem, what can be done about it, and how to implement effective prevention and intervention programs. With this book, we sought to bring together research and practical knowledge that have accumulated to date and to make this evidence accessible to those engaged in efforts to prevent and treat bullying and victimization among children and adolescents from an evidence-based perspective. It is clear that bullying and victimization are complex problems with no simple solutions. Individual characteristics, family processes, school social environments, and community and cultural factors all play important roles.

Each chapter of this book provides a piece to understanding this complex puzzle. Chapters in Part 1 present central concepts and emerging evidence on the multiple characteristics of individuals and environments associated with bullying and victimization. Contributions to Part 2 present options for assessing and intervening at various levels from individual to school. Chapters in Part 3 provide practical advice related to policy and implementation in various contexts. This final chapter summarizes major take-home points regarding best practices and policy implications given what is currently known about bullying and what types of efforts work best to address it. Because gaps still exist in the research base for understanding how to prevent and treat bully–victim problems, we acknowledge these limitations in our discussion of practice implications. At the same time, sufficient progress has been made to generate evidence-informed recommendations for best practices. We summarize these here.

Comprehensive and Coordinated Multilevel Efforts Have the Best Chance of Success

Bullying is clearly a complex phenomenon that is influenced by numerous people and environmental circumstances. As many of the authors in this book point out, bullying is a relational problem that involves an imbalance or misuse of power. This misuse of power is often enabled and sustained by social processes that potentially can be changed, such as peer or adult acceptance of coercion and humiliation. Although personal characteristics such as emotional reactivity, social skills difficulties, or low empathy appear to contribute to involvement in some instances, approaches that focus exclusively on individuals are not likely to be successful in stopping bullying. This is because action (or inaction) of bystanders is such a powerful influence in setting the stage for bullying to occur.

One implication of this fact is that anyone trying to "go it alone" in addressing bully–victim problems, without broad and active support for changes in the social climate, is likely to become frustrated quite quickly. Anecdotally, we have known parents, teachers, principals, children, and adolescents who have expressed such frustration. More importantly, research shows that a comprehensive, multilevel approach has the best likelihood of success. As described by Craig and colleagues (Chapter 9), comprehensive efforts include programming that all children receive regardless of their involvement in bullying (universal, or Tier 1, prevention efforts), more intensive prevention efforts for those at risk for greater involvement (selected, or Tier 2, interventions), and most intensive efforts for those youth already highly involved (indicated, or Tier 3, interventions). For example, a multitiered intervention to help children who are frequent victims of bullying may include adopting school-wide policies and rules to promote respectful social relationships that apply to all students and staff (Tier 1), school-based skill-building groups for children who struggle to develop positive peer relationships (Tier 2), and individual or family-oriented interventions aimed at helping children address emotional and behavioral problems that may interfere with social relationships, such as anxiety, depression, or attention deficits (Tier 3).

Although multitiered comprehensive programs seem most likely to produce meaningful changes, schools typically lack sufficient resources to develop and provide these programs on their own. In other words, schools cannot solve bully–victim problems without substantial, active support from the communities in which they operate. Conversely, community-based efforts to address bully–victim problems or related problems of youth violence must include active partnerships with schools in order to make a meaningful difference.

Fortunately, research on efforts to design and implement bully–victim programs is beginning to shed some light on the conditions under which meaningful changes are likely to emerge.

Evidence-Based Approaches to Implementation Follow Key Principles

Several key principles apply to evidence-based bully–victim prevention and intervention efforts at all levels or tiers. These principles offer a template for planning and measuring the impact of interventions. Importantly, they also highlight strategies that help generate sufficient support and local ownership of intervention efforts to bring about durable changes.

Plan Carefully and Monitor Progress

Evidence-based practice not only involves using information gained from the systematic study of bullying and interventions that work, it also includes careful assessment before beginning a prevention or intervention effort and ongoing assessment while implementing it to monitor the degree to which the intervention is being implemented as intended, to track progress, and to guide adjustments. This gathering of information happens in multiple steps:

Assess and Plan

As described by Singh and colleagues (Chapter 10), any intervention effort should begin with a careful assessment to guide intervention selection and planning. Knowledge about the extent of bullying and possible contributing factors as well as familiarity with general best practices will aid the selection of interventions with the greatest likelihood of success in a particular situation. Attention should also be paid to the perspectives of key stakeholders (e.g., children, parents, teachers, and other school staff), because perceptions and attitudes can influence buy in and the relative ease (or difficulty) in orchestrating a coordinated, multitiered effort.

Educate and Inform

Twemlow and Sacco (Chapter 12) emphasize how *buy in* is crucial to any antibullying effort. They offer practical advice on how to gauge buy in at the outset (see Table 12.2) and also how to draw attention to power dynamics and school climate as central issues in addressing bully–victim problems. Clear communication about the extent and seriousness of the situation, the reasons for intervening, and the approach chosen can influence buy in and willingness of multiple parties to work together in a coordinated plan (Stevens, Van Oost, & De Bourdeaudhuij, 2001).

Implement the Intervention and Monitor Fidelity and Progress

Make a commitment to proper implementation. Even with the best intentions and resources, interventions may not be implemented fully, which can undermine their effectiveness (Biggs, Vernberg, Twemlow, Fonagy, & Dill, 2008; Stevens et al., 2001). Monitoring fidelity to the selected treatment approach can alert interventionists to areas that may require additional education or support to achieve proper implementation. Ongoing assessment of key outcomes such as bullying, victimization, and attitudes toward aggression provides feedback necessary for knowing if intervention plans are having the intended effects.

Recommendations for Tier 1 Efforts

Universal, or Tier 1, prevention efforts are most commonly implemented as whole-school programs and typically aim to promote a peaceful environment characterized by mutual respect and valuing of all members of the school community. Multiple authors throughout this volume have emphasized the complex social dynamics behind bullying problems and give practical guidance informed by both research and experience in implementing whole-school programs. A few key points are listed in the next sections.

Start with a Thoughtful Definition of the School's Mission

Singh and colleagues (Chapter 10) describe a process that can be used to draft a school's mission statement based on the universal values held by students and school staff. Interventions should be clearly linked to the universal values reflected in the school mission. Student and staff involvement in this process is vital. The idea is that those who see that intervention efforts address their concerns and values will be more likely to support them and invest the energy to foster their success.

Knowing the extent of bullying can draw attention to the need for intervention. A careful assessment of the environment can help identify aspects of the school climate that need to be addressed. Roseth and Pellegrini (Chapter 7) describe multiple options for assessing students' involvement in bullying and related attitudes. Key points are to assess multiple perspectives (e.g., teachers, students, parents), use multiple approaches (e.g., observations, surveys, focus groups), and to assess environmental factors (e.g., adult supervision, bystander behaviors) associated with bullying. As emphasized in Chapters 2 and 13, tolerance of bullying and pro-aggression attitudes are extremely important factors contributing to the pervasiveness of bullying. In addition to assessing involvement in bullying, victimization, bystander behavior, and attitudes about bullying, aspects of the school climate should also be assessed. Are there strong and meaningful relationships and connections among people in the school across statuses (e.g., student, teacher, administrator)? Are the school building and grounds inviting and safe? Do school members enjoy being at school? Do students and educators feel motivated to excel in their learning and teaching activities?

Foster "Buy in" from the Entire School and Community

Fostering buy in includes identifying and involving natural leaders in the school and community (Twemlow & Sacco, Chapter 12). As defined by Twemlow and Sacco, natural leaders are motivated by altruism to act for the good of the group and lead by example. Singh and colleagues give strategies to gain support and input from students. The time and effort to get key people on board is likely important to garnering the necessary commitment and energy to get a program off the ground and to keep it running (Whitted & Dupper, 2005).

Select a Program Consistent with Best Practices

Programs with the greatest demonstrated success share some common characteristics. First, they take a coordinated and systematic approach and aim to change the culture and climate of the school (Whitted & Dupper, 2005; see also Chapter 9). Second, they include curricula to teach skills for helping others and knowledge, attitudes, and skills to deal more effectively with bullying behavior and to help those involved in bullying (Chapter 9). Finally, effective programs tend to involve parents and work cooperatively with them (Chapter 9).

Proper implementation of any intervention effort takes time, money, and other resources. Obtaining the needed resources may require garnering support from sources, including school district, community, and grants from government agencies and private foundations. In addition, Twemlow and Sacco (Chapter 12) point out that it is the commitment to mount a sustained effort and allocate time to address issues of school climate that seems to be important rather than the amount of money spent. Time is a precious commodity and schools must be convinced that efforts made to address school climate issues on a regular basis will pay off in terms of reducing interpersonal problems and fostering more successful educational outcomes.

Recommendations for Tier 2 Efforts

Tier 2 programs address the needs of children and adolescents who have been identified as involved in bullying or at increased risk for involvement based on characteristics strongly associated with bullying or victimization. Chapters 3, 4, and 5 provide detailed information about the individual and family characteristics commonly associated with bullying and victimization. Understanding how individuals may become involved in increasingly negative interactions with peers is important for assessment and intervention. Chapters 6 and 7 provide practical guidance for assessment at the school and individual levels.

There are a few important caveats to consider at Tier 2. First, the methods that are currently available for assessing individuals' involvement in bullying come from research studying bullying at a broader level, and their use at the individual level has not been carefully evaluated. Unlike clinically oriented behavior rating scales for problem behaviors (e.g., Reynolds & Kamphaus, 1992), bully–victim measures generally lack normative data needed to determine whether the amount of aggression or victimization reported is within normal limits, above average, or extremely high. In terms of treatment, very few Tier 2 interventions have been developed and tested specific to reducing bullying behavior or protecting individuals from peer victimization. At this point, many of the options that seem most reasonable are interventions developed for related problems such as aggressive behavior (not specifically bullying) or internalizing symptoms (e.g., anxiety, depression), which are associated with victimization. With these caveats under consideration, we highlight key points related to Tier 2 efforts.

Children and adolescents in need of Tier 2 programs may be identified in the whole-school assessment process or by referral from teachers, parents, school nurses, other caring adults, or perhaps even from the youths themselves. Roseth and Pellegrini (Chapter 7) describe assessment approaches that can be used at the school level. Grills-Tachequel and colleagues (Chapter 6) describe a number of assessment options that can be used by professionals to assess the extent of involvement with individual children. In addition, it is also important to assess broad behavioral and emotional functioning, considering that both bullying and victimization are associated with a number of behavioral and psychological problems.

Match the Intervention to the Characteristics of the Individual

Flanagan and Battaglia (Chapter 8) discuss intervention options according to whether children are predominantly aggressive or victimized. Furthermore, for aggressive youth, it is important to assess whether their aggressive behavior is reactive or instrumental in nature, because the intervention focus varies depending on this distinction. Most interventions for aggressive behavior have been designed to address emotion regulation problems, social skills deficits, and social interaction attribution biases (e.g., jumping to conclusions that someone is being hostile) that characterize reactive, or "hot-blooded," aggression. These interventions may not be effective with bullying among children who are socially adept and instrumental in their aggression. In these cases, greater attention may need to be given to changing the circumstances that make bullying attractive to these youth, such as the payoff of getting material goods or esteem from peers. Be mindful that it is fairly common for children and adolescents to be involved as both bully and victim. In determining what intervention approach is best, think about the unique skills and deficits of the child or adolescent and consider a combination of interventions.

Form Groups of Children with Similar Needs and Monitor Group Dynamics

The group format is a nice option for addressing the needs of youth at Tier 2, because a fairly large number of youth can be involved relative to staffing and time demands for running the groups. In addition, the group format also provides opportunities to practice new skills with peers and, with careful attention from group facilitators, can also provide opportunities for social support. However, as pointed out by Flanagan and colleagues (Chapter 8), it is particularly important to monitor the group dynamics of aggressive youth closely because it is possible for participants to encourage and "one-up" each other's aggressive and antisocial attitudes and behavior, creating a group culture that is likely to foster rather than discourage bullying.

Include Lots of Practice

When learning new skills, children and adolescents need ample opportunity to practice. Praise and reward their efforts to implement the skill correctly. To help participants generalize skills outside of the group, include plenty of practice with peers during group meetings and set up ways for participants to practice (and be rewarded for using) skills outside of group sessions. Frankel describes an approach to social skills training that provides both structured in-session practice and explicit instruction to parents on how to support their children's generalization of skills to the "real world" (Chapter 11).

Involve Parents

Parents can be very important agents of change if they are involved in the teaching of the skills their child is learning. As described in detail by Frankel (Chapter 11), parents can facilitate practice of new skills, monitor the success of implementation, and provide important corrective feedback and reinforcement. More broadly, parents and families influence children's social behavior in a number of ways, including developing age-appropriate skills for self-assertiveness and autonomy, modeling attitudes and behaviors around the use of aggression, and providing a sense of being loved and valued (Chapter 4). Inclusion of parents provides opportunities for school and home to get on the same page. Ignoring parents could undermine the effectiveness of an intervention by increasing the chances that children will receive conflicting messages about aggression at home and school.

Coordinate Tier 2 and Tier 1 Efforts

Materials and concepts used for Tier 1 and Tier 2 interventions should complement each other. For example, bullying and victimization can be defined the same at both levels and basic messages regarding norms and expectations for social behavior should be consistent. Tier 2 interventions would provide greater opportunity to understand and master thoughts, feelings, and behaviors related to relationships with peers and adults for students who struggle to avoid the roles of submissive victim, aggressive victim, or bully.

Recommendations for Tier 3 Efforts

Tier 3 interventions are reserved for youth with significant and persistent involvement with bullying and victimization. Often, serious behavioral or emotional problems contribute to (or follow from) their involvement in antagonistic peer interactions. For example, children and adolescents with serious emotional disturbances are often among the most socially rejected or neglected students in schools (Greenbaum et al., 1996). They may be involved with multiple health, social service, and mental-health providers. Many perform poorly academically, further excluding them from peers and weakening their ties with teachers and other school staff. These children and adolescents are likely to need intervention and support beyond universal, school-wide programming and group-based skills groups. In Chapter 6, Grills-Tachequel and colleagues provide detailed recommendations for working individually with youth who frequently bully, are victimized, or both. Dempsey and Storch (Chapter 5) describe how specific health and mental-health problems increase risks for victimization or aggression. Readers will also find Chapters 3 and 4 helpful for understanding individual, family, and developmental factors that often contribute to a child becoming frequently victimized or a frequent perpetrator of bullying. When working with children and adolescents who have serious and persistent health or mental-health problems, it is especially important for the multiple providers to be aware of what others are doing and to coordinate services with the family and school. In this regard, Chapters 2 through 5 provide helpful insights into key peer, school, and family factors that need to be assessed and possibly targeted in treatment.

It may be possible to draw an example from evidence-based interventions for children and adolescents with more severe and persistent emotional disturbances, who often experience peer rejection and victimization at school (Vernberg, Roberts, & Nyre, 2008; Vernberg et al., 2008). Effective intervention generally involves service coordination with multiple providers with an emphasis on adequate school performance, close friendships, peer acceptance, and family relationships. The practical implications for working with a child who is deeply involved in bullying are to build communication among adults in the child's life, such as parents, teachers, school counselors, therapists, coaches (of course, with signed parent/guardian authorization when required by law), and coordinate efforts so that all parties offer consistent messages and coordinated support to the child. For example, regular communication among parents, school staff, and mental-health workers can keep all up to date on the child's behavior and interactions with peers. Therapists working individually with children can integrate language, skills, and rules from school-based programming into treatment plans. Communication between therapists/counselors and teachers can help children generalize skills learned in individual or group therapy to the classroom and playground, just as communication with parents is needed to generalize skills to home and social interactions in the community. Here are a few of the main points to keep in mind for Tier 3 interventions.

Start with a Careful Assessment

Use a multi-informant, multimethod approach to assess for multiple types of involvement (submissive victim, bully, aggressive victim, aggressive bystander), especially when conducting "high-stakes" assessments (see Chapter 7). Also assess for health problems and commonly comorbid mental-health difficulties such as conduct problems among children who bully and internalizing problems among frequent victims (Chapters 5, 6, and 8). In some cases, children and adolescents may be referred for treatment because of their involvement in bullying. In other cases, the reason for referral may be concern about emotional, behavioral, or academic difficulties.

Develop a Comprehensive Treatment Plan That Addresses Bullying and/or Victimization as Well as Behavioral and Emotional Problems

Whereas there are a few promising group treatments for involvement in bullying, we currently do not have any individual treatments developed specifically to help submissive victims or aggressive victims. At this time, our best guess for what might be helpful is to use treatments that have been found to work in treating the types of behaviors, thoughts, and symptoms associated with either bullying or victimization. When working with children who are bullies or bully victims, treatments for general aggressive behavior and conduct problems show promise and typically teach nonaggressive alternatives to accomplish social goals, problem solving, and self-talk skills. These also include parents and teachers in structuring the environment to encourage nonaggressive behavior with behavior management techniques. When working with submissive victims or aggressive victims, current recommendations are to address internalizing problems (e.g., anxiety, depression), emotion regulation, coping skills, and self-assertion skills that likely contribute to ongoing victimization (Chapter 6). In addition, helping victimized children and adolescents develop friendships with well-functioning peers may help protect them from continued victimization or buffer its effects (Chapter 11).

Garner Support from Family and School Staff to Generalize Skills

A particular challenge of working with individual children and adolescents is facilitating the generalizing of skills to environments outside of the treatment setting. Children can learn skills within the session by seeing them modeled by the therapist and then practicing them in role plays. This type of practice is helpful for first teaching a skill, but it will not automatically lead to children using these skills effectively in the environments where they matter most (e.g., with peers at school). It is important that parents learn the skills as well (the child or adolescent could assist the therapist in teaching them to parents to consolidate skill acquisition) and also learn how to provide helpful practice at home and with familiar peers and to encourage their child's use of the new skills in daily life. Communicating with teachers and/or school counselors who have frequent interaction with the child is also important. As with parents, therapists could provide information on what new skills the child is practicing and how to prompt and encourage their use. Coordination among home, school, and therapist's office could include a reward system administered by parents and school staff in collaboration with the therapist in which the child could be prompted and rewarded for using new skills across multiple settings.

Coordinate with the Family and School to Provide Protection from Bullying and Consequences for Engaging in Bullying

Because bullying is a contextual problem, teaching victims social and coping skills is not likely to be effective in isolation. Even worse, focusing solely on the victim could make victims feel blamed and helpless in changing their plight. Likewise, teaching chronic bullies nonaggressive alternatives and problem-solving skills is not likely to change their behavior unless the cost of these behaviors is greater than the benefit they provide in the environment. Therefore, it is imperative for therapists working individually with children and adolescents to collaborate with school staff and parents in changing environmental circumstances that may be contributing to bullying.

Future Directions
Increase the Clinical Utility of Assessment Tools

As noted in Chapters 6 and 7, numerous assessment options currently exist to measure bullying. Currently lacking are normative data and clinically useful cut-off points for these tools. Clearly, no level of perpetration or receipt of bullying is acceptable; yet at what point should there be heightened concern and referral for Tier 2 or 3 interventions? These determinations may be best made based on a combination of factors such as the frequency or intensity of involvement, the chronicity of those problems, and the degree of social and emotional impairment or distress experienced by the individual. Schwartz and colleagues (Chapter 2) describe how definitions and prevalent forms of bullying vary across cultures. Thus, the threshold for intervention likely needs to be defined in light of these cultural differences. However, ample correlational research across many countries, both cross-sectional and longitudinal, suggests that the greater the involvement in bullying, the greater the adjustment difficulties. Additional research suggests that the chronicity of bullying may compound the adjustment difficulties of victims (e.g., Biggs et al., in press; Kochenderfer-Ladd & Wardrop, 2001). The clinical utility of current tools could be greatly enhanced by research that establishes norms by gender and age and investigates the relative sensitivity and selectivity of various cut-off scores for identifying youth at greatest risk.

Further Develop Tier 2 and Tier 3 Interventions and Test Their Efficacy and Effectiveness

The last few decades have seen great advances in the development and evaluation of Tier 1 school-based programs to address bullying. Considering the complex social context of bullying, these initial intervention efforts have done much to show that change is possible. Empirical evaluation of intervention outcomes further supports the use of comprehensive approaches to bullying that address the entire school as well as families and communities (Chapter 9). Continued development of intervention options to address the needs of youth with substantial involvement in bullying (Tier 2) and those with significant behavioral and psychological impairment or distress in addition to involvement in bullying (Tier 3) is needed. For example, in their review of Tier 2 group intervention options, Flanagan and Battaglia (Chapter 8) found only two programs specifically designed to address bullying and victimization: the Social Skills Training (SST) Programme developed by Fox and Boulton and the

Social Skills Group Intervention (S.S.GRIN) developed by DeRosier and colleagues. Both programs are in their early stages of evaluation and show promise in addressing behavioral and social skills deficits among victims. S.S. GRIN has additionally demonstrated some benefit for aggressive children. Both programs were developed for elementary age youth, although an adolescent version of S.S.GRIN has been developed and shows initial promise (Harrell, Mercer, & DeRosier, 2009). At this time, empirically evaluated Tier 2 options for adolescents and Tier 3 options specifically designed and evaluated for youth with both significant involvement in bullying and mental-health concerns are sorely lacking.

The limited intervention options currently available at the Tier 2 and 3 levels, like the Tier 1 programs, have been implemented and evaluated primarily in school settings. Although ample evidence links family characteristics with significant involvement in bullying (Chapter 4), little guidance currently exists for involving families in Tier 2 and 3 interventions. Frankel's parent-assisted social skills training program (Chapter 11) is one exception that provides practical direction for involving parents and for running social skills training groups in a clinic setting. Currently, school counselors and therapists working in clinic settings are left to piece together treatment plans for youth involved in bullying by combining evidence-based practices for psychological and behavioral symptoms with best guesses for addressing bullying or victimization (see Chapters 6 and 8). Further development and evaluation of manualized group and individual treatment approaches could provide much needed systematic and empirically based treatment approaches for children and adolescents who bully or are bullied by others.

Identify Developmentally and Socially Valid Responses to Bullying

A common question we have encountered in treatment of children and adolescents who report being bullied by peers is: How should we teach them to respond? The selection of social skills taught in programs such as S.S.GRIN, the SST Programme (reviewed in Chapter 8), and the Parent-Assisted Social Skills Training (described in Chapter 11) is typically informed by research into the behaviors associated with peer acceptance and/or rejection and victimization. However, the identification of responses to victimization and styles of coping that are associated with changes in victimization and/or adjustment is yet in its infancy. Kochenderfer-Ladd and Ladd (Chapter 3) describe some of the research addressing this issue. Our own research efforts suggest that, at least among teenagers who report frequent peer victimization, changing one's internal response to the situation (e.g., positive thinking, distraction) is likely more helpful than publicly visible responses such as actively trying to change the situation or expressing one's emotions (Nelson, Biggs, Vernberg, & Little, submitted). Unfortunately, not enough is known at this point to make definitive recommendations. Rather, what is becoming clearer in this line of research is that determining which actions would be most helpful is likely to depend on the victim's age, gender, and social context. For example, requesting assistance from a teacher might be effective at young ages but could be socially damaging and exacerbate victimization among older youth.

Increase Attention to Implementation and Dissemination

Meta-analyses of school-based bullying prevention programs (Merrell, Gueldner, Ross, & Isava, 2008) and whole-school programs (Smith, Schneider, Smith, & Ananiadou, 2004), which make up the majority of empirically evaluated interventions, indicate that effects are modest at best and that meaningful changes are often not observed across all targeted outcomes (see also Chapter 9). Some intervention researchers have wondered whether inconsistencies in implementation have hampered effectiveness in some cases; however, without explicit measurement of intervention fidelity, such dose–effect hypotheses cannot be tested. We have tried to address this gap in our own work by measuring fidelity across the multiple aspects of a whole-school approach called Creating a Peaceful School Learning Environment (CAPSLE) (Fonagy et al., 2009). As speculated, we have found that adherence to the classroom management aspect of CAPSLE varied across teachers and schools (Biggs et al., 2008). In addition, our findings indicated that teachers' reported adherence was related to their attitudes toward the intervention program and about classroom management generally. Kallestad and Olweus (2003) have reported similar associations between teacher attitudes and adherence. Of note, teachers' level of reported adherence to CAPSLE also predicted changes in their students' attitudes about and responses to bullying (as measured by students' self-report and peer nomination, respectively; Biggs et al., 2008). The "dose" of an intervention students actually receive may also matter, as may the gender of participants. For example, we have found that the number of defensive martial arts skill-building lessons that boys attended as part of the CAPSLE program was related to changes in their self-reported aggressive and helpful bystanding behaviors (Twemlow et al., 2008). However, similar effects were not observed among girls. More consistent measurement and reporting of implementation fidelity and dose–effect relations in the empirical evaluation of anti-bullying programs would clarify whether interventions were delivered and received as intended and whether the effectiveness of promising programs could be improved by increasing fidelity to their implementation.

Fidelity data would also be useful in evaluating dissemination. Interestingly, only 14 of the 48 studies reviewed by Craig and colleagues (Chapter 9) reported the availability of external resources to assist with successful implementation and maintenance. Useful and interesting questions related to dissemination that will be important to address are as follows:

1. What can be done to maximize buy in and implementation?
2. How are anti-bullying programs perceived by school personnel, students, families, and communities?
3. Which programs and components are easiest and most difficult to replicate?

A group of researchers at the Institute for Families in Society have been working on the replication of Olweus' Anti-bullying Program in the United States since the mid-1990s. These researchers (Limber, Nation, Tracy, Melton, & Flerx, 2004) identify a train-the-trainer model, training and ongoing consultation, an onsite coordinator, and staff discussion groups as important for successful dissemination beyond program schools. Additional ideas regarding dissemination can be found in the clinical psychology literature. Proposed models to guide dissemination of evidence-based practices include Weisz's deployment-focused model (Weisz, Chu, & Polo, 2004) and the multilevel contextual model proposed by Schoenwald and Hoagwood (2001). Common to both models is attention to the characteristics of the people and location where the intervention is to take place. Translated to school-based anti-bullying programs, these dissemination frameworks caution against a "top-down" approach to implementation and emphasize the importance of working with the school personnel to fit the intervention with the cultural context of the school and surrounding community. Consistent with this notion are Singh and colleagues' suggestions such as centering interventions on identified universal values (Chapter 10) and Twemlow and Sacco's thoughts regarding the importance of buy in (Chapter 12).

Gather Data on Cost-Effectiveness

Comprehensive anti-bullying programs cost money, and budgets are often limited. Data on the resources required for implementation versus the potential costs—financial, academic, psychological, and otherwise—are needed to make the case to tax payers, school districts, legislators, and philanthropic organizations to fund them. Further research to identify essential and highest yielding intervention elements could also serve to maximize the efficiency of interventions and allocations of resources.

Develop Cross-Cultural Research and Culturally Valid Interventions

As noted by Schwartz and colleagues (Chapter 2), bullying is a worldwide phenomenon whose prevalence and characteristics can reflect the culture of the region. Despite the apparent worldwide prevalence of bullying, intervention research has been largely limited to countries with significant economic resources. For example, the interventions reviewed in Part 2 of this book have occurred almost exclusively in Australia, Europe, and the United States, although Twemlow and Sacco (Chapter 12) mention their efforts to develop a bullying prevention program in Jamaica and Paraguay. Although cross-cultural implementation issues were not a focus of their chapter in this volume, we hope to see greater development of systematic evaluation of assessment and intervention approaches in countries that have thus far received little attention.

Adopt a Stronger Developmental Perspective

Although some attention is given to development throughout the bullying literature, the importance of a developmental perspective can never be emphasized enough. A large proportion of the research on bullying, peer victimization, and related constructs like aggression has been conducted with youth in primary school, particularly middle childhood. Findings from these studies do not automatically translate to adolescence. As argued by Schwartz and colleagues (Chapter 2) and Dempsey and Storch (Chapter 5), the risk for victimization is increased by characteristics that make an individual stand out from the social norm in a way that is viewed negatively by peers. Social norms and expectations change with development. For example, socializing with members of the opposite sex might be socially stigmatizing in middle childhood but provide a boost to one's social currency in adolescence. Similarly, it is an empirical question whether programs designed for primary schools can be successfully implemented in secondary schools. Programming that works with younger youth could be dismissed by adolescents as juvenile or even "hokey" or "stupid" (or whatever disapproving term is popular in a particular time and place). As the field moves forward, we would like to see more explicit attention given to the developmental periods represented in studies identifying risk and protective factors and in reporting which interventions work for which ages. A commonly held belief that also makes sense to us is that early intervention is important for shaping attitudes, behaviors, and an overall culture that promote peaceful learning and social environments. Long-term follow-up studies can provide valuable information regarding the longevity of effects from early intervention programs. For example, do students who participated in an intervention during primary school continue in secondary school to endorse more peaceful attitudes and have less involvement in bullying relative to students in a control condition? Similarly, are climates of secondary schools positively affected when a substantial number of students received early intervention?

Closing Comments

Bullying is a complex issue with no simple solutions. With this book, we have taken an evidence-based perspective to addressing this issue by asking contributors to translate the most current scientific knowledge about bullying and interventions into practical guidance for intervening. Although we have much more to learn, existing scientific evidence indicates that efforts to prevent or reduce bullying and its effects are most likely to succeed if they are comprehensive, multilevel, and well coordinated across the multiple domains of children's and adolescents' lives. We hope that readers will find this information useful and inspiring in their efforts to reduce and prevent bullying. Considering the well-documented outcomes associated with bullying and being bullied, we believe this goal is well worth pursuing.

References

Biggs, B. K., Vernberg, E. M., Fonagy, P., Twemlow, S. W., Little, T. D., & Dill, E. J. (in press). Peer victimization trajectories and their association with children's affect in late elementary school. *International Journal of Behavioral Development.*

Biggs, B. K., Vernberg, E. M., Twemlow, S. W., Fonagy, P., & Dill, E. J. (2008). Teacher adherence and its relation to teacher attitudes and student outcomes in an elementary school-based violence prevention program. *School Psychology Review, 37*(4), 533–549.

Fonagy, P., Twemlow, S. W., Vernberg, E. M., Nelson, J. M., Dill, E. J., Little, T. D. et al. (2009). A cluster randomized controlled trial of child-focused psychiatric consultation and a school systems-focused intervention to reduce aggression. *Journal of Child Psychology and Psychiatry, 50,* 607–616.

Greenbaum, P. E., Dedrick, R. F., Friedman, R. M., Kutash, K., Brown, E. C., Lardieri, S. P., & Pugh, A. M. (1996). National Adolescent and Child Treatment Study (NACTS): Outcomes for children with serious emotional and behavioral disturbance. *Journal of Emotional & Behavioral Disorders, 4,* 130–146

Harrell, A. M., Mercer, S. H., & DeRosier, M. E. (2009). Improving the social behavioral adjustment of adolescents: The effectiveness of a social skills group intervention. *Journal of Child and Family Studies, 18,* 378–387.

Kallestad, J. H., & Olweus, D. (2003). Predicting teachers' and schools' implementation of the Olweus Bullying Prevention Program: A multilevel study. *Prevention & Treatment, 6,* [np].

Kochenderfer-Ladd, B., & Wardrop, J. L. (2001). Chronicity and instability of children's peer victimization experiences as predictors of loneliness and social satisfaction trajectories. *Child Development, 72,* 124–151.

Limber, S. P., Nation, M., Tracy, A. J., Melton, G. B., & Flerx, V. (2004). Implementation of the Olweus Bullying Prevention Program in the Southeastern United States. In P. K. Smith, D. Pepler, & K. Rigby (Eds.), *Bullying in schools: How successful can interventions be?* (pp. 55–79). Cambridge, England: Cambridge University Press.

Merrell, K. W., Gueldner, B. A., Ross, S. W., & Isava, D. M. (2008). How effective are school bullying intervention programs? A meta-analysis of intervention research. *School Psychology Quarterly, 23,* 26–42.

Nelson, J. M., Biggs, B. K., Vernberg, E. M., & Little, T. D. (2009). *Coping and involuntary stress responses to peer victimization in adolescence: Victimization stability and change in depressive symptoms.* Manuscript submitted for publication.

Reynolds, C. R., & Kamphaus, R. W. (1992). *Behavior assessment system for children.* Circle Pines, MN: American Guidance Service.

Schoenwald, S. K., & Hoagwood, K. (2001). Effectiveness, transportability, and dissemination of interventions: What matters when? *Psychiatric Services, 52,* 1190–1197.

Smith, J. D., Schneider, B. H., Smith, P. K., & Ananiadou, K. (2004). The effectiveness of whole-school antibullying programs: A synthesis of evaluation research. *School Psychology Review, 33,* 547–560.

Stevens, V., Van Oost, P., & De Bourdeaudhuij, I. (2001). Implementation process of the Flemish antibullying intervention and relation with program effectiveness. *Journal of School Psychology, 39,* 303–317.

Twemlow, S. W., Biggs, B. K., Nelson, T. D., Vernberg, E. M., Fonagy, P., & Twemlow, S. W. (2008). Effects of participation in a martial arts-based antibullying program in elementary schools. *Psychology in the Schools, 45,* 947–959.

Vernberg, E. M., Roberts, M. C., Jacobs, A. K., Randall, C. J., Biggs, B. K., & Nyre, J. E. (2008). Outcomes and findings of program evaluation for the Intensive Mental Health Program. *Journal of Child and Family Studies, 17,* 178–190.

Strategies for Implementing Best Practices

Vernberg, E. M., Roberts, M. C., & Nyre, J. E. (2008). The Intensive Mental Health Program: Development and structure of the model of intervention for children with serious emotional disturbances. *Journal of Child and Family Studies, 17,* 169–177.

Weisz, J. R., Chu, B. C., & Polo, A. J. (2004). Treatment dissemination and evidence-based practice: Strengthening intervention through clinician-researcher collaboration. *Clinical Psychology: Research & Practice, 11,* 300–307.

Whitted, K. S., & Dupper, D. R. (2005). Best practices for preventing or reducing bullying in schools. *Children and Schools, 27,* 167–175.

Appendices

Table A.1
Study Descriptions (Chapter 9)

Researchers/ Date/Country of Origin	Program Title	Treatment Type	Length of Treatment	Participants	Constructs Assessed	Description	Results (+/−/=)	Total Scientific Merit
Bierman, K.A., Coie, J.D., Dodge, K. A., Foster, E.M., Greenberg, M.T., Lochman, J.E. McMahon, R.J., Pinderhughes, E.E.; Conduct Problems Prevention Research Group (2002); USA	FAST Track; http://www.fasttrackproject.org/	Systemic; multimodal	Ongoing; 10-year program	Grades 1–10	Bullying, victimization, aggression	Six components in the elementary phase for grades 1–5: PATHS, parent training groups, home visits, friendship groups, tutoring for reading, peer pairing; adolescent phase for grades 6–10 has standard and individualized activities for high-risk youth and families. Group-based interventions were de-emphasized to avoid deviancy training.	+ Home, classroom, and playground behavior	17
Rahey, L., & Craig, W. M. (2002); Canada	Bully Proofing Your School; http://www.oakland.k12.mi.us/resources/bullyproof.html	Systemic; interactional; model/based on Bully Proofing Your School	12 weeks	Grades 1–8, parents and teachers: 240 students, 184 parents, 23 teachers of students	Bullying and victimization	Classroom-based psychoeducational program was led by seven graduate students and topics on bullying and victimizations were learned through role playing and puppet shows; peer mediation program; groups for referred students for involvement in bullying and victimization	+ Girls bullying, − boys bullying; + victimization	13

(continued)

Table A.1
(Continued)

Researchers/ Date/Country of Origin	Program Title	Treatment Type	Length of Treatment	Participants	Constructs Assessed	Description	Results (+/–/=)	Total Scientific Merit
Olweus, D. (2005, 1992, 1991); Norway	Olweus Bullying Prevention Program	Multilevel, multicomponent, and systemic	Approx. 3 years	2500 students, 300–400 teachers, 1000 parents	Bullying	All school staff need to participate for a half a day or full day of training session, read Teacher Handbook, and hold weekly classroom meetings	+ Bullying	13
Ortega, R, Del Rey, R., & Mora-Merchan, R.A., 2004; Ortega, R., & Lera, M. J. (2000); Spain	The Seville Study (SAVE model)	Universal, community approach	5 years	910 students aged 8–18 years	Bullying; victimization	Educational program about interpersonal relationships; promote democratic values, cooperative group work, empathy and concern for others	Bullying (+); victimization (+)	13
Eslea, M., & Smith, P. K. (1998); UK	DFE Sheffield Anti-Bullying Project; http://www.gold.ac.uk/euconf/poster/england.html	Systemic/based on Olweus' principles	Ongoing	Primary and secondary students and head teachers	Olweus Bully Questionnaire Interviews with head teachers	Whole-school policies, awareness raising, consultation, playground intervention, videos, books, quality circles, and lunch hour supervision	Bullying (boys +) (girls –)	12

Twemlow, S. W., Fonagy, P., Sacco, F. C., Gies, M. L., Evans, R., & Ewbank, R. (2001); USA	Social systems psychodynamic antiviolence intervention	Zero-tolerance policy; discipline plan for modeling appropriate behavior; physical education plan for self-regulation skills; mentoring program	156 weeks (3 years)	46 experimental, 64 control; observed at baseline in 3rd grade and again 3 years later in 5th grade	The Metropolitan Achievement Test (Psychological Corp, 1993): a measure of academic achievement; a measure of the disciplinary referrals from the principals	A school-based policy intervention to prevent violence was implemented. Policy included four components: a zero-tolerance policy for behavioral disturbances (including bullying), a discipline plan designed to encourage appropriate behavior, a physical education plan designed to teach self-regulation, and a mentoring program	+ T>C · 12
Soutter, A., & McKenzie, A. (2000); Australia	Reviewed a number of initiatives at schools in Australia; http://Spi.sagepub.com/cgi/framedreprint/21/1/96	Not specified	High schools	Australian primary and secondary schools	Bullying and victimization	School 1 developed policy. Parents introduced to Bully Buster/Peacekeepers Program; School 2, importance of staff as role models; School 3, drama to relay message; School 4, safe and happy playgrounds; School 5, Peer Relations Questionnaire to grades 7, 9, 10, and 11. Whole-school policy developed to deal with bullying. School 6, comprehensive set of actions in whole-school approach. Contains surveys, staff development, reporting and monitoring procedures, strategies, and interventions.	Bullying (+); victimization (−) · 10

(continued)

Table A.1
(Continued)

Researchers/ Date/Country of Origin	Program Title	Treatment Type	Length of Treatment	Participants	Constructs Assessed	Description	Results (+/-/=)	Total Scientific Merit
Pepler, D. J., Craig, W.M., Ziegler, S. & Charach, A. (1994); Canada	Toronto Anti-Bullying Intervention	Systemic anti-bullying program	18 months	1000 kids at four elementary schools	Bullying; victimization	School designed own bullying intervention, ranging from whole-school to education initiatives	Victimization (+); bullying (–)	10
Salmivalli, C., Kaukiainen, A., & Voeten (2005); Finland	Salmivalli Group Intervention	Social-cognitve-emotional approach; systemic; focus on participant roles	Not specified	Grade 4, 5, and 6	Bullying; victimization; attitudes toward bullying; efficacy beliefs; participant roles	Intervention targets classes and focuses on the roles peers play in bully–victim interventions. It does so by raising awareness, encouraging self-reflection, and providing opportunities to commit to anti-bullying behavior	(+) Decreased bully–victim problems for grade 4 students in intervention; (+) self-efficacy beliefs; (=) bystander behaviors	10

Hirschstein, M. K., Edstrom, L. V. S., Frey, K. S., Snell, J. L., & MacKenzie, E. P. (2007); Frey, K. S., Hirschstein, M. K., Snell, J. L., Edstrom, L. V. S., MacKenzie, E. P., & Broderick, C. J. (2005); USA; Committee for Children (2001), UK	Steps to Respect	Social-emotional; education for adults; cognitive behavioral-modeling prosocial behavior	14 weeks	Grade 3–6	Behavioral observations of students; teacher rating of peer interaction skill; bullying and attitudes about bullying; bystander responsibility	Steps to Respect contains whole-school components, classroom lessons, and parent engagement. The program entailed training school staff and administering school curricula. Classroom curricula focus on skill building and emotional regulation.	(+) Decrease in bullying behavior among individuals that engaged in bullying pretest; (+) increased bystander encouragement; (=) no decrease in self-reported bullying; (−) self-reported victimization higher at posttest; (+) stable bystander responsibility in intervention group, versus decreasing responsibility in controls; (=) no increase in teacher reported peer interaction skills

Table A.1
(Continued)

Researchers/ Date/Country of Origin	Program Title	Treatment Type	Length of Treatment	Participants	Constructs Assessed	Description	Results (+/-/=)	Total Scientific Merit
DeRosier, M. (2007); USA	Peer Connections (some elements of S.S.GRIN)	Peer processes; cognitive-behavioral	10 weeks	943 total; 193 identified as highly disliked by peers or experienced a significant level of bullying; 4th grade students	Peer rejection; victimization; bullying; social interactions; anxiety; depression	This intervention is part of the Safe Schools Initiative and combines pretreatment assessment of school climate with the cognitive, social, and coping strategy training of the S.S.GRIN	(+) Social acceptance over time; (+) less aggressive behavior over time; (+) less bulling by peers over time; (+) aggressive children showed a decline in aggressive/ bullying behavior; (+) aggressive children showed no marked increase in antisocial affiliation compared to increase found in children not in S.S. GRIN	10

Reference; Country	Program	Approach	Duration	Sample	Outcome measures	Program description	Results	
Jennifer, D., & Shaughnessy, J. (2005); UK	UK-001 CONECT	Universal; systemic	1 year	Children and youth of all ages (primary, elementary, secondary, and special schools)	Bullying and overt aggression; frequency of be bullied; remainder were observations, diaries, and interviews; school compliance and commitment	UK-001 CONECT includes conflict resolution, peer support, health promotion, anger management, and self-auditing tools. The self-auditing tools include assessments of home, school, community, and individual.	(=) 3 out of 5 schools experienced decreases in overt aggression and bullying; (−) level of support in the school was not adequate to run the program	10
O'Moore, A. M., & Minton, S. J. (2005); Ireland	The Donegal Primary Schools' Anti-Bullying Project; http://www.titles.cambridge.org/	Whole-school approach	2 years	Grades 1–6; ages 6–11 years	Modified Olweus Bully/Victim Questionnaire	Trains teachers in prevention of bullying, parents given bullying resources, and awareness-raising campaigns for students	Bullying (−)	9
Meyer, N., & Lesch, E. (2000); South Africa	Not specified	Behavioral approach	10 nonconsecutive weeks	54 bullying boys (3 schools, 18 boys each) in schools in the suburbs	Bullying behavior	Token economy system, self-observation, positive reinforcement, homework, role play, modeling	Bullying behavior (=)	9
Stevens, V., Bourdeaudhuij, I. D., & Oost, P. V. (2000); Belgium	The Flanders; http://www.ncab.org.au/pdfs/peacepack_slee.pdf	Developmental models of aggression and behavior modification, authoritative child-rearing method applied to school	Not specified	1104 students; 18 primary and secondary schools	Bullying; victimization	Three conditions: program with extra help from research group, program only, and control group interventions	Bullying and victimization: primary (+); secondary (=)	9

(continued)

Table A.1
(Continued)

Researchers/ Date/Country of Origin	Program Title	Treatment Type	Length of Treatment	Participants	Constructs Assessed	Description	Results (+/-/=)	Total Scientific Merit
Cross, D., Hall, M., Hamilton, G., Pintabona, Y., & Erceg, E. (2004); Australia	Friendly Schools Project	Multilevel and multicomponent whole-school bullying reduction intervention	3 years	4th grade students aged 8–9 years, their parents, and teachers	Questionnaire based on Olweus' principles; perceptions of social support/ attitudes toward victims; outcome-expectancies if bullied others;	Curriculum-based student education on bullying; cognitive-based teaching and learning activities addressing social support, reinforcement, and outcome expectancies; self-efficacy and cognitive skills, friendship building, conflict resolution, self-esteem building, decision making, assertiveness training, and encouraging and supporting reporting of bullying	Bullying (slight −)	9
Maines, B., & Robinson, G. (1998); UK	No Blame Approach; http://www.luckyduck. co.uk/approach/ bullying	Student teacher interaction; social system	Not specified	Two middle school, 1 junior high, 8 secondary school (5 schools had parents involved)	Not specified	Teacher talks with the victim and meets the bullies and bystanders to express the victims' feelings but does not allocate blame on the group but responsibility	Bullying (+)	9

Study (authors, year; country)	Program	Approach	Duration	Sample	Measures	Description	Outcomes	Rating
Teglasi, H., & Rothman, L. (2001); USA	STORIES (Structure/Themes/Open Communication/Reflection/Individuality/Experiential learning/Social Problem Solving	Social-information processing training in small groups with narratives as discussion stems; problem-solving strategies	15 weeks	Two 4th and 5th grade classes in two elementary schools; total 59 students (31 males, 28 females)	Normative beliefs about aggression; externalizing behavior	Children identified as aggressive and a few others participated in the STORIES program (small group discussions about stories regarding bullying, victimization, and being bystanders) designed to improve social problem solving for aggressors, victims, and bystanders	Externalizing behavior (+); NOBAG (+)	9
McLaughlin, L., Laux, J.M., & Pescara-Kovach, L. (2006); USA	Multimedia Intervention	Increasing media	8 weeks	Three groups of 3rd graders from 3 schools in the same district; 36 in control group, 34 in intervention 1, and 40 in intervention 2	Overt aggression; relational aggression; self-perceived; bullying and victimization	All three classes were given counselor/teacher intervention based on Olweus (2003); after being trained counselor/teacher met with class 1 hour a week for 8 weeks; role playing a definition of bullying emphasized; the second and third group were also shown three age-appropriate videos on reducing bullying over 4 weeks; the third group was given a commercially produced CD-ROM during week 3.	(+)Number of children in normal category increased; (+) number of students in clinically elevated category decreased; (=) moderately severe and frequent victim categories remained similar	9

(continued)

Table A.1
(Continued)

Researchers/ Date/Country of Origin	Program Title	Treatment Type	Length of Treatment	Participants	Constructs Assessed	Description	Results (+/–/=)	Total Scientific Merit
Beran, T. N., Tutty, L., & Steinrath, G. (2004); Canada	Dare to Care Program	Systemic; multimodal	3 months	Four schools; 197 students grades 4–6	School climate; frequency of bullying; frequency of witnessing bullying; responses to witnessing bullying; strategies during bully episodes; provictim scale	197 4th–6th graders were given the Dare to Care: Bully Proofing your School program; there were 3-month, 1-year, and 2-year program schools as well as one control school	(+) Frequency of witnessing bullying decreased; (=) reports of being bullied did not decrease; (=) no improvement in school climate	9
Heydenberk, R. A., Heydenberk, W. R., & Tzenova, V. (2006); USA	Peace Center	Self-efficacy (social skills training); self-regulation; conflict resolution	Seven 1-hour treatments	437 at 1 yr pilot and 236 at 2 years	School safety; bullying frequency; generalization of learned skills; quality of peer relationships	Peace Center trainers give an intervention targeting vocabulary and social skills to two schools; a pilot study at 1 year is implemented as well as a 2-year study	(+) Reduced physical bullying; (+) prosocial problem solving; (+) sense of safety; (+) teachers and students reported increased use of conflict resolution and decreased fighting	9

| Atria, M. & Spiel, C. (2007); Austria | Viennese Social Competence Training | Social information-processing theory | Six lessons of 1.5 hours each; 1 year for intervention | Four classes in one school; disadvantaged adolescents age 15–19 | Measures of group processes or democracy; Bully/Victim Questionnaire | Program trains nonteachers to administer lessons that focus on the group dynamics, social information processing, and execution of a group's plan | (+) Short-term and medium-term increase in perceived democracy of class treatment; (=) no difference in short-term aggression for treatment; (+) medium term decrease in aggression for treatment | 9 |
| Teglasi, H., Rahill, S., & Rothman, L. (2007); USA | STORIES Program and Skillstreaming | Peer group processes; experiential learning; targeting risk factors | 45 minutes once a week for 25 weeks | 35 in treatment group, 28 in skillstreaming; Grades 2–6 | Behavioral Symptoms Index; Behavioral Assessment System for Children; social competence; antisocial behavior | Both programs contained aspects of modeling, role playing, and skill identification, but the STORIES also includes stories with pictures. The stories are used to examine inner and outer worlds of characters, which is then generalized to the group members' concerns. | (+) More favorable BSI index scores for STORIES group; (=) no difference between groups on BASC and Social Competence; (=) no difference between groups on "bully" behaviors; (+) change in cognitive level was favored in the STORIES | 9 |

(continued)

Table A.1
(Continued)

Researchers/ Date/Country of Origin	Program Title	Treatment Type	Length of Treatment	Participants	Constructs Assessed	Description	Results (+/−/=)	Total Scientific Merit
Alsaker, F.D., & Valkanover, S. (2001); Switzerland	The Bernese Study on Victimization in Kindergarten	Universal teacher training	4 months	319 kindergarten students	Interviews with children and teacher nominations; attitudes toward bullying	Enhance teachers' capabilities of handling bully–victim problems; intensive focused supervision	Bullying (+)	8
Tremblay, R. E., McCord, J., Boileau, H., Charlebois, P., Gagnon, C., LeBlanc, M., et al. (1991); Canada	The Montreal Longitudinal Study of Disruptive Boys; http://www.hamfish.org/progams/27.html	Contingent	2 years	249 disruptive boys in kindergarten	Not specified	The experimental condition received parent training and social skills training.	Bullying (+)	8

| DeRosier, M. E. (2004); USA | Social Skills Group Intervention (S.S.GRIN) program | Social learning and cognitive-behavioral techniques in small group settings with targeted students | 11 weeks – ongoing evaluation | 381 students in 11 schools; aged 7.8–11 years | Measure based on change in sociometric status scores (Coie, Dodge, & Coppotelli, 1982) and change in self-reported researcher designed Social Interactions Survey; Self-efficacy (Ollendick & Schmidt, 1987); Social Anxiety Scale for Children-Revised (La Greca & Stone, 1993); Social Self-Worth Subscale (Harter, 1985) | Used a researcher-designed social skills intervention to target children experiencing peer dislike, social anxiety, and bullying. Build basic behavioral and cognitive skills; reinforce prosocial attitudes and behavior; build adaptive coping strategies for social problems of teasing and peer pressure | Victimization (+) | 8 |

(continued)

**Table A.1
(Continued)**

Researchers/ Date/Country of Origin	Program Title	Treatment Type	Length of Treatment	Participants	Constructs Assessed	Description	Results (+/-/=)	Total Scientific Merit
Hunt, C. (2007); USA	Australian School Anti-bullying Intervention	Systemic; multimodal; minimalist	Not specified	6 schools; 155 intervention; 289 controls	Peer relations (nature/extent of bullying problems); attitude to victim; attitude to bullying; prevalence of bullying at school; perceived school safety, likelihood of telling someone about being bullied, perceived ability to stop others from bullying, attempts to stop others from bullying, perceived ability to join others bullying, actually bullying as part of a group, bullying alone	Information about bullying reported by students in the initial survey was given in parent and teacher meetings; strategies for intervention at individual level and school level discussed; school staff gave discussion of bullying activities to students from an anti-bullying workbook (Murphy & Lewers, 2000); intervention was designed to minimize school/staff resources for the program	(=) No change in intervention group; (=) no change in attitudes toward bullying or victims across time relative to controls; (=) stable pro-bullying attitudes across time for both groups; (=) no difference in degree of change in bullying incidents over time; (+) decrease in number of students having bullied others in one school (male students in a co-educational school); (=) no decreases in bullying others for female students	8

Study	Program	Approach	Duration	Sample	Outcome measure	Intervention	Effects	
Melton, G.B., Limber S.P., Cunningham, P. Osgood, D.W., Chambers, J., Flerx, V., Henggeler, S., & Nation, M. (1998); USA	Anti-bullying Program in rural communities; http://www.njbullying.org/documents/misdirections.pdf	Systemic/school classroom and individual-level intervention based on Olweus' model	2 years	39 schools; 6250 students in grades 4–6 (aged 9–11 years)	Presumably bullying and victimization rates	Including core intervention measures at all three levels of school, classroom, and individual. Addition of supportive materials for school staff involvement of members of the local community in the anti-bullying initiative	Bullying (+)	7
Peterson, L., & Rigby, K. (1999); Australia	The New South Wales study; http://www.education.unisa.edu.au/bullying/pubs.html	Student helpers/empowering of students	Ongoing	Grades 7, 9, 10, and 11	Bullying	Emphasis upon peer involvement in anti-bullying work and the use of the Method of Shared Concern by staff	Bullying: youngest students (+), older students (−)	7
Menesini, E., Codecasa, E., Benelli, B., & Cowie, H. (2003); Italy	Befriending Approach (Peer Support model)	Befriending intervention/based on theory of social complexity levels (Hinde, 1992)	1 school year (October 1998 to May 1999)	Middle school students in central Italy; 115 control, 178 experimental; grades 6–8	Victimization; bullying; attitudes toward victimization	1st phase: class interventions; 2nd phase: selection of peer supporters; 3rd phase: training; 4th phase: working in the class; 5th phase: transmitting the training and passing the roles	Victimization (+); bullying (+)	7
Baldry, A.C., & Farrington, D. P. (2004); Italy	"Bulli & Pupe" (Bullies and Dolls) video program	Teaches participants about negative effects of bullying, helping them to determine alternatives to aggression by enhancing empathy and perspective taking	3 weeks	236 students aged 10–16 years in 3 schools	Italian version of Olweus' measure of prevalence and nature of bullying and victimization in schools	Viewing of three anti-bullying videos aimed at enhancing awareness of violence and its consequences. Directed toward individual and peer group; aims to enhance awareness about violence and its negative effects.	Bullying (+older; −younger); Victimization (+older; −younger)	7

(continued)

Table A.1
(Continued)

Researchers/ Date/Country of Origin	Program Title	Treatment Type	Length of Treatment	Participants	Constructs Assessed	Description	Results (+/-/=)	Total Scientific Merit
Newman–Carlson, D., & Horne, A., 2004; USA	Bully Busters: A Teaching Manual for Helping Bullies, Victims, and Bystanders	Systemic; teacher focused	13 weeks	15 teachers with 6th, 7th, and 8th grade classes (15 "controls"– attrition)	Teacher skills; teacher efficacy; teacher knowledge of bullying intervention skills; disciplinary offences of students	Teachers are given overall bullying education training, then split into groups of 7–8 for supYeYyesport and weekly meetings	(+) increase of bullying knowledge in treatment teachers when compared to controls; (+) use of bullying interventions in treatment teachers when compared to controls; (=) no difference between control and treatment teachers' self-efficacy; (+) decrease in student disciplinary offenses in treatment group	7

Freeman, H. S. & Mims, G. A. (2007); USA	Get Real about Violence	Targeting bystanders	Four lessons: Two 45-minute classes	198 treatment and 160 control; program was K-12, but the evaluation was an even distribution of 4 high school grades (fewer seniors in control group)	School safety survey: beliefs and experiences around aggression; school experience; frequency of witnessing different types of bullying; peer and school (adult) norms; behavioral intent of bystander and victim	GRAV targets bystanders by creating awareness about the contribution made by nonaction. It also focuses on changing norms regarding violence. GRAV was given as 3–6 lessons.	(+) Treatment group showed a change in perception of the bystander roles and subsequent actions; (+) treatment group were more confident in adult responses to violence; (+) treatment group was more confident in their own ability to respond in prosocial means to violence; (=) treatment group maintained hostility toward the whistleblower (peer norms)

(continued)

Table A.1
(Continued)

Researchers/ Date/Country of Origin	Program Title	Treatment Type	Length of Treatment	Participants	Constructs Assessed	Description	Results (+/-/=)	Total Scientific Merit
Galloway, D., & Roland, E. (2004); Norway	Not specified	Teachers increase quality of teaching and attention to students	4 years	1st graders from 9 schools	Questionnaire assesses students' social behavior, attitudes, behavior, and bullying	Teachers attend sessions focusing on the influences of quality care for students. Education on prevention of bullying and group discussions about program concepts	Bullying (−)	6
Beale, A. V., & Scott, P. C. (2001); USA	Bullybusters; http://www.insideouted.com.au	Psycho-educational	Not specified	Elementary school students, staff, parents	Not specified	The students were shown "Bullybuster" performed by their peers with special focus on the victims' feelings and suggestions on how to combat the problem.	Bullying (+)	6
Young, S. (1998), UK	Kingston upon Hull Special Educational Needs Support Service (SENSS) Anti-bullying project; http://www.hullcc.gov.uk/education/sen_antibully.php	Support group/ based on No Blame Approach by Maines and Robinson (1991, 1992)	Not specified	50 referrals from 51 primary schools and 4 secondary schools of victimization	Bullying	Seven steps of intervention based on the No Blame Approach. Interviews, support groups, empathy building, education about bullying, review of group progress	Bullying (+)	6

Study	Program	Description	Duration	Sample	Measures	Program details	Outcomes	Quality
Fox, C. L., & Boulton, M. J. (2003); UK	Social Skills Training Programme	Social skills building programme for children who are victimized by bullying	8 weeks	28 children in 4 schools; aged 9–11 years	Researcher designed Peer Nomination Inventory; Revised Children's Manifest Anxiety Inventory; Children's Depression Inventory; Harter's Self Perception Profile for Children	Program intended to support victims of bullying by improving social skills (and thus reduce a child's individual risk for victimization); via teaching listening, having conversations, asking to join in, body language, assertiveness training as well as dealing with the bully.	Victimization (+)	6
Kim (2006); Korea	Korean Reality Therapy and Olweus	Reality therapy for victims	5 weeks	16 children from grade 5 to grade six	Self-responsibility; peer victimization	Sessions aimed at victims of bullying that focused on improving victims' responsibility and reducing victimization. Sessions included the feeling of belonging, we are able to choose even better situations, pictures of reality, five basic needs, total behavior, learning self-control strategies, making cooperating masterpiece, messages to get what I want, inviting peers to play, new start and saying good-bye.	(+) Self-responsibility; (+) decreased victimization for treatment group	6

(continued)

Table A.1
(Continued)

Researchers/ Date/Country of Origin	Program Title	Treatment Type	Length of Treatment	Participants	Constructs Assessed	Description	Results (+/−/=)	Total Scientific Merit
Baldry, A. C., & Farrington, D. P. (2004); Italy	Bulli & Pupe	Systemic; multimodal; peer intervention; domestic violence and cycle of violence focus	3 days	239 students 11–15 years old	Prevelance and frequency of bulling and victimization; types of bullying/ victimization	131 students were given Bulli & Pupe while 106 served as controls both groups from the same school; the program focuses on bullying among peers, children witnessing domestic violence, and cycle of violence. These messages were delivered in the form of videos and booklets administered by professionals.	(+) Older (14–16) youth reported reductions in bullying/ victimization; (=) younger students in the control group reported reductions as well; (−) on single-item bullying question younger students reported increased bullying after interventions	6

Reference	Program	Type	Duration	Sample	Outcomes measured	Description	Results	
Slee, P. T., & Mohyla, J. (2007); Australia	PEACE Pack	Universal; systemic	1 year	954 children from 4 schools	Experiences in bullying; knowledge of school initiatives; confidence regarding addressing bullying individual	The PEACE program identifies school staff to run programs, runs preliminary school assessments, develops policies for schools, implements lesson plans, give information to parents, gives feedback to schools, and has ongoing monitoring of progress.	(+) 1/5 of students reported being bullied less as a result of the intervention; (+) gains in knowledge of how to stop being bullied; (−) percentage of participants reported being bullied more after intervention	6
McMahon, S. D., Washburn, J., Felix, E. D., Yakin, J., & Childrey, G. (2000); USA	The Second Step Program; http://www.cfchildren.org/ssf/ssf/ssindex	Violence prevention curriculum; universal	20 sessions in 10–20 weeks; 20–50 minutes per session	Children in 5 classes in preschool and kindergartens aged 3–7 (designed for grades K–9)	Skills; knowledge behavior	Use of curriculum to develop knowledge and skills related to bullying behavior. Violence prevention curriculum teaching social skills to reduce impulsive and aggressive behavior in children and increase level of social competence; skills promotion, building school-family-community partnership	Aggressive behaviour (+); knowledge (+)	5
Boulton, M. & Flemington, I. (1996); UK	"Sticks and Stones" video intervention; http://www.ohiou.edu/perspectives/9702/bully2.htm	Video	Pretest, 1 week; video: 1 week posttest	82 girls and 88 boys (170 in total) Semi-rural secondary school in the UK	Level of bullying, students' definitions of bullying, attitudes toward bullying	Filled out questionnaire before and after video. Video shown halfway through 2 weeks of intervention; short discussion after the video	Bullying (=)	5

(continued)

Table A.1
(Continued)

Researchers/ Date/Country of Origin	Program Title	Treatment Type	Length of Treatment	Participants	Constructs Assessed	Description	Results (+/–/=)	Total Scientific Merit
McGurk, B. J., & McDougall, C. (1991); Scotland	The Prevention of Bullying among Incarcerated Delinquents	The officers kept close watch over all the inmates and punished those who were found to be bullied	7 months	Young offenders in dormitories for bullies	Not specified	Officer visited dorm once per day. Color TVs in each room, body checks each morning, inmates used checklist to complain about bullying and severe punishments	Bullying (+)	5
Cowie, Naylor et al., 2002; Naylor & Cowie, 1999; UK	Peer Support System	Universal, peer support system	2 years	413 9- and 11-year-old students who had been in the original program when 7- and 9-year-olds (204 former victims; 209 former non-victims); 34 teachers	Structured and semi-structured interviews with students and teachers about the peer support system and its impact on reduction of bullying	The peer support system had three parts: befriending scheme, conflict resolution scheme, and counseling-based scheme.	Helpful system (+); school climate (+)	4
Brier, J., & Ahmad, Y. (1991); UK	Developing a school court as a means of addressing bullying in schools	Not specified	Not specified	Not specified	Not specified	Two teachers and 5 peer-elected children make up the "bench." The elected children make up the rules for the consequences of bullying.	Bullying (+); victimization (–)	4

Researchers/Date	Program Title	Treatment Type	Length of Treatment	Participants	Constructs Assessed	Description	Results	Total Scientific Merit
Salmivalli, C. (2001); Finland	Happy Face Week	Peer-ed intervention	1 week	Program was implemented in whole school but only 196 7th and 8th graders participated and 8 peer counselors	Bullying: victimization	Campaign with bullying information, short drama	Bullying (+)	4
Cowie, H., & Olafsson, R. (2000); UK	Peer support in helping victims of bullying in a school with high levels of aggression; http://www.mhf.org.uk/peer/psn/resource.html	Peer Support Service	7.5 months; training 2.5 days for students and four workshops in the fall term; Olweus questionnaire administered in Nov. and Jun	High school boys only, UK problem school; 9 peer supporter; 420 boys	Used Olweus Questionnaire Peer support service	Trained teachers met regularly with peer supporters for supervision and help. Service advertised via posters in school and school assembly. Room was available during the lunch hour.	Bullying (=)	4
Murphy, Hutchinson, & Bailey (1983); US	Structured playground activities; http://www.byu.edu/peaceableschools/PDF %20files/ TECBD2002Playground.pdf	Behavioral program of structured play time	1 month	5–8-year-olds	Not specified	Organized games and adult supervision of entire playground; praise paired with time-outs	Aggression, property abuse, rules violations (+)	0

Researchers/Date: Researchers and/or the authors of the program; *Program Title*: Title or brief descriptor of the program; *Treatment Type*: Primary method and/or theory of implementing the program; *Length of Treatment*: How long the program is to be implemented, or how long it was implemented in the empirical study; *Participants*: Who participated in the empirical study or who the program is intended for; *Constructs Assessed*: What type and content of information were collected in the empirical study; *Description*: Brief description of the program; *Results (+/−=)*: How did the program fair? A (+) represents a positive outcome on the indicated behavior/issue, A (−) represents a negative outcome on the indicated behavior/issue, A (=) represents no change on the indicated behavior/issue; *Total Scientific Merit*: Total elements present; see Appendix A.2 for rating criteria.

Table A.2
Rating of Scientific Merit (Chapter 9)

Researchers/ Date	Multiple Sites (Y/N)	Control Group (Y/N)	Follow-up at 24 months (or more) (Y/N)	Pre-Post Evaluation (Y/N)	Multiple Infor- mants (Y/N)	Replication Possible (Y/N)	Random Assign- ment (Y/N)	Large Sample	Attrition Rate	Validity and Reliability	Bullying Outcomes	Victi- mization Outcomes	School Climate	Systemic Outcome	Tailored	Experi- menter Bias
Bierman, K.A., Coie, J.D., Dodge, K. A., Foster, E.M., Greenberg, M.T., Lochman, J.E. McMahon, R.J., Pinderhughes, E.E.; Conduct Problems Prevention Research Group, (2002)	Y	Y	Y	Y	Y	Y	Y	Y	N/A	Present	N/A	N/A	N/A	I, F, P, CL, Co, T, S	Y	N
Rahey, L., & Craig W.M. (2002)	Y	Y	Y	Y	Y	N	N	Y	N/A	Present	–Girls; +boys	+Older kids; – young kids	Y	I,P,S,T,F	Y	N
Olweus, D. (2005)	Y	Y	Y	Y	N	Y	N	Y	N/A	Present	+	+	Y	I, CL, S	Y	Y
Ortega, R, Del Rey, R., & Mora-Merchan, R.A., 2004; Ortega, R., & Lera, M. J. (2000)	Y	Y	Y	Y	N	N	Y	Y	N/A	Absent	+	+	N	I,P,T,S,CO	Y	Y
Twemlow, S. W., Fonagy, P., Sacco, F. C., Gies, M. L., Evans, R., & Ewbank, R. (2001)	Y	Y	Y	Y	Y	N	N	Y	N/A	Absent	+	+	+	I,S	Y	N

Study															
Eslea, M., & Smith, P. K. (1998);	N	Y	Y	Y	Y	N	Y	N/A	Present	+	+	+	I	Y	N
Committee for Children (2001) Hirschstein, M. K., Snell, J. L., Edstrom, L. V. S., MacKenzie, E. P., & Broderick, C. J. (2005);	Y	NR	Y	Y	Y	Y	Y	Y	Present	+/=	−	N	I T	N	N
DeRosier, M. (2007)	N	N	Y	Y	N	Y	Y	61 qualified, but did not get parent consent	Absent	+	+	+	I P	Y	N
Jennifer, D., & Shaughnessy, J. (2005);	Y	Y	Y	Y	N	Y	Y	NR	NR	=	NR	=	I C L T S	Y	N
Salmivalli, C., & Kaukiainen, A. (2000)	N	NR	Y	Y	N	Y	Y	NR	Present	+	+	N	I T	Y	N
Soutter, A., & McKenzie, A. (2000)	N	Y	Y	N	N	Y	Y	N/A	Absent	=	+Grade7; −grade 9	Y	I,S,F,	Y	N
Pepler, Craig, Ziegler, & Charach (1994)	N	N	Y	N	N	Y	Y65	N/A	Absent	−	=	Y	I,F,P,T	Y	N
McLaughin, Laux, and Pescara-Kovach (2006)	Y	N	Y	Y	N	Y	Y	NC	Present	+	+	N/A	I	N	N

(continued)

**Table A.2
(Continued)**

Researchers/ Date	Multiple Sites (Y/N)	Control Group (Y/N)	Follow-up at 24 months (or more) (Y/N)	Pre-Post Evaluation (Y/N)	Multiple Informants (Y/N)	Replication Possible (Y/N)	Random Assignment (Y/N)	Large Sample (Y/N)	Attrition Rate	Validity and Reliability	Bullying Outcomes	Victimization Outcomes	School Climate	Systemic Outcome	Tailored	Experimenter Bias
Beran, T. N., Tutty, L., & Steinrath, G. (2004);	Y	Y	N	Y	N	Y	N	Y	NR	Present	+/=	+	=	I S	N	N
Heydenberk, R. A., Heydenberk, W. R., & Tzenova, V. (2006);	Y	Y	N	Y	Y	Y	N	Y	NR	NC	+	N/A	+	I T	N	N
Atria, M., & Spiel, C. (2007);	N	Y	N	Y	Y	Y	Y	Y	NR	Present	=	=	N/A	I T	Y	N
Teglasi, H., Rahill, S., & Rothman, L. (2007)	Y	Y	N	Y	Y	Y	N	N	NR	Present	=	N/A	N/A	I T CL	Y	N
O'Moore, A. M., & Minton, S. J. (2005)	Y	N	NR	Y	Y	Y	N	Y	N/A	Absent	+	+		I T	Y	N
Teglasi, H. & Rothman, L. (2001)	Y	Y	N	Y	Y	Y	N	N	9%	Present	+	N/A	N/A	I,CL	Y	NC
Meyer, N., & Lesch, E. (2000)	Y	Y	N	Y	Y	N	Y	Y	NR	Absent	=	=	Y	S	Y	N
Stevens, V., Bourdeaudhuij, I. D., & Oost, P. V. (2000)	Y	Y	N	Y	N	Y	Y	Y	6.5%–10.5%	Present	Mixed	=	N	I	Y	N

Study														
Cross, D., Hall, M., Hamilton, G., Pintabona, Y., & Erceg, E. (2004)	Y	Y	Y	N	N	Y	Y	18%	Present	–	=	N	I	Y	N
Maines, B. & Robinson, G. (1998)	N	NR	Y	Y	Y	N	N/A	NR	Absent	+	N/A	Y	I,P,T	Y	N
Hunt, C. (2007)	Y	N	Y	N	Y	NC	Y	Two schools	Present	+/=	=	N/A	I	Y	NC
Alsaker, F.D., & Valkankover, S. (2001)	Y	N	Y	Y	N	Y	Y	NR	Absent	–	+, –verbal	N	I, T	N	N
Naylor, P. & Cowie (1999); Cowie, H., Naylor, P., Talamelli, L, Chauhan, P., & Smith, P.K. (2002)	Y	NR	Y	Y	N	N	Y	16.40%	Present	=	=	N	I,P,T	Y	Y
DeRosier M.E. (2004)	Y	N	Y	Y	Y	Y	N	NR	Absent	N/A	+	N/A	I	N	N
Tremblay, R.E., McCord, J., Boileau, H., Charlebois, P., Gagnon, C., LeBlanc, M. et al. (1991)	N	N	Y	N	N	Y	Y	NR	Absent	+ age 9	N/A	N	I,T	Y	N
Newman-Carlson, D., & Horne, A. (2004);	Y	N	Y	Y	Y	N	N	2	Present	+			T S	N	N

(continued)

Table A.2 (Continued)

Researchers/ Date	Multiple Sites (Y/N)	Control Group (Y/N)	Follow-up at 24 months (or more) (Y/N)	Pre-Post Evaluation (Y/N)	Multiple Infor- mants (Y/N)	Replication Possible (Y/N)	Random Assign- ment (Y/N)	Large Sample	Attrition Rate	Validity and Reliability	Bullying Outcomes	Victi- mization Outcomes	School Climate	Systemic Outcome	Tailored	Experi- menter Bias
Freeman, H. S. & Mims, G. A. (2007);	Y	Y	NR	N	N	Y	Y* seniors excluded from control on school request	Y	NR	Present	N/A	N/A	=	I P	N	N
Peterson, L., & Rigby K. (1999)	N	N	NR	Y	N	N	N	Y	N/A	Present	+	+	N	I	Y	N
Menesini, E. Codecasa, E. Benelli, B., & Cowie, H. (2003)	N	Y	N	Y	Y	Y	N	Y	N/A	Absent	+	=	N	I	N/A	Y
Melton, G.B., Limber S.P., Cunningham, P. Osgood, D.W., Chambers, J., Flerx, V., Henggeler, S., & Nation, M. (1998)	Y	Y	N	Y	Y	N	N	Y	N/A	Absent	+	=	N	I	N/A	N
Baldry, A. C., & Farrington D.P. (2004)	Y	Y	N	Y	N	Y	Y	Y	0%	N/A	−younger; + older	−younger; + older	N/A	I	N	Y

Author															
Kim. J. (2006)	N	Y	I	N/A	+	N/A	Absent	NR	N	Y	Y	N	Y	N	N
Baldry, A. C., & Farrington, D. P. (2004)	NC	N	I	NA	+/=	+/-	NC	2	Y	Y	Y	N	Y	N	N
Slee, P. T., & Mohyla, J. (2007)	N	Y	I	N/A	+/-		NC	NR	Y	N	Y	N	Y	Y	Y
Galloway, D., & Roland, E. (2004)	Y	N/A	I,S	Y	N/A	+	Absent	N/A	N	N	N	N	N	Y	Y
Beale, A.V., & Scott, P.C. (2001)	Y	Y	I	+	–grade 7, +grade 9	+grade 7, – grade 9	Present	N/A	Y	N	N	N	Y	Y	N
Young, S. (1998)	N	Y	I	N	=	=	Absent	N/A	Y	N	n	n	Y	N	Y
Fox, C.L., & Boulton, M.J. (2003)	Y	N	I	N/A	+	N/A	Present	N/A	N	N	N	Y	Y	N	N
McMahon, S.D., Washburn, J., Felix, E.D., Yakin, J., & Childrey G.(2000)	N	Y	I	N	N/A	N/A	Absent	N/A	N/A	N	N	N	Y	Y	Y
Boulton, M., & Flemington, I (1996)	N	N/A	I	N	+	+	Absent	N/A	N	N	N	N	Y	Y	N
McGurk, B.J., & McDougall, C. (1991)	Y	Y	I,P	N	+ girls	+Girls; – boys	Absent	N/A	Y	N	N	N	Y	N	N
Brier, J., & Ahmad, Y. (1991)	N	Y	I	N	N/A	+	Absent	N/A	N/A	N	N	N	Y	N	N
Salmivalli, C. (2001)	Y	N/A	T, CL	N	N/A	+	Absent	N/A	N	N	N	N	Y	NR	N

(continued)

Table A.2
(Continued)

Researchers/ Date	Multiple Sites (Y/N)	Control Group (Y/N)	Follow-up at 24 months (or more) (Y/N)	Pre-Post Evaluation (Y/N)	Multiple Infor- mants (Y/N)	Replication Possible (Y/N)	Random Assign -ment (Y/N)	Large Sample	Attrition Rate	Validity and Reliability	Bullying Outcomes	Victi -mization Outcomes	School Climate	Systemic Outcome	Tailored	Experi -menter Bias
Cowie, H. & Olafsson, R. (2000)	Y	N	NR	Y	N	N	N	Y	N/A	Absent	=	=	N	N/A	N	N
Murphy, H.A., Hutchinson, J.M., & Bailey, J.S. (1983)	N/A	N/A	NR	N/A	N/A	N/A	N/A	N/A	N/A	N/A	N/A	N/A	N/A	N/A	N/A	N/A

Multiple Sites (Y/N): Was the program implemented at more than one school or location? Received 1 point for the presence of multiple sites; *Control Group* (Y/N): In experimental evaluation design, a group of participants that is essentially similar to the intervention (i.e., experimental) group but is not exposed to the intervention. Participants are designated to be part of either a control or an intervention group through random assignment. Received 1 point for presence of a control group; *Follow-Up at 24 months or more* (Y/N): Length of time following the implementation of the program when an assessment of the program's effectiveness was undertaken. Received 1 point if at least 24 months; *Pre-Post Evaluation* (Y/N): Pretest: The collection of measurements before an intervention to assess its effects. Posttest: The test administered at the end of the data gathering sequence of an evaluation (usually after the program or activity being evaluated has been completed). Received 1 point if both a pretest and posttest was conducted; *Multiple Informants* (Y/N):When information on one aspect is obtained from multiple sources, such as having self-report, peers, teachers, and parents report about a child's bullying behavior. The presence of multiple informants received 1 point; *Replication Possible* (Y/N): Is it possible to replicate the study/program based on the information provided by the study/program package? The presence of possible replication received 1 point; *Random Assignment* (Y/N): The process through which members of a pool of eligible study participants are assigned to either an intervention group or a control group on a random basis such as through the use of a table of random numbers; *Large Sample*: Samples that include 100 or more participants. Large sample sizes received 1 point. *Attrition Rate:* An unplanned reduction in size of a study sample due to participants' dropping out of the evaluation (e.g., they moved away from the study location). No points were allocated for attrition rates; this was included for descriptive purposes only. *Validity & Reliability–Validity:* The extent to which a measure of a particular construct/concept actually measures what it purports to measure. For example, is "slapping a peer" a valid measure of aggression? *Reliability:* The consistency of a measurement, measurement instrument, form, or observation over time. The consistency of results (similar results over time) with similar populations, or under similar conditions, confirms the reliability of a measure. When researchers reported measures of the validity and reliability of their assessment tools, 1 point was given. *Bullying Outcomes:* Did the researchers report outcomes for bullying behavior and if so, were they positive (+), were they negative (–), or unchanged (=)? Positive outcomes received 1 point; *Victimization Outcomes:* Did the researchers report outcomes for victimization and if so, were they positive (+), negative (–), or unchanged (=)? Positive outcomes received 1 point. *School Climate:* Were outcomes reported for multiple systemic levels, including individual (I), peer (P), classroom (CL), family (F), teacher (T), school (S), and community (CO). The presence of one level received no points. Two levels received 1 point, three levels received 2 points, and so on for a total of 7 possible points; *Tailored:* Was the program tailored to the needs of the population based on the pretest results? An answer of 'yes' received 1 point; *Experimenter bias:* Did the author of the program conduct the program evaluation? A "no," indicating a lack of experimenter bias, received 1 point. N/A - not applicablei. NR - insufficient information provided to make judgment.

Table A.3
Program Content (Chapter 9)

Researchers/Date	Program Name	Approach	Target Population	Target							
				Individual	Peer/Classroom	Parent	Teachers	Community	Cognitive	Social	Emotional
Bierman, Coie, Dodge, Foster, Greenberg, Lochman, McMahon, Pinderhughes; Conduct Problems Prevention Group (2002);	FAST Track	Systemic/multimodal	Grades 1–10	Y	Y	Y	Y	Y	Y	Y	Y
Rahey & Craig (2002)	Bully Proofing Your School; http://www.oakland.k12.mi.us/resources/bullyproof.html	Systemic, interactional model	Grades 1–8	Y	Y		Y		Y	Y	Y
Olweus, et al. (2005)	Olweus Bullying Prevention Program	Whole-school approach; systemic; universal	Elementary school	Y	Y	Y	Y	Y	Y	Y	Y
Ortega, Del Rey, & Mora-Merchan (2004)	The Seville Study (SAVE model)	Ecological perspective systematic	Ages 8–18 years	Y	Y		Y		Y	Y	Y
Eslea, & Smith, (1998)	DFE Sheffield Anti-Bullying Project	Whole-school approach; systemic; schools have choice of all programs	All grades; all students	Y	Y	Y	Y	Y	Y	Y	Y
Twemlow, Fonagy, Sacco, Gies, Evans, & Ewbank (2001)	Social systems psychodynamic antiviolence intervention	Whole-school approach; universal	Elementary school students	Y	Y		Y				Y

(continued)

Table A.3
(Continued)

Researchers/Date	Program Name	Approach	Target Population	Individual	Peer/ Classroom	Parent	Teachers	Community	Cognitive	Social	Emotional
DeRosier, (2007)	Peer connections	Pretreatment assessment of school climate and peer interactions; peer-rejected and victimized targeted; social skills	Grade 4	Y					Y	Y	
Jennifer & Shaughnessy, (2005)e	UK-001 CONNECT	Systemic; multimodal; checkpoints online questionnaire	Primary, secondary, and special schools		Y		Y		Y	Y	
Soutter, & McKenzie, (2000)	Reviewed a number of initiatives at schools in Australia	Best practices whole-school approach	High schools	Y	Y	Y	Y	Y	Y	Y	Y
Pepler, Craig, Ziegler, & Charach, 1994	Toronto Anti-Bullying Intervention	Changing behavior; disadvantaged boys; social-interactional model; systemic	Disadvantaged boys	Y	Y						Y
Salmivalli, & Kaukiainen, (2000)	Salmivalli Group intervention	Providing information and motivation for bystanders to intervene	Grade 4, 5, and 6		Y		Y		Y	Y	Y
Hirschstein, Snell, Edstrom, MacKenzie, & Broderick. (2005)	Steps to Respect	Whole-school, systematic	Grades 3–6	Y	Y	Y	Y	Y	Y	Y	Y
McLaughin, Laux, & Pescara-Kovach, 2006	Multimedia Intervention	Increasing media	3rd graders	Y	Y		Y		Y	Y	

Citation	Program	Approach	Grade/Age						
Beran, Tutty, & Steinrath, (2004)	Dare to Care	Systemic	Grades 4–6	Y	Y	Y	Y	Y	Y
Atria, & Speil (2007)	Viennese Social Competence Training Program	Group dynamics; input from participants on action plans	15–19 years	Y	Y	Y		Y	
Teglasi., Rahill, & Rothman. (2007)	STORIES	Narrative stories	Grades 2–6	Y	Y (special education classrooms)		Y	Y	Y
O'Moore, & Minton. (2005)	The Donegal Primary Schools' Anti-Bullying Project	Bullying awareness campaign; educational and peer social support	Grades 1–6; ages 6–11 years	Y	Y	Y	Y	Y	Y
Meyer, & Lesch (2000)	Not specified	Social interactional model; behavioral approach	Grades 6 and 7; ages 12–16 years	Y	Y				Y
Stevens., Bourdeaudhuij, & Oost (2000)	The Flanders Study	Restructuring of social environment	Primary and secondary schools	Y	Y	Y	Y	Y	Y
Cross, Hall, Hamilton, Pintabona, & Erceg (2004)	Friendly Schools Project	Empowers teachers, students, and parents to deal with bullying; whole-school approach	Grade 4; ages 8–9 years	Y	Y	Y	Y	Y	Y

(continued)

Table A.3
(Continued)

Researchers/Date	Program Name	Approach	Target Population	Individual	Peer/ Classroom	Parent	Teachers	Community	Cognitive	Social	Emotional
Melton, Limber, Cunningham, Osgood, Chambers, Flerx, Henggeler, & Nation (1998)	Anti-bullying Program in rural communities	Whole-school approach based on Olweus' approach; systematic	4th–6th graders	Y	Y		Y	Y	Y	Y	Y
Teglasi & Rothman (2001)	STORIES (Structure/Themes/ Open Communication/ Reflection/Individuality/ EYperiential learning/Social Problem Solving	Targeted social problem-solving training	4th and 5th grade students	Y	Y					Y	Y
Heydenberk, Heydenberk, & Tzenova (2006)	Peace Center	Conflict resolution	3rd–5th graders		Y		Y		Y	Y	
Maines & Robinson (1998)	No Blame Approach	Whole-school approach; dangers of labeling	Middle, junior, high schools	Y	Y		Y		Y	Y	Y
Hunt (2007); USA	Australian School Antibullying Intervention	Systemic; minimalist	12–15 years		Y	Y	Y		Y	Y	
Alsaker & Valkankover (2001)	The Bernese Study on Victimization in Kindergarten	Train teachers to use anti-bullying techniques; quality teaching to reduce bullying	Kindergarten	Y	Y		Y				Y

Citation	Program	Approach	Age/Grade							
Naylor & Cowie (1999); Cowie, Naylor, et al. (2002)	Peer Support System	Peer support systems; social-contextualism	N/A		Y		Y		Y	
Tremblay, McCord, Boileau, Charlebois, Gagnon, et al. (1991)	The Montreal Longitudinal Study of Disruptive Boys	Parent training and social skills training for children; theoretical learning	Age 7	Y		Y		Y	Y	Y
DeRosier (2004)	Social Skills Group Intervention (S.S.GRIN) Program	Targets victimized individuals	Ages 7.8–11 years	Y				Y	Y	Y
Newman-Carlson, & Horne (2004)	Bully Busters: A Teacher's Manual for Helping Bullies, Victims, and Bystanders	Systemic; teacher	6th–8th graders				Y	Y	Y	
Freeman, & Mims (2007)	Get Real about Violence	Changing peer norms; bystander	K–12	Y	Y			Y	Y	
Peterson & Rigby (1999)	The New South Wales study	Empowering students to make the change	Grades 7, 9, 10, and 11	Y	Y	Y	Y	Y	Y	Y
Menesini, Codecasa, Benelli, & Cowie (2003)	Befriending Approach (Peer Support model)	Ecological approach; theory of social complexity	Middle schools	Y	Y		Y	Y		Y
Baldry & Farrington (2004)	"Bulli & Pupe" (Bullies and Dolls) video program	Universal, whole-school approach	10–16 years	Y	Y				Y	
Kim (2006)	Korean Reality Therapy and Olweus	Reality therapy	5th–6th graders	Y				Y		

(continued)

Table A.3
(Continued)

Researchers/Date	Program Name	Approach	Target Population	Individual	Peer/ Classroom	Parent	Teachers	Community	Cognitive	Social	Emotional
Baldry, & Farrington, (2004)	Bulli & Pupe	Systemic; family (domestic abuse)	11–15 years		Y				Y	Y	Y
Slee, & Mohyla, (2007);	PEACE Pack	Systemic; multimodal; assessment throughout	5.4–13.5 years		Y	Y	Y		Y	Y	
Galloway & Roland (2004)	Not specified	Increase quality of teaching; educational approach	Ages 6–11 years		Y		Y			Y	
Beale & Scott (2001)	Bullybusters	Psychoeducational using drama to empower students	Elementary schools	Y	Y		Y		Y	Y	Y
Young (1998)	Kingston upon Hull Special Educational Needs Support Service (SENSS) Anti-bullying project	Support groups; no blame, or shared responsibility is best	Primary and secondary schools	Y	Y		Y		Y	Y	Y
Fox & Boulton (2003)	Social Skills Training Programme	Targets victimized individuals	Ages 9–11 years	Y					Y	Y	Y
McMahon, Washburn, Felix, Yakin, & Childrey (2000)	The Second Step Program	Teaches skills to decrease aggression and increase prosocial behavior; social skills and behavior approach	Grades K–9		Y		Y			Y	Y

Citation	Program	Approach	Target Population	Participants					Individual Processes		
Boulton & Flemington (1996)	"Sticks and Stones" video intervention	Bullies' behavior definitions and attitudes; one trial learning	Secondary students	Y					Y	Y	Y
McGurk & McDougall (1991)	The Prevention of Bullying among Incarcerated Delinquents	Increase monitoring of young offenders to reduce bullying; numerous environmental strategies were used	Young offenders in dormitories for bullies	Y					Y		
Brier & Ahmad (1991)	Developing a school court as a means of addressing bullying in schools	Bully courts helped children understand need for rules and laws; peers used to determine appropriate punishments	N/A	Y	Y		Y		Y		
Salmivalli (2001)	Happy Face Week	Peers as mediators	Middle school	Y					Y	Y	
Cowie & Olafsson (2000)	Peer support in helping victims of bullying in a school with high levels of aggression	Role of peer support and peer influence	High school – boys only	Y	Y				Y		Y
Murphy, Hutchinson, & Bailey (1983)	Structured playground activities	Behavioral program of structured play time for approach to violence prevention; universal program	Grades K–2; ages 5–8 years	Y		Y			Y		Y

Approach: a set of prevention strategies that typify a program and can be employed in an intervention setting without adopting the program in total; *Target Population:* the group of persons whom program interventions are designed to reach; *Participants:* who is involved and included in the program (individual, peer/classroom, parent, teacher, community); *Individual Processes:* what processes are targeted for change (cognitive, social, emotional-behavior)

Table A.4
Implementation Rating (Chapter 9)

Program Name	Manual (Y/N)	Training (Y/N)	Deliverer	Program Maintenance (Y/N)	Assessment	Additional Comments
Bierman, Coie, Dodge, Foster, Greenberg, Lochman, McMahon, Pinderhughes; Conduct Problems Prevention Group (2002)	Y	Y	Teachers, professionals	Y	Y	
Rahey, & Craig (2002)	Y	Y	Graduate students	Y	Y	Integrates well with curriculum; short
Olweus (2005)	Y	Y	Teacher	N	Y	Entire school and community involvement, low cost
Ortega, Del Rey, & Mora-Merchan (2004	Y	Y	Teacher	Y	Y	Integrates well with curriculum
Eslea, & Smith (1998)	Y	Y	Teacher	N	N	Faced a range of problems, materials fit into curriculum
Twemlow, Fonagy, Sacco, Gies, Evans, & Ewbank (2001)	NR	Y	Teachers/school staff	Y	Y	Measured success with academic achievement
Slee, & Mohyla (2007)	Y	N	Teachers and school staff	Y	Y	
Jennifer, & Shaughnessy (2005)	NR	NC	Teachers	NR	Y	
Soutter, & McKenzie (2000)	N	Y	Teacher and student	N	Y	Students and staff were trained to lead anti-bully support groups and activities

Reference			Facilitator			Notes
Pepler, Craig, Ziegler, & Charach (1994)	NR	Y	Teacher	N	Y	Integrates well with curriculum
Salmivalli & Kaukiainen (2000)	N	Y	Teacher	NR	Y	
Hirschstein, Snell, Edstrom, MacKenzie, & Broderick (2005)	Y	Y	Teacher	Y	Y	Integrates with curriculum
McLaughlin, Laux, & Pescara-Kovach, 2006	Y	Y	Counselor/teacher	NR	NR	
Beran, Tutty, & Steinrath (2004)	NR	Y	Teacher	NR	NR	
Freeman & Mims(2007)	Y	Y	NC	NR	NR	
Teglasi, Rahill, & Rothman (2007)	Y	Y	School counselors and support staff	NR	NR	
DeRosier (2007); USA	Y	Y	School counselors	NR	Y	
O'Moore, & Minton (2005)	Y	Y	Teachers	N	Y	Not curricular based
Meyer, & Lesch, (2000)	NR	Y	Psychology students	Y	Y	Program is separate from curriculum. Takes up a lot of school time
Stevens, Bourdeaudhuji, & Oost (2000)	N	Y	Teacher	N	N	Integrates well with curriculum, short
Cross, Hall, Hamilton, Pintabona, & Erceg (2004)	NR	Y	Teachers	N	N	Integrates well, involves parents
Maines, & Robinson (1998)	NR	Y	Teachers	N	N	Focus on students involved in bullying, education for all students

(continued)

Table A.4
(Continued)

Program Name	Manual (Y/N)	Training (Y/N)	Deliverer	Program Maintenance (Y/N)	Assessment	Additional Comments
Teglasi, & Rothman (2001)	N	Y	NR	N	N	
Hunt, (2007)	Y	Y	School psychologist and school staff	NR	NR	
Alsaker & Valkanover (2001)	NR	Y	Teacher	Y	NR	Intensive training of kindergarten teachers over a 4-month period
Tremblay, McCord, Boileau, Charlebois, Gagnon, LeBlanc et al. (1991)	NR	Y	Parent	NR	N	Provides parents with training to monitor child's behavior
DeRosier (2004)	Y	Y	School counselor and undergrad psychology student	Y	Y	
Newman-Carlson & Horne (2004)	Y	Y	Teacher	NR	Y	
Atria & Speil (2007)	NR	Y	Trainer from outside school	NR	NR	
Melton, Limber, Cunningham, Osgood, Chambers, Flerx, Henggeler, & Nation (1998)	Y	N	Teacher	N	N	Anti-bullying policy integrated into aspects of school

Citation						
Peterson & Rigby (1999)	N	Y	Student	N	Y	Activities are extra-curricular, minimal training needed
Menesini, Codecasa, Benelli, & Cowie (2003);	N	Y	Teacher and student	N	N	Long; requires student training and in class activities
Baldry & Farrington (2004)	Y	Y	Professionals; researcher	N	Y	
Kim (2006)	NR	NR	Counseling specialist	NR	NR	
Baldry & Farrington (2004)	Y	Y	Professional	NR	NR	
Heydenberk, Heydenberk, & Tzenova (2006)	Y	Y	Peace Center trainers	NR	NR	
Galloway & Roland (2004);	NR	Y	Teacher	Y	Y	Increases teachers' competencies and confidence
Beale, & Scott (2001)	N	N	Teachers, students	N	N	Integrates well with curriculum; anti-bully performance by students
Young (1998)	N	Y	Teacher	Y	N	Integrates well with curriculum. Targets bullying through support groups
Fox & Boulton(2003)	Y	Y	NR	Y	Y	
McMahon, Washburn, Felix, Yakin, & Childrey (2000)	NR	Y	Project staff and teachers	Y	Y	Short weekly lessons that teach social skills and anger management
Boulton & Flemington (1996)	N	N	Video and teacher	N	Y	Short, quick implementation
McGurk & McDougal (1991)	N	Y	Corrections officers	NR	Y	Corrections officers increased surveillance of inmates

(continued)

Table A.4
(Continued)

Program Name	Manual (Y/N)	Training (Y/N)	Deliverer	Program Maintenance (Y/N)	Assessment	Additional Comments
Naylor & Cowie (1999); Cowie, Naylor et al. (2002)	NR	Y	Teacher and students	NR	N	Time consuming for teachers
Brier & Ahmad (1991)	NR	NR	Teachers and students	Y	NR	Students involvement helps them to learn the importance of rules
Salmivalli (2001)	NR	Y	Students	N	N	Integrates well with curriculum. Short
Cowie, H., & Olafsson, R. (2000); UK	NR	Y	Student	Y	N	Training intensive (16 hours), students volunteer to support peers
Murphy, Hutchinson, & Bailey (1983)	N	N	Playground monitor	N	N	No training needed

NR indicates insufficient information available to make rating

Index

Note: Page numbers followed by *f* and *t* indicate figures and tables, respectively.

Asthma, 113–14
Attachment
    caregiver–child, 63–64
    insecure-resistant, 92–93
    parent–child, 63, 79–80
Attention-deficit/hyperactivity disorder
        (ADHD), 119, 121–23, 122*t*
Attribution theory
    behavioral self-blame (BSB), 54
    characterological self-blame (CSB), 54
Autism spectrum disorders (ASD), 273–74

Back Off Bully Program, 256
Behavioral disorders, 117–19, 123–24,
        346–47
Behavioral observation methods, for
        bully–victims
    direct, 139–40, 164–65
    indirect, 165, 170, 173, 175, 176, 177
BMI. *See* Body mass index
Body mass index (BMI), 112
Boys
    bullying, 218–19
    as frequent-fighters, 271
    obesity/overweight of, 260
    parental valuing of aggression, 88, 89
    parent's psychological control over, 82
    severity of bulling in, 57–59
Brain Power program, 199, 206*f*
Brave Kits, 126*f*
BreakAway, 259
Bullies
    existing group interventions for
        future directions, 202–3
        practical implications, 204, 208
        resources, 205–7*f*
        social skills group intervention
            programs, 189–90
        social skills training programme,
            189–90
    potential group interventions for,
        197–202

future directions, 202–3
    practical implications, 204, 208
    resources, 205–7*f*
Bully Busters Program, 256
Bullying, 273–74
    age-related concerns of, 168
    aggression as, 5–7
    boys, 218–19. *See also* Boys
    cultural influence and, 31–33
    cyber-bullying, 260–61
    defined, 5, 245, 273
    emotional and behavioral disorders,
        risk of, 7–8
    ethical concerns of, 168–70
    evidence–based research on, 1–15
        goals of, 14–15
    family environment and, 146
    friendship and, 66
    gender and, 145
    girls, 218–19. *See also* Girls
    holistic approach to preventing, 245–62
        practical implications, 261–62
    Internet, 261
    interventions for, 10–13
        potential barriers to implementation,
            13–14
    LGBTQ, 259–60
    myths and fallacy about, 300
        elimination solves problem, 307
        generation gap, 305–6
        kid thing, 309
        money to operate more effectively,
            307–9
        problem kids, 309–10
        school problems, 303–4
        size matters, 305
        too good/bad school, 301–2
        zero tolerance, 304–5
    of obese students, 260
    pediatric illness and, 115–16
    physical, 261
    power dynamics and, 298–99

Cognitive-behavioral therapy (CBT), 123, 235
   for childhood aggression, 142–44
Communication, 169, 315
   parent–child, 94–95
   teacher–teacher, 236–37
Community(ies)
   bullying prevention and, 224
   involvement in bullying prevention programs, 234
   organization and school functioning, 30–31
   resources of, 29–30
Comorbid depressive symptoms, in children, 145
Competition, 13, 310
Computer-presented parenting dilemmas (CPPD), 84
Confidentiality, 169
Coping Cat, 149
Coping Power, 144
Coping strategies, of victimized children, 47, 55–59, 193
Corporal punishment and negative child development, link between, 81–82
Corruption, 308
CPPD. See Computer-presented parenting dilemmas
Creating a Peaceful School Learning Environment (CAPSLE), 350
Culture influence on bullying/victimization, 31–33
CWD-A. See Adolescent coping with depression
Cyber-bullying, 260–61. See also Bullying; Internet bullying
Cystic fibrosis, 110, 124–25

Depression, 58, 118, 194
   in children, 123, 124, 127, 148
   parental, 78, 83–84, 97

Diabetes, 114–15
   type I, 114, 115
   type II, 114
Diaries, 165, 170, 173, 175, 176, 177
Dinosaur Child Training Curriculum, 199, 207f
Dinosaur Social, Emotional, and Problem Solving Child Program, 199–200

Early adolescents. See also Adolescents
   bullying as proactive aggression, 172–73, 175–77
Ecological systems theory, 8, 17–37, 18t
   community characteristics, 29–31
   guidelines for intervention
      with peer group organization, 19–23
      with teachers and educational professionals, 23–27
   neighborhood, 30
   school structure, 27–29
   sociocultural setting, 35–36f
Educators, role in bullying prevention programs, 235–37. See also Teachers
Emotional and behavioral disorders, 7–8, 346–47
Emotionality and peer victimization, 52–53
Emotional reactivity, 7, 44, 52, 53, 118, 338. See also Bullying
Empathy, 84–87
   affective, 86, 87
   cognitive, 86, 87
   total, 87
Empowerment, 245–62
   defined, 248
   evaluation of, 252–53
   interventions, components of, 258–59
Endocrine disorders, 114–15
Ethnicity, in school environment, 28
Evidence-based practice, for bully–victim behavior assessment, 339–47

interpersonal skills, addressing, 192–94

practical implications, 204, 208

resources, 205–7f

social skills. *See* Social skills interventions

youth empowerment, components of, 258–59

Interviews, 140

Intrusive-demandingness, 94–95

Kids health, 126f

Learning disabilities, 116–17, 123–24

Lesbian, gay, bisexual, transgender, and queer (LGBTQ) bullying, 259–60. *See also* Bullying

LGBTQ. *See* Lesbian, gay, bisexual, transgender, and queer bullying

Loneliness, 55, 125, 148, 194

Love-withdrawal disciplinary technique, 86

Maternal depression, 83–84. *See also* Parent(s/ing)

Measuring Violence-Related Attitudes, Behaviors, and Influences among Youths: A Compendium of Assessment Tools, 252

Mental health disorders, 124–27

Multidimensional Peer Victimization Scale, 137

National Center for Injury Prevention and Control, 252

National School Climate Survey 2005, 259

Normative Beliefs about Aggression Scale, 325

Obesity and bullying, 111–13, 260

Obsessive-compulsive disorder (OCD), 119–20, 127

OCD. *See* Obsessive-compulsive disorder

Olweus' Anti-bullying Program, 351

Parent(s/ing)

accepting aggressive nature of children, 88–89

angry, hostile
and children, interaction between, 78

attachment relationship between children and, 79–80

communication between children and, 94–95

corporal punishment to children, 81–82

empathy of, 84–87

harsh overactive, 79, 95

influence in children's social behavior, 344

involvement in bullying prevention programs, 233–34

overprotection/intense emotional closeness, 92

participation in social skills interventions
child's behavior problems, 276–77
child's friendships, 277–78

psychological control to children, 82

role as advisors/consultants, 89

styles, 64–65

valuing of aggression, 87–89

Parent-Assisted Social Skills Training, 349

Parental control, 63

Parental involvement, 79, 93–94

Parental monitoring, 82–83

Parental responsivity, 95

Parental warmth, 78–79, 84

Parent/Child Reunion Inventory, 80

Passive victims. *See also* Victims
family profile of, 89–95

Peaceful Schools Project, 256

Pediatric illness, 115–16, 124

Pediatric Network, 126f